For Reasons of State

NOAM CHOMSKY

For Reasons of State

VINTAGE BOOKS
A Division of Random House, New York

FIRST VINTAGE BOOKS EDITION, 1973

Portions of this book originally appeared in *Abraxas, Journal of Contemporary Asia, Holy Cross Quarterly, New York Review of Books, Ramparts*, "The Rule of Force in International Affairs" reprinted by permission of The Yale Law Journal Company and Fred B. Rothman & Company from *The Yale Law Journal*, Vol. 80, pp. 1456–1491. "The Role of the University in a Time of Crisis," from *The Great Ideas Today*, 1969, reprinted by permission of Encyclopaedia Britannica, Inc.

Library of Congress Cataloging in Publication Data
Chomsky, Noam.   For Reasons of State.
CONTENTS: The Backroom Boys.—The Wider War.—The Rule of Force in International Affairs. [etc.]
1. Vietnamese Conflict, 1961–   —United States.
2. United States—Politics and government—1969–
3. Political science—Addresses, essays, lectures.
I. Title.
[DS557.A63C48 1973]   320.9′73′0924   72–12385
ISBN 0–394–71895–X

Manufactured in the United States of America.
by American Book–Stratford Press, New York

The State is the organized authority, domination, and power of the possessing classes over the masses . . . *the most flagrant, the most cynical, and the most complete negation of humanity*. It shatters the universal solidarity of all men on the earth, and brings some of them into association only for the purpose of destroying, conquering, and enslaving all the rest. . . . This flagrant negation of humanity which constitutes the very essence of the State is, from the standpoint of the State, its supreme duty and its greatest virtue. . . . Thus, to offend, to oppress, to despoil, to plunder, to assassinate or enslave one's fellowman is ordinarily regarded as a crime. In public life, on the other hand, from the standpoint of patriotism, when these things are done for the greater glory of the State, for the preservation or the extension of its power, it is all transformed into duty and virtue. . . . This explains why the entire history of ancient and modern states is merely a series of revolting crimes; why kings and ministers, past and present, of all times and all countries—statesmen, diplomats, bureaucrats, and warriors—if judged from the standpoint of simply morality and human justice, have a hundred, a thousand times over earned their sentence to hard labor or to the gallows. There is no horror, no cruelty, sacrilege, or perjury, no imposture, no infamous transaction, no cynical robbery, no bold plunder or shabby betrayal that has not been or is not daily being perpetrated by the representatives of the states, under no other pretext than those elastic words, so convenient and yet so terrible: *"for reasons of state."*

Michael Bakunin

Contents

Introduction

In early April 1972, Admiral Thomas Moorer, testifying before the House Armed Services Committee, explained that "if domestic restraints were relaxed the US would have the option of bombing Haiphong harbor in North Vietnam and launching amphibious assaults behind North Vietnamese lines."[1] The domestic restraints that Moorer had in mind, according to Congressman Michael Harrington, were "the activities of the peace movement and the press."

The chairman of the Joint Chiefs of Staff is no doubt correct. There is evidence, to which I will return, that the activities of the peace movement and the work of some honest correspondents have, to some unknown degree, restrained the criminal violence of the American government in Indochina. Those who have marched and protested and resisted can compare what is with what would have been, and credit themselves with the difference. We can each of us consider what we have not done, and credit ourselves with a corresponding share of the agony of Indochina. There are not too many people who can undergo this self-examination with equanimity.

The point is more general. An American historian points out that "by 1971 it was noticed on all sides that the students at American universities, who had been rioting on the campuses two years before because of Vietnam, Cambodia, and the military-industrial complex, were forgetting almost all of their zeal and no longer found such public issues interesting."[2] That students were no longer interested is not obvious; it is possible that they were simply no longer willing to endure beatings, imprisonment, vituperation, and idiotic denunciations for what was in fact courageous devotion to principle.[3] But the barely concealed hint is to the point. If their "rioting" will only cease, then aggressive wars of counterinsurgency and the diversion of scarce resources to waste and destruction can proceed without annoying impediments.

Whatever the outcome in Indochina, the framework of ideology and policy making, political culture and popular attitude, has not been substantially modified by this catastrophe, and significant changes in the system of institutions and doctrine that gave rise to it are most unlikely. We cannot lightly dismiss recent history in the hope that it will prove to be some mad aberration of little consequence for the international order that is emerging. America is weary of this war, and in the narrow groups that determine foreign policy there are many who see it as pointless, a failed venture that should be liquidated. But official doctrine nevertheless prevails. It sets the terms of debate, a fact of considerable importance. And as long as victims are designated as "Communists," they are fair game. Virtually any atrocity will be tolerated by a population that has been profoundly indoctrinated.

An allied official describes the current B-52 strikes as "the most lucrative raids made at any time during the war."

> Every single bomb crater is surrounded with bodies, wrecked equipment and dazed and bleeding people. At one such hole there were 40 or 50 men, all in green North Vietnamese uniforms but without their weapons, lying around in an obvious state of shock. We sent in helicopter gunships, which quickly put them out of their misery.[4]

No speech by the president is complete without a denunciation of the Communist barbarians for their alleged mistreatment of captured American pilots in defiance of the Geneva Conventions, which require that "members of armed forces who have laid down their arms and those placed *hors de combat* by sickness, wounds, detention, or any other cause, shall in all circumstances be treated humanely." In the case cited, the victims were soldiers, North Vietnamese, people driven—as Saigon intellectuals see it—by "the same feelings of nationalism that motivated heroes of the past to sacrifice their lives."[5] But the B-52s make no subtle distinctions among

Vietnamese. Years ago, the United States command made it perfectly plain that it would render uninhabitable any settled area under Communist control.[6]

High-ranking officers in the theater of operations report: "There is nothing inviolate"; "This time we are not pulling our punches. We've told the world that we're going to be the winners."[7] No literate person can be unaware of the nature of the air war in North and South Vietnam, and few can mistake its purpose. On much less substantial grounds, Americans have in the past properly condemned the atrocities of others.

In fact, the savagery of the American attack on the people of Indochina is often condemned, but a more fundamental question is rarely raised in the mainstream of opinion. When the president comments that "you have to let them have it when they jump on you," few of the critics of his infantile rhetoric emphasize the crucial point: they are "jumping on us" in their land, not in Kansas or Hawaii or even Thailand. Successful interventions are quickly forgotten. As long as such attitudes prevail,[8] we can expect new interventions in Southeast Asia and beyond, and if indigenous resistance is again miscalculated, then such domestic restraints as can be imposed will remain the major barrier to unlimited terror.

Admiral Moorer's testimony was reported on the day of one of the first spring actions against the war. It turned out to be a fairly quiet one. About a thousand people gathered in Lafayette Park directly across from the White House. With dispatch and courtesy, several hundred were arrested for assembling peaceably, without a permit, to protest the crimes of the state. The demonstrators, as usual, were mostly young. There were quite a few Vietnam veterans among them. One was in a wheelchair, no limbs, a stump and a head. As the demonstrators were driven away in police buses, they could see the remains of this man, alone in Lafayette Park, his view of the White House no longer obstructed by demonstrators and mounted police. The White House, in its majesty, was serene and undisturbed, concerned with more important matters than just another collection of bums. In the police station, a few hours later, arrested demonstrators heard the latest news: B-52s were bombing Haiphong.

The lead story in the press the next day informed us that

United States warplanes had "destroyed petroleum tanks and pumping stations in the city of Haiphong in 1966." So they had—and also factories and homes and the people who lived in them. One of those arrested was Bob Eaton, released not long before from several years in prison as a resister. He had sailed his boat into Haiphong harbor in 1967, and not long before the latest news was received, happened to be describing the bombing damage he saw then: large residential areas entirely wiped out, the local Chinese neighborhood in ruins. The American and foreign press carried eyewitness reports from Western correspondents that the western zone of Haiphong was a "wasteland" (April 1967), that whole neighborhoods had been demolished, homes gutted, much of the city pocked with craters, the enamel and cement factories totally destroyed, food-processing and rice-husking plants damaged.[9] But the United States government asserts that only military targets were attacked, and the press, its memory short and its instincts subservient, duly reports as fact what the government proclaims.

The first B-52 raid on Haiphong took place at night with no ground control and no spotter planes to guide the selection of targets. Eyewitness reports confirmed what any sane person knew must be true:

> There is much evidence of the extremely heavy bombing Haiphong has sustained over the last month. A visitor sees areas flattened like German cities that were subjected to strategic bombing in World War II. . . . A large series of apartment blocks . . . is almost completely smashed. . . . The three buildings that make up the [Thai Phien] school are now a total wreck. . . . The school and the workers' housing are perhaps a mile from the port. A hospital hit by the recent bombing is not near any visible military target. . . . Hundreds of acres are virtually flat with just a wall standing here or there.[10]

A senior American officer informed newsmen in Saigon that the targets in Haiphong are "all logistical in nature—oil storage areas, some transshipment points, railroad marshaling yards, all large targets and far away from populated areas."[11] The vice-president, in a television newscast the same day, stated that the strikes against "communications and logistical systems" in the North have improved Southern morale. What a pity that Goebbels could not have lived to see his final triumph over his enemies.

Bombing of a city by B-52s is another first for the president and his genial adviser, though cities and towns have been leveled throughout North Vietnam and B-52 raids on populous areas in the South were reported as early as 1965. These are sheer terror tactics. The first of Admiral Moorer's options was implemented the very day it was announced. Nixon and Kissinger, who are already responsible for more bombing than any other leaders in the history of warfare, may now take pride in yet another act of "steely nerves" and "political courage."

One might think that it is self-defeating for official spokesmen to insist that only military targets are struck, when observers on the scene can prove the opposite. What could the Pentagon hope to gain by flatly denying that American bombers had attacked the remote village of Phuc Loc, when Anthony Lewis could visit a few days later and see that this "small island in a sea of rice fields" had been devastated?[12] What purpose is there in blandly insisting that United States planes strike only military targets in Laos, in the face of overwhelming evidence that the "bombings were aimed at the systematic destruction of the material basis of the civilian society"?[13] As I write, the Swedish ambassador and Western newsmen in Hanoi describe the bombardment of dikes and dams in North Vietnam. But the administration states that the reports are inaccurate and offers the miserable pretense that if there is a catastrophe, it will be the fault of the North Vietnamese, who have not properly repaired the dikes after last year's floods. Reporters are challenged to prove that the planes they witnessed bombing dikes were not aiming at some hidden oil pipeline—and of course, they cannot.[14]

The government does not really hope to convince anyone by its arguments and claims, but only to sow confusion, relying on the natural tendency to trust authority and to avoid complicated and disturbing issues. How can we be sure of the truth? The confused citizen turns to other pursuits, and gradually, as government lies are reiterated day after day, year after year, falsehood becomes truth.

The mechanism has been perceptively described by James

Boyd in connection with the strange story of Dita Beard, Richard Kleindienst, and ITT. The evasions were "transparent and ridiculous," but that is irrelevant: "The idea is to bring the public to a point of bewilderment. . . ." The lawyer seeks "not to convince, but to confuse and weary."[15] In the same manner, the state is content to lose each debate, while winning the propaganda war.

Shortly after the Pentagon Papers appeared, Richard Harwood wrote in the *Washington Post* that a careful reader of the press could have known the facts all along, and he cited cases where the facts had been truthfully reported. He failed to add that the truth had been overwhelmed, in the same pages, by a flood of state propaganda. With rare exceptions, the press and the public finally accepted the framework of government deceit on virtually every crucial point. Hawks and doves alike speak of the conflict as a war between North Vietnam and South Vietnam, with the United States coming to the defense of the South—perhaps unwisely, the doves maintain, and with means disproportionate to the just ends sought. It was a tragic miscalculation—the implication being that had limited means sufficed, the American intervention would have been legitimate. The situation is complex: "there are elements of a Greek tragedy in Vietnam: two rights are in conflict with one another; the value of peace is at loggerheads with the value of democracy."[16] Or we read, in a strong editorial statement against the war:

> This is not to say that Americans, including the political and military commands and the G.I.'s themselves, did not originally conceive their role quite honestly as that of liberators and allies in the cause of freedom; but such idealistic motives had little chance to prevail against local leaders skilled in the art of manipulating their foreign protectors.[17]

Here we have the image of the American political leadership, noble and virtuous, bewildered and victimized, but not responsible, never responsible for what it has done. The corruption of the intellect and the moral cowardice revealed by such statements, which abound,[18] defy comment. What they plainly reveal is that nothing fundamental has changed in the mainstream of public opinion as the piles of corpses grow higher in Indochina. Others were to blame; the American political leadership was merely a victim of factors beyond its control, not an active agent of disruption in world affairs. Therefore it is free to try again elsewhere, when circumstances are more propitious.

It has long been a deeply rooted premise in American political culture that the United States has the right to intervene in the internal affairs of others. Writing in 1947, A. A. Berle, a typical member of the American ruling elite, presented the "revolutionary" thesis that the world is entering a new stage in which the rights of peoples take precedence over the rights of sovereign governments. The United States must serve as the guarantor of the rights of peoples, intervening if necessary to defend these rights, acting with the same solicitude it has always shown to the nations protected from harm by the Monroe Doctrine ("for nearly a century" the United States has maintained its "dominant objective" of securing world peace). Why are we justified in taking on this exalted role, replacing even the United Nations if it proves ineffective? The reason is simple. Along with Great Britain, the United States is more representative of the people than other powers, and therefore naturally pursues the popular demand for world peace—a refutation of Marxist doctrine, he sagely observes. To illustrate the necessity for intervention in defense of the rights of peoples, Berle cites the case of Greece, where "Russian-inspired aggression" is implemented by "subsidized bands of irregulars and local renegades acting under local leaders, but directed from abroad."[19] Despite the important challenge to American conservative ideology in the past few years, such views largely maintain their hold on American opinion, and Berle's disdain for historical fact is no less typical of contemporary "leaders of opinion."

With regard to the Vietnam war, there are the "optimists," who believe that with persistence we can win, and the "pessimists," who argue that the United States cannot, at reasonable cost, guarantee the rule of the regime of its choice in South Vietnam. These are the two positions that appear in the secret "Kissinger papers," released by the *Washington Post*, April 25, 1972. The pessimists expect "pacification success in 13.4 years," while the interpretation of the optimists "implies that it will take 8.3 years to pacify the 4.15 million contested and

VC population of December 1968." As always, the pessimists differ from the optimists in their estimate of how long it will take to beat the Vietnamese resistance into submission— nothing more.

It is not very surprising that within the National Security Council there is no one to express the view that the United States *should not* (rather than *cannot*) pacify Vietnam or secure the rule of the quisling regime it has instituted. But it is perhaps somewhat surprising that outside the government the debate so commonly remains within the same channels, a fact that I have documented at length elsewhere. There are the Joseph Alsops who believe that victory is within our grasp, and the Arthur Schlesingers who "pray that Mr. Alsop will be right," but doubt it. Much the same, apparently, is true in Great Britain. A left-liberal journal gives the following editorial analysis of the current phase of the conflict:

> The anti-communists have argued that the North Vietnamese may well lose in this desperate last gamble, and will henceforward be unable, or unwilling, to repeat it. The critics of American policy have argued that the South Vietnamese look the more likely losers, and that South Vietnam may crumble like a house of cards. Such arguments have some force; according to one's politics one can pick the first or the second.[20]

The assumptions of United States government propaganda are adopted here without qualification. The North is fighting the South—long since forgotten is the fact that the war has been waged by the United States and the local forces it assembled against much of the rural population of South Vietnam. According to one's politics, one may be a hawk or a dove, an Alsop or a Schlesinger, a pessimist or an optimist in the sense of the National Security Council. But "one's politics" cannot reflect a commitment to the principle that the United States has no right to play any role in the internal affairs of Indochina.

It is curious, and of some importance, that within a substantial component of Anglo-American opinion, opposition to forceful intervention by the United States is regarded as a "radical" or "extremist" view. One has to cross the English Channel to find it generally characterized, more accurately, as a moderate position, established in international law and "solemn treaty obligations," hence in domestic United States law as well. Such is the power of endlessly repeated lies linked with overwhelming force in a political culture that so easily adopts the long-standing premises of imperialist doctrine and patterns of thought.

One mark of a culture in the firm grip of ideological controls is that what must be believed to justify state policy will be believed, regardless of the facts. The American war in Indochina offers many examples, from the start, when the United States undertook to restore Western rule. The former chief of the Division of Southeast Asian Affairs in the State Department (1945–1947) has recently stated:

> I have never met an American, be he military, OSS, diplomat, or journalist, who had met Ho Chih Minh who did not reach the same belief: that Ho Chih Minh was first and foremost a Vietnamese nationalist. He was also a communist and believed that communism offered the best hope for the Vietnamese people. But his loyalty was to his people. When I was in Indochina it was striking how the top echelon of competent French officials held almost unanimously the same view.[21]

The internal record in the Pentagon Papers reveals that United States government analysts recognized that Western intervention must destroy the most powerful nationalist movement in Indochina. But a victory of the forces of revolutionary nationalism in Indochina was regarded as inconsistent with American global objectives, and therefore it was necessary to define the Viet Minh as agents of foreign aggression, while the French were defending the independence of Indochina. The necessary premise was soon embodied in state ideology, and rarely questioned thenceforth in internal documents or official propaganda.

In passing, I might note that it is quite misleading to describe the Pentagon Papers as a record of lies, as many commentators have. There is a striking similarity of internal to external rhetoric and expressed beliefs. What had to be believed for the justification of American policy was, apparently, efficiently internalized. "Lying" is not quite the right term for this kind of behavior.

The United States undertook at once to subvert the Geneva Accords of 1954, quite explicitly, as we shall see. But it was necessary to believe that this government committed to the rule of law was concerned only to restore the status quo as established at Geneva. The required premise became official doctrine, reiterated endlessly by political commentators.

To justify American escalation under Kennedy, it was necessary to believe that an American victory was of cosmic importance. The appropriate premise was duly adopted. As the "legendary" General Lansdale expressed it:

> If Free Vietnam is won by the Communists, the remainder of Southeast Asia will be easy pickings for our enemy, because the toughest local force on our side will be gone. A communist victory also would be a major blow to U.S. prestige and influence, not only in Asia but throughout the world. . . .[22]

Official pronouncements elevated Vietnam to a "test case"; the outcome of the struggle there would virtually determine the course of world history. When Canadian member of the International Control Commission Blair Seaborn conveyed United States warnings to Hanoi in July 1964, he "cautioned that U.S. stakes in resisting a North Vietnamese victory were high, since the United States saw the conflict in Southeast Asia as part of a general confrontation with guerrilla subversion in other parts of the world."[23] Later the alleged aggressive expansionism of Communist China was offered as a reason for the United States escalation. Fantasy piled on fantasy, in accordance with the exigencies of policy.

There is ample evidence that the success of the National Liberation Front can be traced to the appeal of its constructive programs to the peasantry (see chapter 1, note 215). But to concede this would discredit the American enterprise (though it is permissible to concede the point in retrospect; only fanatics are concerned with ancient history). Accordingly, government spokesmen and the press, generally, speak only of the "control" of the peasants by the Viet Cong. The same inability to perceive facts that are inconsistent with the requirements of official propaganda is a common feature of intelligence analyses,[24] which one might have expected to be immune to such distortion. To cite one case, peasant discontent was recognized as a factor in the deterioration of Diem's position in 1960, but in a revealing manner. According to intelligence, "most of the Vietnamese peasants are politically apathetic," but they do have grievances against the government, specifically "lack of effective protection from Viet Cong demands."[25] Defense Department analyses took this "lack of security" to be "the single significant peasant grievance, or the overwhelmingly predominant one, or the basis of the others," so the Pentagon historian reports; but CIA and the State Department, more perceptive, recognized that the oppressiveness of the Diem regime was another factor.[26] At issue, then, was the question whether the inability of the government to protect the peasants from the Viet Cong was one among many grievances, or the basis for all grievances. That the peasants might have some positive reason for supporting the NLF was a possibility too remote for consideration, though there are hints. For example, SNIE 63.1–60 reports that the Viet Cong "have exploited the tendency of the largely passive population to accommodate to their presence and thereby avoid reprisals," though "in some areas of operations . . . they have obtained the active cooperation of the local population,"[27] for reasons that go unreported, at least in the available record.

The effectiveness of NLF programs was, to be sure, tacitly conceded. In Vietnam, as in Laos, the United States has sought to mimic some of the achievements of the revolutionary nationalists in an effort to gain support for its accomplices. This homeopathic character[28] of United States programs for treating the Viet Cong infection has some intriguing consequences. Thus a recent survey shows that the Saigon land reform is progressing in areas where "the Viet Minh and the Viet Cong broke the landlords' hold years ago," so that the program "appears to some merely to confirm a distribution of land already made by the Communists." Where the Communists had not paved the way, "landlords have intimidated their tenants and made deals with local officials," and the reforms are at a standstill. The land reform differs from that of the Communists in that it excludes farm laborers, the poorest peasants.[29] Though it owes such success as it has achieved to the Viet Minh and NLF, the program is hailed as a major accomplishment of the United States and the Saigon government. "One feature of the new law considered highly progressive and revolutionary," a Saigon-based observer writes, "is that which gives those peasants formal entitlement to the land they have been tilling in recent years"[30]—that is, the land reportedly given to them in the NLF land redistribution.

It should be noted that other popular "grievances" are directly attributable to United States intervention. For example, the Can Lao, in effect the regime's secret police,[31] "was largely the brain-child of a highly respected, senior U.S. Foreign Service professional," General Lansdale reports; "I cannot truly sympathize with Americans who help promote a fascistic state," he adds, "and then get angry when it doesn't act like a democracy."[32]

By 1964 it was evident that even with extensive United States involvement the American-instituted regime would be unable to control the Southern insurgency.[33] Therefore the United States took over the war directly, invaded South Vietnam, ultimately devastating the peasant society. In so doing, it was again defending free Vietnam from "aggression from the North." At the same time, the United States began the sustained bombing of North Vietnam in an effort to compel the North Vietnamese government to use its alleged "directive powers" to call off the insurgency. When the DRV dispatched regular armed forces to the South, this reaction was incorporated into the structure of state propaganda, quite effectively, as a proof of North Vietnamese aggression. The press and the public generally conformed.

In the spring of 1972, the "enemy"—now the NLF–Provisional Revolutionary Government and the DRV after seven years of full-scale American war—was once again on the verge of victory. The administration thus shifted to a broader, international confrontation in which it hoped to prevail. The sinking of a Russian ship in the first air strike on Haiphong, the attack on two Russian ships several weeks later,[34] and the mining of Haiphong harbor signaled that the leaders of the free world are prepared to risk general war to achieve their objectives. The president seeks the cooperation of the Soviet Union and China to enable him to impose a noncommunist regime. Like his predecessors, he rejects any thought of an accommoda-

tion among Vietnamese. Whether the Nixon-Kissinger diplomacy will succeed, one cannot predict, though it is most unlikely
that China and the Soviet Union will be so foolhardy as to
test the willingness of the president and his chief adviser—
who long ago urged that we must be prepared to "face up to
the risks of Armageddon" in pursuit of our objectives—to
blow up the planet if necessary. Whatever the outcome of this
particular confrontation, it may well recur in some not too
different form, so long as the resistance is not crushed and the
United States continues to reject a settlement among Vietnamese.

Meanwhile, as in 1965, the United States intensifies its
attack on Indochina within the context of a heightened confrontation, and state propaganda records another triumph as
American and British moralists brood over the relative blame
that attaches to the Americans and the North Vietnamese for
the incredible carnage. The violence of the Saigon Army
against the people of South Vietnam is mysteriously absent
from these calculations, and as to the NLF-PRG, the American reader is generally spared any knowledge of its existence.
Exploring Nazi archives, one might find angry denunciations
of the Anglo-American invaders in 1944, who compounded
their aggression with brutal attacks on civilians in the peaceful
French countryside.[35] Why then be surprised when American
officials indignantly denounce North Vietnamese aggression—
in regions laid waste by American violence years before, in
regions where a marine colonel described one of the milder
American exercises as not war but genocide?[36]

The analogy, to be sure, should not be pressed too far. The
Anglo-American invaders were foreign forces. What is more,
they were most assuredly intent on conquering France,
whereas the alleged North Vietnamese objective of conquering South Vietnam or even part of its territory is, again,
asserted not on the basis of any evidence that has been produced but rather because of the necessary role of this hypothesis in the system of state propaganda. North Vietnamese
tactics appear consistent with those of earlier years:[37] to draw
the forces of the United States and the army it created away
from populated areas, so that the indigenous guerrillas will
have an opportunity to rebuild the structure that was severely

damaged by the terror tactics of the post-Tet "pacification" programs, with their innumerable atrocities, of which My Lai is the best-known example.[38] More revealing was the massacre at nearby My Khe, with scores of civilian dead, revealed by the Peers Panel investigation of My Lai. General Peers falsely stated to newsmen that no evidence had been presented of another massacre. Proceedings against the officer in charge of the operation were dismissed on the grounds that there had been no massacre, merely a normal operation in which a village was destroyed and its population forcibly relocated.[39] His exoneration for this routine operation tells more about the war in Vietnam than a dozen books. The accidental discovery of the My Khe massacre also bears a message. Consider the likely density of atrocities, given the manner in which this event was discovered. Still more significant were the tactics of General Ewell in the Mekong Delta, where thousands were murdered in routine operations in NLF-controlled areas (see chapter 1, note 149).

The fact is that after the Tet offensive of January–February 1968, the United States command, which had already torn much of the country to shreds in its effort to eradicate the NLF, undertook campaigns of unprecedented savagery. We shall probably never know the scale of this frenzied attack. Coupled with the massive terrorism of the Phoenix program and other US-GVN operations, this war of annihilation reportedly restored "security" to the countryside, seriously weakening the NLF.

It is in this context that we must consider the contributions of the subtle moralists who condemn both sides. Consider this rather typical example:

> The North's attack was not merely immoral; it has demonstrated that Hanoi has not persuaded the people of the South to throw off the yoke of Washington's "puppets" in Saigon to embrace their "liberators." The North Vietnamese armies are winning hegemony over the South by right of conquest, not popular demand (the refugees are fleeing South, not North).[40]

The tacit presupposition is clear: the "moral approach" for the DRV would have been to stand back while the United States imposed the rule of its collaborators by the means just described,[41] crushing the remnants of the Southern resistance whose victory was blocked by United States force in 1965. As for the miserable refugees, once again driven from their homes, I would not presume to assess their preferences and desires, having no more information than those who speak so confidently of their deepest wishes. The fact that they were fleeing south rather than remaining in their homes or fleeing north to be wiped out by the most vicious aerial assault in history seems less than compelling proof that they prefer the Saigon regime to Communist rule, as a moment's reflection might suggest.

Throughout, the underlying assumption, variously expressed, is that United States intervention is uncontroversial if only it can succeed without too great a cost. Thus it is immoral for Vietnamese to resist American aggression or to come to the aid of resistance forces that cannot withstand its savagery. It should be clear that to insist upon the malicious character of this pervasive assumption is to imply nothing about the tactics used by any group of Vietnamese.

Needless to say, the assumption is a commonplace of technical studies. To cite one example, consider the comments of Dennis Paranzino on research that appeared to show a correlation between unequal land tenure and government control in South Vietnam. The implications he finds disturbing: "First and foremost, they call into question the desirability of an important class of land reform programs."[42] Why? Evidently, concern for social justice must be subordinated to the overriding principle that the rule of the United States–backed regime must be imposed. Happily, Paranzino concludes from a careful analysis of the data that "greater equality is positively associated with government control." Therefore, we need not enforce traditional injustice and can proceed to ratify parts of the NLF program.

Since the time when hope was abandoned that the Viet Minh could be dislodged in North Vietnam, American policy has been directed to destroying all centers of power except two: North Vietnam, and the United States as represented by regimes composed of collaborators drawn from the urban elite. By now, much of the population has been forcibly concentrated in areas that the United States has some hope of controlling, through the local police and military forces it has established. To win, the United States must now offer to the remnants of South Vietnamese society, as the sole means of survival, absorption into the East Asian system that it hopes to dominate. At the same time, the United States must seek to create a regional conflict of the sort that its propaganda always claimed to exist, as it carried out its direct assault upon the rural society of South Vietnam. I will return to further details below (see chapter 4). My point here is merely to underscore the obvious: the hawks who believe that the imperial strategy shows some signs of succeeding and applaud this outcome are at least honest. In contrast, it is rather cynical to urge that we take a "balanced view," condemning both the "North Vietnamese aggression" and the escalated American air war in "response" to this "aggression."

Nixon and Kissinger have pursued a variant of the strategy implicit in the long-term United States commitment to the imposition of Western-oriented regimes, a variant foreshadowed in the policy debates of 1967–1968. Like their predecessors, they have been free to murder and destroy without fear of reprisal. Since much of the "responsible" criticism is easily neutralized, for reasons already discussed, the domestic restraints have been limited. Well before the expanded air war of 1972, it had been demonstrated that the level of American violence tends to increase as domestic restraints diminish. In the limiting case, where the restraints are null, the destruction will be total. Consider the Plain of Jars in northern Laos. The press was unaware or silent. United States military activities were the focus of no peace-movement activity. The Plain of Jars is now a deserted wasteland, probably uninhabitable for decades to come.[43]

Nixon and Kissinger may or may not be able to achieve their ends, but they have amply demonstrated that they can exact a horrendous price for the refusal to submit. If their efforts collapse, the carnage may exceed all bounds. Limited and malicious men, trapped in the wreckage of their schemes, may be driven to unimaginable extremes of violence. The events of the past years serve as a fair and compelling illustration of what will be done by a system of centralized power, relatively free of restraints, immune from retaliation. Those who are concerned to save Indochina from further destruction will listen carefully to the chairman of the Joint Chiefs of Staff when he speaks of the domestic restraints that so distress him. And if the torture of the people of Indochina will somehow end, Americans who can liberate themselves from the grip of official doctrine will remember these words when the next Vietnam takes shape, whatever its scale.

Some believe that the Nixon-Kissinger diplomacy spells an end to the global interventionism of the postwar period, but this seems a most dubious interpretation. The new diplomacy is an effort to institutionalize the cold-war system with more rational controls. The cold war was never simply a zero-sum game, a conflict between the superpowers in which the gain of one is the loss of the other. Rather, it has functioned as a marvelously effective device for mobilizing support, in each superpower, for ventures that carry a significant cost, economic and moral. The citizen must agree to bear the burdens of imperial wars and of government-induced production of waste, a critical device of economic management.[44] He has been whipped into line by the fear that we will be overwhelmed by an external enemy if we let down our guard.

The case of Vietnam, once again, is instructive. It would have been difficult to convince Americans that Ho Chi Minh posed a threat to their welfare or survival. The Soviet Union or Dean Rusk's billion Chinese are another matter. Government doctrine therefore identified Ho as an agent of a Kremlin-directed conspiracy or Chinese militant expansionism. The pattern has been as persistent in international affairs as the fakery with regard to bomber and missile gaps. The utility of the external enemy was illustrated once again at the outset of the spring offensive of 1972. The reflex response of the administration was to warn that the United States will not stand quietly by while the Soviet Union abets aggression. In fact, United States intelligence estimates indicate that Russian military aid to North Vietnam in 1971 was less than one-fifth of what it was in 1967; military and economic assistance to the DRV from all Communist countries was $775 million in 1971 ($1.02 billion in 1967), trifling amounts when one considers the costs of defense against air attack and reconstruction, or as compared with the vast American expenditures in Indochina.

The United States is reportedly spending well over $1 billion a year in the effort to "neutralize" the "Viet Cong infrastructure," a small component of the American war in South Vietnam. There is a $2.25 billion military-assistance program for Vietnam and Laos that is not even listed under Indochina expenditures in the government budget (in addition to the many billions that are). In two and a half months of combat in 1972 the United States spent more than $400 million on munitions alone.[45] But such facts do not deter administration spokesmen, who blame the great global enemy for the collapse of the Saigon military forces, exploiting the proven technique of the cold-war system of imperial domination.

A conservative alliance of great powers, each free to control its own domains, with arrangements (such as the recent SALT agreements) for a controlled expansion of the system of military production, offers definite advantages to the great powers. Its international consequences are not obscure.

> The day of the maverick states—North Vietnam, and North Korea, Albania and Cuba, Egypt and Israel—appears to be ending; no longer can aggressive adventures which threaten the greater peace rely on the automatic ideological and material support of the communist giants. Those small nations which have been willing to play a role in international affairs similar to that of aircraft hijackers are finding that they no longer have *carte blanche* to threaten the safety of the majority in pursuit of their own fanatical minority goals.[46]

Here we see a clear expression of the ideology of imperialism: it is North Vietnam that is aggressive and fanatic, not the country that deployed half a million ground troops to destroy the NLF and dropped more than six million tons of bombs on Indochina. More important, it is a fair assessment of the intent of the Nixon-Kissinger diplomacy by an informed observer who is sympathetic to its goals. The fanatics who seek independence and social change are to be crushed by their respective imperial masters, with no fear of great-power conflict.

Rational control of the cold-war system by high-level diplomacy may reduce the danger of nuclear war, which can be calmly faced only by the criminally insane.[47] It should also reduce the freedom of bargaining of weaker states that might hope to play one great power against the other in pursuit of their "fanatical minority goals." But there are also potential difficulties. It may not be quite so simple a matter to invoke the external enemy in times of need. This problem is more severe in a more democratic society, where public opinion is a more potent force and a potential brake on policy. A possible solution is to transform the United States into a more disciplined and controlled society. The Nixon administration has taken steps in this direction, with its flagrant defiance of congressional directives, the authoritarian reconstruction of the Supreme Court, and the attack on the media for occasional departures from official doctrine.

It is useful to bear in mind, however, that the commitment to a tightly managed, centrally controlled society finds its place in liberal (and so-called "socialist") ideology as well. Consider, for example, some of the views of Robert McNamara on social organization. "Vital decision-making," he holds, "particularly in policy matters, must remain at the top." Apparently, this is a divine imperative.

> God—the Communist commentators to the contrary—is clearly democratic. He distributes brain power universally, but He quite justifiably expects us to do something efficient and constructive with that priceless gift. That is what management is all about. Its medium is human capacity, and its most fundamental task is to deal with change. It is the gate through which social, political, economic, technological change, indeed change in every dimension, is rationally spread through society.
> . . . the real threat to democracy comes not from over-management, but from undermanagement. To undermanage reality is not to keep it free. It is simply to let some force other than reason shape reality . . . if it is not reason that rules man, then man falls short of his potential.

And reason is to be identified as centralization of decision making at the top, in the hands of management. Popular involvement in decision making is a threat to liberty, a violation of reason, a surrender to "unbridled emotion," "greed," "aggressiveness," and so forth. Management is "a mechanism whereby free men can most efficiently exercise their reason, initiative, creativity and personal responsibility." We must therefore strengthen the institutions in which management can function successfully in its "adventurous and immensely satisfying task."[48]

This is, in fact, the authentic voice of the technical intelligentsia, whether in the service of private capital, or of state power under state capitalism of the American variety, or associated with statist forces of the left. The Dutch Marxist Anton Pannekoek remarked, shortly before World War II:

> The aim of the Communist Party—which it called world-revolution—is to bring to power, by means of the fighting force of the workers, a layer of leaders who then establish planned production by means of State-Power; in its essence it coincides with the aims of social democracy. The social ideals growing up in the minds of the intellectual class now that it feels its increasing importance in the process of production: a well-ordered organization of production for use under the direction of technical and scientific experts —are hardly different.[49]

The technical intelligentsia find their natural place in a state management, organizing society for purportedly liberal and humane ends.

The focus of the essays that follow is not Indochina but rather the United States. The longest is devoted primarily to the Pentagon Papers, which are of considerable value as a source of insight into the exercise of power by the United States executive, a matter of great importance for the future. The documentary record, and the Pentagon history itself, bear only indirectly on the "disagreeable" war in Indochina, as Cyrus Sulzberger calls it,[50] and offer a valuable opportunity to turn our attention to Washington, for us the far more important matter. The other essays are also concerned with state power and ideology and with the image of the United States as reflected in its Southeast Asian war—a distorted image, fortunately, or there would be little hope for the future, but an image that reveals facets of reality that no serious person will ignore. They are concerned with certain problems of law and justice and the responsibility of the citizen in the face of state crimes; with the universities, the main center of intellectual life in the current phase of industrial society; with the contributions of academic fraud to the ideology of control, and more interesting, with the justification of injustice produced by scientists who cannot perceive that the force of their arguments derives from tacit acceptance of the most vulgar principles of the prevailing ideology. Finally, they touch on the libertarian critique of centralized political and economic power, and on the possibilities for a social theory that will be grounded in a science of human capacities, needs, and behavior that does not now exist, contrary to pretentious and irresponsible claims by scientists who always evade the simple challenge: Produce a system of nontrivial empirical hypotheses on behavior or the factors that give rise to it, supported by evidence, with some demonstrable bearing on matters of human concern.

The cultural and institutional barriers that block the way to a more just and humane society are immense. There are, nevertheless, long-term tendencies that threaten the hegemony of coercive institutions and ideologies. It is likely that significant groups in the Third World will recognize the destructive impact of integration in the global economy dominated by the industrial powers and will organize revolutionary struggles against the imperial powers and their local associates. Or consider, as a case in point, the problem of limits of growth, now the topic of much debate. As such limits are approached, an effective technique of social control will be lost. It is not irrational for culturally determined "economic man" to accept the existing system of inequity when it appears possible that as the pie grows larger, his share will grow with it. As such possibilities decline, he no longer has such reasons for tolerating a system of injustice and may turn to a closer examination of its ideological assumptions, for example, the belief that everyone gains when a few are rewarded, or that rewards accrue to those who somehow serve the public welfare. It is possible, furthermore, that the degrading assumptions of capitalist ideology will be challenged seriously by people who recognize that there is more to life than consumption of commodities and that creative and intrinsically rewarding work, freely chosen, is a fundamental human need, along with others that cannot be satisfied in a world of competing individuals.

The demand for redistribution of wealth and power, if it passes beyond rhetoric, will not be tolerated by the privileged. If the demand becomes serious, or if the challenge goes deeper still, only massive force, which may well be available, will prevent a social upheaval in the industrial societies. The outcome will be determined by the state of understanding and effectiveness achieved by popular organizations committed to the principles of a new society, perhaps some form of libertarian socialism.

I know of no concrete and substantive programs for bringing about badly needed and technically feasible social change. The political system offers few possibilities. The centers of power lie elsewhere, and will continue to set the limits for change "within the system" so long as their authority and domination persist unchallenged. There are small groups engaged in important efforts in community organization and workers' control. Multiplied by a large factor, such efforts might offer some hope of raising a serious and broadly based challenge to the centralized control of economic and political institutions.

The ferment of the 1960s provided opportunities for critical analysis of the institutions of industrial society and the imperial consensus, and some limited possibilities for popular participation in social planning. The dogmatic refusal to analyze American foreign policy by the standards applied to all other powers no longer stifles discussion. With the weakening of ideological controls, radicals are no longer virtually excluded from academic life—a development which leads to the cry that the left has taken over the universities, just as proposals for limiting the "defense" budget are described as a call for unilateral disarmament. The colleges are mass institutions, and will no doubt remain so. In an advanced industrial society, scientists, engineers, professionals of various sorts, obviously have a critical social role. These strata of society must surely be involved in any meaningful process of social change, though if they were to attain the position of a dominant "vanguard" or a new elite or ruling class, the promise of revolution or significant reform would once again have been betrayed.

Notes

1 Thomas Oliphant, "Harrington Says Admiral Discussed N. Viet Invasion," *Boston Globe*, April 15, 1972.

2 Robert H. Ferrell, "The Merchants of Death, Then and Now," *Journal of International Affairs*, vol. 26, no. 1 (1972). To be clear, Ferrell is not advocating what is implied by this observation.

3 We read that student activism results from a need for instant gratification, or is an exercise in irrationality or an outburst of left fascism. One can no doubt find cases to which such charges apply, but those who castigate the student movement as dominated by such tendencies are either unaware of the facts or are playing a more cynical game. For discussion, see Julius Jacobson, "In Defense of the Young," *New Politics*, vol. 8, no. 1 (1970); and my "Revolt in the Academy," *Modern Occasions*, vol. 1, no. 1 (1970).

4 Malcolm W. Browne, "B-52 Attacks on Highlands Slow Enemy and Buy Time," *New York Times*, May 6, 1972. The chief American adviser in the highlands, John Paul Vann, told reporters that "the B-52 strikes are turning the terrain into a moon landscape. . . . You can tell from the stench that the strikes have been effective." "Bodies are everywhere," he reported, adding that "Americans put more value on life than do the Vietnamese." William Shawcross, "Vietnam: The Breakdown of Advice and Leadership," *Sunday Times* (London), April 30, 1972; "Life and Death of a Hawk," *New Statesman*, June 16, 1972.

5 Benjamin Cherry, "Balance of Weakness," *Far Eastern Economic Review*, July 1, 1972. Meanwhile, American helicopters flying medical evacuation missions are supplied with tear gas and electric cattle prods ("used regularly on missions in the An Loc area") to prevent South Vietnamese troops, with little taste for the American war, "from mobbing the aircraft and attempting to flee the battle zone." The dangerous missions are flown by Americans while ARVN helicopters "sit idle on their pads, their crews lounging and sleeping." "They have tremendous lack of motivation," an American officer complains. Where ARVN does fly, "rich Vietnamese families . . . loaded electric fans and even Hondas onto helicopters" while "Saigon army soldiers pushed crying women and children off helicopters to provide room for their buddies and baggage," deserting the front. "US Copters get 'Cattle Prods,'" UPI, *Boston Globe*, July 17, 1972; Sydney H. Schanberg, "Saigon's Pilots Shun Dangers of Anloc," *New York Times*, June 24, 1972; Judith Coburn, "Vietnam Refugees: Hostages of Kontum," *Village Voice*, May 18, 1972.

[6] See Sydney H. Schanberg, "Quangtri Villagers Tell of Fleeing Bombing," *New York Times*, July 5, 1972; Daniel Southerland, "Quang Tri Refugees: 'B-52's—Terrible,'" *Christian Science Monitor*, July 7, 1972. Weeks earlier, AFP had reported in *Le Monde* (May 28–29) that according to refugees, "it is the fear caused by the constant attacks, day and night, by American aviation, the guns of the 7th fleet, and the artillery, which has provoked their flight, more than fear of the communists." American firepower, used as it was after National Liberation Front victories in the Tet offensive of 1968, has reached new levels and, as always, dwarfs anything available to Vietnamese on either side.

[7] Editorial, *New York Times*, May 27, 1972.

[8] Given the way national policy is set, one may question the import of this fact.

[9] See Jon M. Van Dyke, *North Vietnam's Strategy for Survival*, pp. 148–52.

[10] Anthony Lewis, *New York Times*, May 18, 1972. See also the report by Claude Julien from Haiphong during the bombing, *Le Monde*, May 12.

[11] Craig R. Whitney, "B-52 Relied upon More Than Troops to Blunt Foe's Offensive in Vietnam," *New York Times*, May 19, 1972.

[12] Anthony Lewis, "The Cost of Phucloc," *New York Times*, June 12, 1972. See also his "Death in Phucloc," *New York Times*, May 22, 1972, on the result of B-52 raids in this village "in the middle of nowhere."

[13] Belgian United Nations Adviser George Chapelier; see references of chapter 2, section I.

[14] Seymour Hersh, "French Newsman and U.S. Differ on Bombing of Dikes," *New York Times*, July 13, 1972. Ambassador Jean-Christophe Oberg stated on returning to Stockholm from Hanoi that "he has no doubt whatsoever that these attacks [on dams, dikes, and locks with rockets and 'smart bombs'] are deliberate and precise." He reported that the United States is pursuing "a policy of annihilation," not only bombing industrial targets but also dropping antipersonnel bombs on housing areas, schools, and hospitals. *Dagens Nyheter*, June 29, 1972; "Civilian Targets?" Reuters, *Christian Science Monitor*, June 29, 1972; "Bombing Criticized by Swedish Envoy," *New York Times*, June 30, 1972.

[15] James Boyd, "Following the Rules with Dita and Dick," *Washington Monthly*, July, 1972.

[16] Michael Harrington, chairman of the Socialist Party, *Village Voice*, July 2, 1970. Harrington does not go on to explain who, in his view, represents "the value of democracy" in Vietnam. For some discussion, see my "Revolt in the Academy."

[17] Editorial, *New York Times*, May 7, 1972.

[18] For example, former United Nations Ambassador Charles W. Yost writes that the United States has "suffered a setback in Vietnam," but the failure "is not ours, except as we made an error of judgment. . . . The decisive failure lies with our Vietnamese allies who, from lack of political will and dedication, did not take sufficient advantage of the enormous help we supplied over a period of seven [sic] years" (*Christian Science Monitor*, May 12, 1972).

19 A. A. Berle, "The Formulation and Implementation of American Foreign Policy," in J. C. Vincent *et al.*, *America's Future in the Pacific*. On Berle's role, see G. William Domhoff, *The Higher Circle*.

20 "War with No End," *New Society*, April 13, 1972.

21 Mimeographed testimony of Abbot Low Moffat before the Senate Foreign Relations Committee, May 11, 1972. See the staff study for the committee by Robert Blum *et al.*, *The United States and Vietnam: 1944–47*, for an informative review of United States attitudes during these years. We return in chapter 1, section V and VI (subsection 7), to the documentation in the Pentagon Papers, which reveals that American planners were well aware of the character of the forces they were committed to destroy. It is remarkable that a well-informed observer can still write that American policy led to "disaster in Vietnam" because "we did not as a nation perceive the peculiar circumstances of Ho Chi Minh's brand of Communism." (Chalmers M. Roberts, "How Containment Worked," *Foreign Policy*, vol. 2, no. 3 [1972]). The people responsible for the propaganda that largely determined what "we as a nation" perceived had ample information, and at crucial moments in their planning, few illusions, though they easily entangled themselves in the myths they fabricated.

22 Memorandum for the secretary of defense after a visit to South Vietnam in January 1961, in U.S. Department of Defense, *United States–Vietnam Relations, 1945–67* (henceforth cited as *DOD*), bk. 2, IV.A.5, tab 4, p. 66. This is the government edition of the Pentagon Papers.

23 *DOD*, bk. 4, p. 2. Seaborn further warned of "the greatest devastation" for North Vietnam if it persisted in the "DRV-assisted pressures against South Vietnam." United States planners were aware that "regroupees provided virtually all the infiltrators in the period 1959–64" (*DOD*, bk. 2, IV.A.5, tab 3, p. 32) and that the insurgency was Southern-rooted.

24 For a striking example, see chapter 1, section V, p. 51; also note 202. When intelligence reports are available, we sometimes discover significant qualifications that disappear from the second-order record. Thus there is much ado about alleged North Vietnamese aggression in Laos from 1959, but when we investigate sources more closely, a different picture emerges. See my "The Pentagon Papers as Propaganda and as History," in *The Pentagon Papers*, Senator Gravel Edition, vol. 5, *Critical Essays*, eds. Noam Chomsky and Howard Zinn. To cite another example, not mentioned there, we discover that what is called the "NVA 335th Division," the DRV command post allegedly set up in 1959 near the Laos border, "had been formed from the 'Lao volunteers' regrouped to the DRV in 1955" (*DOD*, bk. 2, IV.A.5, tab 3, p. 62). In this connection, see also Bernard Fall, *Vietnam Witness*, p. 249; he states that the 335th Division included many Montagnards who lived in the border region.

25 SNIE 63.1–60; *DOD*, bk. 2, IV.A.5, tab 4, p. 49.

26 *Ibid.*, p. 54. On this factor, see General Lansdale's observation, cited on p. xviii.

27 *Ibid.*, p. 51.

[28] Alexander Woodside's apt phrase. "Ideology and Integration in Post-colonial Vietnamese Nationalism," *Pacific Affairs*, vol. 44, no. 4 (1971–2).

[29] Daniel Southerland, "Saigon Land Reform: Still Doubtful," *Christian Science Monitor*, April 1, 1972. See also Jeffrey Race, *War Comes to Long An*, pp. 272–3. It is common to refer to the horrors of totalitarian collectivization under communism, but while such critics properly condemn the killings in the early stages of land reform in the DRV, they rarely note the circumstances, or the fact that the land reform laid the basis for overcoming widespread starvation and injustice. For discussion, see my *At War with Asia*, pp. 280–2, and "Revolt in the Academy." In *At War with Asia* I noted that Hoang Van Chi's *From Colonialism to Communism*, on which much of the discussion of the land reform is based, is an extremely dubious source with many errors and hopeless bias. I had no idea at the time how "dubious" it really is. Chi cites many alleged documents and slogans of North Vietnamese origin to support his conclusions, and other commentators have relied on this documentation. D. Gareth Porter has recently investigated the originals and discovered that much of Chi's documentation is fabricated or seriously mistranslated, including the most damaging portions. Confronted with these facts, Chi's response was that he "tried to convey the real meaning more than the literal translations," and it is safe to predict that United States government supporters will rely on this defense now that still another effort to brainwash the American public has been exposed. Chi's book was written with a grant from the Congress for Cultural Freedom and its publication was secretly subsidized by USIA. Formerly, he was an employee of USIA in Saigon and of the Saigon Government Ministry of Information, which partially subsidized his first book on land reform. See Porter, *The Myth of the Bloodbath: North Vietnam's Land Reform Reconsidered*.

[30] Phi Bang, "Land: Theory and Practise," *Far Eastern Economic Review*, April 23, 1970.

[31] Cf. Dennis Duncanson, *Government and Revolution in Vietnam*, p. 402; Joseph Buttinger, *Vietnam: A Dragon Embattled*, vol. 2, p. 947.

[32] Memorandum cited in note 22; another small revelation of the Pentagon Papers.

[33] See chapter 1. The point is generally conceded. See *At War with Asia*, chap. 1, p. 41, n. 72.

[34] William Beecher, "Washington, Discouraged, Hints at Wider Bombings," *New York Times*, May 3, 1972; Claude Julien, *Le Monde*, May 12; Joel Henri, "Thirty Minutes in Hanoi: A Sky Alive with Planes," AFP, *New York Times*, May 11, 1972.

[35] For an eyewitness report of a napalm attack on a French village, which left many dead, see Howard Zinn, *Vietnam: The Logic of Withdrawal*, p. 51.

[36] William Corson, *The Betrayal*, p. 71. Corson is referring to population removal near the DMZ in May 1967. Corson notes that none of the United States officials present "batted an eye over the fact that out of the 13,000 [people moved] only about a hundred were males between the ages of sixteen and forty-five."

[37] See Frances FitzGerald, *Fire in the Lake*, pp. 307, 342–3. It seems

implausible that Giap expected regular forces to move far from base areas, given the overwhelming United States firepower advantage and total control of the air. The one provincial capital captured, Quang Tri, actually seems to have been abandoned before combat. United States policy in the Tet offensive was to wipe out at once urban areas captured by the NLF. The policy remains in force, making it unlikely that DRV forces would attempt to capture cities. Judith Coburn, "Vietnam Refugees," quotes the Buddhist venerable Tu Quang in Kontum: "What will happen when the Communists come into the town? The Saigon army will pull out and Kontum will be destroyed by bombs and artillery. It has already happened in An Loc and the refugees from Tan Canh and Dak To tell us it has just happened there."

38 Minor in context, though instructive. While the nation agonized over the Calley verdict, a new ground sweep in the area drove perhaps as many as 16,000 from their homes. A year later, the camp where the My Lai remnants were relocated was largely destroyed by ARVN air and artillery bombardment; the destruction was attributed to the Viet Cong. Henry Kamm, "New Drive Begins in Area of Mylai," *New York Times*, April 1, 1971; Martin Teitel, "Again, the Suffering of Mylai," *New York Times*, June 7, 1972.

39 "Ten Get Jail for Raiding a Draft Office [sic]," *New York Times*, June 10, 1970; Seymour Hersh, *Cover-up*; Hersh, "The Army's Secret Inquiry Describes a 2nd Massacre, Involving 90 Civilians," *New York Times*, June 5, 1972.

40 "Cohorts in Immorality," editorial, *Far Eastern Economic Review*, May 6, 1972. I select this example among many because the journal is one of the most independent and best informed. On the objective approach for which the editors pride themselves, see chapter 3, note 25.

41 Elsewhere, the editors explain that "Nixon had demonstrated that he wanted to disengage from the war" (*ibid.*, May 13, 1972). The demonstration failed to persuade the *Review*'s own correspondents, among others. See chapter 4, note 1. But the editors were convinced, and by failing to agree, the leaders of the DRV became cohorts in immorality.

42 Dennis Paranzino, "Inequality and Insurgency in Vietnam: A Further Re-analysis," *World Politics*, vol. 24, no. 4 (1972).

43 See chapter 2, section I. Cf. also the record of the Pentagon Papers with regard to the bombing of North and South Vietnam, discussed in chapter 1, sections I and VI.

44 For my views on this matter, see *At War with Asia*, chap. 1. See also Michael Reich and David Finkelhor, "Capitalism and the Military-Industrial Complex: The Obstacles to Conversion," *Review of Radical Political Economics*, vol. 2, no. 4 (1970).

45 "Soviet Arms Aid to Hanoi is Down," AP, *New York Times*, April 13, 1972; chapter 1, section VI, subsection 3, p. 93 below; testimony of Earl Ravenal, Senate Foreign Relations Committee, April 19, 1972; John W. Finney, "Laird Projects Big Rise in Cost of Vietnam War," *New York Times*, June 6, 1972. R. H. Shackford points out that "Russian and Chinese military aid to North Vietnam during the last seven years is so small it would hardly pay one year of

interest on the more than $100 billion the U.S. has spent on the war in Southeast Asia" (*Washington Daily News*, April 21, 1972).

[46] Editorial, *Far Eastern Economic Review*, June 24, 1972. The analysis should not be discounted merely on the basis of the examples cited (Albania will terminate its aggressive adventures? Israel can no longer rely on Communist support?).

[47] This is not to imply that the risks of Armageddon have not been boldly faced. See my *Problems of Knowledge and Freedom*, pp. 106ff. On Kissinger's remarkable views, see Virginia Brodine and Mark Selden, eds., *Open Secret*.

[48] Robert S. McNamara, *The Essence of Security*, pp. 109–10. Others offer equally persuasive justifications for managerial authority. Historian William Letwin explains that "no society whatsoever can get along without business managers," whose function is "making ultimate arbitrary choices in production." He fails to point out that on his theory, the manager can be replaced by a random-number table ("The Past and Future of the American Businessman," *Daedalus*, winter 1969). The weakness of arguments commonly given for centralized control is of some interest. In fact, little is known, and there is ample room for social experimentation. It is unfortunate that such experimentation proceeds largely in countries that are barely beyond the first stages of development, rather than in the United States, which could easily bear the costs of failures and, under a different social organization, might pursue successes to dramatic results.

[49] Anton Pannekoek, *Lenin as Philosopher*, pp. 78–9. For more extensive discussion, see my *American Power and the New Mandarins*, chap. 1; "Knowledge and Power," in Priscilla Long, ed., *The New Left*; *Problems of Knowledge and Freedom*, chap. 2.

[50] C. L. Sulzberger, "Through the Looking Glass," *New York Times*, July 5, 1972.

For Reasons of State

CHAPTER 1

The Backroom Boys

I. INTRODUCTION

If the next edition of the Pentagon Papers is to contain an epigraph, I would suggest a remark by a war correspondent who is unusual, if not unique, in her concern for the Vietnamese and her detailed reporting on the meaning of the war to them. A year of exposure to the Nixon-Kissinger war, the one that is winding down, left her with "a deep, angry suspicion and scorn" for the White House, the Pentagon, the army, the diplomats, the experts in Vietnam, "for among them are some stunning lunatics and liars who have done their own country much damage, and nearly killed this one."[1]

The Pentagon Papers have a cool and antiseptic quality that readers may find revolting if they are at all aware of the reality that seems so remote from the minds of the planners in Washington. At least, that was my personal reaction. Perhaps that is why, after closing volume IV, I found myself thumbing through a study of the real Vietnam by the British photographer-writer Philip Jones Griffiths.[2] His technique is simple and effective. On one page there is a photograph of a serious looking American pilot with a skull on his helmet, and facing it, a victim of napalm, with a brief text:

> Some of its finer selling points were explained to me by a pilot in 1966: "We sure are pleased with those backroom boys at Dow. The original product wasn't so hot—if the gooks were quick they could scrape it off. So the boys started adding polystyrene—now it sticks like shit to a blanket. But then if the gooks jumped under water it stopped burning, so they started adding Willie Peter [WP —white phosphorus] so's to make it burn better. It'll even burn under water now. And just one drop is enough, it'll

keep on burning right down to the bone so they die anyway from phosphorus poisoning."

The Pentagon Papers do not deal with murder and destruction. They are not—nor do they purport to be—a history of the war or of the American involvement in Indochina. But they do provide much insight into the thinking and machinations of the backroom boys who bear the primary responsibility for a catastrophe of which they seem unaware. The study deals, not with the war, but with the perception of the war in Washington, a rather different matter. The account is sometimes inaccurate and misleading, reflecting what the policy makers persuaded themselves to believe. The relative attention given to various phases of the conflict also reflects the perception of Washington, rather than the significance of the events themselves.

There is, for example, much agonizing over the air war in North Vietnam. In contrast, the bombing of the South, far greater in scale, is barely mentioned. *"It takes time to make hard decisions,"* John McNaughton wrote. "It took us almost a year to take the decision to bomb North Vietnam."[3] The decision is studied in painstaking detail. There is scarcely a word about the decision to bomb South Vietnam, at greater than triple the intensity by 1966 (IV, 49). A few remarks prior to February 1965 indicate some interest in "explicit use of US air in South Viet-Nam" (III, 618—inexplicit use of helicopters and tactical air support for combat operations is reported from 1960 and was extensive by early 1962[4]). These remarks are so insignificant that the Pentagon historians—properly, given a narrow interpretation of their task—do not enter them into their record of planning in Washington.

In February 1965, "for the first time, U.S. jet aircraft were authorized to support the RVNAF in ground operations in the South without restriction" (III, 391), and the roof fell in on the rural population of South Vietnam. From the third week of February, "jet bombers commenced attacks against Southern targets on a daily basis."[5] This was the fundamental policy decision of early 1965. As Bernard Fall pointed out not long after, "what changed the character of the Vietnam war was *not* the decision to bomb North Vietnam; *not* the decision to use American ground troops in South Vietnam; but the decision to wage unlimited aerial warfare inside the country at the price of literally pounding the place to bits."[6] But of this decision, we learn next to nothing. And only a few scattered sentences indicate the effects of the bombing.

The contrast is all the more remarkable given the fact that South Vietnam, beginning in early 1965, was subjected not only to massive aerial attack but also to artillery bombardment which may well have been even more destructive. There is an extensive RAND Corporation study that provides detailed evidence on United States air and artillery tactics and their effects on peasant attitudes and "Viet Cong morale", based on interviews with prisoners, defectors, and refugees. It may well be an extension of the study introduced by Robert McNamara in congressional testimony in January 1966.[7] This report is concerned "especially to highlight some VC vulnerabilities which appear to provide opportunities for exploitation," for example, the vulnerability to bombardment by B-52s, "the most devastating and frightening weapons used so far against the VC"; "VC soldiers and civilians said that they felt there is no protection against these attacks." The report states: "The air and artillery attacks—the latter being far more frequent than the former—while disrupting VC activities and intensifying the cleavage between the population and the VC, often appear to cause [deleted] damage and casualties to the villagers [deleted]." The [deleted] damages and casualties lead the villagers "to move where they will be safe from such attacks . . . regardless of their attitude to the GVN." This is very helpful. "The effects of the departure of large numbers of villagers for GVN areas are beginning to be felt," with a consequent reduction in manpower available to the Viet Cong and the threat of "a major deterioration of their economic base." The report quotes a Viet Cong cadre: "Each person that moves out [of a Viet Cong area] will cause one VC to die of hunger." Viet Cong units find that they are "unable to buy food in abandoned villages." Thus the popular sea in which the guerrillas swim "is receding." Things are looking up for our side.[8]

The public record provides ample evidence that by late 1965 the United States command appreciated the logic of this analysis. In December 1965, General Westmoreland, in a

briefing for war correspondents, explained that previously the
peasant had three options: he could "follow his natural instinct" and remain in his home, or move to a government-
controlled area, or join the Viet Cong. But now, with the
escalated war, "if he stays put there are additional dangers."
"The VC can't patch up wounds," and they "no longer have
secure areas," because of B-52 bombings and other tactics.
Asked whether this gives the villager "only the chance of
becoming a refugee," Westmoreland replied, "I expect a
tremendous increase in the number of refugees,"[9] an expectation that was rapidly fulfilled.

The contrast in the Pentagon Papers between the attention
to the decision to bomb the North and the decision to conduct extensive aerial and artillery bombardment of the South
is striking. The reason for this seems clear enough. The
bombing of North Vietnam was highly visible, very costly to
the United States, and quite dangerous, with a constant and
perceived threat of general war. The far more vicious bombing
of the South, on the other hand, was merely destroying the
rural society of South Vietnam, and thus did not merit the
attention of the backroom boys.

The Pentagon Papers are a study of decision making, nothing more. They do not deal with the results of decisions,
except in terms of military success and cost—cost, that is, to
the planners and the interests they represent. There are no
memoranda on bombs that tear the flesh with tiny arrows,
designed to cause maximum pain and impossible to extract
without grave injury. There are no scenes of cratered fields and
poisoned rice paddy,[10] no smell of burning flesh. We find no
description of an old woman searching the rubble of her
napalmed "hooch," or of a child, chained to a hospital bed,
insane since the age of two when his mother was killed by a
helicopter gunship as she held him in her arms. Nor is there a
word of comment on the wreckage of the village society of
Vietnam, or on life in the densely packed urban slums to
which villagers have fled because "they don't like our artillery
and air strikes,"[11] or because they are starving, or because they
have been moved by force. Such sentimentality is far from the
minds of the men whose thoughts are recorded in the Pentagon study.

The sense of remoteness from reality conveyed by the documentary record is heightened by the accompanying analysis. Two of the authors have commented on

> the well carpeted stillness and isolation of those govern-
> ment offices where some of the Pentagon Papers were first
> written. The efficient staccato of the typewriter, the anti-
> septic whiteness of nicely margined memoranda, the affable,
> authoritative and always urbane men who wrote them—
> all of it is a spiritual as well as geographic world apart from
> piles of decomposing bodies in a ditch outside Hue[12] or a
> village bombed in Laos, the burn ward of a children's
> hospital in Saigon, or even a cemetery or veteran's hos-
> pital here.[13]

The essence of the Pentagon Papers is conveyed in a summary and analysis of the situation after the Tet offensive of
1968 (II, 414–15). The analyst ponders the question whether
the United States can

> overcome the apparent fact that the Viet Cong have
> "captured" the Vietnamese nationalist movement while the
> GVN has become the refuge of Vietnamese who were allied
> with the French in the battle against the independence of
> their nation? Attempts to answer this questions are com-
> plicated, of course, by the difficult issue of Viet Cong al-
> legiance to and control by Communist China.

He goes on to muse over "the question of the adequacy of
counterinsurgent theory and doctrine" and the problem of "its
transformation into operational reality," a "difficult, frustrat-
ing business," where "there exists no 'control' by which laboratory comparisons of alternative courses can be made," but a
problem that must be studied "in order better to guide future
policy."

The United States, in short, is supporting the former agents
of French colonialism against the nationalist movement captured—by implication, illegitimately—by the Viet Cong, like
the Viet Minh before it. Twenty years earlier, a State Department policy statement noted that the Communists under Ho
Chi Minh had "captur[ed] control of the nationalist movement," thus impeding the "long-term objective" of the United
States, "to eliminate so far as possible Communist influence in
Indochina."[14] The biographies of Thieu, Ky, and Khiem

indicate the continuity of policy; all served with the French forces.[15] This poses no moral dilemma, but rather a technical one. As Dean Acheson once explained, "Question whether Ho as much nationalist as Commie is irrelevant." He is an "outright Commie," and that is all that matters (besides, "All Stalinists in colonial areas are nationalists"; *DOD*, bk. 8, p. 196). At worst, this fact poses one of those dilemmas of counterinsurgency, and as the theorists are quick to point out, "All the dilemmas are practical and as neutral in an ethical sense as the laws of physics."[16] If the children in a burn ward in the Quang Ngai hospital disagree, well, they probably don't understand the laws of physics either. By defining the problems as technical, one appears hardheaded and realistic, any moral considerations are displaced, and the public is effectively excluded, since clearly technical problems are to be left to experts.

Furthermore, the technician who is concerned with transforming counterinsurgent theory into operational reality in the absence of laboratory control need not concern himself with the origin of the idea that the Viet Cong may be Chinese agents. This "issue," a hypothesis originating in someone else's department, merely sets the terms of the technical problem, which the counterinsurgent theorist is therefore free to address, understanding nothing. Facts are no more relevant to him than they were to Dean Acheson when he urged aid and recognition for the Bao Dai government in May 1949 to safeguard Vietnam from "aggressive designs Commie Chi" (*DOD*, bk. 8, pp. 190–1).

In fact, the function of the hypothesis is transparent: by assuming it, one can squarely face the problem of repressing the nationalist movement of Vietnam, untroubled by sentimental moral qualms, since the enemy is really China (or perhaps the Kremlin, which is directing a "coordinated offensive" against Southeast Asia),[17] not Vietnam. This kind of thinking, if that is the right word, goes a long way towards explaining the barbarism of the Vietnam war, in which the world's most advanced technology is pitted against the nationalist movement "captured" by the Viet Cong. If the backroom boys at Dow were forced to walk through the burn ward of a children's hospital, they might think twice about what they are doing in their laboratories. It is conceivable that even the modern Metternich might be shaken by a face-to-face confrontation with refugees from the Plain of Jars, if one of his jaunts happened to bring him to the place where the fun and games are "transformed into operational reality." The same is true more generally of the planners in Washington and academia, insulated from the facts, posing as technical experts and problem solvers.[18]

The analyst noted above is, finally, perceptive in recognizing that the technical problem must be studied "in order better to guide future policy" in Indochina and elsewhere, in pursuit of a stable world order in which the rights of the privileged will be guaranteed. Vietnam was seen as a great experiment, challenging and almost exhilarating, a laboratory of counter-insurgency and a test of the feasibility of "wars of national liberation"—by definition, inspired by "international communism" when they take place within the "free world." Under the Kennedy administration, "there was an emphasis on counterguerrilla and counterrevolutionary training."[19] Kissinger's doctrine of "limited war," extricated from its rationalization in terms of great-power conflict, is a natural theme of United States political-military global policy, given the relations between the industrialized countries and the developing world. Advanced technology makes a dual contribution. On the one hand, it provides the antipersonnel weapons, electronic battlefield, automated fire-control systems, and the like, all designed for wars against the weak. It also provides an intellectual framework to protect the decision maker from any realization of what he is in fact doing and to deflect the attention of the public—an important matter, since most people are not gangsters by nature and tend to be unhappy about murder and destruction. It is difficult to plot aggression "under the klieg lights of a democracy."[20] How much more convenient it is merely to face technical problems, as neutral in an ethical sense as those of physics.

The technical pose also allows the Pentagon historians to slip into unquestioning acceptance of the assumptions that guide the thinking of the policy planners themselves. Following Secretary McNamara's guidelines, the Pentagon historians do not undertake to inquire seriously into the American role in world affairs and its long-term motives and objectives, nor do they try to place the material that they investigate within the general context of postwar history. Thus the analysts describe the variants of the "domino theory" that appear throughout the record. The director of the study, Leslie Gelb, points out that "this theory, whether more or less completely articulated, appears in the relevant NSC papers of the Indochina war period, and underlies all major U.S. policy decisions taken relevant to the area."[21] But the Pentagon historians do not analyze the implicit content of the domino theory—the fact, as Gabriel Kolko expresses it, that "translated into concrete terms, the domino theory was a counterrevolutionary doctrine which defined modern history as a movement of Third World and dependent nations—those with economic and strategic value to the U.S. or its capitalist associates—away from colonialism or capitalism and toward national revolution and forms of socialism."[22] Nor do they take note of the important fact that the same domino theory was formulated for other areas as well, in rather similar terms, as when Secretary of State Marshall told a group of key congressional leaders in February 1947 that "if Greece should dissolve into civil war," Turkey might then fall, and "Soviet domination might thus extend over the entire Middle East and Asia."[23]

Furthermore, the interpretation given by the analysts generally reveals an unspoken but prevailing commitment to the faith that the position of the United States was defensive and responsive, that it was not an active disruptive agent in world affairs. At times this general stance leads to a serious misrepresentation of the documentary record. To mention one crucial case (see pp. 100–103), the documentary record reveals plainly that the United States intended to undermine the Geneva Agreements from the start, but the Pentagon historians do not accurately report the content of the basic document and speak only of the United States "response" to the prevailing situation, giving a generally inaccurate account of events in Vietnam and Laos at the time. Similarly, the Pentagon history underplays or entirely fails to mention clandestine American activities in Indochina. It does not take note, for example, of the fact that in late 1963 and early 1964 there was a marked expansion of American and American-sponsored military actions in all of the countries of Indochina, or of the coincidence of American-sponsored subversion in Laos and in Cambodia in the late 1950s. United States initiatives elsewhere in Southeast Asia, particularly in Thailand, also go unreported, though it is only by considering this broader context that one can hope to gain any real insight into evolving American plans for Southeast Asia.

Nevertheless, these limitations of the Pentagon Papers as history, like the exclusive preoccupation with the question of cost to the imperial power, provide a faithful and often revealing reflection of the limitations within which the designers of policy themselves operate, at least at the secondary level that is richly illustrated by the documentary record presented here. It is hardly surprising that policy planners raise no searching questions about the people whose lives and fate they manipulate, about the validity of their own beliefs or their own vision of a properly organized society, or about their right to act upon these beliefs to impose social and economic arrangements on others. Correspondingly, the planners tend not to see themselves as imperialist aggressors, a hostile and disruptive force in some foreign land; rather, they defend civilized values and the status quo. They seek peace and order. They are victims, not agents, and merely respond to the acts of their great-power rivals or of the obstinate, recalcitrant, and perverse elements in foreign lands who do not bend to the will of the superpower, reject its vision of their future, and even forcefully resist its intrusions, thereby becoming violent aggressors in their own homes. The technician who merely studies the day-by-day moves of the imperial planners can also easily avoid the painful questions that arise at once for anyone who extricates himself from the framework of official ideology.

The issues raised by the Pentagon Papers fall into several categories. There are, in the first place, questions relating to the public release of the material and the government response: the matter of executive privilege, the scope of the First Amendment, the rights and duties of a citizen (section II below). The contents of the study also bear directly on problems of law and conscience and legitimate social action (section III). It is also important to explore the broader lasting value of this collection of documents and analyses as a contribution to the historical record (section IV) and to the understanding of the objectives of American global strategy (section V), as well as for the insight it provides into the mentality of the planners and the functioning of government (section VI). All of these matters merit extensive study. I would like to comment on each of them, in the sequence indicated.

II. ON THE PUBLIC RELEASE OF
THE PENTAGON PAPERS

Senator Sam Ervin, who has been conducting an inquiry into the separation of powers, observed recently:

> Throughout history, rulers have imposed secrecy on their actions in order to enslave the citizenry in bonds of ignorance. By contrast, a government whose actions are completely visible to all of its citizens best protects the freedoms embodied in the Constitution.[24]

Ervin is referring specifically to the doctrine of executive privilege, invoked with increasing frequency as a device for withholding information from Congress and the public so that "those who govern are not accountable for their actions." On this matter, Senator Ervin takes his stand within a distinguished tradition. Thomas Jefferson warned that if citizens "become inattentive to the public affairs," then the government "shall all become wolves"[25]—a perceptive remark, and an accurate prediction. The story revealed by the Pentagon Papers is just what we should expect of a system of centralized power insulated from public scrutiny and democratic control, and unmindful—perhaps even ignorant—of the human consequences of its acts.

For a generation, there has been a contrived inattention to public affairs in the domain of foreign policy. Government secrecy has been a contributing factor, far outweighed in importance by the intense indoctrination that had rendered the public inert until very recently, when the Vietnamese resistance awakened some degree of skepticism and open-mindedness with regard to the behavior of the state executive and its official claims. With the partial collapse of the ideological consensus of the postwar years, it is much easier to undertake some serious inquiry into the United States role in world affairs. The release and publication of the Pentagon Papers are in part a result of this more healthy intellectual climate, and should contribute to it, one may hope.

Naturally, the government response is to try to shore up the dikes. The Nixon-Kissinger administration has gone even beyond its predecessors in invoking the "inherent executive power," in particular the proclaimed right to withhold information from Congress and the public. This is consistent with the Nixon ideology of radical authoritarianism (often mislabeled "conservatism") and Kissinger's belief in the need for tight central management in foreign policy.[26]

A related matter is the flagrant disregard for law on the part of the Nixon administration, perhaps even beyond that of its predecessors. As a revealing if minor illustration, consider the use of Thai mercenaries in Laos, recently the subject of some acid commentary in Congress. An executive session of the Senate was called to consider the CIA war in Laos, particularly the fact "that the United States is currently paying for foreign troops, for mercenaries if you will, despite legislation which, by letter as well as intent, was designed to prohibit any such practice."[27] Despite repeated efforts on the part of Senator Fulbright, information was withheld until reporters determined that thousands of Thai troops, recruited and funded by the CIA, were fighting in Laos under Thai officers in a new phase of the decade-long war conducted under CIA direction "without the authorization of the Congress; and largely without the knowledge—therefore obviously without the consent —of either the Congress or the American people."[28] With these acts, the administration moves another step towards realizing the proposal of George Ball in 1965: "Securing the Mekong Valley will be critical in any long-run solution, whether by the partition of Laos with Thai–U.S. forces occupying the western half or by some cover arrangement" (IV, 618; Ball has been widely praised for his appreciation, in this memorandum, of the difficulties of fighting an unpopular war against a large part of the population of South Vietnam).

In Senate hearings Alexis Johnson, speaking for the administration, was asked whether he considered Thais in Laos to be local forces, as required by law. "I do consider them local forces," he replied. Asked further whether he believed that under the terms of the legislation it would be permissible to "recruit Cambodians and Malaysians, Australians or anybody you felt, by calling them local forces," Mr. Johnson explained that he did indeed; they would then become "Lao forces or local forces," as required by the legislation restricting funds to local Lao forces.[29]

In the face of such blatant violation of law, Senator Symington raised the question, "If we pass a law and the law can be honored in the breach, what real reason is there to be a Senator of the United States?"[30] And Senator Fulbright noted, "I and some of my colleagues have almost been reduced to the situation where it makes no difference what is put into law, the administration will not abide by it," adding that perhaps someday "this country will return to its senses and we will then have an opportunity to resurrect the basic principles of law on which this country was founded."[31]

The example is, to be sure, a minor one in the context of general executive lawlessness in Indochina, but it serves to indicate why the administration must continue to "enslave the citizenry [and Congress as well] in bonds of ignorance." It is no surprise, then, that there was an effort at prior restraint, the first in American history, followed by an indictment alleging a conspiracy involving Daniel Ellsberg, Anthony Russo, and others, with further indictments pending. The point was captured succinctly in a Mauldin cartoon showing a worried Nixon whispering to LBJ, "If I let them print the truth about you, I'd be their next victim." What the administration fears is a breakdown in the system of secrecy that has so facilitated the planning and execution of policies that cannot be defended before the public.

In an important study of the First Amendment, Thomas Emerson points out that "limitations of expression are by nature an attempt to prevent the possibility of certain events occurring rather than a punishment of the undesired conduct after it has taken place."[32] In the present instance, this observation applies with a slight modification. The punishment is intended to prevent efforts to inform the public about events still to occur. Reviewing earlier efforts to restrict First Amendment rights, Emerson concludes, I think correctly, that in each case the alleged need for restriction upon freedom of expression was seriously exaggerated, administration of the limitations created an "obnoxious" enforcement apparatus, and, most significantly, "in practice the restrictions were employed to achieve objectives quite different from the theoretical purposes of the laws," with social losses that proved significant. The response to the publication of the Pentagon Papers is a case in point.

The central issue in this case is that, legalisms aside, there is an element of absurdity in any investigation or prosecution of those who released the Pentagon Papers to the American public. Any indictment of those involved in making this information available represents nothing more than an effort on the part of the government to punish the exposure of its crimes. We may ask whether it is the law itself that is absurd, in that it permits such proceedings, or whether the law is again being contravened.

It can be plausibly argued that the First Amendment provides a proper framework for exposing the absurdity of the proceedings. The government alleges that release of this material to the American public violates various statutes, for example, the sections of the Espionage Act which prohibit the transmission of documents "relating to the national defense" or of "information relating to the national defense which information the possessor has reason to believe could be used to the injury of the United States or to the advantage of any foreign nation."[33] Congress has, however, passed no law prohibiting the release of documents or information relating, not to the national defense, but to a history of aggression (the executive, of course, will always characterize aggression as "national defense"); or prohibiting the release of information which the possessor has reason to believe will be used to the advantage of the United States—that is, the people of the United States and the Congress. If it was not the intent of the Espionage Act to protect the executive from embarrassing disclosures, or to permit it to conceal its actions from the public and from Congress, there is no reason to suppose that release of the Pentagon Papers, in an effort to inform the American people about the acts—perhaps criminal acts—of successive administrations, is in violation of the Espionage Act.

It might be argued further that under the First Amendment, no congressional statute can inhibit transmission of information to the press. The courts, however, have never adopted a strict interpretation of the First Amendment. They have held, rather, that the press cannot, for example, publish "the sailing dates of transports or the number and location of troops,"[34] appealing to the First Amendment for protection against prosecution. Several cases that might fall under this proscription are mentioned in the Pentagon Papers. The White House called off a planned attack on the Tchepone barracks in southern Laos in December 1964 (it was "deleted as a secondary mission") "because a Hanson Baldwin article had named it as a likely target" (III, 255). Later, strikes against North Vietnamese petroleum facilities at Haiphong were temporarily canceled when the Dow Jones news wire reported the plans, "an extremely serious leak, because of the high risk of U.S. losses if NVN defenses were fully prepared" (IV, 106). In another incident, the president seems to have announced the Tonkin Gulf "retaliatory strike" before American planes were intercepted by North Vietnamese radar. The reason, according to Anthony Austin's important study, is that although "if the President spoke too soon he would be tipping off Hanoi," nevertheless "if he delayed much longer he would lose his audience on the whole Eastern seaboard" (the hour being past 11 P.M. Washington time).[35]

In recent years, the courts have held that First Amendment rights must be balanced against other interests. Emerson suggests that this "balancing" test has been construed so broadly that the First Amendment may be reduced "to a limp and lifeless formality . . . threatened with disintegration."[36] However one regards the balancing doctrine, it applies in the present case only if the government represents some legitimate public interest in its efforts to prosecute those who released the Pentagon study to the American public. If so, then one might ask whether this interest, whatever it may be, outweighs the First Amendment. But the question does not even arise if the government represents no legitimate public interest. In this instance, the public interest lies squarely in the strict and literal interpretation of the First Amendment, which affords the citizen some protection against the state, in that inquiry may reveal secret plans that might be criminal, or might simply be condemned by an informed public. Such considerations are particularly important in a political system with no opposition party in the domain of foreign affairs and no system of parliamentary questioning. Deprived of the information revealed by a press that is substantially free, the citizen has no defense against the conniving of the state executive. It is therefore essential for the press to play an adversary role, as the First Amendment permits. To the extent that the press is inhibited by ideological constraints, intimidation, or simply the concentration of wealth and power, fundamental rights are infringed. The government can make no legitimate claim to abridge these rights in the interest of "enslaving the citizenry in bonds of ignorance." The First Amendment alone suffices to block the government's current efforts to intimidate the press and restrain its further investigations by prosecuting and otherwise harassing individuals who expose its ugly secrets.

In the case of the Pentagon Papers, the issue is particularly clear because the government is seeking to punish the release of historical information. But the same would be true in the more interesting case of plans for the future. For example, on February 26, 1966, the president stated: "We do not have on my desk at the moment any unfilled requests from General Westmoreland."[37] In fact, there was at this time a request to double the troop commitment, and the president had on his desk a memorandum from the secretary of defense stating that with deployments of the kind recommended (to about 400,000 by the end of 1966 and perhaps more than 600,000 in the following year), Americans killed in action could be expected to reach 1,000 per month (IV, 309, 623–4). The president and his advisers did not consider it appropriate that the American people should be aware of what was in store for them. To cite another case, when Secretary Rusk spoke on television on January 3, 1965, "ruling out . . . a major expansion of the war" (III, 138, 263), the basis for the escalation that soon followed had already been solidly laid, as he knew. He also knew the possible consequences, whatever his personal estimate of the probabilities may have been. A National Security Council working group had predicted that the commitment "to maintain a non-Communist South Vietnam" would "involve high risks of a major conflict in Asia," which would "almost inevitably involve a Korean-scale ground action and possibly even the use of nuclear weapons at some point."[38] Earlier, Secretary Rusk himself had emphasized to General Khanh that the United States "would never again get involved in a land war in Asia limited to conventional forces," and that "if escalation brought about major Chinese attack, it would also involve use of nuclear arms" (II, 322; May 1964).

To those in power, it seems obvious that the population must be cajoled and manipulated, frightened and kept in ignorance, so that ruling elites can operate without hindrance in "the national interest," as they choose to define it. The citizen should be informed of only "the things he needs to know to be a good citizen and discharge his functions," as Maxwell Taylor explained in commenting on the peoples' "right to know," after the release of the Pentagon Papers.[39] If policies are to be modified, then "a conditioning of the U.S. public" is necessary, and where this cannot be done expeditiously, the executive may find itself trapped by its own earlier misrepresentations.[40]

But officials of the government have no legal authority to act in accordance with their contempt for the public and to lie with impunity.[41] And under a reasonable interpretation of the First Amendment, they have no authority to prosecute the exposure of their deceit and their acts.

The Pentagon Papers provide documentary evidence of a conspiracy to use force in international affairs in violation of law. One may debate the sufficiency of the evidence, but hardly its existence. The Justice Department, which initiates criminal investigation and prosecution, is at the service of the conspirators. Naturally, instead of investigating a possible conspiracy to involve the United States in an expanding war of aggression in Indochina, with continual and recognized risks of nuclear war (see above, pp. 17–18),[42] it will rather try to protect the inheritors of these policies from scrutiny and will prosecute those who bring the facts to the public, which must know these facts if it is to act to restrain the executive. In short, it will seek to demonstrate that Proudhon was quite right when he wrote that laws are "spider-webs for the powerful and the rich, chains that no steel can break for the small and weak, fishing nets in the hands of the government."[43]

The Bill of Rights represents an effort of great historical significance to protect the citizen from state power. The true content of these formal rights is determined by the willingness of the public to defend them. One essential element in the protection of the citizen is his access to information about the acts and plans of the state executive. It will require energy and determination to overcome the natural tendency of the state executive to conceal its doings. This, it seems to me, is the fundamental issue raised by the release of the Pentagon Papers and subsequent events relating to that release.

III. CRIMES AGAINST PEACE

The contents of the Pentagon Papers, not merely the circumstances of their release, bear directly on problems of law and conscience and legitimate social action. The Pentagon study is not concerned with the character of United States military and police activities in Indochina, and therefore provides little information about war crimes in the narrow sense: forced evacuation, destruction of the land, massacres, and so on. But it does provide important documentation with respect to a second category of possible crimes, namely, the "planning, preparation, initiation or waging of a war of aggression or a war in violation of international treaties, agreements or assurances," or a conspiracy to this end, in the wording of Nuremberg.[44]

It is important to be clear about the issues that are at stake in an inquiry into the legality of the American war in Indochina. It is not in dispute, among rational people with some concern for the facts, that the United States command is responsible for major crimes in the layman's sense of this term. What we may reasonably ask is whether the acts that are documented beyond dispute are also crimes in the lawyer's sense, recognizing that when we raise this question, it is not the war that is on trial but the law. We are asking—if we are serious—whether the law is a sufficiently precise and delicate instrument so that it can label a monstrous crime as a violation of law. Similarly, in considering the legality of the intervention itself (apart from the means employed), a person who is serious about the matter is not examining the propriety of the act, but rather the adequacy of the law. Suppose we were to determine that international law does not condemn the United States intervention as criminal in the technical sense. Then a rational person will regard the law, so understood, with all the respect accorded to the divine right of kings.[45] In fact, it seems to me that the law is not so deficient as to be unable to rule this intervention illegal, but it is, again, important to be clear about what is at stake when the issue is raised.

The fundamental treaty obligation of the United States is to the United Nations Charter, to which other treaties, such as SEATO, are explicitly subordinate. The United Nations Charter, which as a valid treaty is part of the supreme law of the land, specifies a series of "peaceful means" (negotiations, etc.) that must be employed in the event of a dispute that might endanger peace (article 33). It is the sole responsibility of the United Nations Security Council to "determine the existence of any threat to the peace, breach of the peace, or act of aggression" and to determine what measures shall be taken (article 39). Member states are required to "settle their international disputes by peaceful means" and to "refrain in their international relations from the threat or use of force against the territorial integrity or political independence of any state, or in any other manner inconsistent with the Purposes of the United Nations"; and even the United Nations is not authorized "to intervene in matters which are essentially within the domestic jurisdiction of any state" (article 2), in particular, domestic insurgency and civil war. There is only one exception: "Nothing in the present Charter shall impair the inherent right of individual or collective self-defense if an armed attack occurs against a Member of the United Nations, until the Security Council has taken the measures necessary to maintain international peace and security" (article 51). The distinction between "aggression by means of armed attack" and threats "other than by armed attack" (including "subversive activities directed from without") is written into the SEATO treaty, which permits only consultation in the latter case, while reaffirming the right of collective self-defense in the case of "armed attack." Article 51 is consistent with the remainder of the Charter on the assumption that "armed attack" is construed narrowly, for example, as an attack that is "instant, overwhelming, and leaving no choice of means, and no moment for deliberation," in a classic formulation.[46]

The law is reasonably clear and straightforward. The open questions have to do with historical interpretation. The questions concern the "state of South Vietnam," a state established and maintained in existence by United States force; a state which claims, in its 1967 Constitution, that "Viet-Nam is a territorially indivisible, unified and independent republic," thus extending from the borders of China to the Camau Peninsula (article 1; this is, furthermore, the only provision of the Constitution not subject to amendment or deletion),[47] as the Geneva Agreements of 1954 also stipulate. The question is, Was this state subjected to a sudden and overwhelming attack, leaving no opportunity for the Security Council to determine the existence of a threat to peace, so that the United States was entitled to intervene in collective self-defense under article 51 of the United Nations Charter?

We hardly need the Pentagon study to refute this claim. This study merely provides further and still more conclusive evidence that the alleged "aggression from the North," far from constituting an armed attack, was claimed by the United States executive to be a matter of "support and direction" for the domestic insurgency at a time when the United States was directly engaged in combat operations in South Vietnam[48] and was providing "our leadership, and our officer direction, and equipment as we can furnish them."[49] It also adds supporting evidence to the conclusion that direct North Vietnamese military involvement followed upon the regular bombardment of all Vietnam and the invasion of South Vietnam by an American expeditionary force in early 1965,[50] a consequence that was always anticipated by American planners. It further reveals that each step of American escalation was undertaken to sustain a regime incapable of withstanding a rebellion that was overwhelmingly indigenous, and that American policy was to avoid "premature negotiations" which would enable the "enemy," holding all the cards, to achieve his objectives through peaceful means.

The United States executive is granted no authority to determine that the North Vietnamese involvement it believed to exist constituted armed attack, or to respond to the Southern insurgency by deployment of United States military force from the early 1960s. It had no authority to implant a terroristic dictatorship in South Vietnam in 1954 (or even a benevolent democracy), or to carry out covert activities or direct military action elsewhere in Indochina.

The war planners were never in doubt about these issues. They understood that article 51 of the United Nations Charter is the only possible basis for a defense of the legality of United States intervention and that appeal to it would require "a major public relations effort" (III, 229). The public-relations effort had several facets. One component was outright misrepresentation with regard to "North Vietnamese aggression," as in testimony by Secretary Rusk before the Senate Foreign Relations Committee. State Department legal experts developed the theory that the return of Southern regroupees to their homes from 1959 (to take part in the ongoing struggle against the terror of the American-imposed regime that had refused to abide by the Geneva Accords) constituted an "armed attack" against "South Vietnam." Still more subtle minds devised the concept of "internal aggression," used earlier by Dean Acheson with respect to the Viet Minh. It was even claimed that political activity contrary to United States goals constituted aggression. To disguise the absurdity of these formulations, it was alleged that the "internal aggressors" were agents of a foreign Communist power. Lack of evidence was never a problem.

More significantly, before the ink was dry on the Geneva Agreements of 1954, the National Security Council set forth an explicit program to undermine the agreements and undertake the use of force in violation of law. In later years, the planners developed an explicit (and patently illegal) policy of exercising force prior to the recourse to peaceful means, to compensate for the political weakness of the American position in Indochina.

We will return to all of these matters in section VI, with explicit documentation.

It should be noted that the defense of the American intervention has given rise to some curious constructions by the more inventive geopoliticians. At one stage of the twenty-five-year war it was necessary to defeat the Vietnamese Communists to prevent Kremlin rule over Indochina, at another, to save the Vietnamese people from the alien influence of China, and at still another, to prevent the militant Chinese ideology from gaining ascendance over the more moderate Kremlin version within the Communist world. Tomorrow, we shall very likely hear that the United States must continue to pound Indochina to dust to further the common United States–Chinese interest in preventing Soviet hegemony over South and Southeast Asia. It is noteworthy that as the premises replace one another in rapid succession, nevertheless the conclusion deduced from them remains constant: Kill Cong.

It must also be emphasized that the direct involvement of DRV ground forces in South Vietnam was a response to American escalation of the ground and air war in the South and the bombing of the North, and that Russian and Chinese involvement in Indochina was a response to American escalation from 1964. But once the "intervention" had taken place, government propagandists were quick to exploit it as a justification for still further American escalation to save the people of South Vietnam from aggression.

It is possible to devise a defense for United States intervention that is less disreputable intellectually than the appeal to article 51 of the United Nations Charter, and probably this defense will be heard more frequently now that the Pentagon Papers have further undermined the argument based on the inherent right of collective self-defense against armed attack.[51] It might be argued that the Charter does not explicitly prohibit a government from calling on its allies to suppress an indigenous rebellion. Under this interpretation, it is legitimate to use force to destroy an indigenous movement within the territory of another state on request of the incumbent government. It is necessary, under this interpretation, to argue that such use of force is consistent with article 2(7) of the Charter, which forbids even the United Nations to intervene in matters of the domestic jurisdiction of any state, and that it is consistent with the purposes of the United Nations (see article 2(4)), which include the commitment to peaceful means for settlement of disputes, respect for self-determination of peoples, and so on. The defense must further reject the position taken by the General Assembly that "no State had the right to intervene, directly or indirectly, for any reason whatever, in the internal or external affairs of any other State," or to "interfere in civil strife in another State."[52] But at least it does not fly in the face of historical facts, and it can appeal to some ambiguity in the Charter as well as to a tradition granting rights to incumbent governments.

The primary virtue of this defense is that it avoids hypocrisy. The interpretation of law that underlies it is explicitly counterrevolutionary and expresses the fact that regardless of the law, great powers will do as they wish to achieve the objectives of their ruling elites ("the national interest"), restrained only by cost or competing force. The Bangkok Conference of Asian Jurists (1965) concluded that "in the former colonial territories, the Rule of Law is viewed more as a malevolent instrument of tyrannical rule than as a force of emancipation or of protection of human rights."[53] As a general conclusion, this is accurate enough.

"The right to aid incumbent governments," whether claimed by the United States in South Vietnam or the Soviet Union in Hungary, is merely a flimsy disguise for imperial ambition. The same is true of the concept of "limited sovereignty" developed by the United States in the Caribbean, and later, in almost the same terms, by the Soviet Union in Eastern Europe. In both cases, the essence of the doctrine is that "a regional organization may designate a particular sociopolitical ideology as alien to the region," and its advocacy by indigenous groups a form of aggression.[54] In accordance with this doctrine, Guatemalans, Vietnamese, Hungarians, and Czechs become aggressors in their own country if they are inspired by an ideology held to be alien and intolerable by the great power dominating that sphere of influence.

Under a reasonable interpretation of the United Nations Charter, intervention under these conditions is not permissible, but this fact in no way inhibits great-power practice. The conclusion is similar to that of section II above. There is a reasonable interpretation of the existing body of laws under which the law is not absurd and the behavior of the state executive is improper, even criminal. But state power will construct, and seek to implement, a different interpretation under which it suffers virtually no restraints. The law, so conceived, has no legitimacy. Which interpretation prevails, in the international sphere at least, is determined not by legal or historical argument—much as we may deplore the fact—but by the distribution of power.

It is in this connection that the Pentagon Papers raise some uncomfortable questions concerning legitimate social action. Confirming other evidence, they indicate that fear of domestic disruption was an effective constraint on policy. The analyst recognizes that one of the more serious problems for the administration was "the massive anti-war demonstration organized in Washington on October 21 [1967]," with the "massive march on the Pentagon": "the sight of thousands of peaceful demonstrators being confronted by troops in battle gear cannot have been reassuring to the country as a whole nor to the President in particular" (IV, 217, 197). McNaughton was concerned that escalation of the land war beyond South Vietnam might lead to massive civil disobedience, particularly in view of opposition to the war among young people, the underprivileged, the intelligentsia, and women (IV, 482, 478). In considering additional troop deployments to Vietnam after the Tet offensive, the Joint Chiefs had to make sure that "sufficient forces would still be available for civil disorder control" (IV, 541). A memorandum in the Defense Department a few weeks later was concerned that increased force levels would lead to "increased defiance of the draft and growing unrest in the cities," running the risk of "provoking a domestic crisis of unprecedented proportions" (IV, 564).

Considerations of cost are the sole factors inhibiting policy makers, so these volumes indicate. I have found no exception to this conclusion. Among the effective costs are those just noted. It was and still remains within the power of American citizens to raise these costs and thus to restrain the criminal violence of the state.

IV. THE PENTAGON STUDY AND
THE HISTORICAL RECORD[55]

Though in no sense a history of American involvement in Indochina, the Pentagon study adds important details to the historical record. As a general assessment, it seems fair to say that it corroborates reasonable inferences drawn in the most critical literature on the war. The Pentagon historians do at times try to distinguish the evidence they present from the conclusions in the critical literature, but unsuccessfully: they misrepresent the views of the critics of the war whom they discuss, and severely distort the historical record as well.

Not surprisingly, the Pentagon historians, in case after case, reiterate United States government claims as if they were established fact. Often they go far beyond government propaganda in attempting to justify United States policy and to uphold the view that North Vietnam was the disruptive and aggressive force in Indochina, sometimes even misrepresenting the documentation on which their account is based. Their reasoning, when they go beyond the documentary record, also reveals the extreme progovernment bias that one would naturally expect in a study of this sort. To cite one case, consider the interpretation of the post-Geneva period (presumably by the study director—cf. note 21). In his view, the United States and the GVN, though not "fully cooperative," nevertheless "considered themselves constrained by the Accords" and did not "deliberately . . . breach the peace." "In contrast, the DRV proceeded to mobilize its total societal resources scarcely without pause from the day the peace was signed, as though to substantiate the declaration" of Pham Van Dong that "we shall achieve unity" (I, 250). Thus by mobilizing its total societal resources for social and economic reconstruction, the DRV clearly demonstrated its intent to upset the accords, in contrast to the peace-loving United States and GVN, who were merely maintaining the status quo as established at Geneva as they rejected the central elections provision of the accords and launched a murderous repression of the Viet Minh and other opposition elements, in violation of article 14(c) of the accords. The DRV could have demonstrated its sincerity only by succumbing to the famine that appeared imminent in 1954 (cf. *At War with Asia*, p. 282), refraining from economic development, and permitting the United States to succeed in its efforts to undermine it. The logic of the historian is rather like that of Dean Acheson when he declared in 1950 that recognition of Ho Chi Minh by China and the Soviet Union "should remove any illusion as to the nationalist character of Ho Chi Minh's aims and reveals Ho in his true colors as the mortal enemy of native independence in Vietnam" (I, 51). To Acheson, apparently, Ho could prove his nationalist credentials only by capitulating to the French, who, as Acheson saw it, were defending liberty and national independence in Vietnam against Viet Minh aggression (see pp. 115–16 below).

On similar ideological premises, the analyst states that "no direct links have been established between Hanoi and perpetrators of rural violence" in the 1956–1959 period (I, 243). By "perpetrators of rural violence" he means the resistance forces in South Vietnam who undertook measures of self-defense (contrary to the policy of the Vietnamese Communists) in response to the reign of terror instituted by President Diem and his associates, who organized massive expeditions to peaceful Communist-controlled areas, killing innumerable peasants and destroying villages by artillery bombardment, killing, torturing, and imprisoning tens of thousands of dissidents.[56] In this regard, the analyst merely states that "at least through 1957, Diem and his government enjoyed marked success with fairly sophisticated pacification programs in the countryside" (I, 254), though he affirms that Diem instituted various "oppressive measures" (I, 253, 255). But he concludes that the Diem regime "compared favorably with other Asian governments of the same period in its respect for the person and property of citizens" (I, 253; in particular, for the property of the 2 percent of landowners who owned 45 percent of the land by 1960; I, 254). Diem and his associates are not described as "perpetrators of rural violence." There is, incidentally, little difficulty in establishing "direct links" between Washington and the organizers of the "sophisticated pacification programs," a fact not discussed in this connection.

When the Pentagon study appeared there was loud protest

that it was biased, misleading, a chorus of doves. In a sense, this is correct. The Pentagon historians do, in general, seem to believe that the United States involvement in Vietnam may well have been a costly error. At the same time they tend to accept uncritically the framework of official ideology and rarely question government assertions. As the term has been used in American political discourse, they are doves, by and large, and they have naturally been subjected to much criticism on that account by the statist ideologues who are scandalized when the mass media or scholarship or public opinion shows the slightest signs of intellectual independence or skepticism with regard to official dogma.

The general bias of the analysts must be appreciated by anyone who hopes to make serious use of this material. Disinterested scholarship on contemporary affairs is something of an illusion, though it is not unusual for a commitment to the prevailing ideology to be mistaken for "neutrality." Such naiveté is not infrequently apparent in these analyses, though no more so than in most professional work. Nevertheless, no reader will fail to learn a great deal about the United States involvement in Vietnam, and the attitudes and goals that underlie it, from a careful study of the analyses and the documentation on which they are based.

The most striking feature of the historical record, as presented in the Pentagon study, is its remarkable continuity. Perhaps the most significant example has to do with the political premises of the four administrations covered in the record (and we may now add a fifth). Never has there been the slightest deviation from the principle that a noncommunist regime must be imposed, regardless of popular sentiment. True, the scope of the principle was narrowed when it was finally conceded, by about 1960, that North Vietnam was "lost." Apart from that, the principle was maintained without equivocation, the record indicates. Given this principle, the strength of the Vietnamese resistance, the military power available to the United States, and the lack of effective constraints, one can deduce, with almost mathematical precision, the strategy of annihilation that was gradually undertaken.

In May 1949, Acheson informed United States officials in Saigon and Paris that "no effort should be spared" to assure the success of the Bao Dai government (which, he added, would be recognized by the United States when circumstances permitted) since there appeared to be "no other alternative to estab[lishment] Commie pattern Vietnam." He further urged that the Bao Dai government should be "truly representative even to extent including outstanding non-Commie leaders now supporting Ho."[57] Of course, Acheson was aware that Ho Chi Minh had "captured control of the nationalist movement."[58] But to Acheson, Ho's popularity was of no greater moment than his nationalist credentials.

In May 1967, McNaughton and McNamara presented a memorandum that the analyst takes to imply a significant reorientation of policy, away from the early emphasis on military victory and towards a more limited and conciliatory stance. McNaughton suggested that the United States emphasize "that the sole U.S. objective in Vietnam has been and is to permit the people of South Vietnam to determine their own future." Accordingly, the Saigon government should be encouraged "to reach an accommodation with the non-Communist South Vietnamese who are under the VC banner; to accept them as members of an opposition political party, and, if necessary, to accept their individual participation in the national government."[59] Precisely Acheson's proposal of eighteen years earlier (restricted now to South Vietnam).

The final words of the Pentagon Papers analysis describe a new policy, undertaken after the Tet offensive of 1968 had shattered the old: "American forces would remain in South Vietnam to prevent defeat of the Government by Communist forces and to provide a shield behind which that Government could rally, become effective, and win the support of its people" (IV, 604). Again, the same assumption: the United States must provide the military force to enable a noncommunist regime, despite its political weakness, corruption, and injustice, somehow to manage to stabilize itself. Nowhere is there the slightest deviation from this fundamental commitment.[60] The same policy remains in force today, despite tactical modifications.[61]

Small wonder, then, that many Vietnamese saw the Americans as the inheritors of French colonialism. The analyst cites studies of peasant attitudes demonstrating "that for many, the struggle which began in 1945 against colonialism continued uninterrupted throughout Diem's regime: in 1954, the foes of nationalists were transformed from France and Bao Dai, to Diem and the U.S. . . . but the issues at stake never changed" (I, 295; see also I, 252). Correspondingly, the Pentagon considered its problem was to "deter the Viet Cong (formerly called Viet Minh)" (May 1959; DOD, bk. 10, p. 1186; also II, 409).[62] Diem himself, on occasion, seems to have taken a rather similar position. Speaking to the departing French troops on April 28, 1956, he pledged that "your forces, who have fought to defend honor and freedom, will find in us worthy successors."[63] In January 1964 General Minh warned of the "colonial flavor to the whole pacification effort." The French, he said, in their worst and clumsiest days never went into villages or districts as the Americans were about to do. (Note the date.) In response to Lodge's argument that most of the teams were Vietnamese, General Minh pointed out that "they are considered the same as Vietnamese who worked for the Japanese." The United States reaction was to reject Minh's proposals as "an unacceptable rearward step" and to extend the adviser system even below "sector and battalion level" (II, 307–8). A year and a half later, it was quite appropriate for William Bundy to wonder whether people in the countryside, who already may be tempted to regard the Americans as the successors to the French, might not "flock to the VC banner" after the full-scale United States invasion then being planned (IV, 611).

The Thieu regime today has a power base remarkably like Diem's, perhaps even narrower.[64] By now, substantial segments of the urban intelligentsia—"the people who count," as Lodge put it (II, 738)—regard American intervention as blatant imperialism. Of course, one may argue that the popular mood counts for less than in former years, now that the United States has succeeded, at least partially, in "grinding the enemy down by sheer weight and mass" (Robert Komer; IV, 420).

V. VIETNAM AND UNITED STATES GLOBAL STRATEGY

With regard to long-term United States objectives, the Pentagon Papers again add useful documentation, generally corroborating, I believe, analyses based on the public record that have been presented elsewhere.[65] In the early period, the documentary record presents a fairly explicit account of more or less rational pursuit of perceived self-interest. The primary argument was straightforward. The United States has strategic and economic interests in Southeast Asia that must be secured. Holding Indochina is essential to securing these interests. Therefore we must hold Indochina. A critical consideration is Japan, which will eventually accommodate to the "Soviet bloc" if Southeast Asia is lost. In effect, then, the United States would have lost the Pacific phase of World War II, which was fought, in part, to prevent Japan from constructing a closed "co-prosperity sphere" in Asia from which the United States would be excluded. The theoretical framework for these considerations was the domino theory, which was formulated clearly before the Korean War, as was the decision to support French colonialism. The goal: a new "co-prosperity sphere" congenial to United States interests and incorporating Japan.

It is fashionable today to deride the domino theory, but in fact it contains an important kernel of plausibility, perhaps truth. National independence and revolutionary social change, if successful, may very well be contagious. The problem is what Walt Rostow and others sometimes call the "ideological threat," specifically, "the possibility that the Chinese Communists can prove to Asians by progress in China that Communist methods are better and faster than democratic methods."[66] The State Department feared that "a fundamental source of danger we face in the Far East derives from Communist China's rate of economic growth which will probably continue to outstrip that of free Asian countries, with the possible exception of Japan," a matter of real as well as psychological impact elsewhere (*DOD*, bk. 10, p. 1198; June 1959). The Joint Chiefs repeated the same wording two weeks later (p. 1213), adding further that "the dramatic economic improvements realized by Communist China over the past ten years impress the nations of the region greatly and offer a serious challenge to the Free World" (p. 1226). State therefore urged that the United States do what it can to retard the economic progress of the Communist Asian states (p. 1208),[67] a decision that is remarkable in its cruelty.

A few years later, in the midst of the fall 1964 planning to escalate the war, Michael Forrestal argued that we must be concerned with Chinese "ideological expansion," its need "to achieve ideological successes abroad," and the danger that any such ideological success will stimulate the need for further successes. Therefore "our objective should be to 'contain' China for the longest possible period" (III, 592; November 4, 1964); or, as the analyst puts it a bit more accurately, paraphrasing Forrestal, "the U.S. object should be to 'contain' Chinese political and ideological influence" (III, 218). William Sullivan picked up the same theme, viewing "Chinese political and ideological aggressiveness . . . as a threat to the ability of these peoples to determine their own futures, and hence to develop along ways compatible with U.S. interests" (III, 218; analyst's paraphrase).

Note the typical assumption that self-determination is compatible with United States interests, an assumption that is more than usually insipid in the light of what the Pentagon Papers reveal about the actual American response to Vietnamese efforts at self-determination. The same assumption, in effect, appeared much earlier in the important State Department policy statement of September 1948, mentioned earlier, which took note of "our inability to suggest any practicable solution of the Indochina problem." This inability arose from the incompatibility of our long-term objectives with certain unpleasant facts. One long-term objective is to eliminate Communist influence so far as possible and to prevent Chinese influence, and "the unpleasant fact [is] that Communist Ho Chi Minh is the strongest and perhaps the ablest figure in Indochina and that any suggested solution which excludes him is an expedient of uncertain outcome." What is particularly interesting is the reason why we must "prevent undue Chinese penetration and subsequent influence in Indochina." The reason is "so that the peoples of Indochina will not be hampered in their natural developments by the pressure of an alien people and alien interests."

This laudable concern for the "natural developments" of the people of Indochina, free from alien interests, is coupled with the statement of another long-term objective of United States policy: "to see installed a self-governing nationalist state which will be friendly to the US and which . . . will be patterned upon our conception of a democratic state," and will be associated "with the western powers, particularly with France with whose customs, language and laws [the peoples of Indochina] are familiar, to the end that those peoples will prefer freely to cooperate with the western powers culturally, economically and politically" and will "work productively and thus contribute to a better balanced world economy," while enjoying a rising standard of income (*DOD*, bk. 8, pp. 148, 144). The United States and France, in short, do not constitute "alien people and alien interests" so far as the peoples of Indochina are concerned, and association with them does not hamper "natural developments."

The National Security Council working group of November 1964, in discussing the domino theory, pointed out the danger that mainland Southeast Asia might fall to Communist domination if South Vietnam does, noting that "if either Thailand or Malaysia were lost, or went badly sour in any way, then the rot would be in real danger of spreading all over mainland Southeast Asia" (III, 627). The Joint Chiefs added that they were "convinced Thailand would indeed go." The NSC working group was further concerned with the "effects on Japan, where the set is clearly in the direction of closer ties with Communist China, with a clear threat of early recognition"; and with the possibility that "if the rest of Southeast Asia did in fact succumb over time," the effects might be "multiplied many times over" and might, "over time, tend to unravel the whole Pacific defense structure." The Joint Chiefs added that the loss of South Vietnam alone would have these effects, that the United States would not be able to prevent the rot from spreading, very likely, except through "general war," and that the time-frame for the unraveling of the whole Pacific defense structure would be brief.

Shortly after, William Bundy and John McNaughton noted that the "most likely result" of the least aggressive option they were considering (option A) "would be a Vietnamese-negotiated deal, under which an eventually unified Communist Vietnam would reassert its traditional hostility to Communist China and limit its own ambitions to Laos and Cambodia." They added: "In such a case . . . whether the rot spread to Thailand would be hard to judge." It would, however, be likely that the Thai "would accommodate somehow to Communist China even without any marked military move by Communist China," because they would "conclude we simply could not be counted on" (III, 661).

Option A was unacceptable: the United States was unwilling to accept its "most likely result," a Vietnamese-negotiated deal leading to a unified Vietnam, Communist-led and hostile to China, its ambitions limited to Laos and Cambodia. Therefore the planners quickly moved to heightened aggression. They are vague as to just how the rot will spread to Thailand or why they fear a Thai "accommodation" to China. This imprecision cannot be an oversight; these are, after all, the crucial issues, the issues that led the planners to recommend successive stages of aggression in Indochina, at immense risk and cost. But even internal documents, detailed analyses of options and possible consequences, refer to these central issues in loose and almost mystical terms. Occasionally, as in the document just cited, the planners make it clear that military conquest is not the mechanism by which the rot will spread. Surely they did not believe that Ho Chi Minh was going to conquer Thailand or Malaya or set sail for Jakarta or Tokyo. One must assume they were sufficiently in touch with reality to comprehend that Vietnamese support for guerrilla movements could hardly be very significant in Thailand or Malaya (and would be of no significance beyond). Such movements could succeed only if they had powerful roots and were capable of rallying the local population. If nothing else, repeated failures to incite resistance in North Vietnam would have sufficed to establish this fact. And it is difficult to believe that the planners, not ignorant men, feared Chinese aggression in Southeast Asia. As we see from the cited document, they regarded even a unified Vietnam that would be hostile to China as a danger to their plans, and anticipated that the mysterious Thai "accommodation" would take place even without any overt military moves by China.

In fact, the American political leadership desperately sought some indication that China had aggressive intentions. A case in point was their interpretation of Lin Piao's statement of September 1965, which emphasized that national liberation movements must be self-reliant and cannot count on China for meaningful support. To McNamara, Rusk, and others, this was a new *Mein Kampf*.[68] The response of the Kennedy intellectuals to Mao's talk about the East Wind prevailing over the West Wind,[69] or to Khrushchev's statements of support for wars of national liberation, was of the same order. It would be misleading to say that such statements inspired fear or concern in Washington; rather, ideologists eagerly seized upon them in an effort to justify programs that they wished to undertake or had already set in motion. As we shall see directly, United States intelligence agencies made determined (though unavailing) efforts to unearth evidence that would prove the Viet Minh to be agents of "international communism," after having decided, with certain qualms, to support the reconquest of Indochina by France.

There is only one rational explanation for these and many similar incidents, and for the imprecision of the planners with regard to the spreading of the rot and the accommodation that they so feared. The "rot" is the Communist "ideological threat," which must be combatted by direct intervention against local Communist rebellion, whether or not armed attack is involved (see p. 101 below). The Thai elite, they fear, will "conclude we simply could not be counted on" to help them prevent internal social change in Thailand or to suppress a domestic insurgency. The only "threat" posed by a unified Vietnam, hostile to China and limiting its ambitions to Laos and Cambodia, is the threat of social and economic progress within a framework unacceptable to American imperial interests. This is the rot that may spread to Thailand, inspiring a Communist-led nationalist movement there. But no skillful ideologist would want to see the implications spelled out too clearly, to himself or others. Consequently the central factors noted are left a mystery, apart from occasional comments such as those just cited.

Recall that in this period there was much talk of competition between the Chinese and the Indian models of development (see note 66). In this context, fear of Chinese "ideological expansion" gave substance to the domino theory, quite apart from any fantasies about Chinese troops roaming at will through northern Thailand or Kremlin-directed aggression by the Viet Minh (see note 210 and pp. 40, 115–16 below).

It is important to be clear about what is at stake in discussion of the domino theory and related matters. The reality of perceived dangers is, of course, irrelevant to determining the motivation of policy makers. The fact that threats were perceived and taken seriously suffices to establish motive. The question of the reality of the threats is nevertheless of interest, for a different reason. If, in fact, foolishness or ignorance led to the perception of imaginary dangers, as is often alleged (see notes 86, 97, 98), then policy could be "improved" (for whose benefit is another question) by replacing the policy makers by others who are more intelligent and better informed. The issues are sometimes not kept separate, with much resulting confusion.

In Southeast Asia, the threat was heightened by a look at the allies of the United States. When Lyndon Johnson returned from Vietnam in May 1961, he spoke of the problem of reassuring our friends: in addition to Diem, these were Chiang, Sarit, and Ayub (II, 56). Such friends as these—the only ones mentioned—surely were endangered by the "ideological threat" that Rostow and others perceived. The threat would be enhanced if Vietnam were to be united under communist leadership and successful in mobilization of the population for social and economic development, as might well have occurred had United States force not been introduced.

The comparison of development in South and North Vietnam was not particularly encouraging to the United States in this regard. An intelligence estimate of May 1959 concluded that "development will lag behind that in the North, and the GVN will continue to rely heavily upon US support to close the gap between its own resources and its requirements" (*DOD*, bk. 10, p. 1191). In the North, the standard of living is low and "life is grim and regimented," but "the national effort is concentrated on building for the future." The South has a higher standard of living (and "there is far more freedom and gaiety"—for whom is not specified, nor is there discussion of the distribution of wealth), but "basic economic growth has been slower than that of the north." The alleged higher standard of living in the South was not unrelated to the more than $1 billion of American nonmilitary aid, the bulk of which financed import of commodities (*DOD*, bk. 10, pp. 1191–3). In a similar context a few years later, an NSC working group took note of the discouragement in South Korea "at the failure to make as much progress politically and economically as North Korea" (III, 627).

Perhaps the threat has now diminished, with the vast destruction in South Vietnam and elsewhere and the hatreds and social disruption caused by the American war. It may be that Vietnam can be lost to the Vietnamese without the dire consequence of social and economic progress of a sort that might be meaningful to the Asian poor. Perhaps the "second line of defense" of which American planners spoke can be held, at least for a time. On such assumptions, the United States government might be willing to reverse its long-standing opposition to a political settlement among Vietnamese.

If our friends were toppled by popular movements, perhaps ultimately leading Japan to realign, influencing India, affecting even the oil-rich Middle East and then Europe, as the domino theory postulated, there would be a serious impact on the global system dominated by the United States and United States–based international corporations. Although some of the formulations of the domino theory were indeed fantastic, the underlying concept was not. Correspondingly, it comes as no surprise to discover that it is rarely challenged in this record. The analyst regards support for the French against Ho Chi Minh as "the path of prudence rather than the path of risk"; it "seemed the wiser choice," given the likelihood that all of Southeast Asia might have fallen under Ho's leadership (obviously not by military conquest, say, in Indonesia). This he regards as "only slightly less of a bad dream than what has happened to Vietnam since" (I, 52). The domino principle, he notes "was at the root of U.S. policy" since Chiang's defeat. It was also at the root of French policy, though the dominoes they were concerned with were in North Africa (I, 54). The domino theory was firmly reiterated by McGeorge Bundy in mid-1967 (IV, 159; cf. p. 116 below), and by many others.

In the years between, there is debate only over timing and probability. A CIA analysis of June 1964 has frequently been described as a challenge to the validity of the domino theory.[70] However, this analysis (III, 178) merely states that the surrounding nations probably would not "*quickly* succumb to communism as a result of the fall of Laos and South Vietnam" (my emphasis) and the spread of communism would not be "inexorable" and might be reversed, though the loss of South Vietnam and Laos "would be profoundly damaging to the U.S. position in the Far East," and might encourage the "militant policies" of Hanoi and Peking.

The documentation for the pre-Kennedy period gives substantial support to this interpretation of United States motives. By April 1945 the United States had publicly supported the reconstitution of French authority, somewhat evasively, while a "more liberal" pattern, specifically "liberalization of restrictive French economic policies," was recommended "for the protection of American interests" (*DOD*, bk. 8, pp. 6–10). The American interest in Indochina ("almost exclusively a French economic preserve, and a political morass") was considerably less than in Indonesia, where "extensive American and British investments . . . afforded common ground for intervention" (I, 29). It was urged that France move to grant autonomy to its colonies (or the people "may embrace ideologies contrary to our own or develop a Pan-Asiatic movement against all Western powers") and that open-door policies be pursued (*DOD*, bk. 8, p. 23). By December 1946, it was noted that "French appear to realize no longer possible maintain closed door here and non-French interests will have chance to participate in unquestioned rich economic possibilities" (p. 87). Although the resources of Indochina itself are repeatedly mentioned (e.g., p. 183), it was of course the whole region (on the hypothesis of the domino theory) that was the primary consideration: "if COMMIES gain control IC, THAI and rest SEA will be imperiled" (p. 220; June 1949).

A National Security Council report of December 1949 went into the situation in some detail (NSC 48/1; *DOD*, bk. 8, pp. 226–7). The problem is that now and for the foreseeable future, the Soviet Union threatens to dominate Asia, an area of significant political, economic, and military power. The "Stalinist bloc" might achieve global dominance if Japan, "the principal component of a Far Eastern war-making complex," were added to it. "Whether [Japan's] potential is developed and the way in which it is used will strongly influence the future patterns of politics in Asia." "In the power potential of Asia, Japan plays the most important part" by reason of its economic potential and strategic position. "The industrial plant of Japan would be the richest strategic prize in the Far East for the USSR." Communist pressure on Japan will mount, because of proximity, the indigenous Japanese Communist movement which might be able to exploit cultural factors and economic hardship, and "the potential of Communist China as a source of raw materials vital to Japan and a market for its goods." Japan requires Asian food, raw materials, and markets; the United States should encourage "a considerable increase in Southern Asiatic food and raw material exports" to avoid "preponderant dependence on Chinese sources." Analogous considerations hold for India. Furthermore, these markets and sources of raw materials should be developed for United States purposes. "Some kind of regional association . . . among the non-Communist countries of Asia might become an important means of developing a favorable atmosphere for such trade among themselves and with other parts of the world."

As John Dower among others has emphasized, "the United States has never intended to carry the burden of anti-Communist and anti-Chinese consolidation alone. It has always seen the end goal as a quasi-dependent Asian regionalism."[71] The Pentagon Papers enrich the available documentation on this matter in a rather interesting way.

Continuing with NSC 48/1, it is recommended that under certain restrictions, trade with Communist China should be permitted, for the health of the Japanese and American economies. The industrial plant of Japan and such strategic materials as Indonesian oil must be denied to the Soviet Union and kept in the Western orbit. The particular problem in Southeast Asia is that it "is the target of a coordinated offensive directed by the Kremlin" (this is "now clear"), and has no responsible leaders, outside of Thailand[72] and the Philippines. If Southeast Asia "is swept by communism we shall have suffered a major political rout the repercussions of which will be felt throughout the rest of the world, especially in the Middle East and in a then critically exposed Australia."

The general lines of this analysis persist through the Truman and Eisenhower administrations. NSC 64 (I, 361–2) concluded that Thailand and Burma would "fall under Communist domination" and the rest of Southeast Asia would be "in grave hazard" if Indochina were "controlled by a Communist-dominated government." The Joint Chiefs urged "long-term measures to provide for Japan and the other offshore islands a secure source of food and other strategic materials from non-Communist held areas in the Far East" (I, 366; April 1950; they also recommended military aid and covert operations). A State Department policy committee interpreted NSC 64 as asserting that "the loss of Indochina to Communist forces would undoubtedly lead to the loss of Southeast Asia" (DOD, bk. 8, p. 351; October 1950). NSC 48/5 saw the Soviet Union as attempting to bring the mainland of East Asia and eventually Japan under Soviet control (pp. 425–6; May 1951). Given Asian population, military capacity, critical resources, and Japanese industrial capacity, it is essential to block this program. An NSC staff study of February 1952 warned:

> The fall of Southeast Asia would underline the apparent economic advantages to Japan of association with the communist-dominated Asian sphere. Exclusion of Japan from trade with Southeast Asia would seriously affect the Japanese economy, and increase Japan's dependence on United States aid. In the long run the loss of Southeast Asia, especially Malaya and Indonesia, could result in such economic and political pressures in Japan as to make it extremely difficult to prevent Japan's eventual accommodation to the Soviet Bloc. [I, 375]

It went on to speak of the importance of Southeast Asian raw materials (for example, Indonesian oil, and the significance of Malaya, the largest dollar earner of the United Kingdom, to Britain's economic recovery) and United States strategic interests, developing the domino theory in detail.

NSC 124/2 in June 1952 identified China as the main enemy and gave a clear formulation of the domino theory, emphasizing again the problem of raw materials and the threat of Japanese accommodation to communism (I, 83–4, 384–5). The same themes persist, with added and even clearer emphasis, under the Eisenhower administration. It was emphasized that Japan is the keystone of United States policy and that the loss of Southeast Asia (a likely consequence of the loss of Indochina, or even Tonkin) would drive Japan to accommodation with the Communist block, permitting Red China (now the main culprit, though some analyses still refer to "the Soviet Communist campaign in Southeast Asia"; cf. *DOD*, bk. 9, p. 214; January 1954) to construct a military bloc more formidable than that of Japan before World War II. The world-wide effects would be disastrous. Therefore Indochina must be saved and its countries encouraged to integrate themselves into the "free world" system and to stimulate the flow of raw-material resources to the free world, Japan being the critical factor (see I, 436, 438, 450, 452). In June 1956, John F. Kennedy gave a clear formulation of the basic thesis:

> Vietnam represents the cornerstone of the Free World in Southeast Asia, the keystone to the arch, the finger in the dike. Burma, Thailand, India, Japan, the Philippines and, obviously, Laos and Cambodia are among those whose security would be threatened if the red tide of Communism overflowed into Vietnam. . . . Moreover, the independence of Free Vietnam is crucial to the free world in fields other than the military. Her economy is essential to the economy of all of Southeast Asia; and her political liberty is an inspiration to those seeking to obtain or maintain their liberty in all parts of Asia—and indeed the world. The fundamental tenets of this nation's foreign policy, in short, depend in considerable measure upon a strong and free Vietnamese nation.[73]

Intelligence estimates repeated, with various nuances, the general assumptions of the domino theory (see *DOD*, bk. 10,

p. 999, September 1955, for a qualified statement). Memoranda of the NSC and of the Joint Chiefs of Staff also elaborate the same assumptions consistently, adding conventional recommendations that the investment climate for United States capital be improved (p. 1206) and that Southeast Asian countries be integrated into the free-world economic system (pp. 1206, 1228, 1234, 1288).

It is sometimes argued that at best, "citation of these views [which can now be documented extensively from internal documents as well as the public record] proves no more than conviction, and a mistaken conviction at that," and therefore the "radical argument" that Japanese relations with Southeast Asia were a dominant consideration in American planning can be discounted.[74] The argument is an obvious nonsequitur, a particularly clear example of the fallacy noted earlier (p. 136 above). Documentation of the *conviction* suffices to establish motive; its *accuracy* is clearly irrelevant to the determination of motive. Robert W. Tucker compounds his logical fallacy with a factual error when he states that "the radical argument of Japanese dependence on Southeast Asia is difficult to take seriously." This is not a "radical argument" but rather the expressed conviction of United States policy makers. By arguing merely the irrelevant question of the accuracy of the conviction, Tucker in effect concedes the actual "radical argument" while appearing to reject it. To make matters still worse, when he turns to the question whether the conviction was held, he hedges, claiming only that "at least after 1964" one cannot attribute Vietnam policy to this conviction. Again irrelevant, since what has actually been argued is that this was the operative factor through the 1950s, of diminishing importance in later years as deepening American involvement became self-motivating and increasingly irrational on imperialist grounds, leading finally to serious disenchantment on the part of rational imperialists and a "split in the ruling class." From every point of view, then, Tucker's discussion of this point is entirely inept, yet it is the only attempt I know of to respond seriously to what Tucker calls "the radical argument."[75]

In the 1960s, there is an increasing component of irrationalism and posturing, with much talk of psychological tests of will, humiliation, the American image, and so on. The insistence that the other fellow blink first is not without its ironic aspects. Thus the analyst regards 1961 as "a peculiarly difficult year" for the United States because of "the generally aggressive and confident posture of the Russians . . . and the generally defensive position of the Americans" (II, 21). It was therefore difficult to make concessions or to give ground to the Soviets, a matter which indirectly affected Vietnam. Anything, anywhere, that "was, or could be interpreted to be a weak U.S. response, only strengthened the pressure to hold on in Vietnam." Chester Cooper believes, however, that "Kennedy's foreign policy stance was given an added fillip in late 1962 following his dramatic success" in the Cuban missile crisis. Vietnam then provided an opportunity to prove to Peking and Moscow that their policy of "wars of liberation" was dangerous and unpromising, and also "provided both a challenge and an opportunity to test the new doctrines" of counterinsurgency.[76] Thus whether the United States stance with respect to its great-power rival is defensive or not, the determination to win in Indochina is fortified.

It is, I believe, reasonable to attribute the increasing irrationality of United States Indochina policy in the 1960s at least in part to the influx of technical intelligentsia into Washington and the expansion of the state role in the system of militarized state capitalism that has been evolving in the United States since World War II. The primary allegiance of the technical intelligentsia is to the state and its power, rather than to the specific interests of private capital, insofar as these interests can be distinguished. Furthermore, the claim of the technical intelligentsia to a share in power rests on their alleged expertise. For this reason, it is difficult for them to concede error or to shape state policy in terms of a pragmatic calculation of interests, once a commitment has been made to a particular policy. By admitting error, they concede that their claim to power was fraudulent. These problems are not faced in the same measure by someone whose authority is based on his role in controlling private empires or on an aristocratic heritage. If his policies founder and his judgments prove erroneous, his right to power is not correspondingly diminished and he is therefore somewhat more free to terminate an enterprise that is wasteful, failing, or indecisive.

By early 1964, concern over the effects of the "loss" of South Vietnam reached a peak of what can perhaps properly be called "hysteria." In the analyst's phrase, referring to the February deliberations, "Stopping Hanoi from aiding the Viet Cong virtually became equated with protecting U.S. interests against the threat of insurgency throughout the world" (III, 153). Ralph Stavins hardly exaggerates when he describes the "clouds on the horizon" as seen from Washington in the early 1960s: "Hanoi would overthrow Diem with a few guerrilla bands, and the United States, as a direct consequence, would be forced to retire from the arena of world politics."[77] Such fears were incorporated into the important NSAM 288 of March 1964, which presented what the analyst calls "a classic statement of the domino theory" (III, 3). Throughout the world, it held, "the South Vietnam conflict is regarded as a test case of U.S. capacity to help a nation to meet the Communist 'war of liberation.' Thus, purely in terms of foreign policy, the stakes are high. . . ." The memorandum stated in clear terms that "we seek an independent non-Communist South Vietnam" free to accept outside—meaning American—assistance, including "police and military help to root out and control insurgent elements." And it stated that unless we can achieve this objective, "almost all of Southeast Asia will probably fall under Communist dominance" or "accommodate to Communism," with an increased threat to India, Australia, and Japan and indeed throughout the world, given that the conflict is a "test case" (III, 50–1; II, 459–61). Although these views were modulated later on (cf. III, 220, 658), the essential idea of South Vietnam as a "test case" remained, and the commitment to a noncommunist South Vietnam was never modified.

Despite the hyperbole, the rational core of policy making remained in the early 1960s, and in fact can even be detected in the exaggerated doctrine of Vietnam as a "test case." In one sense, Vietnam was indeed to serve as a test case. Developing countries were to be taught a harsh lesson. They must observe the rules of the international system as determined by the powerful—who, like many a stern disciplinarian, saw themselves as benign, even noble in intention. Developing countries must not undertake "national liberation" on the

Chinese model, extricating themselves from the international system dominated by Western and Japanese state capitalism, with mass mobilization, a focus on internal needs, and exploitation of material and human resources for internal development. If they are so foolhardy as to disobey the international rules, they will be subjected to subversion, blockade, or even outright destruction by the global judge and executioner.

The problem of Japan continued to be a serious though much less central issue. In November 1964 an important NSC working group, considering the problem of escalation, discussed "the effect on Japanese attitudes through any development that appears to make Communist China and its allies a dominant force in Asia that must be lived with." They already perceived a danger that Japan would move towards closer ties with Communist China, and "the growing feeling that Communist China must somehow be lived with might well be accentuated" if the United States were not to prevail in Indochina (III, 623, 627; William Bundy's draft). It is important, in short, that Japan not accommodate to China or drift towards a readiness to live with China. Again in June 1965, William Bundy warned of the importance of considering Japanese views in choosing policy, for fear that Japan may turn to "accommodation and really extensive relationships with Communist China" (IV, 614). We know from other sources that in the 1950s Japan was pressured to break trade relations with China, and that access to Southeast Asia was explicitly offered as an inducement.[78] Japan's need for markets was also an important consideration for President Kennedy.[79] It must, of course, be kept in mind that Japan in those years was not generally perceived as an immediate rival; in fact, until 1965 Japan always had an unfavorable trade balance with the United States.[80] Japan was perceived as a potential threat if it drifted from the United States global system and began to "live with" China.

Failure to appreciate the historical circumstances and the range of options actually available to policy makers sometimes leads to superficial commentary on this matter. For example, Charles Kindleberger argues that Japan is a "difficult counter-example" to the theory that American economic foreign policy is motivated by self-interest,[81] specifically to the theory that "foreign aid to less developed countries is to keep these countries dependent" and that United States policies "are designed to use the dollar as a main instrument of control over the capitalist world." Putting aside the question whether the theory is defensible, consider the logic of Kindleberger's argument: why does he regard Japan as a "difficult counterexample"? His reason is that Japan has been assisted by the United States in various ways but is not "a puppet of the United States." By the same logic, we can prove that Soviet aid to China and Rumania was not granted out of self-interest. In fact, Kindleberger's argument holds only on the further assumption that the United States is omnipotent: on this assumption, if American aid is intended to induce some nation to remain within the American-dominated system, then that nation must be a puppet; and if the nation is not a puppet, it follows that American assistance cannot have been intended as a device to maintain control or influence.

In the real world, United States policy makers faced a rather different problem. They had a variety of means at hand to influence postwar Japanese development towards integration into the "free world" system. A possible alternative, which they successfully overcame, was that "the workshop of the Pacific" might undergo revolutionary social change or "accommodate" to the closed systems developing in East Asia (cf. NSC 48/1, discussed above). The option of guaranteeing that Japan would be "a puppet" was not available; whether it would have been chosen had it been feasible is another question.[82]

The results are a mixed blessing to American capital—bad for textiles and a bonanza for oil interests, to mention two examples—but surely preferable to the perceived alternatives. In any event, once Kindleberger's untenable implicit hypothesis is removed, the "difficult counterexample" becomes quite manageable. Reasonable discussion of the matter is impeded by a kind of paranoia that is developing about "Japan, Inc." For example, Zbigniew Brzezinski, in an article which is critical of such exaggeration, nevertheless predicts that Japan will seek to "exclude" computers from its liberalization policy on foreign investment, failing to mention that a wholly owned subsidiary of IBM, IBM Japan, has an estimated 40 percent share of the Japanese computer market (apart from other arrangements between American and Japanese companies in the computer fields).[83] In fact, Japanese liberalization is proceeding, and if the outcome of the competition between American and Japanese capital may be in doubt, it should not be forgotten that quite apart from questions of scale, the United States holds many cards—for example, control of most of Japan's sources of petroleum.[84] Prior to the full-scale United States invasion of South Vietnam, with its vast and unanticipated costs, it was quite reasonable to suppose that Japan would remain for some time a reasonably well-behaved junior partner in the American-dominated system.

Perhaps a word might be added with regard to the commonly heard argument that the costs of the Vietnam war prove that the United States has no imperial motives (as the costs of the Boer War prove that the British Empire was a figment of the radical imagination). The costs, of course, are profits for selected segments of the American economy, in large measure. It is senseless to describe government expenditures for petroleum, jet planes, cluster bombs, or computers for the automated air war simply as "costs of intervention." There are, to be sure, costs of empire that benefit no one: 50,000 American corpses or the deterioration in the strength of the United States economy relative to its industrial rivals. The costs of empire to the imperial society as a whole may be considerable. These costs, however, are social costs, whereas, say, the profits from overseas investment guaranteed by military success are again highly concentrated in certain special segments of the society. The costs of empire are in general distributed over the society as a whole, while its profits revert to a few within. In this respect, the empire serves as a device for internal consolidation of power and privilege,[85] and it is quite irrelevant to observe that its social costs are often great or that as costs rise, differences may also arise among those who are in positions of power and influence. While serving as a device for internal consolidation of privilege, the empire also provides markets, guaranteed sources of inexpensive raw materials, a cheap labor market, opportunities for export of pollution (no small matter for Japan, for example), and investment opportunities. On the assumptions of the domino theory, even in its more rational versions, the stakes in Vietnam in this regard were considerable.

The same fallacy is one of several that undermine the familiar argument that our economic stake in the third world is too slight a fraction of the gross national product to play any significant role in motivating Third World interventions.[86] The private interests that stand to gain from foreign intervention are undeterred by its social costs and will exert their often substantial influence to engage state power in support of their aims, irrespective of the percentage of GNP at stake. Quite apart from this, it is in general impossible to uncouple economic interests in the Third World from those in industrial societies, as the case of Vietnam clearly illustrates, with the long-standing concern of the policy makers over the fate of the farther dominoes such as Japan, and in the early stages, the relationship to the critical problem of reconstructing Western European capitalism (cf. the matter of Malayan dollar-earning capacity, noted above, p. 41; or the matter of French unwillingness to accept West Germany as an unrestricted participant in a Western alliance prior to successful reconstruction of the French imperial system).

Still, it might very well be true that had the costs been anticipated, the Vietnam venture would not have been undertaken. But in the real world, policy makers do not operate with a knowledge of ultimate costs and cannot begin all over again if plans go awry. At each point, they consider the costs and benefits of future acts. On these grounds, the Vietnam involvement might very well have seemed reasonable within the framework of imperialist motives, though by the 1960s, with the influx to Washington of ideologists and crisis managers, it can be argued that other and more irrational considerations came to predominate.

Furthermore, even now that the bill is in, the effort might be judged a moderate success for those segments of American society that have a major interest in preserving an "integrated global system" in which American capital can operate with reasonable freedom. Consider the assessment of the editor of the *Far Eastern Economic Review*, generally committed to economic liberalism. He speaks of "the ring of success stories in East and Southeast Asia," with the Japanese economy serving as "the main factor in pulling the region together and providing the shadowy outlines of a future co-prosperity sphere . . . and neatly complement[ing]" the economies of the rest of the region. "The U.S. presence in Vietnam," in his view, "has won time for Southeast Asia, allowing neighbouring countries to build up their economies and their sense of identity to a degree of stability which has equipped them to counter subversion, to provide a more attractive alternative to the peasant than the promises of the terrorist who steals down from the hills or from the jungles at night"—or on different ideological premises, allowing these countries to become more securely absorbed within the neocolonial global system. Whatever premises one adopts, the fact is that "American businessmen . . . are convinced of the potential of Asia and the Pacific Basin as the world's third largest and fastest growing market area," and are moving rapidly into the region, a process that is continuing "since the initiation of 'Vietnamisation'." American investments now total nearly 70 percent of all foreign investments in the region.[87]

The imperial drive that is clearly expressed in many documents may have been blunted by the unexpected resilience and obstinacy of the Vietnamese resistance. Nevertheless, it has partially achieved its aims, though in retrospect it might be argued that other means would perhaps have been more efficacious.

To be sure, the imperial drive is often masked in defensive terms: it is not that we are seeking to dominate an integrated world system incorporating Western Europe and Japan, but rather that we must deny strategic areas to the Kremlin (or "Peiping"), thus protecting ourselves and others from their "aggression." The masters of the Russian empire affect a similar pose, no doubt with equal sincerity and with as much justification. The practice has respectable historical antecedents, and the term "security" is a conventional euphemism. The planners merely seek to guarantee the security of the nation, not the interests of dominant social classes.

There is, in fact, a sense in which the "defensive" rhetoric is appropriate. It is natural for the managers of the world's most advanced industrial superpower, organized more or less along capitalist lines, to seek free and open competition throughout the world in fair confidence that the interests they represent will tend to predominate. Thus they seek only to deny various areas to closed systems, national or imperial. The United States, like Britain in the period of its world dominance, tends towards the "imperialism of free trade," while maintaining the practice of state intervention for the benefit of special interests and demanding special rights (as in the Philippines) where they can be obtained.[88]

Many commentators deny that United States policy was determined or even influenced by long-term imperial objectives, and argue that the Pentagon Papers reveal no imperial drive. A case can be made for this view, specifically in the 1960s. Leslie Gelb makes the interesting point that "no systematic or serious examination of Vietnam's importance to the United States was ever undertaken within the government."[89] He attributes the persistence of the Vietnam venture, in the face of this oversight, to multiple factors: the stranglehold of cold-war assumptions, bureaucratic judgments, anticommunism as a force in American politics and other domestic pressures, and so on.[90] He points out that although the view that "Vietnam had intrinsic strategic military and economic importance" was argued, it never prevailed; properly, of course, since Vietnam has no such *intrinsic* importance. Rather its importance derives from the assumptions of the domino theory, in his formulation the theory "by which the fall of Indochina would lead to the deterioration of American security around the globe." "It was ritualistic anticommunism and exaggerated power politics that got us into Vietnam," he maintains, noting that these "articles of faith" were never seriously debated (*New York Review*). Nor, we may add, is there any record of a debate or analysis of just how American "security" would be harmed by a victory of the Communist-led nationalist movement of Indochina, or just what components of "American security" would be harmed by the triumph of a nationalist movement which, it was expected, would be hostile to China and would limit its ambitions to Laos and Cambodia (see p. 34 above).

Hannah Arendt has discussed a variety of rather different irrational factors that impelled policy makers in Vietnam.[91] "The ultimate aim," she concludes, "was neither power nor profit . . . [nor] particular tangible interests," but rather "image making," "something new in the huge arsenal of human follies." "American policy pursued no real aims, good or bad, that could limit and control sheer fantasy," in particular no imperial strategy. Ignorance, blind anticommunism, arrogance, and self-deception lie behind American policy. She is certainly correct in noting these elements in the Pentagon history. Thus in the face of all historical evidence, the American authorities persisted in the assumption, a point of rigid doctrine, that China was an agent of Moscow, the Viet Cong an agency of North Vietnam, which was in turn the puppet of Moscow or "Peiping" or both, depending on the mood of the planners and propagandists, who surely had more than enough information at hand to refute these assumptions, or at the very least to shake their confidence in them. A kind of institutionalized stupidity seems a possible explanation.

There is ample material in the Pentagon Papers to support such interpretations, from the time when Dean Acheson, in a cable to Saigon, spoke of the need to aid the French and the Associated States of Indochina "to defend the territorial integrity of IC and prevent the incorporation of the ASSOC[iated] States within the COMMIE-dominated bloc of slave states" (I, 70; October 1950), and on to the present. One of the most remarkable revelations of the Pentagon study is that the analysts were able to discover only one staff paper, in a record of more than two decades, "which treats communist reactions primarily in terms of the separate national interests of Hanoi, Moscow, and Peiping, rather than primarily in terms of an overall communist strategy for which Hanoi is acting as an agent" (II, 107; an intelligence estimate of November 1961). Even in the "intelligence community," where they are paid to get the facts straight and not to rant about helping the French defend the territorial integrity of Indochina from its people and the Commie-dominated bloc of slave states, it was apparently next to impossible to perceive, or at least express the simple truth, that North Vietnam, like the Soviet Union, China, the United States, and the NLF, has its own interests, which are often decisive.

It is amusing to trace the efforts to establish that Ho Chi Minh was merely a Russian (or Chinese) puppet—as obviously must be the case. The State Department, in July 1948, could find "no evidence of direct link between Ho and Moscow" (but naturally "assumes it exists").[92] State Department intelligence, in the fall, found evidence of "Kremlin-directed conspiracy . . . in virtually all countries except Vietnam." Indochina appeared "an anomaly." How can this be explained? To intelligence, the most likely explanation is that "no rigid directives have been issued by Moscow" or that "a special dispensation for the Vietnam government has been arranged in Moscow" (I, 5, 34). In September 1948, the State Department noted: "There continues to be no known communication between the USSR and Vietnam, although evidence is accumulating that a radio liaison may have been established through the Tass agency in Shanghai" (*DOD*, bk. 8, p. 148, grasping at straws). American officials in Saigon added: "No evidence has yet turned up that Ho Chi Minh is receiving current directives either from Moscow, China, or the Soviet Legation in Bangkok." "It may be assumed," they conclude from this, "that Moscow feels that Ho and his lieutenants have had sufficient training and experience and are sufficiently loyal to be trusted to determine their day-to-day policy without supervision" (p. 151). By February 1949, they were relieved to discover that "Moscow publications of fairly recent date are frequently seized by the French," indicating that "satisfactory communications exist," though the channel remains a mystery (p. 168); also, "there has been surprising[ly] little direct cooperation between local Chinese Communists and the Viet Minh."

"We are unable to determine whether Peiping or Moscow has ultimate responsibility for Viet Minh policy," an intelligence estimate of June 1953 relates (I, 396), but it must be one or the other—that is an axiom. In the context of a discussion of Chinese Communist strategy, Intelligence concludes that the Communists are pursuing their present strategy in Indochina because it "diverts badly needed French and US resources from Europe at relatively small cost to the Communists" and "provides opportunities to advance international Communist interests while preserving the fiction of 'autonomous' national liberation movements, and it provides an instrument, the Viet Minh, with which Communist China and the USSR can indirectly exert military and psychological pressures on the peoples and governments of Laos, Cambodia, and Thailand" (I, 399). Might there be another reason why the Viet Minh fight on?

It is tempting to use such evidence to support the claim that ignorance, mythology, and institutionalized stupidity led United States policy makers into a series of disastrous errors. If only they had realized that Stalin was lukewarm or negative towards Mao and the Greek guerrillas, that there was no "pattern of Communist conquest . . . manifest" in Guatemala in 1954,[93] that the Vietnamese were conducting their own struggle for national liberation. If only William Bundy had had a course in Vietnamese history at Yale. But ignorance and paranoia obscured the facts.

This theory, however, leaves too many questions unanswered. To mention only the simplest: Why were policy makers always subject to the same form of ignorance and irrationality? Why was there such a systematic error in the delusional systems constructed by postwar ideologists? Mere ignorance or foolishness would lead to random error, not to a regular and systematic distortion: unwavering adherence[94] to the principle that whatever the facts may be, the cause of international conflict is the behavior of the Communist powers, and all revolutionary movements within the United States system are sponsored by the Soviet Union, China, or both.[95] Why was the latter assumption so far beyond challenge that no examination of Vietnam's importance was ever undertaken (Gelb)? Ignorance and stupidity can surely lead to error, but hardly to such systematic error or such certainty in error. And there is a second and even more obvious question: Why is the United States anticommunist?

With respect to the first question, whether it is Acheson, Rostow, Stevenson, Kissinger, or whoever, one generally finds the same distortion as in the sorry record of the "intelligence community." From one or another such source we hear that Stalin supported Mao and incited the Greek guerrillas and Ho Chi Minh, China attacked India, the Viet Cong are agents of international Communist aggression, and so on. These are, indeed, articles of faith. The crisis managers do not argue these claims; they merely intone them. All are at best highly dubious and probably false, so the available record indicates, but questions of fact are beside the point in theological disputation.

What is not beside the point is that these articles of faith are highly functional. The fact is that anticommunism provides a convenient mythology to justify colonial wars, and to gain the popular support that is often hard to rally, given the grisly nature and substantial costs of such endeavors. But to explain the United States attack on Vietnam on grounds of anticommunist delusions would be as superficial as explaining the Russian invasion of Czechoslovakia or Hungary merely on grounds of fear of West Germany or Wall Street. No doubt at some level the Soviet leadership believes what it says and is bewildered at the bitter reaction to its selfless and benevolent behavior. Perhaps Russian public opinion indeed "is proud of its country's armed power in Prague and speaks of Czechoslovak weakness, ingratitude, irresponsibility, etc."[96] Similarly, Washington claims to be defending democracy and warding off "internal aggression" or subversion by agents of international communism when it helps to destroy a mass popular movement in Greece, supports an invasion of Guatemala, invades the Dominican Republic, and devastates the peasant societies of Indochina. Its defenders, and many critics as well, are at most willing to concede error if the costs mount too high, and cannot conceive that any "responsible" or "qualified" observer might have a rather different view. Some still insist that for the most part the United States pursues its foreign policy "for reformist, even utopian goals," and that this policy can be faulted only for being "callow, sentimental, savagely stupid . . . too little the work of an intellectually serious leadership."[97] It is remarkable how difficult it is, even for those who see themselves as critics, to interpret United States behavior by the standards of evaluation and analysis that would, properly, be applied to any other great power.

The fact that policy makers may be caught up in the fantasies they spin to disguise imperial intervention, and may sometimes even find themselves trapped by them, should not prevent us from asking what function these ideological constructions fulfill—why *this* particular system of mystification is consistently expounded in place of some alternative. Similarly, one should not be misled by the fact that the delusional system presents a faint reflection of reality. It must, after all, carry some conviction. But this should not prevent us from proceeding to disentangle motive from myth.

The efforts of the "intelligence community" to establish the thesis that the Viet Minh were agents of international communism reveal quite clearly the function of the "international Communist conspiracy" in postwar American foreign policy. There is no doubt that the Soviet Union, within the limits of its power, established its harsh and oppressive imperial rule. But it was not this fact that determined American policy in Southeast Asia. Contrary to the fantasies of Walt Rostow (see note 192) and others, the United States did not first discover that the Viet Minh were agents of a Kremlin-directed conspiracy and then proceed to help France beat back Russian aggression against Southeast Asia. Rather, the United States merely applied in Indochina the general policy of establishing Western-oriented regimes that would cooperate ("freely") with the West and Japan, "culturally, economically, and politically," and "contribute to a better balanced world economy"—the "world economy" in question being, of course, that of the "free world" (cf. p. 33 above). In its essentials, the policy was not fundamentally different from, say, American policy in Italy in 1943, or in Greece and Korea shortly after.[98] To implement this policy in Vietnam, it was necessary to destroy the forces that had "captured the nationalist movement," since these forces had a different model of social and economic development in mind. But this would have appeared too cynical, if stated frankly. Therefore it was necessary to recast the issue in "defensive" terms, and to establish that these nationalist forces were really the agents of aggression by an international conspiracy, aimed ultimately at destroying the freedom of the United States itself. The "intelligence community" thus was assigned the task of demonstrating the thesis that was required as the ideological underpinning of the American intervention. It is interesting, but not very surprising given the background, that the failure of intelligence to establish the needed link in no way impeded the ideologists, who simply continued to insist that the required thesis was correct, accepting and proclaiming it as an article of faith. The same pattern has appeared elsewhere, with predictable regularity.

Turning to the second question: Why is the United States anticommunist? A conventional answer is that the United States opposes communism because of its aggressive, expansionist character. Thus it is argued that we do not seek to overthrow communism where it represents the status quo, as in Eastern Europe; and that when President Kennedy, in an often-quoted remark, said that we would always prefer a Trujillo to a Castro,[99] he meant that "the power requirements of the struggle with the Soviet Union took precedence over the commitment to a 'decent democratic regime.'" As to China:

> The containment of China has not been pursued simply because China has a communist government, but because of China's outlook generally and her policy in Asia particularly. It is China's insistence upon changing the Asian status quo, and the methods she has used, that explain American hostility.[100]

Such proposals cannot withstand analysis. It is true, but irrelevant, that the United States will not risk nuclear destruction to roll back communism; again, one should not overlook the objective limits on American power. Tucker's interpretation of Kennedy's remark seems to presuppose that American hostility towards Castro was a consequence of his turn towards the Soviet Union, which is of course untrue. Perhaps one can argue that American hostility was not a determining factor in this move, but that it preceded it is beyond argument.[101] With respect to China, Tucker's argument is weaker still. What methods did China use in changing the status quo beyond its borders? In what respect were these methods "objectionable" in comparison with American methods in the Far East? In what sense was the forceful reimposition of French colonialism, in opposition to a Communist-led Vietnamese nationalist movement, an attempt to preserve the status quo after World War II? Why the effort to demonstrate that the Vietnamese revolutionaries—or the backers of Arbenz or Bosch—were Russian or Chinese agents, despite the evidence at hand, leading ultimately to the religious faith that this must be so? The answers to these questions entirely undermine Tucker's effort to "explain American hostility."

Tucker is in fact mistaken about what counts as an explanation of policy. He is nearer the mark when he points out that Castro "would refuse to do our bidding" and "would stand as a challenge to our otherwise undisputed hegemony in this hemisphere," but he does not pursue these observations to the degree of specificity that any serious discussion of policy must achieve. In what respects would Cuba refuse to do our bidding and challenge our hegemony? This question Tucker does not answer, or even pose. He says merely that "America's interventionist and counterrevolutionary policy . . . may be accounted for in terms of a reasonably well-grounded fear that the American example might become irrelevant to much of the world," along with the "will to exercise dominion over others." Tucker is in error when he states that "a radical critique cannot *consistently* accept this explanation."[102] It would, however, be quite accurate to say that no serious critique can accept such proposals *as an explanation of policy*. Rather, any serious critique will pursue the matter further, asking what elements of "the American example" a foreign society must adopt to allay these fears. Was it fear that Guatemala would choose soccer rather than baseball as its national sport that precipitated the 1954 intervention? Was the Bay of Pigs invasion rooted in the fear that Cuban intellectuals would prefer Continental phenomenology to American-style analytic philosophy? Is it our concern that the model of American political democracy might prove "irrelevant" that explains why the United States executive so prefers Brazil to Chile under Allende? Again, a serious look at real historical examples reveals at once the emptiness of Tucker's proposals. He believes himself to be offering a more cogent alternative to a "radical critique," whereas in fact he is offering no alternative at all, but merely abstracting away from the particular specific questions that must be faced by any serious effort, radical or not, to explain the American policy of counterrevolutionary intervention.

Tucker's failure to come to grips with the real problems follows a familiar pattern. It is commonly argued that American interventionism is not attributable to the normal workings of state capitalism, but to some deeper motive, such as the "drive for power." The reasoning is shoddy, and it is important to see why. The failure of the argument does not lie in the identification of the "power drive" as the cause of imperialist intervention; this premise is sufficiently vague so that we can grant it to be true without fear of refutation. Rather, the argument fails because it does not recognize that a generalization is not refuted by rephrasing it in terms that are logically equivalent, or even by tracing it to deeper theses from which it derives. Thus suppose one were to argue that the normal behavior of a businessman is not governed by the pursuit of profit (or, say, growth, assuming this to be an empirically distinguishable thesis), but rather by a "deeper" drive for power. Again, we may accept the claim that the normal behavior of the businessman is explained by a drive for power, which manifests itself in a capitalist society in the pursuit of profit. This claim merely restates, and does not contradict, the hypothesis that the behavior of a businessman in a capitalist society is governed by the pursuit of profit.

Much the same is true of the vague musings about a "generalized drive for power" which often appear in discussions of American foreign policy. It may well be true that any autocratic system of rule will support and intensify the "drive for power" and give it free rein. In a capitalist society, the operative form of autocratic rule is the private control of the means of production and resources, of commerce and finance, and further, the significant influence on state policy of those who rule the private economy, and who indeed largely staff the government. Elements of the private autocracy who have a specific concern with foreign affairs will naturally tend to use their power and influence to direct state policy for the benefit of the interests they represent. Where they succeed, we have imperialist intervention, quite commonly.

It might be argued that a healthy democracy would impede imperial planners, for two reasons: in the first place, considerations of self-interest would serve as a brake on imperial ventures with their often substantial social cost; and secondly, a functioning democracy might foster other values beyond domination and power—solidarity, sympathy, cooperative impulses, a concern for creative and useful work, and so on. The prevailing ideology tends to downgrade and scoff at such motives, often appealing to the alleged discoveries of the "behavioral sciences," but this farce need not detain us here (see chapter 7). The important point is that the resort to a "power drive" as the explanation of imperial intervention is not false, but irrelevant, once its true character is laid bare. It is fair, I think, to suggest that this "alternative explanation" merely serves as a form of mystification; it serves to obscure the actual workings of power.

The question remains: Why is American ideology and policy anticommunist? Or a further question: Why has the United States been antifascist (though selectively)? Why was fascist Japan evil in 1940, while fascist Greece and Portugal (preserving the status quo with American arms in Africa) are quite tolerable today? And why is the United States generally anticolonialist, as in Indonesia shortly after World War II, when the conservative nationalist leadership appeared at first to favor foreign investment, but (reluctantly) not in Indochina, where the alternative to a barely disguised French colonialism was an indigenous Communist resistance?

It is not too difficult to discern a criterion that serves rather well to determine which elements in foreign lands receive support and which are labeled enemies. It is surely not the humanitarian impulse (see p. 62 below); nor is it the prospects for development that determine the official United States response: China or Cuba might well have profited from capital grants for development—more so, at least, than from blockade, invasion, and harassment. Nor is it the fear of our great-power rivals that leads us to intervene halfway around the world, as is plainly shown by the determined effort to prove that Russia and China were responsible for the "internal aggression" in Vietnam, in the face of the evidence that they were not, and analogous efforts in the Caribbean and elsewhere. Nor do democratic or authoritarian rule, bloodthirstiness, aggressiveness, or a threat to United States security (in the proper sense of the term) provide a plausible criterion. Brazil and South Africa are as vicious as they come. The horrendous Indonesian massacre of 1965 was greeted with calm. China has been the least aggressive of the great powers.

The Viet Minh and the Pathet Lao are hardly a threat to United States security. Fascist Japan was no doubt an aggressive power—in some ways, not unlike the United States today[103]—but the United States was prepared to seek a *modus vivendi* in 1939 provided that its rights and interests on the mainland were guaranteed. And fascist Greece is quite all right today; it plays its NATO role, provides bases for American naval forces,[104] and as an added attraction there is—as Secretary of Commerce Maurice Stans put it so lyrically not long ago—"the welcome that is given here to American companies and the sense of security the Government of Greece is imparting to them."[105]

Friends and enemies can be identified, to a rather good first approximation, in terms of their role in maintaining an integrated global economy in which American capital can operate with relative freedom. The so-called "Communist" powers are particularly evil because their "do-it-yourself" model of development tends to extricate them from this system. For this reason, even European colonialism, which was bad enough, is preferable to indigenous communism. For the same reason, Washington will prefer a Trujillo to a Castro.

The study group of the Woodrow Wilson Foundation and the National Planning Association was perceptive, and more honest than many contemporary ideologists, when it described the primary threat of communism as the economic transformation of the Communist powers "in ways which reduce their willingness and ability to complement the industrial economies of the West,"[106] their refusal to play the game of comparative advantage and to rely primarily on foreign investment for development. If the "developing nations" choose to use their resources for their own purposes, or to carry out internal social change in ways which will reduce their contribution to the industrial economies of the state capitalist world, these powers must be prepared to employ sufficient force to prevent such unreasonable behavior, which will no doubt be described as aggression by agents of international communism. The Soviet Union reacts no differently when Czechoslovakia seeks a degree of independence or social change.

At a much different level of domination, British auto workers must not be permitted to demand too great economic benefits or a share in management in the Ford plant, and must remain subject to the threats that can be wielded quite effectively by an international corporation.[107] In East Asia, which many regard as a most promising region for the "internationalization of production" as well as for supplying raw materials (see chapter 4), the problems will be particularly acute. Surely such considerations lie at the very core of American foreign policy. Though they are far from the sole operative factors in United States policy, and are often overwhelmed by the impact of ideological commitments which themselves grow out of such concerns, it is surely the beginning of wisdom to recognize their crucial role.

It is often maintained that United States policy is motivated by a commitment to political democracy. To test the force of this concern, we can consider how United States policy typically evolves when political democracy is destroyed, while American economic intervention is freed from constraints— and we can compare such policy with the typical United States reaction when an economy is closed to American economic penetration, whether or not political democracy is more or less maintained. Latin America provides an ample set of test cases. Considering American policy towards Brazil and Chile, Guatemala for the past two decades, the Dominican Republic in 1965, and so on, there can be little doubt as to the outcome of such an investigation. Gordon Connel-Smith puts the matter in terms that seem quite adequate:

> . . . United States concern for representative democracy in Latin America is a facet of her anti-communist policy. There has been no serious question of her intervening in the case of the many right-wing military coups, from which, of course, this policy generally has benefited. It is only when her own concept of democracy, closely identified with private, capitalistic enterprise, is threatened by communism that she has felt impelled to demand collective action to defend it.[108]

Those who are called upon to implement and defend United States policy are often quite frank about the matter. The director of USAID for Brazil, to take one recent and very important case, explains clearly that protection of a favorable investment climate for private business interests is a primary

United States objective. To be sure, he mentions other objectives as well: our "humanitarian interests" and our "security objectives." As to our humanitarian interests, they seem a bit selective, and correlate remarkably well with "the protection and expansion, if possible, of our economic interests, trade and investment, in the hemisphere."[109] Thus our humanitarian interests in Brazil, as measured by the aid program, showed a marked upsurge after the April 1964 "revolution" which, among other achievements, overcame the "administrative obstacles to remittance of income developed under the Goulart regime" (pp. 185–7, 215). Another achievement that correlated with the vast flow of aid was the rise of private investment from 50 percent to 75 percent of total investment.[110]

Or perhaps our humanitarian interests, as measured by the aid flow, were stirred by the incidence of state violence and torture in Brazil under the new regime, or by the significant decline in the share of GNP of the bottom 80 percent of the population,[111] and the reported decline in wages for most workers that accompanied the significant rise in production under "a dictatorship, established to protect the privileges of a small property-owning class and to assure the growing control of the nation's economy by imperialistic interests."[112] As for the security objectives, the fear that Brazil under Goulart posed a security threat to the United States seems a bit farfetched; and as far as Brazil itself is concerned, the military perceive no external threat to the country,[113] so that the extensive American military aid is clearly either for "internal security"—that is, protection from its own population of the regime whose acts have so awakened our humanitarian concerns—or for threats against Brazil's neighbors, in particular those neighbors who might choose to jeopardize the closely related economic interests of the Brazilian privileged elite and American investors. We are, I am afraid, reduced to the first objective: the protection and expansion of "our" economic interests in the hemisphere.

Before we attribute this or that misadventure to "blind anticommunism," we would do well to distinguish several varieties of anticommunism. Opposition to indigenous movements that might pursue the so-called Communist model of development, extricating their societies from the international capitalist system, is not "blind anticommunism," strictly speaking. It may be "anticommunism," but it is far from blind. Rather, it is rational imperialism which seeks to prevent the erosion of the world system dominated by Western and Japanese capital. On the other hand, reference to a "coordinated offensive directed by the Kremlin" against Southeast Asia in 1949 (NSC 48/1) or to the "militant and aggressive expansionist policy advocated by the present rulers of Communist China" (George Carver of the CIA; IV, 82; April 1966) is indeed blind anticommunism—or to be more precise, it is perhaps blind, but it is not anticommunism at all. Rather, it is pure imperial ideology, beyond the reach of evidence or debate, a propaganda device to rally support for military intervention against indigenous Communist-led movements. (The device is no doubt useful for the self-image of the policy makers themselves.) In Vietnam, the first form of anticommunism motivated United States intervention, while the second was called upon to justify it—as elsewhere, repeatedly.

It may be argued, with justice, that this view is no more than a first approximation to a general understanding of foreign policy, and that it omits many second-order considerations. Thus it would not be correct to claim that formation of foreign policy is in the interests of a monolithic corporate elite. On the contrary, there are conflicting interests. But we would expect to find—and do find—that those interests that are particularly concerned with foreign policy are well represented in its formation.[114] By similar dynamics, regulatory agencies tend to fall into the hands of industries that are particularly concerned with their decisions. It is, furthermore, no doubt true that at some point ideology takes on a motive force of its own. There are other interacting and for the most part mutually supportive factors: the interest of the "state management" in the Pentagon in enhancing its own power;[115] the role of government-induced production of rapidly obsolescing luxury goods (largely military) as a technique of economic management, with a resulting need to secure strategic raw materials; the usefulness of an external enemy as a device to whip the taxpayer into line, in support of the production of waste and the costs of empire; the heady sense of power, to which academic ideologues in particular seem to succumb so readily. Such factors as these produce a fairly stable system to support the basic imperial drive, which is second nature to the men of power in the state executive in any event.[116] There are many specific factors that must be considered in a detailed examination of particular decisions, such as those that led us ever more deeply into Indochina. Nevertheless, it seems reasonably clear that American policy, like that of any great power, is guided by the "national interest" as conceived by dominant social groups, in this case, the primary goal of maximizing the free access by American capital to the markets and human and material resources of the world, the goal of maintaining to the fullest possible extent its freedom of operation in a global economy. At the same time, ideologists labor to mask these endeavors in a functional system of beliefs.

It is interesting that such analyses of foreign policy, which incorporate the material interests of private or quasi-private capital as a central factor interacting with others, are often characterized as "vulgar economic determinism" or the like when put forth by opponents of the system of private control of resources and the means of production. On the other hand, similar formulations receive little attention when they appear, as they commonly do, in official explanations of state policy. What is more, explanations that emphasize, say, vague emotional states, or ideological elements, or error, are not similarly characterized as "vulgar emotional (ideological) determinism" or "vulgar fallibilism."

The term "vulgar economic determinism" is particularly surprising, given that those segments of (quasi-) private capital that are particularly affected by foreign-policy decisions are generally well represented in the formation of state policy. One would therefore expect that the view mislabeled "vulgar economic determinism" would serve as a kind of null hypothesis. Since it is, furthermore, quite plausible as an explanation for basic foreign policy decisions (and not infrequently, the justification offered for them), the reaction becomes still more curious. The label too often serves to deflect attention from the proposed explanations, which are much easier to ignore when misrepresented. This is a standard reaction to analysis that raises questions about prevailing ideology. Compare much of the response to "revisionist" work on the cold war several years ago.[117] Many illustrations can be given; in fact, there is an interesting literary genre, worthy of investigation in itself, devoted to the refutation of nonexistent arguments attributed to "radicals"—such as argument that capitalism needs war to survive, or that the United States bears sole responsibility for the cold war.

It is possible to give some useful advice to an aspiring political analyst who wants his work received as thoughtful and penetrating—advice which surely applies to any society, not merely to ours. This analyst should first of all determine as closely as possible the actual workings of power in his society. Having isolated certain primary elements and a number of peripheral and insignificant ones, he should then proceed to dismiss the primary factors as unimportant, the province of extremists and ideologues. He should rather concentrate on the minor and peripheral elements in decision making. Better still, he should describe these in terms that appear to be quite general and independent of the social structure that he is discussing ("power drive," "fear of irrelevance," etc.). Where he considers policies that failed, he should attribute them to stupidity and ignorance, that is, to factors that are socially neutral. Or he may attribute the failures to noble impulses that led policy makers astray ("tragic irony"), or to the venality, ingratitude, and barbarism of subject peoples. He can then be fairly confident that he will escape the criticism that his efforts at explanation are "simplistic" (the truth is often surprisingly simple). He will, in short, benefit from a natural tendency on the part of the privileged in any society to suppress—for themselves as well as others—knowledge and understanding of the nature of their privilege and its manifestations.

In the particular case of Vietnam, anticommunism served as a convenient device for mobilizing the American people to support imperial intervention. After a time, they were no longer willing to bear the costs or were appalled at the consequences. At this point, the propaganda device, no longer effective, is discarded. We now hear laments about the cold-war myths that led us to a "Greek tragedy" in Vietnam. But the war goes on.

The motive force for the American war in Indochina lies, it seems to me, where it was located in the earliest internal documents of the state executive: in the perceived significance of Southeast Asia for the integrated global system that was to be organized by American power—and, under reasonable assumptions, dominated by American power for the primary benefit of those who possess that power. Although in the 1960s other and more irrational considerations may have come to predominate, nevertheless the continuing effort by the United States to achieve a Korea-type solution in Indochina, whatever the cost to its people, can still be traced in part to the same fundamental objectives.[118]

VI. THE MENTALITY OF THE BACKROOM BOYS

Perhaps the most significant contribution of the Pentagon study is the insight it provides into the mentality of the planners. Since there is no reason to expect changes in this regard in coming years, it is particularly important to examine the attitudes that are revealed by their decisions and debate.

1. The Bombing of North Vietnam

The callous disregard of the planners for the victims of American terror is illustrated, in a fairly typical way, when one of the backroom boys explains that a program of sustained bombing of the North "seems cheap," despite its higher cost in American casualties—particularly, since a reprisal policy "demonstrates U.S. willingness to employ this new norm in counter-insurgency." Thus it will "set a higher price for the future upon all adventures of guerrilla warfare, and it should therefore somewhat increase our ability to deter such adventures."[119] The importance of Operation ROLLING THUNDER (RT), the analyst explains, was that "breaking through the sanctuary barrier had been accomplished" (IV, 53). This was an important achievement, since the United States had previously been a staunch defender of the "sanctuary barrier," as when United Nations Ambassador Adlai Stevenson emphasized American disapproval of "retaliatory raids, wherever they occur and by whomever they are committed" after the

British raids against Yemen in reprisal for Yemeni attacks.[120]

But, it is important to add, though the "sanctuary barrier" was effectively broken, the genocide barrier still remained,[121] for reasons that are most informative. A CIA analysis of March 1966 explicitly recommended intensification of RT, directed largely against "the will of the regime as a target system." But agriculture and manpower as target systems were "not recommended at this time"—the genocide barrier stands. The sole reason is, "the effects are debatable and are likely to provoke hostile reactions in world capitals."[122] And John McNaughton urged:

> Strikes at population targets (per se) are likely not only to create a counterproductive wave of revulsion abroad and at home, but greatly to increase the risk of enlarging the war with China and the Soviet Union. Destruction of locks and dams, however—if handled right—might (perhaps after the *next* Pause) offer promise. It should be studied. Such destruction does not kill or drown people. By shallow-flooding the rice, it leads after time to widespread starvation (more than a million?) unless food is provided—which we could offer to do "at the conference table." [IV, 43]

This was January 18, 1966. A report of the air war at that time states that only eight locks and dams were targeted as "significant to inland waterways, flood control, or irrigation," and one had been hit and heavily damaged (IV, 56). There is no further information here on the follow-up, if any, to McNaughton's proposal that the United States engage in explicit war crimes of the sort punished after World War II.[123] The DRV, however, reports attacks on dams in Thanh Hoa Province (April 4, 1965; the Pentagon history reports only attacks on Thanh Hoa bridges from April 2–8; III, 285) and Nghe An Province (June 26–28, 1965, and many later occasions) and elsewhere.[124] These attacks increased sharply after 1965.[125] Eyewitness reports have occasionally appeared in the American press, and bombing of the irrigation and hydraulic system in South Vietnam has been frequently reported.[126] The Pentagon Papers contain no information on the latter, as on most aspects of the American war in South Vietnam.

What is interesting, in the present connection, is McNaughton's reason for not breaching the genocide barrier in

the North. Much the same considerations are stressed by
McNamara when he argues that bombing of population centers in the North should be avoided because of the risk that it
might precipitate Soviet or Chinese direct intervention and
"appall allies and friends" (IV, 28–9), a most unfortunate
consequence.

The analyst is under the illusion that "populated areas were
scrupulously avoided" in the North (IV, 18). This is nonsense, as any visitor to the DRV quickly discovers as soon as
he leaves Hanoi. The CIA estimated that by 1966, after
161,000 tons of bombs had fallen, there had been almost
30,000 civilian casualties (IV, 136). Note also that the figure
of 1,000 killed or seriously wounded a week, cited below, refers
to the bombing of North Vietnam. As early as December
1965, Bernard Fall reported that "at least one hospital [in
North Vietnam] had been completely destroyed by bombers,"
as "verified by non-Communist outside observers," and that
"Canadian officials who recently returned from North Viet-
Nam also told me that the city of Vinh was 'flattened' "—a
city of 60,000, he notes.[127] I myself have seen the ruins of
towns and villages not far from Hanoi and the remains of the
hospital in Thanh Hoa city, destroyed, according to the North
Vietnamese, in June 1965.[128] Testimony on this matter is by
now so voluminous that it is amazing, a real tribute to the
power of government propaganda, that one can still read that
the bombing of the North scrupulously kept to military
targets. The appalling destruction in the North, which has
suffered less than 10 percent of the total bombing through
1971 (and of course none of the still more destructive shelling,
apart from naval bombardment), is small only in comparison
with the accomplishments of our government elsewhere in
Indochina.

United States government propaganda has tried to give the
impression that aerial bombardment achieved near-surgical
accuracy, so that military targets could be destroyed with
minimal effect on civilians. Technical military documents give
a different picture. For example, Captain C. O. Holmquist
writes:

> One naturally wonders why so many bombing sorties are re-
> quired in order to destroy a bridge or other pinpoint target.

. . . However, with even the most sophisticated computer system, bombing by any mode remains an inherently inaccurate process, as is evident from our results to date in Vietnam. Aiming errors, boresight errors, system computational errors and bomb dispersion errors all act to degrade the accuracy of the system. Unknown winds at altitudes below the release point and the "combat degradation" factor add more errors to the process. In short, it is impossible to hit a small target with bombs except by sheer luck. Bombing has proved most efficient for area targets such as supply dumps, built-up areas, and cities.[129]

The American government claim that the bombing of North Vietnam was directed against military targets does not withstand direct investigation. But even if one were to accept it, considerations such as those mentioned by Captain Holmquist indicate that this was to a large extent a distinction without a difference.

Later, McNaughton and McNamara were to raise other objections to bombing.

The picture of the world's greatest superpower killing or seriously injuring 1000 non-combatants a week, while trying to pound a tiny backward nation into submission on an issue whose merits are hotly disputed, is not a pretty one. It could conceivably produce a costly distortion in the American national consciousness and in the world image of the United States—especially if the damage to North Vietnam is complete enough to be "successful." [IV, 172; 484]

The most important risk remains "the likely Soviet, Chinese and North Vietnamese reaction." The question whether there might conceivably be some other objection to killing or maiming 1,000 noncombatants a week, apart from its potential costs to us, is not raised.

The same logic underlies the CIA advocacy of an "unlimited campaign" as "the most promising" in January 1967 (IV, 139–40; analyst) but with the proviso that although "bombing the levee system which kept the Red River under control, if timed correctly, could cause large crop losses," nevertheless the military effects might be short-lived. A draft memo of the Clifford Group in March 1968 argued against "a change in our bombing policy to include deliberate strikes on population centers and attacks on the agricultural population through the destruction of dikes" on the sole grounds that this "would further alienate domestic and foreign sentiment" and might lose European and other support (IV, 251). For this reason, the genocide barrier must stand. Not that everyone agreed: see the proposals from CINCPAC (Commander in Chief, Pacific) and Air Force Secretary Harold Brown (IV, 261).

In an informative analysis of the management of the air war in the North, Ralph Stavins points out some differences, determined by interviews, among the planners. Paul Warnke "opposed the bombing to the hilt" and sought to restrict targets. According to Alvin Friedman of the Pentagon, he came "from a different geological age compared to the likes of McNaughton, M. Bundy, McNamara and Rusk." McNaughton, in particular, was quite uncritical in recommending targets. "Warnke himself said his disagreement with McNamara arose over the possibility that the bombing would draw the Communist superpowers into the war," throughout, a major factor in deterring all-out bombing of the major population centers.[130]

2. Military Operations in South Vietnam

South Vietnam, of course, has borne the brunt of the American attack in Indochina. As noted above, the facts of the American war in South Vietnam are barely discussed in the thousands of pages of documents and analyses, and, the record suggests, were not a matter of great interest or concern to the backroom boys. For example, from the analysis of United States ground strategy, the reader can learn that "in the estimation of the MACV staff [Operation CEDAR FALLS] gained outstanding results, capturing large numbers of weapons, ammunition and other war materials, plus nearly a half-million pages of enemy documents" and destroying the Iron Triangle as a "secure base area."[131] But he will have to look elsewhere to discover that for over a week before this operation, the windows of Saigon were rattling from concentrated B-52 raids in this settled area, or to learn the fate of the inhabitants of Ben Suc, forcibly evacuated from their demolished village to barren camps surrounded by barbed wire, with a sign at the entrance saying "Welcome to Freedom."[132]

On the rare occasions when questions were raised about the

United States attack on South Vietnam, the moral level of the analysis is on a par with the occasional qualms expressed about RT. For example, William Bundy (June 30, 1965) advocated that "our air actions against the South should be carried on a maximum effective rate," including "substantial use of B-52s against VC havens." He recognized only one problem: "we look silly and arouse criticism if these [B-52 raids] do not show significant results" (IV, 612). If the B-52 raids do show significant results, we may turn out to be mass murderers (since in the nature of the case, there could be at best partial information about the targets), but this appears to be no problem at all.[133]

As noted earlier, the Pentagon Papers contain virtually no record of the decision to bomb the South. Perhaps we are to infer that this, like the bombing of the North, was undertaken to raise the morale of the South Vietnamese population. The reader who finds this remark overly cynical may turn to II, 546, where a MACV monthly evaluation appears for February 1965: "*US/GVN strikes against DRV and increased use of U.S. jet aircraft in RVN* has had a salutary effect on both military and civilian morale which may result in a greater national effort and, *hopefully, reverse the downward trend*" (emphasis in original). Not a word on the character of the bombing, which was improving morale in South Vietnam by "literally pounding the place to bits" (see Bernard Fall, pp. 4–5 above). So effective was this pounding that McNamara, in a generally gloomy analysis of July 20, 1965, could at least point to the fact that "US/VNAF air strikes in-country have probably shaken VC morale somewhat" (IV, 620), an important matter given the high morale of the indigenous Viet Cong and the civilian society in which they were embedded.

This is not the place to review once again the bloodbath for which the United States is directly responsible in South Vietnam. To appreciate the scale, recall the estimates presented by Bernard Fall in April 1965—prior to the outright American invasion, prior to the introduction of any regular units of the North Vietnamese so far as Washington was aware: 66,000 Viet Cong killed between 1957 and 1961, that is, before the large-scale combat involvement of American air and helicopter forces (see note 4); 89,000 between 1961 and

April 1965.[134] McNamara estimated another 60,000 of the "enemy" killed by mid-1966 (IV, 348), overwhelmingly South Vietnamese and probably including many civilians (see p. 83 below). "The problem is that American machines are not equal to the task of killing communist soldiers except as part of a scorched-earth policy that destroys everything else as well," so that the task of United States technology must be "to 'bomb the hell out of Indochina,' as one airman put it."[135] Furthermore, it became necessary to demolish the rural society, for reasons to which we return. The consequences are indescribable, and entirely missing from the Pentagon Papers.

The facts, of course, will be denied, no matter how strong the evidence. For example, Brigadier General W. A. Tidwell, chief of the Reconnaissance and Photo Intelligence Division in Vietnam and director of the Target Research and Analysis Center in 1964–1965, writes that he developed many of the bombing techniques (including B-52 bombardment), and assures the reader that there was virtually no possibility that villages were attacked, except during ground combat.[136] And no matter what the facts may be, there will always be a Sidney Hook to claim that Bertrand Russell "plays up as deliberate American atrocities the unfortunate accidental loss of life incurred by the efforts of American military forces to help the South Vietnamese repel the incursions of North Vietnam and its partisans."[137] One can imagine what the same commentator would write if the enemies of the state whose propaganda he so faithfully parrots[138] were to indulge in a small fraction of the savagery of the American attack on the population of South Vietnam.

In an era that has experienced good Germans and apologists for Stalinist terror, it is perhaps not surprising to find some who will depict the horrors inflicted by the United States on Indochina as "unintended consequences of military action." Still, even the most cynical might be somewhat taken aback when such apologetics are coupled with attacks on critics of the American war for overlooking the barbarism of the enemy. One can hear the voice of some party hack berating critics of the Russian intervention in Hungary because they fail to denounce the terror of the resistance. In fact, it was quite proper for Russell, whom Hook castigates for such "omission," to concern himself with atrocities for which Americans bear responsibility, either by their own actions or through their local agents. Consider in contrast Hook's practice: denunciation of Communist atrocities, absolute silence with regard to the far greater GVN atrocities (for which the United States bears a large measure of responsibility), and miserable apologetics with regard to the United States attack on the civilian population, incomparably greater in scale as well as foreign in origin.

In the Pentagon study, the Vietnamese appear only marginally, and then only as items to be controlled by the American-instituted regime, never capable of performing its assigned task; or as infrastructure to be rooted out; or as people who must be permitted to "enjoy the inherent right to choose their own way of life and their own form of government" (John McNaughton, describing the "national commitment" of the United States; IV, 393) within the framework of a constitutional system that "opposes Communism in any form" and prohibits "every activity designed to publicize or carry out Communism" Article 5 of the 1967 Constitution, the proclaimed legal basis of such monstrosities as the Phoenix program—see below, pp. 92–3).

There is occasional recognition that the creatures who inhabit Vietnam may be human, or at least animate. It is assumed, for example, that they have a threshold of pain that can perhaps be reached without too much danger to the United States—we have already noted the reasons why the bombing "was too light, gave too subdued and uncertain a signal, and exerted too little pain" (IV, 20). The bombing of the North, that is.

As for the South, the careful reader can determine from the Pentagon study that it was being bombed. There are scattered statements referring to the fact, side comments in the review of the extensive debate over the American ground invasion, or in the course of the elaborate and detailed discussion of the vicious though far milder bombing of the North, which was the real "attention getter" (III, 431). In comparison to this, the decision to land combat marines in March 1965 "created less than a ripple" (III, 433), although proposals for further build-up "were the center of much private debate in the spring and early summer of 1965" ("behind the scene while the American public was in ignorance of the proceedings"; III, 445), and therefore merit a lengthy chapter in the Pentagon study. The build-up of United States combat forces, like the bombing of the North, was expected to be costly to the United States and was uncertain and dangerous in its further consequences. Therefore, it was worthy of attention.

The decision to pound South Vietnam to bits was the subject of no internal debate, so far as the record indicates. In fact, the decision and its impact were so insignificant that even the lack of concern over it receives no comment (in contrast to the decision to land combat marines). A similar observation applies to "responsible" segments of the peace movement, in large measure. On July 30, 1965, McNamara pointed out to the president, not inaccurately, that the "hue and cry" over bombing relates primarily to the North (III, 387). There were, of course, those whom McGeorge Bundy called the "wild men in the wings,"[139] but their hue and cry over the destruction of the rural society of South Vietnam had not yet come to the attention of Washington, and would not, until it became considerably more strident and indecorous (see above, p. 25).

With regard to scale, we read that "from the first, strike requirements in SVN had first call on U.S. air assets in Southeast Asia" (IV, 18). The analyst refers to "recommendations that had been made previously by COMUSMACV [United States Commander in Vietnam], and especially insistently by CINCPAC, to expand the use of US airpower in SVN" (III, 337). He cites one example from each of these authorities. General Westmoreland, on February 25, 1965, thought that we could "buy time" and reverse the decline in the South by adding three army helicopter companies, flying more close support and reconnaissance missions, and using ground combat troops. Admiral Sharp wrote to General Wheeler the following day that "the single most important thing we can do to improve the security situation in South Vietnam is to make full use of our airpower." These recommendations followed shortly after the initiation of regular and intensive aerial bombardment in South Vietnam (see above, p. 4, and note 140).

In the preceding months there had been a few references to the possibility of bombing the South, and some dispute over its advisability (see III, 562, 581, 587, 591, 618, 634). On January 27, as the political base of the American effort in the South appeared to be collapsing, McNamara agreed that Westmoreland should be authorized to use American jets in the case of "emergencies in South Vietnam" (III, 687). This seems to exhaust the record prior to February, when the bombing of the North was undertaken in a mood of desperation, and American jets were "authorized to support the RVNAF in ground operations in the South without restriction" (III, 391), with consequences already noted.

A cable from Admiral Sharp (CINCPAC) to the Joint Chiefs on February 24 recommended that a squadron of Marine F4s be deployed to Da Nang for close air support for the two marine battalions soon to be dispatched and "for other missions along with primary mission" (III, 419). The "other missions" are not specified. The GVN did not acquiesce in the deployment of a marine tactical fighter squadron until April 6 (III, 455). This reluctance of GVN officials was not unique (another instance of "Vietnamese xenophobia," no doubt). The general pattern through the 1960s was for the United States authorities to decide on appropriate measures of escalation and then to try to convince the GVN to go along. Finally, if agreement was obtained, a news release would be issued, stating typically that "after consultation between the governments of South Vietnam and the United States, the United States Government has agreed to the request of the Government of Vietnam to . . ." (III, 423). The elaborate maneuvering was necessary to maintain the pretense that the United States was responding to the request of the authentic indigenous government for help in resisting aggression. As the analyst states, in commenting on some proposals of President Diem in 1961 which probably caused "the initial reaction . . . of surprise": "The U.S. was not accustomed to GVN initiatives; it seldom sought them" (II, 446–7). In later years, as the façade disintegrated, the problem of gaining GVN acquiescence mounted. In one crucial case, the president's new program of escalation in February 1965 was received "with enthusiasm" by Ambassador Taylor in Saigon, but in his re-

sponse to the president, "he explained the difficulties he faced
in obtaining authentic GVN concurrence 'in the condition of
virtual non-government' [Taylor's phrase] which existed in
Saigon at that moment" (III, 323). Compare Lyndon Johnson's recollection of Taylor's reply (*Vantage Point*, p. 130): "In
his reply Taylor reported that our decision had been received
in Saigon with 'deep enthusiasm.'"

On March 5, CINCPAC again advised General Wheeler that
"the single most important thing we can do quickly to improve the security situation in SVN is to make full use of our
air power" (III, 429). Four days later, restrictions on United
States aircraft "were lifted, permitting their use in combat
operations in South Vietnam with USAF markings and without VNAF personnel aboard" (III, 334)—that is, without the
deception of earlier years (see notes 4, 142; chapter 3, note
14).

At the time that these restrictions on explicit use of United
States air power were lifted, Army Chief of Staff Harold K.
Johnson was leading a "high-ranking team" investigating the
situation in South Vietnam. He returned on March 12 with
twenty-one recommendations, four relating to the use of air
and helicopter forces in the South. The first three, approved
by Secretary McNamara, proposed additional helicopters for
troop mobility, aircraft for intelligence, and target research
and analysis "to utilize increased info effective"—how is not
specified. The fourth recommendation, with a question mark
in the margin added by the defense secretary, is: "Evaluate
effects of COMUSMACV's unrestricted employment of U.S.
fighter-bombers within SVN" (III, 95; General Johnson's
recommendations were approved by the president on April 1;
III, 703). Directly below we read that "on 17 March . . .
refugee problems were mounting in I and II Corps" (III,
97)—perhaps, though nothing is said, a result of unrestricted
bombing. So press reports would indicate. For example, A. J.
Langguth writes that in the spring of 1965 he "watched while
a tribe of hill people near Kontum [II Corps] trudged away
from their village to escape the American bombing," to be
"given a lecture by a Vietnamese officer on the evils of
Communism" upon their arrival at a refugee camp.[140]

In a memo of February 18, William Bundy mentions an

incident "in which Communist agents stirred up a village 'protest' against government air attacks" (III, 692). The incident is not further identified. Perhaps it was similar to one a few weeks later, when after South Vietnamese planes bombed a village, killing 45 (including 37 schoolchildren), villagers carrying coffins marched in protest to Da Nang but were turned back by Vietnamese troops.[141]

Maxwell Taylor, who can always be counted on to add just the right note of black humor, had apparently already completed the evaluation urged by General Johnson. He informed the president on March 11: "The most encouraging phenomenon of the past week has been the rise in Vietnamese morale occasioned by the air strikes against North Vietnam on March 2, the announcement of our intention to utilize U.S. jet aircraft within South Vietnam, and the landing of the Marines at Danang. . . . The press and the public have reacted most favorably to all three of these events" (III, 345; the marines at Da Nang were soon to learn differently—see below, p. 84). It is not recorded whether the ambassador's survey of public opinion included the inhabitants of five hamlets north of Saigon where fifty peasants had been killed in a napalm attack by American-piloted B-26s several months earlier—that is, well before the lifting of restrictions on United States aircraft.[142] We have already noted the February evaluation by COMUSMACV regarding the beneficial effect of United States air strikes in the North and South on Southern morale in February (see above, p. 71; also III, 424–5).

In a draft "plan of action for South Vietnam" on March 24, McNaughton suggested "US/VNAF air & naval strikes against VC ops and bases in SVN" as one element in an elaborate "program of progressive military pressure" (III, 697). General Westmoreland presented what he described as "a classical Commander's Estimate of the Situation" two days later. In this extremely detailed analysis, he stated: "If *basic strategy of punitive bombing in RVN* does not take effect by mid-year additional deployments of U.S. and 3rd Country forces should be considered" (III, 464; my emphasis). The reference to RVN—South Vietnam—rates a *"sic!"* from the analyst.

We know from other sources that the "punitive bombing in

RVN" did take effect in several respects. While "literally pounding the place to bits," it also succeeded in tripling the number of recruits for the Viet Cong. In 1966, unobserved strikes alone succeeded further in providing the "enemy" with about 27,000 tons of dud bombs and shells, more than enough material for mines and booby traps which were the cause of death for over 1,000 American soldiers in that year—a year in which the number of Viet Cong and North Vietnamese killed by these strikes was estimated at probably less than 100.[143]

The tactic of massive bombardment must be labeled "counterproductive" in Pentagonese, and can be attributed only to advanced cretinism, *if* the United States goal had been to restrict American casualties or to win popular support for the Saigon government or to "protect the population." But it is quite rational as a device for demolishing the society in which a rebellion is rooted and takes refuge. Hearts and minds can be left to a later stage, when the population is driven to refugee camps or urban slums with (it is hoped) no way to survive outside of the framework established by United States terror. Then the gentle nation builders can appear on the scene to win the hearts and minds that are left, while the apologists for state violence speak of the "unintended consequences of military action" (see section III, below).

In early March two marine battalions were deployed at Da Nang, joining the 1,300 marines already there (III, 402), the first overt deployment of United States combat forces. Their mission was to protect the Da Nang base, "which was heavily supporting air activity over North and South Vietnam" and was therefore "a lucrative target" for the Viet Cong (III, 424, 389). The mission, in short, was to prevent another "outrageous act" of the Southern rebels such as the attack on the United States air base at Bien Hoa on November 1, 1964 (see p. 121). By April 1–2, the president decided "to get U.S. ground combat units involved in the war against the insurgents" (III, 394). At the Honolulu meeting of April 20 "it was agreed that tasks within *South* Vietnam should have first call on air assets in the area" (III, 359; McNaughton's minutes, his emphasis). According to the analyst, "it seems apparent that Honolulu marked the relative downgrading of pressures against the North, in favor of more intensive activity in the South." A May 4 assessment by Ambassador Taylor noted that North Vietnam might introduce "additional PAVN units on order of several regiments [in the hope of] offsetting US/GVN application of air power" (III, 364). See below, pp. 111, 125-7.

"In line with the April decision to give priority to South Vietnam over North Vietnam in the employment of U.S. air power, a major administration decision was taken after the bombing pause [ending May 18] to assign saturation bombing missions in the South to SAC B-52 bombers . . ." (III, 383). This decision followed some complaints by General Westmoreland (with Taylor's "political endorsement") that massive air attacks on Viet Cong base areas (one on April 15, with 900 tons of ordnance dropped) were inefficient, the topography being "more suitable for area carpet bombing." The first B-52 raid was authorized on June 18. Air attacks "increased significantly in *South* Vietnam" (III, 383-4).

There are occasional further references to proposed "increased use of air in-country, including B-52's" (McNamara, July 20, 1965; IV, 298), but nothing about the scale and character of the air war, or the devastating helicopter and artillery war in the South, as there is virtually nothing said directly about the impact of United States ground operations on the Vietnamese. Thus we learn that "Vietnam changed over from a rice exporter in the years through 1964 to a heavy importer from 1965 onwards" (II, 366), but the reasons remain a mystery, one of the many that did not have sufficient "signal strength" to reach the higher circles of decision making.

One can deduce from the Pentagon study that the American war was not exactly a bed of roses for the Vietnamese. A Roles and Missions study of August 1966 recommended that "the physical and attitudinal consequences of present air and artillery employment policies should be studied" (II, 385). But the follow-up, if any, is missing from this record, though it is presumably to be found in the secret RAND study mentioned above (see p. 5). The same report urged that ARVN Ranger units should be disbanded "because of generally bad behavior," that is, terrorizing the population, but COMUSMACV demurred on grounds that this "would seriously reduce ARVN combat strength."

To pick up the story of the air war in South Vietnam after the April 1965 decision to give priority to the South in employment of air power, we must again turn to other sources. By May 1965 huge sectors had been declared "free bombing zones," and "tens of thousands of tons of bombs, rockets, napalm and cannon fire [were being] poured into these vast areas each week," with heavy casualties, "if only by the laws of chance."[144] But the backroom boys were so bemused by China's aggressive expansionist policies and the like[145] that they could not spare the time for "the heaps of dead in the battle zone includ[ing] many local villagers who didn't get away in time."[146] The displacement of the brute facts by weird geopolitical delusions produces a tone of moral imbecility that is only enhanced when the planners occasionally express some reservations over the policies that they are recommending, invariably on grounds of the sort illustrated above.

Documentation of the air war prior to 1965 is also slight. A CIA report of July 1962 mentions "extensive relocation Montagnards," allegedly resulting from fear of Viet Cong, "and new found respect for power GVN has manifested bombing attacks and use helicopters" (II, 687; in other cases, the CIA tactfully observes, "movement has been at invitation GVN"). The CIA analyst shares the concern of the ambassador, "fearing adverse political impact of bombing non-VC installations and concentrations of people." In December 1962, State Department intelligence noted reports "that indiscriminate bombing in the countryside is forcing innocent or wavering peasants toward the Viet Cong" (II, 706), and estimated that over 100,000 Montagnards had fled Viet Cong–controlled areas,

> due principally to Viet Cong excesses and the general intensification of the fighting in the highlands rather than to any positive measures taken by the GVN to appeal to the tribespeople. The extensive use of artillery and aerial bombardment and other apparently excessive and indiscriminate measures by GVN military and security forces

in attempting to eliminate the Viet Cong have undoubtedly killed many innocent peasants and made many others more willing than before to cooperate with the Viet Cong . . . (II, 708–9).

The report further urged "restriction of the tactical use of airpower" since extensive use of air power and crop destruction may provoke "militant opposition among the peasants and positive identification with the Viet Cong" (II, 714), who recruit locally and are largely dependent on the local population. Their ability to regroup, intact, after GVN military clearing operations "is considerably enhanced by the concealment afforded them, voluntarily or otherwise, by the local population" (II, 696). It is left to the reader to imagine the effects of the use of artillery and air power "to 'soften up' the enemy" (II, 703), an enemy that is concealed by the local population.

Similar concerns were expressed shortly after by Michael Forrestal (II, 717–18), who reported that American advisers, helicopters, air support, and arms have led to "increased aggressiveness" on the part of ARVN. The United States can hardly evade responsibility for the consequences, say, for the fact that "no one really knows . . . how many of the 20,000 'Viet Cong' killed last year were only innocent or at least persuadable villagers," in particular, because of the direct United States involvement (see note 4, and chapter 3, notes 14 and 15).

Dennis Duncanson, a member of the British Advisory Mission and a passionate supporter of the American intervention, reports that the policy of random bombardment of villages in "open zones" was the "principal cause of a huge migration of tribesmen in the summer of 1962," citing estimates from 125,000 to 300,000 (*Government and Revolution in Vietnam*, p. 321).

In April 1966, a task force was set up "to establish a set of interagency priorities." In its "first rank of importance" the task force placed "those activities that persuade the people that RVNAF is wholly on the side of the people and acting in their interests" (II, 580–3). At this point, words fail. For years, RVNAF—the South Vietnamese armed forces, trained, equipped, and advised by the United States—had been driving the people of South Vietnam from their homes and smashing their villages into dust; and now, in April 1966, it is a highest priority task for the United States Mission to persuade the people that RVNAF is on their side and acting in their interests. What kinds of thoughts must pass through the mind of a person capable of producing such a recommendation?

The Pentagon study terminates before the massive escalation of the air war in 1968, to reach its peak of fury in the early months of the Nixon administration, and before the concentrated air attack on Laos and then Cambodia, presumably under the direction of the amiable professor who is said to provide the president with his more profound strategic concepts. One of the final documents in the Pentagon study is a cable to United States ambassadors informing them of the decision to redistribute the bombing on April 1, 1968 (what the analyst describes—tongue in cheek, perhaps—as "the decision to cut back the bombing," IV, 275): "air power now used north of 20th [20th parallel in North Vietnam] can probably be used in Laos . . . and in SVN" (IV, 595), a grim and accurate portent, as the peasants of South Vietnam, Laos, and later Cambodia would soon discover (see note 228 and chapter 2).

In these documents, some policies are regarded as controversial, but not the policy of "elimination of the Viet Cong from . . . the Saigon area and the Mekong Delta," for example. It is the task of United States troops to "vigorously undertake" this program of eliminating Viet Cong forces, known to be indigenous (IV, 301, 302; summer 1965). In the delta, a major center of Viet Cong strength, few NVA forces were reported during the period covered by this study, though American air and later ground forces were heavily engaged in combat, once the United States invasion had reached a scale sufficient "to take on the Delta."[147] "US Army units continued their work in the densely populated Delta provinces," the analyst blandly reports (II, 399; early 1967). We must assume, from his silence, that the documents available to him do not describe "their work." When the United States units were deployed, one commanding officer told correspondent Peter Arnett that they hoped to "drive the Viet Cong out of the area before they have to reduce the whole countryside to

ashes."[148] They failed. Another mistake, with more unintended consequences. By the end of 1969, officials were com-
plaining that pacification efforts were hampered by the
indiscriminate killings of civilians by American soldiers, and
peasants were fleeing the dead gray-and-black fields and
charred ruins of delta hamlets.[149]

By late 1966, the plan was to give "increased emphasis . . .
to identifying and eliminating the VC infrastructure," for
example, by armed river-patrol operations in the delta (IV,
379), which were to prove "significantly successful in depriving the enemy of freedom and initiative in the population and
resources-rich Delta areas" (IV, 539), where "the VC effort is
primarily indigenous" (IV, 487). McNamara explains that it
"has been our task all along" to "root out the VC infrastructure and establish the GVN presence" (November 1966; IV,
376). The Combined Campaign Plan 1967 announces that
"the people are the greatest asset to the enemy," providing
him with "food, supplies, money, manpower, concealment and
intelligence." Conclusion: "During this campaign every effort
will be made to deny these assets to the enemy" (IV, 380).
We call this "protection of the population," just as "identifying and eliminating the VC infrastructure" is defense of the
South Vietnamese people against aggression.

It takes no military genius to predict what will happen to
the people who are being protected in this way. On returning
from a trip to Saigon in October 1966, McNamara informed
the president: *The one thing demonstrably going for us in
Vietnam over the past year has been the large number of
enemy killed-in-action resulting from the big military operations*" (IV, 348; his emphasis). On November 17, he reported
that "U.S. forces in SEA have performed exceedingly well."
The enemy "has lost 114,000 troops in the last year, including
invaluable cadre" (IV, 368). But there is some question as to
just who these enemy "troops" really are: "the VC/NVA
apparently lose only about one-sixth as many weapons as
people, suggesting the possibility that many of the killed are
unarmed porters or bystanders" (IV, 371; see notes 146, 149).
With no comment, the text cites the report by the marines in
late 1966 of "5000 to 6000 NVA troops killed or disabled and
414 weapons lost" (II, 609). In the Tet offensive, 1968, when

the United States command conceded that "the enemy" were overwhelmingly NLF rather than NVA,[150] killed and captured outnumbered captured weapons by a factor of five (IV, 539). By the same criterion, figures presented in IV, 377, suggest that United States forces were killing far more civilians than ARVN forces were.

Without describing American military practices, McNamara further notes that "about 30% of the reported gains [in population under GVN control] probably came from movement of refugees into cities and towns" (IV, 374). It was surely not the attractiveness of the GVN that enticed these refugees to flee the countryside. The same report notes the belief of the rural Vietnamese that "the GVN is indifferent to the people's welfare; the low-level GVN officials are tools of the local rich; and the GVN is excessively corrupt from top to bottom" (IV, 374). This is one reason, no doubt, why the Viet Cong "can replace current losses solely from within South Vietnam" (IV, 371), and why "pacification has if anything gone backward" (McNamara's emphasis) while "the VC political infrastructure thrives in most of the country, continuing to give the enemy his enormous intelligence advantage," and full security exists nowhere, "not even behind the US Marines' lines and in Saigon" (IV, 348). In fact, when the marines were deployed in spring 1965, they discovered "to their own amazement" that "the toughest war for them was the war in the villages behind them," and they turned "away from the enemy to a grueling and painfully slow effort to pacify the villages."[151] Their strategy was derived in part "from their own traditions in the 'Banana Republics' and China" in the 1930s, where many of the top officers had served. They were opposed even by the dominant right-wing political party of the area (II, 535–6).

The point was not lost on Robert Komer, who was in charge of "the other war." His recommendation, on leaving for Saigon in April 1967, was to "step up refugee programs deliberately aimed at depriving the VC of a recruiting base" (IV, 441; emphasis his). Translation into "operational reality": drive the population into the American-controlled areas, thus depriving the enemy of his "greatest asset," namely, the people. Surely Komer understood this, in April 1967. Nicholas

Katzenbach put it more delicately: "We should stimulate a greater refugee flow through psychological inducements to further decrease the enemy's manpower base" (IV, 508; see pp. 5–6 and notes 7–9). Again, we must turn to other sources to learn about the "psychological inducements" used, for example, the 26 billion leaflets that had been dropped over South Vietnam by summer 1971, warning villagers to move to GVN areas or "be considered hostile and in danger"; to "hurry to return to the righteous cause" or "stay to die in suffering and horrible danger"; or warning that "the U.S. Marines will not hesitate to destroy, immediately, any village or hamlet harboring the Vietcong."[152]

By the use of such psychological inducements, along with measures to drive home their reality, it was possible to deplete the recruiting base of the enemy. By the time McNamara visited Saigon in July 1967, army intelligence and General Westmoreland were able to inform him that the war was "becoming more and more an NVA war" because the enemy had been "denied recruits in the numbers required from the populated areas along the coast, thereby forcing him to supply manpower from North Vietnam" (IV, 520, 518). This was the primary reason for the infiltration, as COMUSMACV was aware (see pp. 125–7 below), though as the Tet offensive was to show, his calculations were the result of "wishful thinking compounded by a massive intelligence collection and/or evaluation failure" (IV, 557).

Still, Komer's recommendation was to the point. He writes today that "up through 1967 most of the forces arrayed against Saigon were southern Viet Cong, not regular troops from the North," but "today the VC recruiting base is attenuated."[153] How it was attenuated he does not specify, nor does he recall his recommendation that this be done deliberately. Komer, like McNamara, understands that it was not the attractiveness of the GVN that depleted the Viet Cong recruiting base. On the contrary, "Saigon's record in dealing with the underlying causes of the Viet Cong revolution is still spotty at best," though American firepower was an effective substitute.

In 1966 Komer felt that the growing number of refugees posed a problem, though in some ways it was "a plus" since it helped to "deprive VC of recruiting potential and rice growers." Furthermore, it was "partly indicative of growing peasant desire seek security on our side" (II, 569). How significant and gratifying that the peasants should seek security on our side, joining the righteous cause, instead of remaining in their villages with the Viet Cong "to die in suffering and horrible danger."

The general problem was outlined in a force-requirement study in early 1967. In I Corps in the North, it is necessary to eliminate enemy forces and base areas "and to remove his control over large population and food resources" in areas where "the enemy has operated for years virtually unmolested" (COMUSMACV). "The next most dangerous situation," the analyst summarizes, "appeared to be that in II Corps . . . [where] the enemy, orienting himself on the population, presented a different problem. . . ." in III Corps it is necessary "to expand security radially from the Saigon-Cholon area . . . [with] an intensified campaign conducted to root out the VC infrastructure." United States forces will "provide a protective shield behind which the Revolutionary Development programs could operate," conducting search-and-destroy operations against the indigenous VC forces and "base area clusters" (IV, 433-5). Unless the Viet Cong infrastructure ("the VC officials and organizers") "was destroyed, US-GVN military and pacification forces soon degenerated into nothing more than an occupation Army," a Systems Analysis study concluded. It was never asked "whether or not U.S. forces should be or even could be profitably engaged in pacification" (IV, 513). We know from many other sources, apparently not available to the analyst, that United States forces were profitably engaged in the destruction, massacre, and forced population concentration that was a necessary preliminary for "Revolutionary Development."

The United States command found itself "fighting a war of attrition in Southeast Asia," in accordance with Westmoreland's concept of "a 'meatgrinder' "—"kill[ing] larger numbers of the enemy but in the end do[ing] little better than hold[ing] our own" (IV, 442). "Essentially, we are fighting Vietnam's birth rate," states an official quoted in a "startlingly accurate" newspaper account (IV, 587). Specifically in North Vietnam, "the bombing was unable to beat the birth rate"

(IV, 227). There is only one way to beat the birth rate, in North Vietnam but more crucially in the South, where the primary enemy of the United States, the South Vietnamese peasant, permits the NLF to "orient himself on the population." The method is that succinctly described by General Westmoreland's chief planner: "The solution in Vietnam is more bombs, more shells, more napalm . . . till the other side cracks and gives up."[154]

3. Nation Building and Crimes of War

In the South, the task faced by the United States was to build a nation while rooting out the infrastructure of the organization that had captured the nationalist movement. A difficult task, but perhaps not impossible, given sufficient force and terror. Robert Komer, always an optimist, thought it could be done. He advocated "increasing erosion of southern VC strength" (IV, 391), and cheerily reported to the president (February 1967) that although "few of our programs—civil or military—are very efficient," still "we are grinding the enemy down by sheer weight and mass" (IV, 420). Later, Komer was to explain that "thanks to massive U.S. intervention at horrendous cost," a favorable military environment was created "in which the largely political competition for control and support of the key rural population could begin again" in this "revolutionary, largely political conflict."[155] The "constructive aims" of pacification, Komer explained, are to protect the rural population from the insurgents, "which also helps to deprive the insurgency of its rural popular base," and to generate support for the Saigon regime—not easy, given the character of this regime, as noted by McNamara (see p. 84 above) and others. It was far easier to fulfill the constructive aim of depriving the insurgency of its rural popular base by stepping up the programs of deliberate refugee generation, as Komer proposed.

Komer finds it difficult to comprehend why some regard him as a possible candidate for a war-crimes trial. The issue was raised by Eqbal Ahmad, with reference to a speech in which Komer explained that Vietnam had proved the inefficacy of "gradual escalation" which permitted the "guerrillas to make adjustments"; the lesson of Vietnam, he said, is to escalate ruthlessly and rapidly, to "snow them under." In an outraged reply to Ahmad, Komer reviews his career as special assistant to the president from April 1966 and as "chief pacification adviser to the GVN" from May 1967 to November 1968. The charge, Komer claims, must seem strange to anyone familiar with the post-1966 program, which he helped develop, "one of the more sensible and constructive endeavors which the U.S. belatedly supported in Vietnam." Its first phase "was essentially a nation-building effort, an attempt to help build a viable socio-economic fabric in the middle of a shooting war." From May 1967, when CORDS was set up under Komer's direction, the pacification program *"was wholly Vietnamese manned and commanded"* (his emphasis), his role being only "to provide advice and logistic/financial help" to the GVN effort. The program did not rely on "bombing, napalm, defoliation, and other technological means" and the "pacifiers" opposed and sought to minimize generation of refugees; "the stress was on local self-government, political checks and balances, and rule of law."[156]

In general, Komer explains, his task was clean, bloodless, and constructive: to help the Saigon regime "build a nation." Surely, then, only the ill-informed or malicious could possibly accuse him of complicity in criminal acts.

Noting Komer's laudable concern that "the record of U.S. pacification support and advice need not be hidden behind a classified screen," let us compare his presentation with the record that is available now that the classified screen has been partially lifted.

The "pacifiers," he tells us, did not seek "the displacement and dispossession of the rural population" and sought to minimize refugee generation. As already noted, Komer is one of the few administration officials on record with the explicit recommendation to *"step up refugee programs deliberately aimed at depriving the VC of a recruiting base."*

Komer states that after the establishment of CORDS, the pacification program was *"wholly Vietnamese manned and commanded."*

He fails to mention the fact, documented endlessly by the press, the Pentagon Papers, and others, that rooting out the Viet Cong infrastructure and "denying the villages to the Viet

Cong" was primarily an American responsibility. American armed force was to "provide the shield" behind which ARVN could undertake "pacification" (Westmoreland, August 1966; II, 588). Discussing the CORDS program, headed by Komer as deputy to COMUSMACV, the analyst remarks that the structure of CORDS was "so massive that the Vietnamese were in danger of being almost forgotten" (II, 622). McNamara proposed in September 1966 that COMUSMACV be assigned responsibility for pacification. Komer, supporting this proposal, noted that "the military are much better set up to manage a huge pacification effort," since 60–70 percent of the "real job of pacification is providing local security . . . [which] can only be done by the military" (II, 590). As Komer explains elsewhere,[157] "Given the massive military support required, it made good sense on the U.S. side to put the new unified U.S. advisory structure [CORDS] under military command."

In an announcement drafted by Komer in May 1967, Ambassador Bunker stated that support of RD is "to be neither exclusively a civilian nor exclusively a military function, but to be essentially civil-military in character," involving "both the provision of continuous local security in the countryside—necessarily a primarily military task [—] and the constructive programs conducted by the Ministry of Revolutionary Development [of the GVN], largely through its 59-member RD teams," trained by the CIA (II, 616–17; 567–8). Bunker reported that General Westmoreland would undertake "the responsibility for the performance of our U.S. Mission field programs in support of pacification or Revolutionary Development," with Komer serving as "the single manager for pacification" (II, 428). The Combined Campaign Plan for 1967 of the United States and Saigon military forces (MACV/JGS; II, 495–6) assigned to ARVN regular forces the task of "operations to destroy VC guerrillas and infrastructure in specified hamlet or village areas" in conjunction with provincial military forces and civil intelligence and police. US-FW military forces were to conduct combined operations with the Saigon military and police forces "to destroy VC guerrillas and infrastructure in specified hamlet or village areas," though it was left to the provincial forces and the National Police to carry out "population and resources control" directly. US-FW military forces were also to conduct "military and civic action to help win the support of the people for the government with emphasis to ensure that credit is given to the GVN," a directive observed by Komer in the remarks cited in his "Epilogue."

Komer's remarks on the *wholly Vietnamese manned and commanded* program should also be read in the light of his recommendation that "leverage" must be applied "always in such manner as to keep the GVN foremost in the picture presented to its own people and the world at large" (II, 503–4). We are "applying more leverage in Pacification," he adds. His view was that "increased use of U.S. leverage . . . must be done discreetly" (II, 430; analyst). Perhaps it might be more accurate to say that the United States must pretend that the GVN exists, to ourselves, to the world at large, and to the population that we are trying to win for it.

Komer always emphasized the central military component in pacification: "we must dovetail the military's sweep operations and civil pacification" so as to "secure and hold the countryside cleared by military operations." Komer "put everyone politely on notice" that he had no hesitation in calling on "military resources, which are frequently the best and most readily available" (II, 570). Pacification "demands a multifaceted civil-military response" to provide security, for "*breaking the hold of the VC over the people*," to "*systematize the flow of refugees*," and so on (II, 572–3; his emphasis). The most important problem in pacification, in his constantly reiterated view, is security, a military-police problem. In comparison, his position on land reform, though he pressed for signs of progress and urged that it be accelerated "to consolidate rural support behind the GVN," was that "it was not an important issue in Vietnam." "Far more important was the matter of security in the countryside" (II, 400, 569, 392; IV, 441).

A CORDS report from Bien Hoa Province for the period ending December 31, 1967, gives a bit more insight into the wholly Vietnamese programs that Komer and his American colleagues merely advised. Because of the corruption and inefficiency of the GVN officials (whose "primary interest . . . is money"), "CORDS has had to increasingly rely on the

resources, skills and capabilities of resident US military units."
"CORDS Bien Hoa (as well as the GVN itself) owes a great
deal to these units and their commanders who have unselfishly
devoted themselves to furthering pacification." The "disturbing truth" is that "it still remains for the government [of
South Vietnam], with forceful and meaningful direction from
above, to begin to assume the responsibility for prosecuting
this war and the pacification effort" (II, 407). The Pentagon
study terminates at this point, but we know from many other
sources that in the following months the reliance on the
United States military in preparing the ground for "pacification" increased, the My Lai massacre being only the best-
known and most grotesque example (see note 149). Allan
Goodman writes: "Whatever else the introduction of [Ameri-
can combat troops] may have achieved it is now clear that
their participation in the conflict (particularly in the twelve
months after the Tet offensive of 1968) seriously weakened
the ability of the VC/NVA to conduct effective mobile warfare within South Vietnam."[158] Forced population removal
and massive devastation intensified, laying the groundwork for
Komer's program of constructive nation building.

The same period marked the implementation of another of
Komer's important recommendations: *Revamp and put new
steam behind a coordinated US/GVN intelligence collation
and action effort targeted on the VC infrastructure at the
critical provincial, district, and village levels* (IV, 441; his
emphasis). The problem, he related, is that "we are just not
getting enough payoff yet from the massive intelligence we are
increasingly collecting. Police/military coordination is sadly
lacking both in collection and in swift reaction."

Two months later, on June 14, 1967, in a memorandum for
General Westmoreland entitled "Organization for Attack on
V.C. Infrastructure," Komer recommended "consolidation,
under his direction, of U.S. anti-infrastructure intelligence
effort," and expressed his desire for a "unified GVN/US,
civil/military 'management structure targeted on infrastructure.'" In response, the ICEX (Intelligence Coordination
and Exploitation) structure was developed in July 1967, under
Westmoreland and Komer (II, 429, 585). ICEX, involving
CIA, American military and civilians, and the GVN military-

police-intelligence apparatus, was the immediate predecessor of the Phoenix program, other sources indicate. Early internal directives describe the Phoenix program as an American program of advice, support, and assistance to the GVN *Phung Hoang* program. Later modifications delete reference to "Phoenix" and refer merely to the GVN *Phung Hoang* program, again in line with the approach of "keep[ing] the GVN foremost in the picture presented to its own people and the world at large."

On March 4, 1968, the secretary of defense recommended that "Operation Phoenix which is targetted against the Viet Cong must be pursued more vigorously in closer liaison with the US," while "Vietnamese armed forces should be devoted to anti-infrastructure activities on a priority basis" (IV, 578).

After Westmoreland and Komer's ICEX became Phoenix, the coordinated US-GVN intelligence-military-police programs succeeded in "neutralizing" some 84,000 "Viet Cong infrastructure" with 21,000 killed, according to reported "official figures."[159] According to the same UPI report, Komer is indeed correct when he states ("Epilogue") that United States advisers criticized excesses. One reports that local officials in the delta decided to kill 80 percent of the suspects, but American advisers were able to convince them that the proportion should be reduced below 50 percent. Another American adviser concedes that "naturally, we kill and torture many Vietcong. . . . The only way to combat these people who act like animals is to kill them." We treat them just as they treat us, he adds, failing, however, to list the American towns in which cadres assisted, trained, and paid by the NLF have conducted murder and torture missions. According to the same report, the actual assassinations are largely carried out by former criminals or former Communists recruited and paid by the CIA, which also organizes the provincial interrogation centers where prisoners are tortured. Other reports indicate that CIA-directed teams drawn from ethnic minorities are widely used; that American military men often conduct operations; and that the units often include Nationalist Chinese and Thai mercenaries. An American IVS volunteer reports picking up two hitchhikers in the Mekong Delta, former criminals, who told him that by bringing in a few bodies now and then and collecting the bounty, they can live quite handsomely.[160]

The "pacification" program was reportedly accelerated substantially in March 1971, its "top priority" being neutralization of the political apparatus of the Viet Cong, at a reported cost of considerably more than $1 billion to the United States and an undisclosed amount to the Saigon regime (hence indirectly, the United States).[161] A rare statistic for April 1971 reveals that in that month, of 2,000 "neutralized" more than 40 percent were assassinated,[162] possibly the firstfruits of the accelerated terror program. A United States intelligence officer attached to the Phoenix program in the Mekong Delta states that when he arrived in his district, he was given a list of 200 names of people who were to be killed, and when he left six months later, 260 had been killed, but none of those on his list.[163]

As in other cases of "body count," the numbers given and the identity of the victims raise various questions. There is ample evidence that the operatives and intelligence collectors (heavily infiltrated, quite probably, by the NLF) often avoid the difficulties and hazards of trying to tangle with the NLF infrastructure, meeting their quotas in other ways.[164] As a device for terrorizing the political opposition, however, the Phoenix program may well be effective. Although the actual assassinations, torture, and imprisonment are conducted by operatives trained, advised, and paid by the United States, it would be "double think," Komer insists ("Epilogue"), to criticize the "GVN *Phung Hoang* program" too harshly.

We have noted Komer's insistence that his "pacifiers" are devoted to the rule of law. That may well be true, though the significance of this noble commitment only becomes clear when we explore the system of laws that they uphold. "Security offenses" can be tried by military field courts, and the laws are so severe that virtually any form of overt dissent might be regarded as a violation of national security: undermining public morale, or acts in furtherance of communism or procommunist neutralism, or acts to undermine the anticommunist spirit of the country, all punishable by five years to death.[165]

The problem that Komer always regarded as the most important, namely, "security in the countryside," has been approached by the methods just indicated. Among the most savage were the programs of deliberate refugee generation and "swift reaction" by the military and police under the "coordinated US/GVN intelligence collation and action effort," as explicitly recommended in both cases by Komer, who tells us that he was concerned merely with the constructive tasks of nation building, after United States military force had provided a "favorable military environment" for these benign activities. He is quite right, incidentally, in emphasizing that in the full spectrum of American activities in Vietnam, those that he directed are the least criminal.

4. The Asian Mind—the American Mind

So far as the bombing of the North was concerned, the analyst concludes that the idea was based "on a plausible assumption about the rationality of NVN's leaders," namely, that they would not want to bear its cost (IV, 57). But the guerrillas were "supplying themselves locally, in the main" (IV, 57), and, as McNamara rather prissily explained to a Senate committee, the North Vietnamese leaders' "regard for the comfort and even the lives of the people they control does not seem to be sufficiently high to lead them to bargain for settlement in order to stop a heightened level of attack" (IV, 202). Any Nazi could have said the same about Winston Churchill.

This line of thinking has been extended since by a number of thoughtful commentators. William Pfaff, liberal-in-residence at the Hudson Institute, explains that "ours has been a reasonable strategy," but it was "the strategy of those who are rich, who love life and fear 'costs.' "[166] For us, "death and suffering are irrational choices when alternatives exist." "We want life, happiness, wealth, power. . . ." But we failed to comprehend "the strategy of the weak," who "deal in absolutes, among them that man inevitably suffers and dies." The enemy "stoically accept[s] the destruction of wealth and the loss of lives"; "happiness, wealth, power—the very words in conjunction reveal a dimension of our experience beyond that of the Asian poor." The weak thus invite us to carry our "strategic logic to its conclusion, which is genocide,"[167] but we balk, unwilling to "destroy ourselves . . . by contradicting our own value system." As Hoopes formulated it, we hesitate because we realize "that genocide is a terrible burden to bear." Thus we fail. Neither Pfaff nor Hoopes tells us how he has determined that the Asian poor do not love life or fear costs or seek wealth and happiness. Perhaps this is demonstrated in a classified research study of the Hudson Institute.

Pfaff and Hoopes are rivaled in their understanding of the Asian mind by several secretaries of state. Byrnes, in December 1946, alluded to the problems caused by the "almost childish Vietnamese attitude and knowledge of economic questions and vague groping for 'independence,'" which was causing all sorts of troubles, citing Abbot Moffat (*DOD*, bk. 8, p. 89). These childish attitudes and vague gropings were perhaps still more pronounced because the Vietnamese had "been thoroughly indoctrinated with the Atlantic Charter and other ideological pronouncements" and thus foolishly expected American help (Richard Sharp, reporting remarks of General Philip Gallagher; *DOD*, bk. 8, p. 56). Secretary Marshall, more practical and realistic than the Vietnamese, understood the need for "a continued close association between newly-autonomous peoples and powers which have long been responsible their welfare," as France had been responsible for the welfare of the Vietnamese;[168] and he recognized that "for an indefinite period" the Vietnamese would require not only French material and technical assistance but also "enlightened political guidance," under a voluntary association (*DOD*, bk. 8, pp. 100–1). Still another secretary of state commented that "as with most Orientals Diem must be highly suspicious of what is going on about him" (Dulles, April 1955; *DOD*, bk. 10, p. 909); though apparently Diem was not suspicious enough, as events were to prove in mid-1963.

The National Security Council, equally astute, explained the favorable prospects of the Soviet Union in Asia in part on the grounds that "its protégés deal with Asiatic peoples who are traditionally submissive to power when effectively applied" (*DOD*, bk. 8, p. 239; December 1949)—an insight that has been corroborated so conclusively by the effective application of force to the Vietnamese in the past quarter-century.[169]

Similar perspicacity is exhibited by United States Ambassador Maxwell Taylor, who has been described elsewhere as the "chief adviser, if not *éminence grise*" of the Kennedy administration.[170] He bemoans the "national attribute" which "limits the development of a truly national spirit" among the South Vietnamese, perhaps "innate" or perhaps a residue of the colonial experience. And he then proceeds to speculate about "the ability of the Viet Cong continuously to rebuild their units and to make good their losses"—"one of the mysteries of this guerrilla war"—and their remarkable morale and recuperative powers and continued strength, for which "we still find no plausible explanation" (III, 668; November 27, 1964). The only explanation he can conjure up is the dispatch to the South of "trained cadre and military equipment" and the flow of radio messages. It did not, apparently, occur to him that US-GVN operations in North Vietnam somehow did not have a similar impact. It is, of course, completely beyond his comprehension that the true source of Viet Cong resilience may be precisely a "national attribute," deeply rooted in the peasant society that we have systematically destroyed, an "attribute" that arouses the Vietnamese peasants to continued resistance to colonial domination—the attribute that is repeatedly characterized as "xenophobia" in these documents. The same remarkable foolishness is revealed when overflights for dropping leaflets in North Vietnam were recommended in May 1961 "to maintain morale of North Vietnamese population," as though the people of North Vietnam, enslaved by their Communist masters, were prayerfully awaiting salvation by American bombers, or perhaps by the "networks of resistance, covert bases and teams for sabotage and light harassment" to be formed in North Vietnam, "using the foundation established by intelligence operations" (II, 641).

It would perhaps be unfair to quote the various contributions of the Joint Chiefs, for example, their suggestion that a firm declaration of intent by the United States to block "aggression originating outside of Indochina . . . would in general raise the morale of all peoples in Southeast Asia and in particular would increase the determination of the Indochinese to fight the war to a successful conclusion" against the "Soviet Communist campaign in Southeast Asia" (January 15, 1954; DOD, bk. 9, pp. 214, 216).

In comparison, Eisenhower appears a model of profundity "in commenting philosophically" on the low morale among "democratic forces in Laos" and wondering aloud "why, in interventions of this kind, we always seem to find that the morale of the Communist forces was better than that of the democratic forces" (II, 637). "His explanation was that the Communist philosophy appeared to produce a sense of dedication" not matched among those "supporting the free forces." The problem had been noted much earlier, as in a National Intelligence estimate of June 1953 pointing out the gloomy prospects for the "Vietnamese government" given "the failure of Vietnamese to rally to [it]," the effective Viet Minh "control," the fact that the population assist the Viet Minh more than the French (making it difficult "to provide security for the Vietnamese population"), the inability of "the Vietnam leadership" to "overcome popular apathy and mobilize the energy and resources of the people," and so on (I, 391–2). With hardly more than a change of names, this analysis might be taken for the despairing report from pacification specialists (MACCORDS) on December 31, 1967, cited above, deploring the corruption of the GVN,[171] the "ever-widening gap of distrust, distaste and disillusionment between the people and the GVN," and its growing weakness. With these words, the record of US-GVN relations ends (II, 406–7). *Plus ça change* . . .

Somehow, the United States never managed "to influence the GVN to do the things we believe they must do to save their own country" (II, 623). In October 1966, McNamara lamented "that the US had not yet found the formula for training and inspiring the Vietnamese" (II, 388; analyst): *"the discouraging truth is that, as was the case in 1961 and 1963 and 1965, we have not found the formula, the catalyst, for training and inspiring them into effective action* (IV, 349; McNamara's emphasis; Carver of the CIA disagreed, II, 598). All we seem to be able to do is kill, he adds.

Not that ideas were not put forth as to the proper formula, or catalyst. A memorandum of October 20, 1954, to the director of the CIA suggested that "a psychological operations concept entitled 'Militant liberty'" might do the trick. The concept was later endorsed by General Bonesteel of the NSC

Planning Board (*DOD*, bk. 10, pp. 777, 975), but it then disappears from the record. The Joint Chiefs, in February 1964, while recommending increased crop destruction and other measures, added that it would be helpful to "create a 'cause' which can serve as a rallying point for the youth/students of Vietnam." A "National Psychological Operations Plan" might help, they thought (III, 45).

The technical intelligentsia were also rallied to the effort of finding the proper formula to inspire the Vietnamese to effective action. The journal *Army* (December 1966) discusses a meeting of

> a group of physicists in the so-called Jason division of the Institute for Defense Analyses (IDA), a think factory that works closely with the Department of Defense. . . . Although they concentrated upon such matters as night vision for detecting guerrillas, improved communications, and vulnerability of aircraft to guerrilla gunfire, the scientists finally concluded that the compelling research need was not in the "hard" sciences but in "softwares"—the social sciences.
>
> "We found that it was a very different problem from what we encountered in dealing with strategic weapons which are generally removed from human factors," said Dr. Jack Ruina, former president of IDA and now a vice president at the Massachusetts Institute of Technology. "In nuclear weapons it's machine versus machine. When we started thinking about counterinsurgency we quickly realized that you cannot isolate these problems from people. What did we know about these people—the Viet Cong and the Vietnamese generally? We felt we needed to know a great deal more from the anthropologist, from the social scientists. The greatest insight we have obtained about the Vietnam situation comes from anthropologists who can speak Vietnamese.
>
> "What we concluded at the Jason session was that social and political and cultural knowledge was very important. A systematic and scholarly study of these areas of the world was clearly necessary. There would be serious difficulties in this type of research, some false starts, and some obstacles, but it should be done."

The report goes on to cite some results, for example, a RAND study of the effects of American bombing, "finding that such raids in North Vietnam improved morale in South Vietnam;

that raids in South Vietnam damaged Viet Cong morale and that hostility toward the U.S. did not grow materially in the bombed areas" (see note 8).

Another RAND study "showed Viet Cong recruits in the villages are lured by the promise of their own rifle and a uniform. As a result the Saigon government decided to try to attract youths with flashy uniforms, jaunty with red, yellow or other lively scarves and berets." This idea does not seem to have been quite the answer. Apparently some component is missing; further research is necessary.

Still another RAND study observed: "The communication of a charisma (miraculously acquired powers) or a set of sympathetic symbols has received attention as an effective leadership device to arouse responsiveness in populations of underdeveloped societies. Charisma or similar symbolism is parsimonious of administrative skill, but also unstable and difficult to use in accomplishing complex social cooperation." No doubt the Pentagon is still puzzling over how to translate this advice into an effective catalyst.

One should not laugh at this sort of inanity. When intelligence fails, there is plenty of force in reserve. As the insights from the social scientists proved inadequate, the United States simply extended and intensified its war of machines against people.

American ambassadors in Saigon were in no position to await the results of the research by government intellectuals, and therefore proposed programs of their own for creating a "cause" that would "accomplish complex social cooperation" on the part of the Vietnamese. Ambassador Bunker suggested that the United States should use its influence to get the GVN to "adopt a program and identify it with that of a former national hero"—in his words, "so as to give the new government an idealistic appeal or philosophy which will compete with that declared by the VC" (August 1967; II, 403). But this ingenious proposal met with no better results than the Ten Point Program for Success proposed by Ambassador Lodge two years earlier. The first point: "Saturate the minds of the people with some socially conscious and attractive ideology, which is susceptible of being carried out" (II, 530). Apparently it didn't matter much what the ideology was. At least, nothing further is said. Somehow, these far-reaching concepts never succeeded in overcoming the "idealistic appeal" of the Viet Cong.

Since the United States never succeeded in "saturating the minds of the people" with a sufficiently attractive ideology, it turned to the easier task of saturating the country with troops and bombs and defoliants. A State Department paper observed: "Saturation bombing by artillery and air strikes . . . is an accepted tactic, and there is probably no province where this tactic has not been widely employed . . ." (IV, 398). The only objection raised is that it might be profitable to place greater emphasis on "unconventional war," specifically on winning popular support for the Saigon regime. That United States force should be devoted to winning support for its creation, the Saigon government, apparently seemed no more strange to the author than that the United States should be conducting saturation bombing of all provinces of South Vietnam.

5. "The Parties to Any Dispute Shall Seek a Solution by Peaceful Means" (United Nations Charter)

5.1. *Geneva, 1954*

Given its inability to win popular support for the regime it imposed in South Vietnam, the United States government took a dim view of international conferences, negotiations, elections, and other peaceful means for resolving the conflict. The American attitude towards the Geneva Conference of 1954 foreshadowed a policy that still persists, in essence. Every effort was made to sabotage the Geneva Conference. When agreements were nonetheless reached, the United States government undertook at once to subvert them. The head of the French delegation at Geneva, Jean Chauvel, concluded that the "only purpose of the Geneva agreements, as [the Americans] see them, is to provide a cover for the political, economic, and military preparations for the conquest."[172] The documentation now available gives dramatic confirmation to this conclusion.

Immediately after the Geneva Conference, the National Security Council met and adopted NSC 5429/2 on August 20,

1954 (*DOD*, bk. 10, pp. 731 ff.). This document, which appears only in the government edition and is misrepresented beyond recognition in the Pentagon Papers history, begins by recognizing the disastrous consequences of the Geneva Conference. One major problem is the Communist "appearance of moderation," which gives them "a basis for sharply accentuating their 'peace propaganda' and 'peace program' in Asia in an attempt to allay fears of Communist expansionist policy and to establish closer relations with the nations of free Asia." The "loss of Southeast Asia," apparently regarded as a serious prospect in the light of these Communist successes, "would imperil retention of Japan as a key element in the off-shore island chain." As we have already seen (section V above), the linkage of Japan to Southeast Asia was a central element in over-all American planning in this period.

The document then outlines a variety of proposals for clandestine operations and other pressures. The key passage, repeated verbatim in NSC policy statements of December 1954 and June–July 1959 (*DOD*, bk. 10, pp. 844, p. 1203), is the following (my emphasis):

> If requested by a legitimate local government which requires assistance to defeat local Communist subversion or rebellion *not constituting armed attack,* the U.S. should view such a situation so gravely that, in addition to giving all possible covert and overt support within Executive Branch authority, the President should at once consider requesting Congressional authority to take appropriate action, which might if necessary and feasible include the use of U.S. military forces either locally or against the external source of such subversion or rebellion (including Communist China if determined to be the source).

This doctrine is in clear and explicit violation of the law (see section III above). In effect, NSC 5429/2 and subsequent elaborations announce that the United States is not bound by its fundamental obligations under the United Nations Charter, and make nonsense of the subsequent appeals to article 51 of the charter, farcical in any event, as we have already observed. Since the "legitimacy" of a local government is a matter of unilateral United States decision, the statement implies that the United States will intervene as it sees fit in the internal affairs of other countries, constrained only by the need to obtain congressional authorization (as it did, by fraud, after the Tonkin Gulf incident of 1964) for its illegal use of force, and will prepare to use military force against any state that it regards as responsible for local subversion or rebellion against a government designated by the United States as "legitimate." In keeping with this principle, the statement—in a section "to be considered as a basis for further consideration," not reported in the subsequent record—recommends policies to "reduce the power of Communist China in Asia even at the risk of, but without deliberately provoking, war," for example, "support for Chinese Nationalist harassing actions" and efforts to "create internal division in the Chinese Communist regime and impair Sino-Soviet relations by all feasible overt and covert means."

The NSC policy statement proposes further that Japan be remilitarized and Thailand developed "as the focal point of U.S. covert and psychological operations in Southeast Asia." With respect to Indochina, the United States will proceed to "make every possible effort, not openly inconsistent with the U.S. position as to the [Geneva] armistice agreements, to defeat Communist subversion and influence, to maintain and support friendly non-Communist governments in Cambodia and Laos, to maintain a friendly non-Communist South Vietnam, and to prevent a Communist victory through all-Vietnam elections." The United States should undertake "covert operations on a large and effective scale" in support of these policies throughout Indochina, including North Vietnam, where it should "exploit available means to make more difficult the control by the Viet Minh of North Vietnam."

Goodbye Geneva. August 1954.

This NSC statement formulates in outline the policies then pursued by the United States government in violation of its commitment to "refrain from the threat or use of force to disturb" the Geneva settlement, and in violation of its more fundamental commitment to the United Nations Charter. The basic content of this highly significant document is omitted from the Pentagon Papers history. Worse still, the history cites the document with a fairly detailed exposition of its implied content, little of which actually appears in the document itself (I, 204). In another chapter, the historian discussing the consequences of the Geneva settlement states that "read in context," the formulation of "the corollary objective (stated by the NSC in August and approved by the President) 'to prevent a Communist victory through all-Vietnam elections' did *not* connote American intention to subvert the accords," but "meant that American influence would aim at assuring that the Communists not gain an electoral victory through deceitful, undemocratic methods" (I, 177). He omits the context, cited above, which reveals clearly that the NSC statement approved by the president connotes precisely an American intention to subvert the accords, as part of a general campaign of intervention throughout East Asia. The director of the Pentagon study, summarizing, states only that "almost at once [after Geneva] . . . U.S. policy began to respond to military urgency" (I, 181).

This misrepresentation, it should be noted, is fully in accord with the general failure of the Pentagon history to inquire into the United States' role as an agent of subversion and aggression, its tendency to regard the United States as a victim merely responding to situations created by others (see pp. 10–11 and section IV above).[173] It should also be noted that the Lansdale report on covert operations in North and South Vietnam in 1954 and 1955 (I, 573 ff.; also II, 643 ff., a few years later) was not part of the Pentagon Papers, and was apparently obtained by the *New York Times* in some other manner. Making no reference to Lansdale's sabotage and subversion missions in the North, the Pentagon historian further states, falsely: "Although American policy spoke of taking steps to prevent the complete absorption of the DRV into the Soviet bloc, those steps amounted to nothing more than maintenance of a U.S. consulate in Hanoi" (I, 213). The failure of the Pentagon historian to mention documented examples of subversion and sabotage—indeed, his denial of their existence—leaves us with no further information here with regard to the report by Bernard Fall that small saboteur groups were parachuted or infiltrated into North Vietnam, with small success and high casualties, "at least since 1956."[174] The combination of omissions and falsification, leading to a complete misrepresentation of the origins of the American war in Indochina, reveals in a striking way the effectiveness of the ideological controls that govern the Pentagon Papers history.

As the records of the International Control Commission make clear, the United States and the GVN during the 1950s attempted to make use of the Geneva Agreements selectively, relying on the ICC to protect the fragile Saigon government while obstructing the ICC at every turn in its efforts to implement the agreements, conducting a vast campaign of terror in the South, and excising the most important provision of the agreements, namely, the elections provision for reunifying the country.[175] Virtually everyone expected the DRV to win the elections, and therefore the United States and the GVN "seemed determined from the outset to scuttle the Geneva Agreements," much to the annoyance of Nehru, for example, who pointed out that "the question is of giving effect to the Geneva Agreements [specifically, the elections provision] or of putting an end to them and facing the consequences," namely, a return to armed struggle. By early 1956, the Western powers "disclaimed responsibility for the most important clause of the Geneva Agreements," the elections provision; and the ICC (Canada abstaining) declared that the explicit opposition of the GVN to the Geneva Agreements "naturally amounts to revocation." The British role was particularly ugly.[176] The ICC reported in 1956 that "while the Commission has experienced difficulties in North Vietnam, the major part of its difficulties has arisen in South Vietnam."[177] All discussions that even attempt to be serious note the difference in degree of compliance, easy to explain, given the general expectation that Vietnam would be unified under Communist rule if the accords were observed.

A DOD study of April 1955 concluded that should the Communists permit elections under international supervision, "there is no reason to doubt at this time that they would win easily in the 1956 elections" (DOD, bk. 10, p. 936), and the same fear was voiced, with various qualifications, throughout this period (DOD, bk. 10, pp. 692, 806, 867, 883), though it was later hoped that it would be possible to weaken the Communists in the North and strengthen the government in the South so that the whole country might ultimately be unified under anticommunist leadership (p. 1131; April 1958).

In April 1955 Dulles proposed (p. 892) that the Western powers insist on certain "safeguards" that would be "probably unacceptable to Communists because of provisions for strict compliance to ensure genuinely free elections" (such as those held under the United States aegis in Asia), and as is well known, the United States backed Diem in his refusal to hold elections or even enter into preliminary discussions, as required by the Geneva Agreements, which of course stipulated that the 17th parallel was merely a provisional military demarcation line, not a political or territorial boundary. Diem consistently took the position that his government was not bound by the Geneva Agreements (p. 1077).

It is interesting that none of these facts have prevented Washington, in later years, from claiming that its only wish is to restore the "essential provisions of the Geneva Accords of 1954" (William Bundy, June 1967; IV, 502). The contents of the Geneva Accords have been so thoroughly forgotten that even Chester Cooper, who took part in the Geneva Conference and has remained active in Indochina affairs since, is able to say blandly that the United States' Vietnam aid program was governed by "a strong desire to maintain for the South Vietnamese the independence they were granted at Geneva" (discussing the "basic philosophy of American aid to Vietnam," so "naive and idealistic").[178] Thus are myths created.

5.2 Elections and Democracy

In the late 1960s, the United States backed elections within the GVN, so long as they were held under laws that excluded Communists and neutralists who work directly or indirectly for the Communists or "whose actions are advantageous to the communists."[179] A Vietnamese commentator points out: "The election laws in the Republic of Vietnam are laws designed to exclude all those patriotic people who have made the greatest contribution toward protecting their country and their villages and who will never be cowed by the foreigners."[180] He is elaborating the views of a South Vietnamese judge who had written shortly before: "In a whorehouse society [Vietnam, under allied occupation] if the prostitutes were forced to organize elections to choose their leader, the house's madam can always have them vote for a pimp who can effectively carry out her orders."

Since the publication of the Pentagon Papers and the one-man "election" of October 1971, it has become fashionable to point out that the United States of course never really intended to bring democracy to Vietnam. But it should be recalled that while the illusion could still be popularly maintained, American intervention was consistently justified on just these grounds, to the public and internally as well. See, for example, John F. Kennedy's remarks cited above (p. 41), or the remarks of William Bundy on the "courageous and extremely difficult effort [of South Vietnam] to become a true democracy during a guerrilla war" and the United States commitment to prevent any solution not "acceptable voluntarily to the South Vietnamese Government and people."[181] Such ideas are still expressed, for example, by Sir Robert Thompson, one of Britain's gifts to the Vietnamese people, who writes that "giving the people of South Viet Nam a free choice" is the cornerstone of American policy.[182]

Sir Robert's concept of "free choice" provides a good insight into the colonialist mentality. It is explained by Roger Hilsman in discussing Thompson's concept of strategic hamlets, which were to "create the physical security the villager must have before he could make a free choice between the Vietcong and the government." The plan failed, Hilsman explains, because Diem's brother Nhu did not follow a careful program "in which the loyalties of each area were assured and all Vietcong agents eliminated before the troops and civic action teams moved on to the next." Thus "Vietcong agents remained in place," and a free choice was impossible. For a true "free choice," it was necessary to physically eliminate the opposition. Then the villagers could choose freely between the government and the Viet Cong, in their encampments surrounded by barbed wire and occupied by American-backed government troops.[183]

In a survey of the strategic hamlet program, which the GVN claims resettled a third of the population of South Vietnam by summer 1962,[184] the Pentagon Papers analyst (II, chap. 2) records Thompson's "input," in particular his belief that the program should be "clinical," not "surgical"—emphasizing police rather than military—and that it failed because the Viet Cong infrastructure was not eliminated. The analyst observes that the "physical aspects" of the program were "similar if not identical to earlier population resettlement and control efforts practiced by the French and by Diem"; "all failed dismally because they ran into resentment if not active resistance on the part of the peasants at whose control and safety, then loyalty, they were aimed." This was evident from the start, when the majority of the peasants refused to cooperate and had to be "herded forcibly from their homes" in Operation SUNRISE. Another way of putting it is that the peasants, unaccountably, refused the free choice so generously offered them.

The form of "democracy" envisioned by Americans who were intervening most extensively in the internal affairs of Indochina is revealed in some comments by General Lansdale. Discussing the situation in Laos in 1961, he writes: "There is also a local veteran's organization and a grass-roots political organization in Laos, both of which are subject to CIA direction and control . . ." (II, 647). The concept of a grass-roots organization under CIA direction and control is symbolic of American aims in Indochina, and brings out the reality behind the rhetoric in which they are masked.

The conception of democracy advanced by our various ambassadors also makes interesting reading. Ambassador Durbrow, for example, thought that a liberal press code would be a good idea: "it would be most beneficial to a better understanding of the fruitful efforts being made by your [Diem's] Government on behalf of the people. . . ." Under the system he envisioned, "the Government should only intervene if articles are flagrantly dishonest, inaccurate, or favorable to the Communists" (*DOD*, bk. 10, p. 1354; December 1960). Interchanging a few names, what commissar could disagree?

Ambassador Lodge's contributions are along similar lines. He opposed Diem when it appeared that Diem could not "gain the support of the people who count, i.e., the educated class in and out of government service" (II, 738; August 1963). A few months later, he recognized that the Vietnamese generals obviously "are all we have got" (II, 304), but was undeterred by this insight. In his second tour of duty, Lodge came to support elections, which he felt should be as fair as possible "so as to gain a maximum improvement in the image of the GVN in the United States and internationally." They should "bring together" all noncommunist groups committed to receiving American help (to defend "their country's independence"). With his concurrence, "the approved electoral law gave the Directorate [the Ky regime] ample scope to exclude unwanted candidates, and prevented the Buddhists from putting their symbol . . . on the ballot." Lodge further "unreservedly backed" the exclusion of Buddhists of the Struggle Movement as "moderate measures to prevent elections from being used as a vehicle for a Communist takeover." Lodge regarded the Buddhists "as equivalent to card-carrying Communists," the analyst reports (II, 376–8, 384). Any democracy, after all, must take special measures to exclude communists from the electoral process if they have a chance to win, and also to defend itself from criminal elements; and the Buddhists of Hue and Da Nang, in Ambassador Lodge's considered judgment, were responsible for "criminal violence operating under political, economic and social guise." Their actions demonstrated to him that the Vietnamese are obviously not ready for self-government, and raised the possibility that "we may have to decide how much it is worth to us to deny Viet-Nam to Hanoi and Peking—regardless of what the Vietnamese may think" (IV, 99–100). Lodge also opposed a "constituent assembly" (a "pernicious French phrase") which "stays around and makes trouble for an indefinite period," preferring a "constitutional convention," which "would meet, adopt the constitution and disband" (II, 371).

Perhaps a fair indication of how the United States actually viewed Vietnamese politics is given by the reaction to the elections to the National Assembly of September 27, 1963, "with predictably high turnouts and majorities for Government candidates" (II, 215). At just this period, as the analyst reports, "we variously authorized, sanctioned and encouraged the coup efforts of the Vietnamese generals and offered full support for a successor government" (II, 207), for the reason that the government had so "alienated popular support" that victory over the Viet Cong under Diem was thought to be virtually impossible (II, 201 ff.).

It might be added that the attitude towards American democracy was not too different (see note 39). This is revealed in a striking way during the deliberations of 1964. Plans for the February 1965 escalation were undertaken in 1964 with awareness of the necessity for waiting until the president had a congressional mandate and a popular mandate.

> . . . mid-1964 was not an auspicious time for new departures in policy by a President who wished to portray "moderate" alternatives to his opponents' "radical" proposals. Nor was any time prior to or immediately following the elections very appealing for the same reason. . . . President Johnson had neither a congressional nor a popular mandate to Americanize the war or to expand it dramatically by "going north." [III, 2–4; cf. NSC 5429/2, discussed in subsection 5.1 above]

By June 1964, it was recognized "that only relatively heavy levels of attack on the DRV would be likely to have any significant compelling effect," but most of the president's advisers "recognized the necessity of building firmer public and congressional support for greater U.S. involvement in SEA before any wider military actions should be undertaken" (III, 107). After the Tonkin Gulf incident and the resulting congressional endorsement, and President Johnson's "smashing victory at the polls," his "feasible options increased." He was now "armed with both a popular mandate and broad Congressional authorization" and could therefore proceed (III, 4–6). By September, "there was little basic disagreement among the principals on the need for military actions against the North." At an important meeting of top-level officials (Rusk, McNamara, Wheeler, Taylor, McCone), this view was advanced "with a sense that such actions were inevitable." But "tactical considerations," among them the ongoing election campaign in which the president "was presenting himself as the candidate of reason and restraint," prevented action "for the time being" (III, 111). During the September deliberations, "unity of domestic American opinion" was regarded as a precondition to escalation, but during the November debates, this was "no longer an important factor," though the president remained "cautious and equivocal." In the interim, he had been elected "with an overwhelming mandate" (III, 113–16). Decisions to escalate or to carry out deliberate provocation to justify United States response were to be postponed "probably until November or December." Throughout the deliberations, December or January 1 was regarded as "target D-day" (III, 198–200, 207), that is, after the elections.

It is remarkable that nowhere does the analyst see fit to mention that the popular mandate was *not* to escalate, or that the congressional support was obtained in a rather dubious fashion.[185] It was sufficient that congressional approval was obtained, and that there was a smashing victory at the polls. The obvious conclusion to draw from this history is that peace-minded people should have voted for Goldwater, so that the "mandate" would have been less overwhelming, since apparently it was only its scale and not its character that mattered. The whole affair is a remarkable example of the totalitarian instincts of the planners, accepted as natural by the historian.[186]

5.3. Negotiations

A major reason why the president was "cautious and equivocal" was the fear that a Communist response to American escalation would topple the unstable GVN and that international pressures would bring about "premature negotiations" —that is, negotiations that might lead to a political settlement, hence a Communist victory, given the political strength of the opposing forces. Recall that this was a period when, as Douglas Pike puts it, the noncommunists in South Vietnam, with the possible exception of the Buddhists, could not risk entering a coalition, "fearing that if they did the whale would swallow the minnow."[187]

These fears were expressed early in the year, when plans for direct military action against the North were under serious consideration. Secretary McNamara informed the president that such operations were of an "extremely delicate nature": "There would be the problem of marshalling the case to justify such action, the problem of communist escalation, and the problem of dealing with the pressures for premature or 'stacked' negotiations" (III, 504; March 16, 1964). A few days later, the president informed Ambassador Lodge in Saigon that the immediate task must be "to strengthen the southern base." "For this reason," he went on, the plans for overt military action against the North must be "on a contingency basis at present, and the immediate problem in this area is to develop the strongest possible military and political base for possible later action" (III, 511). Further deliberations remained within this framework until the elections.

It has been argued that there was no real deception during the presidential campaign of 1964, since the plans to escalate were only "contingency plans." The record excludes this interpretation. True, the plans were "on a contingency basis," for the reasons just noted: the need for a popular and congressional mandate, the weakness of the Southern base, the dangers of premature negotiations. To place these deliberations in the category of plans to bomb Moscow or invade Brazil, if circumstances warrant, is patently absurd.

Throughout the fateful year of 1964, planning continued on the assumptions noted. After the election, there was little doubt that escalation would be undertaken. As Ambassador Taylor explained rather neatly on November 27, if the GVN falls, "we should be prepared for emergency military action against the North if only to shore up a collapsing situation"; and "if, on the other hand . . . the government maintains and proves itself, then we should be prepared to embark on a methodical program of mounting air attacks" (III, 241). In short, whatever the situation, bomb. He also added, "Do not enter into negotiations until the DRV is hurting."

The latter assumption was unchallenged, through 1964. McNamara's fear of premature or "stacked" negotiations was reiterated throughout the detailed planning. The DRV might respond with some military action of its own to a direct bombing attack, which "may have to continue through substantial levels of military, industrial, and governmental destruction in the DRV" (III, 620). Such Communist perfidy might topple the collapsing GVN. It might also spur international efforts to achieve a solution by peaceful means. But negotiations, seriously undertaken, would lead to a political solution, hence an American defeat. We have already noted the refusal of the

planners to accept the likely outcome of a Vietnamese-negotiated deal leading to a unified Communist Vietnam hostile to
China (see p. 34 above).

The insistence on using force prior to any negotiations
should be read in the light of the legal obligation, under the
United Nations Charter, to refrain from the threat or use of
force and to employ peaceful means (such as negotiations)
for settling disputes. In a parody of the supreme law of the
land, the cabal insisted that "after, *but only after*, we have
established a clear pattern of pressure" could peaceful means
be considered (William Bundy, August 11, 1964; III, 526;
his emphasis). The same wording was repeated a few days
later in a message from State to Saigon under the heading
"Essential Elements of US Policy" (III, 535). First force,
then talk.

One finds no discussion of the legal obligations of the
United States.[188] Rather, all agencies "saw negotiations as
something that should not be entered into until the pressures
were hurting North Vietnam" (III, 204). As Taylor put it in
February, we must "convey signals which, in combination,
should present to the DRV leaders a vision of inevitable, ultimate destruction if they do not change their ways"; "degree of
damage and number of casualties inflicted gauge the impact of
our operations on Hanoi leadership and hence are important
as a measure of their discomfort" (III, 316). Consistently,
United States policy was to avoid being trapped[189] into reliance on peaceful, legal means until the proper signals had
been conveyed by sufficient damage, casualties, and a credible
threat of ultimate destruction.

Subsequent policy adhered to the principle: First force,
then talk. President Johnson's speech of April 7, 1965, according to the analyst, "was in accord with the 'pressures policy'
rationale that had been worked out in November, 1964, which
held that U.S. readiness to negotiate was not to be surfaced
until after a series of air strikes that had been carried out
against important targets in North Vietnam" (III, 356). For
this reason, "significantly," there had been particularly intensive bombing for the two weeks prior to the president's "initiative." The cynicism of this approach entirely escapes the
analyst. Nor does he, in a later section, draw any connection

between the general "pressures policy" and the odd fact that, repeatedly, apparent DRV peace feelers and negotiations opportunities were undercut by sudden escalation of bombing (IV, 135, 205). To the analyst, the bombing escalation at these moments was "inadvertent" or an "unfortunate coincidence" (though he admits that the DRV leaders must have had "the strong impression they were being squeezed by Johnsonian pressure tactics"). He attributes the failure of negotiations to "North Vietnam's bruised ego," a degree of sensitivity revealed as well by his reference to the "cries of civilian casualties . . . heard long and loud from Hanoi" when the Hanoi power plant was bombed in May 1967 (IV, 153).

Historians who do not unthinkingly accept the framework of government propaganda have taken note of the "unfortunate coincidences," and have suggested possible explanations that need not concern us here.[190] It is possible that all of these instances merely reflected the "pressures policy" rationale of Washington, the general assumption that, in explicit contradiction to the supreme law of the land, threat and use of force must precede efforts at "peaceful settlement" of disputes.

This is not to deny that the consensus of the planners in late 1964 was realistic. It was. There was simply no basis for negotiations, given the balance of political forces. A predominant United States role in determining the economic and social structure of Vietnam is not negotiable as long as nationalist forces that oppose such an outcome are sufficiently strong to continue their resistance. Hence all negotiations are doomed to failure, apart from those leading to a true United States withdrawal, or ratifying the surrender of those who had "captured" the nationalist movement to the United States and its local associates.

The volumes of the Pentagon Papers dealing with negotiations are not yet available to the public, but in the record presented here there are some interesting curiosities. Throughout 1964 and early 1965 there are repeated references to various negotiations efforts, but one is conspicuously missing, namely, the effort by U Thant that was probably the most promising of all. In October 1964, U Thant told United

Nations Ambassador Stevenson that Ho Chi Minh had apparently agreed to negotiations in Rangoon. The proposal seems to have been concealed internally until U Thant threatened to "blow" the story in January, when the United States rejected the proposal.[191] On January 6, 1965, William Bundy reported to the secretary of state that the Soviet Union, China, and the DRV had "called for a Laos conference without preconditions but have refrained from mentioning a conference on Vietnam" (III, 684), and went on to suggest an explanation for the latter omission. Apparently Bundy was unaware of the proposal (as was his brother, according to Cooper). Without further information, it appears that there was a conspiracy within a conspiracy, in this instance.

6. Initiative and Response: Aggression Against South Vietnam

In its official propaganda, the United States government, like most others, presents itself as a status quo power attempting to uphold a stable international order in the face of violence and aggression. As we have seen, the Pentagon historians generally operate within this ideological framework. The documentary record that they were examining, however, reveals that exactly the opposite was the case. At every point, the United States resorted to force to disrupt social and political arrangements that it regarded as detrimental to its global policies. A response by indigenous forces was then labeled "aggression," and presented to the public as a justification for further American escalation.

The essence of the United States position is revealed by public statements explaining the concept of "aggression." Consider, for example, the fairly typical remarks by Adlai Stevenson to the United Nations Security Council, May 21, 1964 (III, 715–16). He observed that "the point is the same in Vietnam today as it was in Greece in 1947." In both cases, the United States was defending a free people from "internal aggression":

> I would remind the members that in 1947, after the aggressors had gained control of most of the country, many people felt that the cause of the Government of Greece was hopelessly lost. But as long as the people of Greece were

prepared to fight for the life of their own country, the United States was not prepared to stand by while Greece was overrun.

Similarly, "The United States cannot stand by while Southeast Asia is overrun by armed aggressors."

Stevenson's historical analogy is more or less to the point. In Vietnam as in Greece, the United States was seeking to block "internal aggression," that is, "aggression" by a mass-based indigenous movement against a government protected by foreign power, where the "internal aggression" has the kind of outside support that few wars of liberation have lacked (for example, the American Revolution, to cite a case where far greater outside support was decisive; cf. chapter 3, p. 245).

In both cases, in utter defiance of available evidence, the United States executive has sought to mask the absurdity of its claims by pretending that the "internal aggressors" were merely agents of a global conspiracy directed by Moscow or "Peiping."[192] As the United States undertook to overthrow the status quo of 1945–1946 by attempting to restore French influence and control over Indochina, the State Department solemnly informed the French government, in June 1949, of the "inevitable intention" of the Viet Minh "to subvert the nationalist cause in the end to the requirements of international Communism." The benighted Vietnamese, unable to comprehend this fact, are impressed by "its effective leadership of the nationalist movement." But the United States understands full well, and therefore takes the "paramount question in Indochina" to be "whether the country is to be saved from Communist control," all other issues being "irrelevant," given the need "to preserve Indochina from a foreign tyranny" (*DOD*, bk. 8, pp. 208–9). Dean Rusk went on to inform the press that the French and the "independent" Associated States are firmly holding the line in "defense of Indochina against communist colonialism," spearheaded by the Viet Minh (p. 397).

The National Security Council (February 1950) held that the French army, along with native troops, "is now in armed conflict with the forces of communist aggression," and is "attempting to restore law and order" (I, 361). The president's Special Committee on Southeast Asia, in early 1954, explained further that the French had demonstrated, by their grant of independence to the Associated States, that "the Viet Minh are not fighting for freedom." The French are fighting "to defend the cause of liberty and freedom from Communism in Indochina." "The cause of Viet Minh," in contrast, is "the cause of colonization and subservience to Kremlin rule as was the cause in China, in North Korea[193] and in the European satellites" (*DOD*, bk. 9, p. 342).

The Viet Minh are the colonialists; the French defend Vietnamese independence.

In his first State of the Union message, President Kennedy warned that "in Asia, the relentless pressures of the Chinese Communists menace the security of the entire area—from the borders of India and South Viet Nam to the jungles of Laos, struggling to protect its newly-won independence."[194] A draft report of the Gilpatric Task Force (May 1961), discussing the deployment of "U.S. battle groups," stated that their purpose would be to deter "*further* Communist aggression from North Vietnam, China, or the Soviet Union, while rallying the morale of the Vietnamese" (II, 48; emphasis mine). On the eve of the escalation of February 1965, John McNaughton, with the agreement of McNamara, described the "U.S. objective in South Vietnam" as "to contain China" (III, 686, 267), and two months later stated a major objective as "To keep SVN (and then adjacent) territory from Chinese hands."[195] A more profound misunderstanding of the content of Vietnamese nationalism, and its Communist leadership, could hardly be imagined. And George Carver, speaking for the CIA in April 1966, proclaimed the objective: "Demonstrating the sterile futility of the militant and aggressive expansionist policy advocated by the present rulers of Communist China" (IV, 82; cf. note 145). Essentially the same view was developed further by McGeorge Bundy, in mid-1967, when he stated that whatever Eastern intellectuals may think, most Americans and "nearly all Asians" know that the domino theory is correct; thus United States intervention "has already saved the hope of freedom for hundreds of millions," no less (IV, 159). Robert McNamara added that the objective of "draw[ing] the line against Chinese expansionism in Asia" had already been attained (IV, 174).[196] And so on.

The notions of the Kennedy intellectuals and the CIA are hardly different from some of the weird views of American military experts. For example, General Van Fleet, reporting on his mission to the Far East in October 1954, charged that "since the end of World War II, the Chinese Communist regime has waged a relentless war against the free world, specifically the United States." "Peace with freedom cannot be restored to Asia as long as the Chinese Communist regime continues to exist" (*DOD*, bk. 10, p. 794). It would be interesting to explore further General Van Fleet's ideas about "restoring" freedom to Asia. The director of the Pentagon study comments that "all U.S. expectations [in 1950] seemed to have been underpinned by the Joint Chiefs' belief that 'attainment of United States objectives in Asia can only be achieved by ultimate success in China'" (I, 179).

Internal documents quite generally refer to the "VC aggression in the South" (e.g., IV, 58, October 1965). Similarly, a Pentagon memorandum described "the obvious and not wholly anticipated strength of the Viet Cong infrastructure" after the Tet offensive of 1968, adding that this "shows that there can be no prospect of a quick military solution to the aggression in South Vietnam"—the aggression, that is, organized by the Viet Cong infrastructure (IV, 581).

On the character of "aggression," there are also interesting comments by the Joint Chiefs. In February 1955, they foresaw "three basic forms in which aggression in Southeast Asia can occur: a) Overt armed attack from outside of the area. b) Overt armed attack from within the area of each of the sovereign states. c) Aggression other than armed, i.e., political warfare, or subversion" (*DOD*, bk. 10, p. 885). The concept of "overt armed attack from within" a sovereign state is Stevenson's "internal aggression." In defining "political warfare" as a form of aggression, the Joint Chiefs reveal that they comprehend with precision and insight the fundamental position of the United States executive.

Notice that it is the same concept of "internal aggression" that Sidney Hook employs in the remarks cited earlier, when he refers to the application of American military force in repelling the "incursions" of the NLF (mere "partisans" of

North Vietnam), for example, by B-52 raids in the Mekong Delta with their "unfortunate accidental loss of life" (p. 72 above).

In January 1959, the Operations Coordinating Board published an "Operations Plan for Viet-Nam," to be implemented by member agencies. As the plan was developed within the Defense Department, the Joint Chiefs of Staff were assigned responsibility to "deter the Viet Cong (formerly called Viet Minh) from attacking or subverting Free Viet-Nam or other neighboring states." They were also to "probe weaknesses of the Viet Cong and exploit them internally and internationally whenever possible" (*DOD*, bk. 10, p. 1186; May 1959). The Pentagon, in short, was to deter "internal aggression" by the nationalist movement of Indochina.

According to the same plan, the Pentagon was to "encourage U.S. training and orientation visits" for Vietnamese, expanding existing programs, and to "encourage fullest assimilation into Vietnamese life (military, economic, social, political and cultural) of returned exchangees, participants and trainees," thus "help[ing] them exercise a pro–Free World influence among fellow Vietnamese." Or, to use the terminology favored by American propagandists, the United States military was to step up its program of infiltrating trained regroupees into South Vietnam to subvert South Vietnam and to place it more firmly under foreign domination. The Operations Plan for Vietnam does not deal with the problem of deterring ongoing "aggression from the North," there being none. Rather, its concern is to implement American intervention in the South, that is, military and other actions against the indigenous "Viet Cong." At the same time the United States military command was to increase its efforts to bring South Vietnam within the American orbit, in accordance with the long-term objectives laid down years earlier.

There is a certain irony in the fact that both the propaganda apparatus of the United States government and independent scholars have given much attention to a meeting that took place in Hanoi in the same month, May 1959, when the Communist Party of North Vietnam—as government spokesmen would have it—set in motion its effort to subvert and conquer its free Southern neighbor. At this meeting, the party is reported to have granted Southern cadres permission to take up arms to defend themselves against the terror of the United States–imposed regime, which had decimated the Southern Viet Minh during the period when Hanoi was urging restraint and abstention from force and violence.[197] The same meeting reportedly authorized Southerners who had regrouped to the North in accord with the Geneva Agreements to return to their homes in the South to participate in the ongoing Southern rebellion. Not even the most extreme advocate of United States intervention claims that the party did more in May 1959 than initiate programs of the sort that the American Joint Chiefs of Staff were given responsibility to *expand* at the same moment. All of this, to be sure, overlooks a fundamental asymmetry: those who were implementing the Operations Plan for Vietnam could hardly be classed as Vietnamese, and the border they were crossing was most assuredly a political and territorial boundary.

The same concept of "internal aggression" was employed with regard to Laos. The president justified the initiation of low-level armed reconnaissance (that is, bombing and strafing) in Laos in May 1964 as a reaction to "new acts of communist aggression in Laos" (III, 720). The "aggressors," in this case, were left-leaning neutralists and Pathet Lao who restored the status quo as of April 1963, possibly responding to a right-wing coup attempt in Vientiane and an effort to integrate left-neutralist forces into the rightist army.[198] In Laos as in South Vietnam, the United States had for many years trained right-wing military forces abroad, then returned them to take part in rebellion and domestic repression. For example, in late 1960 the United States handed over 200 Laotian paratroopers who had been training in Thailand (the "focal point" for American operations in Southeast Asia—see p. 102 above) to Phoumi Nosavan, the favorite of the CIA and the American military, who was then in open rebellion against the Souvanna Phouma government,[199] pro-Western but not sufficiently reactionary to enlist United States support. This was a period when American correspondents reported that "if free elections were held today in Laos, every qualified observer, including the American Embassy, concedes this hermit kingdom would go Communist in a landslide," that the Pathet Lao political party "controls the countryside [and] the odds [in any election] are heavily in favor of that party, which has diligently built up an organization controlling most of the country's ten thousand villages."[200] The dispatch of Lao paratroopers in an effort to overthrow the centrist regime which itself could not withstand the Pathet Lao in open political competition is not regarded by the United States government or the Pentagon historians[201] as aggression or armed intervention, though the return of Southern regroupees to their homes from 1959 was an "armed attack" against South Vietnam which justified United States "response" under article 51 of the United Nations Charter.[202]

In these and many other cases, the concept of aggression employed by the United States executive gives the game away. Indigenous forces are carrying out "internal aggression" against regimes chosen to rule by the Western powers, and protected from their own populations by outside force (acting in "collective self-defense" against this "aggression").

The Pentagon historian traces the "U.S. awareness of the requirement to promote internal stability" to the late 1950s, noting in particular the contribution of the Draper Committee (The President's Committee to Study the U.S. Military Assistance Program) in 1958–1959. The Draper Committee distinguished clearly between two tasks of the military forces assisted by the United States: "countering external aggression" and countering "internal aggression" (II, 435). Perhaps this is the origin of the interesting phrase "internal aggression," later adopted by Adlai Stevenson and others. The Draper Committee's papers also "sought to popularize military civic action programs and to link them to politically acceptable precedents—such as the U.S. Army's role in the development of the American West." The reference is suggestive. The United States Army was protecting the developers of the American West from the internal aggression of the Indians who were being swept off their lands. Taking this as a "precedent," who plays the role of the American Indians in the "military civic action programs" advised and assisted by the United States military in some foreign land? And to whom is the precedent, or its contemporary analogue, "politically acceptable"? Pursuing these questions, we achieve some interesting insights into counterinsurgency doctrines that developed out of the deliberations of the Draper Committee and that so entranced the Kennedy intellectuals.[203]

Occasionally, explicit notice is taken of the fact that "in South Vietnam, the Communists are clearly embarked on a 'national liberation war' of insurgency and subversion from within rather [than] on overt aggression."[204] The distinction is fundamental. It undermines any appeal to the United Nations Charter or to the SEATO treaty, as has frequently been noted. The facts, however, did not prevent President Kennedy from asserting that "the systematic aggression now bleeding that country is not a 'war of liberation'—for Viet Nam is already free" (II, 806; January 1962), as they have never prevented his advisers from saying that the United States was throughout engaged in defending a free people from aggression, or that in 1962 "aggression [was] checked in Vietnam."[205] Misrepresentation becomes absurdity when we realize that in that same year, 1962, American forces were directly engaged in combat operations against the insurgents in South Vietnam.[206] Throughout, the United States, exactly like France, is fighting to preserve the freedom of the Vietnamese from the colonialist Viet Minh and their successors in aggression. On this assumption it is quite proper for Ambassador Maxwell Taylor to sputter with indignation over the "outrageous acts of the Vietcong in South Vietnam, such as the attack on Bien Hoa," the American air base, damaging or destroying 27 of 30 United States B-57s and killing several Americans. To "repay" such outrageous acts, "we could engage in reprisal bombings" against North Vietnam, which we have determined to be responsible (III, 669; II, 341; III, 288; October–November 1964).

On other occasions, administration spokesmen were placed in a position where reference to "internal aggression" would appear too cynical or unconvincing, and they therefore simply asserted that there had been overt aggression by the North Vietnamese prior to United States escalation in February 1965. Secretary Rusk, testifying before the Senate Foreign Relations Committee in January and February 1966, stated that the 325th Division of the North Vietnamese army had entered South Vietnam by January 1965, an act that constituted "aggression by means of an armed attack" and entitled the United States to respond under article 51 of the United Nations Charter. The public record sufficed to disprove this contention, as Theodore Draper demonstrated in a careful analysis at the time.[207] The Pentagon Papers now demonstrate conclusively that when the United States undertook the February escalation, it knew of no regular North Vietnamese units in South Vietnam. In fact, in early July 1965, the assistant secretary of defense was still concerned with the *possibility* that there might be PAVN forces in or near South Vietnam; and a few weeks later, the Joint Chiefs included one regiment of the 325th PAVN Division in their estimate of 48,500 "Viet Cong organized combat units" (the only PAVN unit identified). For comparison, note that the Honolulu meeting of April 20 had recommended that American forces be raised to 82,000 supplemented with 7,250 Korean and Australian troops (2,000 Koreans had been dispatched on January 8, 1965). By June, the United States decided "to pour U.S. troops into the country as fast as they could be deployed" (II, 362), and in mid-July the president approved the request that the United States troop level be raised to 175,000.[208] In the light of these facts, the claim that the United States was defending South Vietnam from an armed attack is merely ludicrous.

Conceivably, one might argue that Secretary Rusk's testimony is not inconsistent with the record presented in the Pentagon Papers and elsewhere. One might speculate that information obtained prior to his testimony, but after the summer of 1965, revealed that the PAVN 325th Division had in fact infiltrated into South Vietnam by January 1965, as Rusk maintained in his Senate testimony.

There are two difficulties in this defense, the only possible one. In the first place, there is no evidence that the speculation is correct. Second and more important, even if it were correct it would be irrelevant. Rusk's testimony was an effort to justify the United States escalation of February as collective self-defense against armed attack. Putting aside a variety of other objections, the justification would have force only if it had been known at the time of the escalation that an armed attack had taken place. The record makes it absolutely clear that this was not the case. Hence the justification fails under any assumption with regard to unknown facts.

Suppose, for example, that after invading Czechoslovakia the Russians had discovered that, unknown to them, some armed attack had taken place against Czechoslovakia, say, by West German forces. They could not have argued that this "discovery" justified their armed intervention on the grounds of article 51. It is therefore clear that Rusk's testimony consisted of either false statements or fraudulent representations, and hence was technically criminal (see note 41). It may also be recalled that the fraudulent nature of Rusk's testimony (and not his alone) was known and demonstrated at once (cf. Draper, *Abuse of Power*), even without the far more extensive confirmation now possible. And finally, we may take note of the homilies on "the rule of law" that are delivered from the judicial bench or in the pages of journals of opinion when citizens undertake minor acts of nonviolent civil disobedience in protest against aggression and mass murder: the fabric of society will dissolve and we will fall into anarchy and barbarism if the law is not uniformly applied.

The Pentagon Papers reveal that United States policy makers believed the NLF to be a creature of Hanoi, and Hanoi to be an agent of "international communism." Under law, they were entitled to express these beliefs and to request the Security Council of the United Nations to determine the existence of a threat to peace. That they did not do so is significant, and self-explanatory. But it is worth mentioning that there is a logical gap between the demonstration that American policy makers expressed (and perhaps even held) such beliefs and the demonstration that the beliefs were correct. The matter has no bearing on the issue of American aggression, but it might be considered nonetheless. It is interesting, for example, that the Soviet Union had virtually cut off aid to North Vietnam from 1962 to 1964 (IV, 116), when this agent of international communism was allegedly engaged in aggression against the free people of South Vietnam. So marginal was the Soviet interest in Southeast Asia prior to the American escalation of 1964 that the NSC working group (November 1964) expressed the view that "Moscow's role in

Vietnam is likely to remain a relatively minor one" (III, 215). But the "period of nearly three years of diligent detachment" came to an end; "the Soviet Union . . . reentered Southeast Asian politics in an active way" with a "reported Soviet pledge in November [1964] to increase economic and military aid to North Vietnam," and subsequent warnings that it would support the DRV in the face of the naval attacks on the coast and United States air attacks in Laos, then approaching the DRV border (III, 266–7). As to the Chinese menace, the United States White Paper of February 1965 was able to report the discovery of three 75-millimeter recoilless rifles of Chinese Communist origin (more is claimed in internal documents—cf. III, 502). The only Chinese directly engaged in Indochina, so far as is known, were the "few Chinese nationalists" involved in covert operations in North Vietnam (III, 500), and those reportedly engaged in clandestine operations under CIA direction in South Vietnam and Laos.[209]

The Pentagon historian observes that Chinese Communist activity in Southeast Asia appeared "ominous" to Washington in late 1964 (III, 267), but he is able to cite as factual basis only "Sukarno's abrupt withdrawal of Indonesia's participation in the U.N.," which led to various speculations. We have already noted the determined efforts, always unavailing, to demonstrate the link to "international communism" in earlier years, and the significance of this quest(see above, pp. 51–5). See also Lyndon Johnson's ludicrous account of the pattern of Communist aggression in Asia in 1964–1965 (*Vantage Point*, pp. 134–6).

As to the matter of the assumed North Vietnamese control over the NLF, it is relevant that the Commander-in-Chief, Pacific (CINCPAC), also believed that Hanoi furnished "support and direction" to the "insurgency in Thailand" (IV, 124), exactly as claimed with regard to the NLF. When pressed, however, United States officials are unable to present evidence that the Thai insurgency was directed by or received more than minimal support from China or North Vietnam, even long after the use of Thailand as the "focal point" for United States covert and direct military operations (including the air war) throughout Indochina.[210] There have been efforts to demonstrate that the Pathet Lao is hardly more than an agency of the DRV, but they are not very impressive.[211] The United States did attempt to prove North Vietnamese aggression in a White Paper of February 1965. But as Chester Cooper observes, this "proved to be a dismal disappointment" because "the actual findings seemed pretty frail."[212] His statement takes on added interest when we learn that Cooper was in charge of preparing the evidence on infiltration for publication (III, 255, 681).

The Pentagon history refers to intelligence estimates allegedly demonstrating North Vietnamese control over the NLF, but no evidence is actually presented.[213] It is useful to recall that United States intelligence is not the only source of information on Indochina and has not been remarkable for its insights. Others with a more intimate understanding of the affairs of Indochina have consistently been more successful in interpreting, explaining, and predicting events there. Turning to such sources, we find considerable skepticism with regard to the belief that the NLF are well-behaved puppets of North Vietnam. "Even a summary acquaintance with Vietnamese realities," two such experts write, "excludes the possibility that the insurrection in the South is directed or even inspired by the North Vietnamese. If Vietnam is one, still regional differences remain and the members of the resistance are too well-informed to fail to take account of this."[214]

Surveying such evidence as exists, United States government claims with regard to DRV control of the NLF prior to 1965 are not compelling, though as DRV forces were drawn into the war by American aggression, and as South Vietnamese society crumbled under the massive American attack, the degree of influence and control exercised by Hanoi undoubtedly increased, as had been anticipated by American planners.

It was, in fact, always understood that heightened American intervention might lead to "DRV ground action in South Vietnam or Laos" in "retaliation" (III, 616; William Bundy, November 1964). The same assumptions underlie the analysis of the "fast/full squeeze," the most aggressive option under consideration in November 1964 (III, 633 ff.). This analysis considers the possible "serious Communist responses to increased military pressures" by the United States against the DRV: "a VC offensive in South Vietnam; DRV or Chicom air attacks in South Vietnam; DRV ground offensives into South Vietnam; and Chicom/DRV offensives into South Vietnam or Laos." These are identified as the possible forms of Communist "retaliation" in response to "a systematic program of military pressures against the north, meshing at some point with negotiation, but with pressure actions to be continued at a fairly rapid pace and without interruption until we achieve our present objective of getting Hanoi completely out of South VN and an independent and secure South VN reestablished." In the event of a DRV ground offensive into South Vietnam in response to the United States attack on the North, the United States would implement CINCPAC OPLAN 32-64, Phase III, which "envisages further an early ground attack northward to seize, liberate and occupy North Vietnam." In the event that Chinese troops join in "retaliation" against American escalation of the war, then the United States would "employ massive US naval and air power against Communist China and her satellites [not further identified] at times and places of our choice to force termination of the aggression [*sic*] . . . including liberation and control of North Vietnam and reunification of Vietnam under a government aligned with the Free World . . . and the curtailment of communist influence in Southeast Asia."

Consider the reasoning of the American planners. The United States initiates a "fast/full squeeze" against the DRV. If the DRV "retaliates" by sending troops to the South (where more than 20,000 American forces are deployed, and American troops have been engaged in combat and combat support against Southern rebels for three years), then the United States will "liberate and occupy North Vietnam." If China joins the DRV in responding to the American aggression, then the United States will attack Communist China and her "satellites" at will, "to force termination of the aggression." Here we see exposed, with full clarity, the thinking of a gang of international outlaws.

Similar fears are expressed by Ambassador Maxwell Taylor in May 1965. He submitted a United States Mission "Assessment of DRV/VC Probable Courses of Action During the Next Three Months," which argued that Hanoi might expand its military action in the South, "including covert introduction of additional PAVN units on order of several regiments," a course that offers "the prospect of achieving major military gains capable of offsetting US/GVN application of air power" (III, 364; on American estimates of PAVN strength in the South at the time, see reference of note 208). An intelligence estimate of July 23, 1965 warned that it was "almost certain" that "additional PAVN forces [would be] employed in South Vietnam on a scale sufficient to counter increased US troop strength" (IV, 25). In July 1967, McNamara was informed by Westmoreland in Saigon that "the enemy" was forced "to supply manpower from North Vietnam" to compensate for the fact that he "has . . . been denied recruits in the numbers required from the populated areas along the coast" in the South, as a result of United States military actions (IV, 518; cf. also III, 397, 621: IV, 484ff.). In short, United States authorities were well aware that their escalation would probably draw the North Vietnamese army into combat in the South. When the expected happened, every hypocrite in Washington would howl in protest, to the accompaniment of much of the press (and with nuances, parts of the "intellectual community" as well), over the infamy of the North Vietnamese aggressors, launching an unprovoked attack against the peace-loving South Vietnamese people and their staunch American allies. With minor variants, the same record has been replayed in response to events elsewhere in Indochina (see chapter 2).

7. Political Force Versus Military Force

Whatever the facts may be about North Vietnamese influence over the NLF, existing sources of information leave little doubt that the NLF was the major political and social force within South Vietnam. The sources of its success, as a nationalist and revolutionary movement with constructive programs and considerable appeal to the overwhelmingly rural population, have been explored at length in valuable studies.[215] There is, furthermore, no question that the successive governments backed by the United States were quite incapable of competing with the indigenous political forces mobilized by the NLF. In Vietnam, as in Laos, this was a constant problem for the United States, another of those ethically neutral dilemmas of counterinsurgency.

In the early years, "the Viet Minh was the main repository of Vietnamese nationalism and anti-French colonialism" (I, 42; cf. State Department analysis, cited above, pp. 7, 29, 32). Acheson noted in March 1950 that the French appear to "understand that success of [military] operation . . . depends, in the end, on overcoming opposition of indigenous population" (*DOD*, bk. 8, p. 301). Recall that these are the same French who are defending Indochina from "foreign tyranny"— or as Acheson put it here, who "are determined to protect IC from further COMMIE encroachments by [political], [economic] as well as [military] measures."

As noted earlier, it was a similar estimate of Communist political strength that led the United States–imposed regime to reject the elections provision of the Geneva Agreements in 1955–1956 (see note 176), and to resort to a campaign of terror and repression to destroy the Viet Minh political structure and other potential opposition groups in the late 1950s, thus precipitating renewed resistance.

By March 1961, intelligence estimated that "VC controlled most of countryside" (II, 417), despite their limited military force.[216] As in the next few years, it was recognized that "vast majority of Viet Cong troops are of local origin" and there was "little evidence of major supplies from outside sources" (II, 72). As to infiltrators, intelligence warned of "experienced guerrilla forces from North Vietnam in guerrilla operations in territory long familiar to them"—that is, South Vietnamese returning to their homes (II, 77; October 1961).

Towards the end of the Diem regime, the analyst concludes that "only the Viet Cong had any real support and influence on a broad base in the countryside" and that the army was "the only real alternative source of political power" (II, 204–5). The "clear and growing lack of legitimacy of GVN" (II, 278, January 1964) is a constant refrain, reiterated as the situation was seen progressively to "deteriorate" through 1964–1965. Offensive action against the North was undertaken partly in the hope that it "might provide at least a partial antidote against the willingness of country boys to join the

VC" (III, 95; analyst, referring to the situation as of March 1965). John McNaughton explained: "Action against North Vietnam is to some extent a substitute for strengthening the government in South Vietnam. That is, a less active VC (on orders from DRV) can be matched by a less efficient GVN" (III, 599; November 6, 1964). Therefore the terms for settlement (under the favored option) should be that "we will stop squeeze on DRV (no promise to withdraw from SVN)" if the DRV not only stops support and direction for the insurgency, but also "must order the VC and PL to stop their insurgencies" (III, 603). As Ambassador Taylor perceived the situation, even in the unlikely event that an effective government were established in the South, to attain United States goals it would not suffice to "drive the DRV out of its reinforcing role"; rather, we will not succeed unless we also "obtain its cooperation in bringing an end to the Viet Cong insurgency." We must "persuade or force the DRV to stop its aid to the Viet Cong and to use its directive powers to make the Viet Cong desist" (III, 668–9).[217]

As the United States prepared to extend the war to the North, intelligence concluded that "the basic elements of Communist strength in South Vietnam remain indigenous" (III, 653; November 24, 1964), though the "high VC morale" is sustained in part by "receipt of outside guidance and support." The question why far greater outside guidance and support fails to sustain GVN morale remains unanswered, even unasked (nor is there an effort to explain why guerrilla operations in the North were such a miserable failure). The fact nevertheless was noted, and dominated discussion as the United States prepared to take over the war. The Principals (Rusk, McNamara, Wheeler, McCone, McGeorge Bundy, Ball) agreed "that the struggle would be a long one, even with the DRV out of it," and, of course, the United States in it (III, 237; November 24). The preceding August, Taylor had reported from Saigon that the Khanh government "has not succeeded in building any substantial body of active popular support in the countryside" and "has about a 50-50 chance of lasting out the year" (III, 82). By the end of the month Vietnamese paratroopers with bayonets had to be called out to restore order in Saigon (III, 86). On September 6 Taylor explained that the politicians in Saigon and Hue feel that "the conflict with the VC belongs to the Americans." The United States must therefore "actively assume . . . increased responsibility for the outcome following a time-schedule consistent with our estimate of the limited viability of any South Vietnamese government." The only alternative would be a political settlement, that is, "development of a popular front, knowing that this may in due course require the U.S. to leave Vietnam in failure," with consequences that would be "disastrous" throughout the Third World (II, 336). "He went on to recommend that escalating pressures on the DRV begin around December 1"—that is, a decent interval after the peace candidate had been re-elected.

By the beginning of the next year, the situation was desperate. William Bundy wrote on January 6 that "the situation in Vietnam is now likely to come apart more rapidly than we had anticipated in November . . . the most likely form of coming apart would be a government of key groups starting to negotiate covertly with the Liberation Front or Hanoi," sooner or later asking us to leave (III, 685). The problem, as the analyst explains, was that "there was no sense of dedication to the GVN comparable to that instilled in the VC" (III, 94). Bundy felt that actions against North Vietnam "would have some faint hope of really improving the Vietnamese situation, and, above all, would put us in a much stronger position to hold the next line of defense, namely Thailand." Therefore we should not accept the present situation, "or any negotiation on the basis of it," but should move "into stronger actions." In early 1965 "the GVN was seen to be well on its way to complete collapse. The most optimistic estimate was that the VC would take over within a year" (III, 390; analyst).

Given its indigenous political strength and the lack of legitimacy of the GVN, the NLF was able to pursue the strategy of gaining a political settlement, that is, one that would reflect indigenous political forces. Or, as Ambassador Taylor expressed the same thought on August 10, 1964: "The communist strategy as defined by North Vietnam and the puppet National Liberation Front is to seek a political settlement favorable to the communists . . . passing first through 'neutralism,' using the National Liberation Front machinery,

and then the technique of a coalition government" (III, 531).
Intelligence reports, shortly after, "estimated that it was the
Communist intention to seek victory through a 'neutralist
coalition' rather than by force of arms" (III, 207). Mc-
Naughton warned in mid-October that the United States
must "watch for Saigon and Vientiane hanky panky with
Reds" (III, 582)—that is, moves towards a political settlement. But a political settlement could no more be considered
by the United States than by the French, since it would mean
a victory for the Communist-led nationalist movement, so it
was always assumed. The president had clearly excluded any
peaceful settlement when he explained to Ambassador Lodge
that his mission was "knocking down the idea of neutralization wherever it rears its ugly head" (III, 511; March 20,
1964). Neutralism, as Ambassador Taylor noted, "appeared to
mean throwing the internal political situation open and thus
inviting Communist participation" (W. Bundy, memorandum of meeting of November 27, 1964; III, 675). According
to the analyst's report of this meeting, George Ball "observed
that a neutralist state could not be maintained unless the VC
were defeated and that the GVN must continue to be free to
receive external aid until that occurred" (III, 242)—an interesting concept of "neutralism," expressed by the administration's official dove. It is possible that "Saigon hanky panky
with Reds" was a factor in the removal of Diem (see note
223). There can be little doubt that the administration was
aware of the publicly announced position of the National
Liberation Front in 1962 calling for neutrality of South Vietnam, Laos, and Cambodia.[218] But neutrality and moves
towards peaceful settlement were obviously incompatible with
the long-term objectives of the United States, as clearly outlined in 1948 and never significantly modified.

The analyst regards it as "ironic" that the NSC Working
Group's "considerations of a negotiated settlement did not
include the problems of a political settlement in the South"
(III, 225). This might appear ironic to someone who takes
seriously government propaganda about the American role in
world affairs and the commitment to the rule of law and
international peace. To a more realistic observer, there is
nothing ironic in the oversight. The political weakness of the

American-imposed regimes as compared with their indigenous rivals ruled out a political settlement or the reliance on pacific means as prescribed by law. This is no more ironic than the Russian unwillingness to permit free elections in Czechoslovakia. The United States "had few bargaining points," the analyst notes, and "it was primarily to fill this lack that many group members and Administration officials favored initiation of direct military pressures against North Vietnam." Quite true. The impending NLF victory in the South compelled the United States to move to a wider confrontation, in the hope that somehow North Vietnam would use its alleged "directive powers" to "make the Viet Cong desist." Furthermore, within this wider confrontation the imperial aggressor could undertake a far more effective war against South Vietnam, with massive aerial and artillery bombardment and a direct invasion by American ground troops to destroy the indigenous NLF and, as proved necessary, the rural society in which it was based. All of this, of course, to protect the free people of South Vietnam from the "aggression from the North" that had for several years been a major theme of government propaganda and most of the mass media. Use of such terms as "ironic" in describing these developments reveals a complete incapacity to comprehend American policy, not only in Vietnam.

We have already noted a certain similarity between the situation of May 1972 and that of late 1964 (see note 217). Furthermore, the United States administration still rejects the concept of a political settlement among Vietnamese, in the South or in Vietnam as a whole (cf. references of note 61). The reasons are those of 1964, of 1962, of 1954, and of 1948. Furthermore, as in 1964–1965, the administration in the spring of 1972 moved to a still more devastating attack on Vietnam within the context of the broader international confrontation it constructed. Only the internal collapse of the American-imposed regime in the South, or some form of domestic or international pressure that does not at the moment seem very likely, will bring about a modification of policies that have not substantially changed, apart from scale, in twenty-five years.

From other sources, we know that the general opinion in

Washington and in the United States Mission in Saigon regarding the political viability of the American-backed regimes was about the same as that revealed in the Pentagon Papers. Chester Cooper, who was close to the center of planning for many years, speaks of "the hope [in 1965] that a South Vietnamese government could be organized that would eventually be able to compete politically with the National Liberation Front."[219] American spokesmen in Saigon outlined the problem of utilizing our vast military power, with its weak political base, to defeat an enemy with enormous political force but only modest military power.[220] In almost the same words, captured documents speak of the "absolute superiority over the enemy in the political field," in contrast to the military superiority of the US-GVN.[221] Western scholars have generally come to the same conclusion. Few would disagree with John McAlister's explanation as to why the pro-Western, urban-oriented (and to be fully honest, Western-imposed) governments have had "no choice but to rely on military force"—foreign military force at that: "Without a means of transforming control over territory into popular political loyalties, these governments have simply not been able to compete on the same plane with their Communist adversaries," who were "successful in mobilizing political power" primarily because of "the relevancy of their values to the lives villagers must lead."[222] Hence the inescapable necessity for the United States to demolish the rural society.

In the same vein, Mieczyslaw Maneli reports a discussion in 1964 with an anticommunist Vietnamese intellectual who chose to support the NLF, regarding its victory as "inevitable," since the Communists "were the only ones to fight for national liberation and meaningful social reforms" and the only possible alternative is "the corrupt regime kept in power by the Americans."[223] A highly placed member of the Lao ruling elite spoke to me in almost exactly the same terms in April 1970 in Vientiane.

To complement the extensive documentation revealing United States opposition to neutralism and a political settlement in the South, we must again turn to sources beyond the Pentagon study, sources which take cognizance of the position of the NLF and the DRV. The official position of the NLF since 1962, with constant DRV backing, has been that South Vietnam, "independent and sovereign," should be nonsocialist and should constitute a neutral zone together with Laos and Cambodia. Reunification of Vietnam is to be a gradual evolutionary process (see note 47). Georges Chaffard presents considerable evidence that the NLF and DRV hoped that the 1962 Geneva Agreements on Laos would serve as a model for South Vietnam as well, with a tripartite government (as in Laos) in which the NLF would constitute one element. The United States rejected any such idea—not surprisingly, given its estimate of the relative strength of political forces in the South (see note 219). For the United States, the Laos settlement was intended to "permit the isolation of the Vietcong infection so that it could be better treated."[224] Chaffard concludes, quite plausibly, that by adopting this attitude the United States and its British ally destroyed any possibility for the success of the "Laotian experiment," while of course never even considering the possibility of neutrality and political settlement in South Vietnam.[225]

In later years, the problem faced by the United States remained basically unchanged. By January 1966, McNaughton reported that "the GVN political infrastructure is moribund and weaker than the VC infrastructure among most of the rural population" (IV, 47); or in simpler words, the NLF is the dominant political force in the rural society of Vietnam. A few months earlier, McNamara reported Prime Minister Ky's estimate that "his government controls only 25% of the population" (IV, 622). In April 1966, McNaughton noted a report from Saigon that "we control next to no territory" and "people would not vote for 'our side'" (IV, 84). After Tet, 1968, General Wheeler reported that "to a large extent the VC now control the countryside," the situation being particularly bad in the delta (IV, 548);[226] and Systems Analysis concluded that "our control of the countryside and the defense of the urban areas is now essentially at pre-August 1965 levels" (IV, 558). And so on.

But these matters were of no concern, apart from the technical difficulties they created. To the imperial mentality, it is perfectly comprehensible that the best-organized political forces in some country are engaged in "internal aggression" against the incumbent government installed and maintained in power by the imperial master who is responsible for the welfare of the misguided and backward population. The assumption is not only expressed constantly by planners, advisers and administrators, and political leaders, but is even implicit in the judgments of the "intelligence community." For example, an intelligence estimate of October 1955 could, with a straight face, speak of Diem's progress "toward establishing the first fully independent Vietnamese government" (I, 297) —namely, the government accurately described by the analyst as "essentially the creation of the United States" (II, 22). Naturally, intelligence discounted the DRV, a mere agency of Communist colonialism.

It is interesting that the PRG position today, with DRV backing, is hardly different from that of ten years ago. Correspondingly, the United States continues to reject any thought of a coalition government in the South incorporating the PRG, and insists rather on a "cease-fire," that is, a surrender by the indigenous revolutionary forces to the massive military and police structure established by the United States, which will continue to maintain "law and order" by the "GVN *Phung Hoang* program" (see above, subsection 3) and other similar devices, under the terms of a cease-fire. The American position is based on the reasonable grounds that if the American-backed army and police apparatus are neutralized, there will be no organized force to oppose the Communists; the generals are still "all we have got," as Ambassador Lodge pointed out in January 1964.

The United States proposal is what Henry Kissinger calls "leav[ing] the determination of the political future to the Vietnamese" (press conference, May 9, 1972). Perhaps, like their predecessors, administration officials will announce their willingness to accept a Communist victory in elections, so long as these elections take place within the legal and constitutional framework described earlier (cf. above, subsections 3, 5.2), and with the country in the firm grip of the apparatus of terror and repression installed by the United States. If, on the other hand, this apparatus is neutralized and a coalition regime of South Vietnamese political groupings is established, the Communists are likely to emerge as the dominant political force within South Vietnam, contrary to long-term United States objectives.

"That is the only issue on which negotiations have broken down," Kissinger explains. "That is what we call the imposition, under the thinnest veneer, of a Communist government." The demand for a tripartite coalition government including the PRG is what the president (May 8) calls the Communist "ultimatum . . . that the United States impose a Communist regime on 17 million people who do not want a Communist government"—a statement worthy of a man who can announce that "the United States has exercised a degree of restraint unprecedented in the annals of war."

As in the past, the conflict in South Vietnam pits a foreign-created military force against an indigenous political force, now weakened (perhaps, as American spokesmen claim, decimated) by the "semi-genocidal counterinsurgent strategy" that is responsible for such "successes" as the United States has achieved in its war in South Vietnam,[227] and now backed by the armed forces of the DRV that were introduced in response to the American aggression in the South and the bombing of North Vietnam.

When Kissinger speaks of "the constant delusion that there is just one formula that has somehow eluded us," he is perhaps being somewhat disingenuous. Averell Harriman is surely correct in stating: "While negotiations have been going on, this Administration has never accepted the concept of a neutral non-aligned south nor has it given up its futile attempt to maintain a pro-American government in Saigon.[228] In fact, the formula of a political settlement among South Vietnamese continues to "somehow elude" Henry Kissinger because of the unresolved dilemma of 1948 (see above, p. 32). An accommodation based on existing political forces, whether in South Vietnam, in Vietnam as a whole, or throughout Indochina, is inconsistent with the long-term United States objective of maintaining Western dominance. Therefore the people of Indochina must continue to massacre one another under a hail of American bombs.

Perhaps a word should be added on the interpretation of this record by certain American commentators. John Roche criticizes the Pentagon study for a "serious gap":

There is no examination of the "neutralization" option, which flourished in the aftermath of the 1962 Geneva Agreement on Laos. In retrospect, the notion of the neutralization of all Indochina under great power auspices was doubtless a fantasy—Hanoi simply would not cooperate. But at the time a number of serious men, both inside and outside the government, took the possibility seriously.[229]

He suggests, as a general corrective to the Pentagon study, that the "conscientious analyst" must turn to "existing commentaries on our Vietnam policy, particularly Lyndon B. Johnson's *The Vantage Point*, with its careful documentation of what occurred in the president's inner circle."

The conscientious analyst will find little of significance in Johnson's self-serving account, with its many examples of distortion and misrepresentation, but he will find a few remarks on the neutralization option.[230] Johnson quotes McNamara's "gloomy" appraisal of December 1963: "Current trends, unless reversed in the next two or three months, will lead to neutralization at best and more likely to a Communist-controlled state." Johnson confirms that " 'neutralization' of Vietnam was in many people's minds at the time, and it had a particular meaning." Namely, it meant the proposal of de Gaulle "that North and South Vietnam be unified and neutralized, and that all foreign forces be withdrawn."[231] But, Johnson continues, "Most thinking people, I believe, recognized that the De Gaulle formula for 'neutralization' would have meant the swift communization of all Vietnam, and probably of Laos and Cambodia as well." He then cites approvingly President Kennedy's sharp response to the de Gaulle proposal, which Kennedy interpreted as the demand that "we all just go home and leave the world to those who are our enemies"—unthinkable, of course. The Kennedy-Johnson view clearly implies that we must, if we can, conquer and reorient any part of the world where indigenous forces pursue a path inimical to "our interests." It was with this "particular meaning" of "neutralization" in mind that Johnson explained to Ambassador Lodge his mission and that the backroom boys expressed their fears about neutralism and political settlement, as outlined above.

In the light of the existing record, it is astonishing that a political scientist can write that "serious men" in Washington "took the possibility [of neutralization] seriously," but that the option was "a fantasy" because "Hanoi simply would not cooperate." As we have seen, the option was indeed a fantasy, but not quite for this reason.

American observers on the scene have hardly been more accurate. To cite one case, not untypical, Robert Shaplen writes that the present (June 1972) outlook in South Vietnam is not "altogether bleak—that is, perhaps the North Vietnamese will settle for half a loaf, including some territorial adjustments, resumed trade and other relations with the South, and an emerging political process that might keep the rest of South Vietnam from going Communist in the immediate future."[232] In short, perhaps the North Vietnamese will settle for considerably more than they have ever demanded ("territorial adjustments" have never been mentioned). As for the NLF-PRG/DRV positions from 1962, it is as if they do not exist. It is the same cheery dismissal of fact that permits the American press, in case after case, to speculate that "Hanoi, scenting military failure, might resume negotiations in a few weeks,"[233] while the news columns report that Hanoi continues to press for reconvening of the Paris talks, while the United States continues to refuse.

Reviewing the ample documentary record on the topics surveyed here, and contrasting it with journalistic and "scholarly" commentary, one has the impression of living in a madhouse.

8. We Must Build a Nation

When the United States took over from the French, a National Intelligence Estimate noted perceptively that "the energy and resourcefulness necessary" for "building national states" in the noncommunist areas of Indochina "will not arise spontaneously among the non-Communist Indochinese but will have to be sponsored and nurtured from without" (DOD, bk. 10, p. 695). On May 1, 1967, the director of Systems Analysis in the Pentagon pointed out: "We are facing the strongest political current in the world today: nationalism." Hence, "we must match the nationalism we see in the North with an equally strong and patient one in the South";

we must "build a nation in South Vietnam" (IV, 463). Typically, he overlooked the nationalist forces in the South that the United States was then attempting to crush. To recognize the true character of the American war in South Vietnam was, as always, beyond the capacity of the commentator.

We must build a nation in the South, to counter the Communist Vietnamese, who seem to be alone in their ability to mobilize the people of Vietnam, North or South, in pursuit of nationalist and revolutionary goals. We must "establish an adequate government in SVN" (Maxwell Taylor; III, 668). We must undertake activities to "add to GVN's strength and image of concern for all its citizens."[234] "I think we're up against an enemy who just may have found a dangerously clever strategy for licking the United States," the director of Systems Analysis warns. "Unless we recognize and counter it now, that strategy may become all too popular in the future" (IV, 466). The strategy was to wage a war of national liberation based on the aspirations of the Vietnamese for independence and social justice.

Somehow, the outside power was never able to compete. The United States could kill and maim, drive peasants from their homes, destroy the countryside and organized social life, but could not build a nation in the approved image. Apparently, only the Vietnamese can govern Vietnam. The United States had taken on a society and a culture that was simply not fit for imperial domination. Therefore, it had to be destroyed. This was worse than a crime; it was a blunder, as the realistic experts soberly explain.

People who are personally acquainted with the individuals whose deliberations are reported in the Pentagon study describe them as humane, liberal, gifted, and sometimes even sincere opponents of the war. Knowing none of them personally, I have no comment on this judgment. Assuming it to be accurate, the Pentagon study serves as a dramatic record of the impact, on anyone, of participation in an odious venture. Decent young men were made into vicious murderers by the circumstances of Vietnam, and many of them have spoken of the process and its consequences with courage and sensitivity.[235] There has been nothing similar from the backroom boys, whose responsibility was incomparably greater and who were, of course, in a far better position to think about what they were doing than a soldier in a village where any ten-year-old child might try to kill him.

Congressman Robert Drinan, on a tour of South Vietnam, was told by a Vietnamese lawyer:

> . . . long after you have left we will conduct our own Nuremberg trials. You will brush these trials off as Communist or Asian propaganda,[236] but you should remember that by one-half of the population the Americans will be thought of as barbarians.[237]

It will be unfortunate for American society if we must await the judgment of the victims.

VII. FINAL COMMENT

To my mind, one of the more depressing paragraphs of the Pentagon study is in the epilogue, where the analyst comments on the change of tactics after the Tet offensive in early 1968 (IV, 603). He reports that "large and growing elements of the American public had begun to believe the cost [of the war] had already reached unacceptable levels and would strongly protest a large increase in that cost." If the analyst is correct, then the public is at one with the executive in its almost exclusive concern with the costs to us of continued aggression. I doubt the accuracy of this assessment, but it seems that the Nixon administration is counting on it, and is hoping that a less costly technological war, with automated fire-control systems and mercenaries in place of GIs, with helicopter gunships and smart bombs in place of Westmoreland's "meatgrinder," may still succeed in destroying the infrastructure of the enemy and guranteeing to the people of Indochina that particular variety of independence that United States global strategy will tolerate. If the analyst is correct in his assessment, the revelations of the Pentagon Papers will have little impact on public attitudes towards Vietnam, or on the global policy of which Vietnam was a particularly disastrous episode. If he is correct, then the McNamara study might just as well gather dust in the vaults of the Pentagon.

Notes

1 Gloria Emerson of the *New York Times*, "Vietnam Diary," *McCall's*, August 1971.

2 Philip Jones Griffiths, *Vietnam Inc.*

3 *The Pentagon Papers*, Senator Gravel Edition, vol. IV, p. 48 [IV, 48] (his emphasis). References henceforth are to this edition, in the style indicated in brackets, except where otherwise noted. Other references are to Department of Defense, *United States–Vietnam Relations, 1945–67*, the government offset edition of the Pentagon Papers, censored but including valuable documents unavailable elsewhere, henceforth referred to as *DOD*. For a comparison of the various editions, see L. Rodberg, in *The Pentagon Papers*, Senator Gravel Edition, vol. 5, *Critical Essays*, eds. Noam Chomsky and Howard Zinn.

4 II, 360. In November 1961, the president authorized "execution of air-ground support," and three helicopter companies were operating by February 1 with 22 helicopters each (II, 656–7). Air force units were also deployed for air-ground support, and the first C-123s were sent for defoliation missions. United States advisory teams were extended to battalion level. In one week of May, air force and United States helicopter units flew about 350 sorties: offensive, airlift, etc. (II, 656–8, 677). During 1962–1963, the United States "provided helicopter companies for rapid tactical transport" and "tactical air and artillery support to assure ARVN firepower superiority over the insurgents." This led to various complaints, such as "that supporting air and artillery were an inducement to rely on indiscriminate firepower as a substitute for aggressiveness" (II, 455). For some of the effects on the population, see below, pp. 80–1. Roger Hilsman describes a January 1962 operation in which American-piloted planes struck a Cambodian village in a "tragic error," then hitting the right village, with civilian casualties in both cases (*To Move a Nation*, p. 437).

For comparison, the French had about 10 operational helicopters at the time of Dien Bien Phu, and in the 56 days of the Dien Bien Phu battle, the French expended less bomb power than the United States did in a single day in 1966–1967 (Bernard Fall, *Street Without Joy*, p. 242; *Last Reflections on a War*, p. 231). Fall adds: "The French aircraft total in all of Indochina . . . was 112 fighters and 68 bombers. That is what the United States flies in a single mission." Following a more classical imperial pattern, the French relied primarily on mercenaries rather than French nationals, and never sent conscripts to Vietnam. There were about 20,000 French nationals fighting in all Indochina in February 1949, about 51,000 (plus 6,000 advisers) in all Indochina as of April 1953 (*DOD*, bk. 8, p. 179; I, 400). Under "Vietnamization," the United States is reverting to the classic pattern, and an Asian mercenary army is being created involving nationals from many countries. See note 198 below for early stages. See also Fred Branfman, ed., *Voices from the Plain of Jars*, and Alfred W. McCoy, *et al.*, *The Politics of Heroin in Southeast Asia*.

5 George McT. Kahin and John W. Lewis, *The United States in Vietnam*, p. 186.

6 Bernard Fall, "Vietnam Blitz," *New Republic*, October 9, 1965.

7 "Vietcong Motivation and Morale," June–December 1965, reprinted in *Vietnam Perspectives*, May 1966, from Senate Armed Services and Appropriations Committee hearings, January–February 1966. Sections of the RAND study dealing with atrocities by the Korean mercenary forces in Vietnam (December 1966) were released by Alternative Features Service, P.O. Box 2250, Berkeley, California, June 9, 1972. Anthony Russo, who was working on the RAND studies in Saigon from February 1965 to September 1966, reports that the interviews revealed the National Liberation Front cadres to be dedicated idealists, intensely committed to freeing Vietnam from foreign control. But regardless of the content of the interviews, the project leader (Leon Gouré, probably the author of the memorandum cited above) would interpret them in such a way as to support his bias in favor of the use of American air power to weaken the NLF. Gouré's conclusion as of summer 1965 that refugee generation was hurting the NLF by depriving them of "strategic support" soon became general United States military policy. Anthony Russo, "Inside the RAND Corporation and Out: My Story," *Ramparts*, April 1972. For selections from the RAND study, now released, see *Ramparts*, November 1972.

8 According to the report, "The interviews do not reveal any deep-seated resentment or hatred of the GVN or the Americans caused by air or artillery attacks on villages. [Deleted]." As Russo notes ("Inside the RAND Corporation"), there may well be a divergence between the content of interviews and the conclusions of the briefer. Nevertheless, the statement may be literally correct. That is, it may be true that refugees interviewed by agents of the military power that has blasted them out of their homes will say that they really didn't mind. I noticed the same, quite predictable phenomenon interviewing refugees from the Plain of Jars in Laos shortly after they had been removed to miserable camps near Vientiane. Quite a few said, at first, that they harbored no resentment against the Americans who had bombed their villages so intensively that they had to hide in tunnels deep in the forest to survive, farming only at night, if at all, because of the ever-present terror from the sky. The refugees, after all, are not imbeciles. See my *At War with Asia*, pp. 69, 241.

9 Cited by Richard Critchfield, *The Long Charade*, p. 173. Referring to the last quote, Critchfield states that "obviously, Westmoreland was trying to balance common humanity against military necessity." Later Critchfield blames the "Hanoi Politburo" for the massive generation of refugees. "This was exactly the effect [they] were trying to produce; it was a skillful, calculated, logical exploitation of human suffering" (p. 177). Many other American observers have taken a similar position: it is the responsibility of Hanoi, a consequence of Communist viciousness, that the United States blasted the people of South Vietnam out of their homes.

10 Six years after its inception, the criminal program of crop destruction was evaluated in a secret RAND report and found "ineffective" against the Viet Cong. See Russo, the author of the report, "Inside the RAND Corporation." The program was continued.

As entirely predictable from the outset, crop destruction "had its greatest effects on the enemy-controlled civilian populations" and "created widespread misery and many refugees" (L. Craig Johnstone, Chief, Pacification Studies Group, Military Assistance Command, Vietnam, 1956–1970, "Ecocide and the Geneva Protocol," *Foreign Affairs*, vol. 49, no. 4 [1971]). Since "neither the crop destruction program nor the defoliation program was anything but a liability to pacification," both have been phased out. Besides, Rome plows are a more efficient tool of destruction. On this matter, see Arthur H. Westing, "Leveling the Jungle," *Environment*, November 1971.

There is only one casual and uninformative reference in the Pentagon study to the crop destruction and defoliation programs. The military regarded it as a "gimmick" from the start, at best an "R&D effort" (II, 658). The victims, had they been asked, might have chosen different terms.

11 Colonel Charles Smith of the 196th Light Infantry Brigade, quoted by Griffiths, *Vietnam Inc.*, p. 67. J.-C. Pomonti of *Le Monde* reports that "a series of urban ghettoes have sprung up" since 1965, containing "at least half the population, whereas in 1960 the country was still 85% rural" ("The Other South Vietnam," *Foreign Affairs*, vol. 50, no. 2 [1972].

12 Reference is to the massacre that took place in February 1968 after the Communist capture of Hue. On this matter, see chapter 3, pp. 230–2.

13 Anthony Lake and Roger Morris, "The Human Reality of Realpolitik," *Foreign Policy*, vol. 1, no. 4 (1971).

14 *DOD*, bk. 8, pp. 144–5. For further discussion of this important statement, see p. 32 below.

15 For biographical data, see Eqbal Ahmad, "Revolutionary War and Counterinsurgency," *Journal of International Affairs*, vol. 25, no. 1 (1971).

16 George K. Tanham and Dennis J. Duncanson, "Some Dilemmas of Counterinsurgency," *Foreign Affairs*, vol. 48, no. 1 (1969); an illuminating remark, with implications that should be carefully considered.

17 NSC 48/1, December 23, 1949; *DOD*, bk. 8, p. 248. See pp. 39–40 below for extensive quotes.

18 See Anthony Russo's account of the "naively carefree attitude" at RAND, "Inside the Rand Corporation."

19 Major-General George S. Beatty, chief of the United States military mission in Brazil, Hearings Before the [Church] Subcommittee on Western Hemisphere Affairs, U.S. Senate, May 1971, p. 86. Henceforth cited as Church Subcommittee Hearings.

20 III, 648; William Bundy, in a memorandum in which he asks, on November 24, 1964, whether the favored escalatory option (option C) can be carried out in practice, "in view of its requirement that we maintain a credible threat of major action while at the same

time seeking to negotiate, even if quietly." On the seriousness of the effort to negotiate, see VI, 5, 7.

[21] I, 187. The "letter of transmittal" (I, xvi) identifies Gelb as the author of the summary and analysis sections, including the one quoted above, p. 7 (II, 414–5).

[22] Gabriel Kolko, "The American Goals in Vietnam," in Chomsky and Zinn, *Critical Essays*.

[23] *Ibid*. Kolko notes that in this case, as in Indochina, it was the farther dominoes that were the really important ones. See Joyce and Gabriel Kolko, *The Limits of Power*, p. 340.

[24] Sam Ervin, "Executive Privilege: Secrecy in a Free Society," *The Nation*, November 8, 1971.

[25] Thomas Jefferson, in a letter of 1787, quoted by Hannah Arendt, *On Revolution*, p. 241.

[26] On this matter, see Virginia Brodine and Mark Selden, "The Kissinger-Nixon Doctrine," in Brodine *et al.*, *Open Secret*.

[27] Senator Stuart Symington, *Congressional Record*, August 3, 1971, p. S12931.

[28] *Ibid*., October 4, 1971, p. S15763. The Thai soldiers describe themselves as regular army troops serving in Laos for extra pay. It was reported that 12,000 would be "available for combat" by March 1, 1972. See stories by Don Ronk and Tammy Arbuckle, reprinted in the *Congressional Record*, October 4, 1971, pp. S15768–9. "Senior U.S. sources" in Bangkok confirm these reports (see *Washington Post–Boston Globe*, January 22, 1972).

[29] Hearings Before the Committee on Armed Services, U.S. Senate, July 1971, pp. 4275–7.

[30] *Congressional Record*, August 3, 1971, p. S12956.

[31] *Ibid*., October 4, 1971, p. S15773–4. It was left to Senator Hart to observe that "all of the screaming about law and order in this country is talking about something minuscule if in fact it is established that one branch of the Government ignores the law of the lawmakers" (August 3, S12955).

[32] Thomas Emerson, *Toward a General Theory of the First Amendment*, p. 20.

[33] *United States Code*, tit. 18, sec. 793d,e. Classified information is continually leaked to correspondents for the particular purposes of the administration, and it is a common practice for ex-officials to release such information and documents in memoirs. An example relevant to the present case is Lyndon Johnson's *The Vantage Point*, which contains, *inter alia*, classified material that appears in the Pentagon Papers, presented, arguably, for personal gain. A former president has no special rights in this regard. Similarly, pledges of secrecy are freely violated by the executive for its own purposes, as when Nixon chose to reveal secret negotiations on Indochina on January 25, 1972. The negotiations volumes of the Pentagon study are still suppressed by the government as supersensitive, but participants are leaking their private versions to the press (as did LBJ), with names and dates. See Benjamin Welles, *New York Times*, February 14, 1972.

We await, with bated breath, the arrest of Lyndon Johnson and others.

[34] Near v. Minnesota, 1931, cited by Justice Brennan, concurring in the

decision against prior restraint in the case of the Pentagon Papers. See Gerald Gold *et al.*, eds., *The Pentagon Papers*, p. 656.

35 Anthony Austin, *The President's War*, pp. 313, 297–8. This is, however, hardly the most grotesque feature of the Tonkin Gulf story.

36 Emerson, *First Amendment*, introduction. For a review of the history of this matter, see Edward G. Hudon, *Freedom of Speech and Press in America.*

37 Cited in Gold *et al.*, *Pentagon Papers*, p. 467. The *Times* commentator (Fox Butterfield) states that "neither General Westmoreland's requests nor President Johnson's approvals were made public." In fact, as usual, the information had leaked to the press, and the request (though not the approval) was mentioned in a *Times* article from Saigon which the Pentagon historian states "reflected thinking of many junior and mid-level officials in both the U.S. Mission and the GVN" (II, 544). This is one of many examples which indicate that an observer with limitless time and energy, who was sufficiently realistic to treat government pronouncements with utter cynicism, might be able to follow events as they unfolded. Another example is the Hanson Baldwin report of the secret BARREL ROLL airstrikes in Laos in 1964, cited above, p. 16.

38 III, 217, 623; November 8, 1964. The Joint Chiefs commented, reassuringly, that the main risk is not to us but to the Chinese. " 'Possibly even the use of nuclear weapons at some point' is of course why we spend billions to have them." Therefore they believed the risk of nuclear war to be low. They added that the loss of South Vietnam would be a disaster, worse even than the loss of Berlin (III, 628), rejecting the view of the NSC working group that "the loss of South Vietnam" only "*could*" be as serious as the loss of Berlin.

39 Quoted, with some appropriate comment, by James Aronson, "The Media and the Message," in Chomsky and Zinn, *Critical Essays.* Taylor develops a similar view in his *Swords and Plowshares*, in discussing "the new Cold War technique directed against the sources of our power," more acute than ever "because of the increasing strength and boldness of the internal revolutionary movement and the mind-numbing power of press and television in their effect on the critical judgment of the public." To "cope with [this threat], we need a new concept of national security broad enough to assure that defensive measures are taken against subversion in this form" (p. 413). Cited and discussed in "The Mind of the Ruling Class," *Monthly Review*, June 1972. For expression of similar concerns on the part of academic intellectuals, see *At War with Asia*, pp. 60–3. Complaints about media bias—that is, occasional departures from government propaganda—are now common among the military. See, for example, Colonel Wesley W. Yale (retired), "On Ignorance of Armies," *Army*, June 1972. He fears that "editorial policy will probably not return to its World War II standards of responsibility by refusing to print material prejudicial to the national interest," as defined by the army, quite properly, since "the Army is the public." This is a serious matter in an era when "expropriation of U.S. properties is damaging both psychologically and economically," and when the population must be made to understand the "painful truth that if you want economic influence

and prosperity for yourself and your children you must not only be prepared to fight for it, but exhibit the will to do so"; "a soft and affluent society must be made to see that all-out war is the most logical path to permanent peace."

[40] William Bundy, commenting on problems of lying, IV, 611.

[41] On the contrary, "false, fictitious or fraudulent statements or representations" by government officials in the area of their jurisdiction is a crime punishable by heavy fines or up to five years imprisonment (*United States Code*, tit. 18, sec. 1001). For discussion, see Peter Dale Scott, *The War Conspiracy*, p. xxiii and elsewhere, a detailed examination of fraud and deception in the course of the Indochina war.

[42] In December 1965, the "intelligence community" estimated at almost fifty-fifty the probability that significant United States escalation would lead to the introduction of Chinese forces, always understood as the trigger for nuclear "retaliation." With the exception of State's INR, intelligence appeared to favor escalation, including strikes against North Vietnamese petroleum reserves (IV, 64–5). Senator Symington, long an advocate of more extensive use of airpower, has recently expressed the view that B-52 raids in northern Laos, far from the Ho Chi Minh Trail and conducted in secrecy, "are dangerous to the security of the United States" and that "any air activity around northern Laos has in it the incipient danger of starting a major war" (*Congressional Record*, August 3, 1971, pp. S12939, S12951).

[43] Proudhon, cited in Daniel Guérin, ed., *Ni Dieu ni Maître*, p. 115.

[44] My own views on this matter, relying on material prior to the Pentagon study, are presented in chapter 3. See the references cited there for extensive discussion. See also the important essays in Richard A. Falk, *Legal Order in a Violent World*, and in Falk, ed., *The International Law of Civil War*.

[45] Noting that this doctrine, too, was devised to protect a tyrant from the right of resistance. See Gerald A. Sumida, "The Right of Revolution," in Charles A. Barker, ed., *Power and Law*, p. 133.

[46] See Lawyers Committee on American Policy Toward Vietnam, *Vietnam and International Law*, pp. 27–8. On SEATO, see chap. 8.

[47] *Congressional Record*, June 6, 1967, S7733–4. Article 1, here also nonamendable, is the first article of the GVN Constitution of 1956. The DRV Constitution of 1960 states (article 1): "The territory of Viet-Nam is a single, indivisible whole from North to South." See Bernard Fall, *The Two Viet-Nams*, apps. 1,2. The NLF has consistently put forward the official view that "the southern zone" of Vietnam is to be "an independent and sovereign state," part of a neutral zone including Laos and Cambodia as well, with reunification to be a matter of slow evolution. Cf. the fourteen-point declaration of August 10, 1962, and other documents and official statements (Georges Chaffard, *Les Deux Guerres du Vietnam*, pp. 266, 255 ff., chaps. 7 and 10, app.). The DRV has repeatedly indicated its acceptance of this position (*ibid.*, pp. 441–2).

[48] Much later the documents commonly use the same terms. In April 1966: "The overall objective is to cause NVN to cease supporting, directing, and controlling the insurgencies in South Vietnam and Laos" (IV, 81). Cf. also IV, 59, 562, etc.

49 Lyndon Johnson, September 28, 1964. Cited in Lawyers Committee on American Policy Toward Vietnam, *Vietnam and International Law*, p. 35.

50 In March 1965, when combat marines were deployed, the Third Marine Expeditionary Force was renamed the "Third Marine Amphibious Force," to avoid offending Vietnamese sensibilities—for what Ambassador Sullivan referred to elsewhere as "cosmetic purposes" (II, 282, 319; 355; III, 462).

51 I disregard certain other arguments that have been offered. For instance, Wilson C. McWilliams observes, with supreme irrelevance, that "Washington did not *think* it was planning an aggressive war." It was guilty only of inaccuracy, not crime. *New York Times Book Review*, September 26, 1971, review of Ralph Stavins *et al.*, *Washington Plans an Aggressive War*—an accurate title for this study, which adds considerable supplementary information to the Pentagon Papers.

52 United Nations, Secretariat, *Annual Report of the Secretary-General, 16 June 1964 to 15 June 1965* (A/6001), p. 48, cited by William Bruce, "The United States and the Law of Mankind," in Barker, *Power and Law*, p. 100. Discussing the same matter, P. E. Corbett concludes that the various General Assembly resolutions "appear to place intervention on behalf of an existing government on the same footing as aid to its rebel opposition," noting, however, that this demands a radical change in the established practice of states. "The Vietnam Struggle," in Falk, *International Law of Civil War*, pp. 374, 402.

53 As reported by John Spencer, in *American Journal of International Law*, vol. 61, no. 3 (1967), cited by Nam-Yearl Chai, "Law as a Barrier to Change," in Barker, *Power and Law*, p. 114. Chai goes on to illustrate how "the rules of law were used as legal barriers by Japan and Western powers to frustrate Korean aspirations for national independence" and to explain why "Koreans regarded law as an instrument of oppression."

54 Edward Weisband and Thomas M. Franck, "The Brezhnev-Johnson Two-World Doctrine," *Trans-action*, October 1971. See also Franck and Weisband, *Word Politics*, for an elaboration of these themes.

55 This section is largely excerpted from my article "The Pentagon Papers as Propaganda and as History," in Chomsky and Zinn, *Critical Essays*, which contains extensive discussion and documentation on the matters mentioned briefly here, and on other related matters.

56 See my essay in Chomsky and Zinn, *Critical Essays*, for references and discussion. See particularly the important study by Jeffrey Race, *War Comes to Long An*. He points out that until 1959 the government had a near monopoly on violence. It was not until the Communists rescinded the prohibition against armed struggle in 1959 that "the threat was equalized for both sides," though in later years as well "the government terrorized far more than did the revolutionary movement," and by so doing, contributed to its growing strength. See also Chaffard, *Les Deux Guerres*, p. 233: in 1959 Hanoi responded to the appeal of the Viet Minh veterans of the South, permitting "violence *only* in self-defense."

57 DOD, bk. 8, pp. 190–1. Characteristically, Acheson added that this

appeared to be the only way to safeguard Vietnam from "aggressive designs Commie Chi[na]."

58 *Ibid.*, pp. 145, 148. State Department policy statement of September 1948, cited above, p. 7.

59 IV, 488–9. He also points out (IV, 487) that in the Delta, with 40 percent of the population, the Viet Cong effort is primarily indigenous and the North Vietnamese main-force units play almost no role (though United States combat forces were operating; see below, notes 133 and 147). Still, he is able to say that our objective is to permit the people of South Vietnam to determine their own future.

60 It might be added that the policy later called "Vietnamization" was recommended in mid-1967 by Systems Analysis; IV, 459, 467. Cf. also IV, 558, option (4); 564.

61 See my articles in *Ramparts*, April and May 1972 (the latter in part incorporated in chapter 4), and in the *New York Review of Books*, June 15, 1972; also Gabriel Kolko, "The Nixon Administration's Strategy in Indochina—1972," Paris World Assembly, February 1972. See section VI, 7 below.

62 Cf. Joseph Buttinger, *Vietnam: A Dragon Embattled*, vol. 2, p. 981: "the National Liberation Front was truly the Vietminh reborn"; there was a "similarity, or better near identity, of the Vietminh and the National Liberation Front." I noticed a similar usage of terminology in Laos, interviewing refugees from the Plain of Jars. They generally referred to the Pathet Lao as "Issara," the name of the independence movement that fought the Japanese and then the French. See Branfman, *Voices from the Plain of Jars*, p. 12. Though there is little doubt that the NLF incorporated much of the former southern Viet Minh, it represented itself as broader in base and not strictly socialist in character. Cf. Chaffard, *Les Deux Guerres*, p. 419. Chaffard and several other independent and highly qualified observers take this seriously, though sources close to the United States government generally do not.

63 Cited from AFP, in Nguyen Khac Vien, ed., *South Vietnam: Realities and Prospects*, p. 27.

64 For a detailed analysis, see Peter King, "The Political Balance in Saigon," *Pacific Affairs*, vol. 44, no. 3 (1971). See also Gareth Porter, "The Diemist Restoration," *Commonweal*, July 11, 1969. A further change in the character of the regime is its profound corruption, far beyond that of the Diem period, a direct consequence of the full-scale American invasion in the mid-1960s. On this matter, see *At War with Asia*, pp. 71–2, 195–6, 205, 257–8; Frances Fitz-Gerald, *Fire in the Lake*, pp. 311, 346 ff.; and McCoy et al., *Politics of Heroin*.

65 Cf. in particular Gabriel Kolko, *The Roots of American Foreign Policy*, and the discussion in Kolko and Kolko, *Limits of Power*; *At War with Asia*, chap. 1; Committee of Concerned Asian Scholars, *The Indochina Story*, pt. 3; and other references cited earlier. See also the articles by Dower, Du Boff, and Kolko in Chomsky and Zinn, *Critical Essays*.

66 See Walt W. Rostow and Richard W. Hatch, *An American Policy in Asia*, p. 7. In Rostow's view, this "ideological threat to our interest . . . is as great as the military threat" posed by Communist China and the Soviet Union. It is essential, Rostow notes, "to emphasize

. . . especially the close link between Japan's dangerous foreign trade problem and the requirements of growth in Southeast Asia" (p. 12), and to remove the "illusory glamor" of trade with the Communist bloc, which "represent[s] a powerful attraction" (though an unreal one), particularly to Japan (pp. 46–7). Furthermore, "The relative performance of India and Communist China over the course of their respective First Five Year Plans may very well determine the outcome of the ideological struggle in Asia" (p. 37). "India and Asia could be won to Communism without a Chinese Communist soldier crossing Chinese borders," if "the Communist bid to win Asia by demonstrating rapid industrialization" is more successful than development in "Free Asian societies" (pp. 51–2). It is also necessary "to learn to deal effectively with subversion and insurrection . . . as now in Southern Vietnam" (p. 7). The book is interesting as the ideological expression of an influential planner of the 1960s, with its emphasis on our fundamental interest in preserving open societies with no "concentrated power" in the state (pp. 4–5, 14; other forms of "concentrated power" go unmentioned). For further discussion, see *American Power and the New Mandarins*, p. 332.

[67] These fears were re-evaluated shortly, when it appeared that China was undergoing an economic crisis, but may well be voiced again in the future.

[68] For some discussion, see Donald Zagoria, "The Strategic Debate in Peking," in Tang Tsou, ed., *China in Crisis*, vol. 2, pp. 249 ff.

[69] See, for example, Roger Hilsman's discussion of this speech in his *To Move a Nation*. For comments, see my *American Power and the New Mandarins*, chap. 3, pp. 262–6.

[70] For example, by Chester Cooper, "The CIA and Decision-making," *Foreign Affairs*, vol. 50, no. 2 (1972).

[71] John Dower, "The Superdomino in Postwar Asia: Japan in and out of the *Pentagon Papers*," in Chomsky and Zinn, *Critical Essays*.

[72] Compare Ho Chi Minh and Phibun Songkhram, the Japanese collaborator who had overthrown the government of Thailand in April 1948 after his poor showing in the elections, "the first pro-Axis dictator to regain power after the war" (Frank C. Darling, *Thailand and the United States*, p. 65). Support from the United States was immediate, one of the measures taken "to deter Communist aggression in Southeast Asia" (p. 67).

[73] Cited in Chester Cooper, *The Lost Crusade*, p. 168. A bit "melodramatic," Cooper feels, but otherwise unexceptionable.

[74] Robert W. Tucker, *The Radical Left and American Foreign Policy*, pp. 116–17.

[75] On Japanese-Southeast Asian relations and their significance, see Jon Halliday and Gavan McCormack, *Japanese Imperialism*.

[76] Cooper, *Lost Crusade*, pp. 410–11.

[77] Stavins *et al.*, *Washington Plans an Aggressive War*, p. 20.

[78] See *At War with Asia*, chap. 1, for references. For general background, see Dower, "The Superdomino in Postwar Asia."

[79] See C. Fred Bergsten, "Crisis in U.S. Trade Policy," *Foreign Affairs*, vol. 49, no. 4 (1971).

[80] For data, see Yasuo Takeyama, "Don't Take Japan for Granted," *Foreign Policy*, vol. 1, no. 2 (1971–72).

81 Or as Kindleberger puts it in his caricature, the theory that "United States economic foreign policy is unrelievedly evil." Review article on *The Age of Imperialism* by Harry Magdoff, *Public Policy*, summer 1971.

82 On the evolution of United States policy in the crucial 1945–1950 period, see John Dower, "Occupied Japan and the American Lake," in Edward Friedman and Mark Selden, eds., *America's Asia*. On the limits of American power in the real world, see Kolko and Kolko, *Limits of Power*.

83 Zbigniew Brzezinski, "Japan's Global Engagement," *Foreign Affairs*, vol. 50, no. 2 (1972); Takeyama, "Don't Take Japan for Granted." For comparison, American firms control about 40 percent of the British computer industry (Raymond Vernon, *Sovereignty at Bay*, p. 240). Excluding table-top machines, IBM has about 70 percent of Japan's computer market (Koji Nakamura, "The Okinawa Payoff," *Far Eastern Economic Review*, August 21, 1971).

84 On this and related matters, see Malcolm Caldwell, "Oil and Imperialism in East Asia," *Journal of Contemporary Asia*, vol. 1, no. 3 (1971).

85 Thus the director of USAID for Brazil finds it quite natural that "we have spent $2 billion [since 1964] on a program one objective of which is the protection of a favorable investment climate for private business interests in this country," while the total investment is about $1.7 billion. Senator Frank Church, in Church Subcommittee Hearings, pp. 165–6. On the other alleged objectives, see below, pp. 62.

86 This is argued, with reference to Vietnam, by Arthur Schlesinger, Jr., in testimony before the Senate Foreign Relations Committee, May 10, 1972; and commonly by others. Schlesinger considers the "more sophisticated" economic argument that defeat in Vietnam would jeopardize American economic interests throughout the Third World, failing to notice that this is only part of the argument offered by those he hopes to refute. Rather, they have generally pointed out that United States policy in Indochina was closely related to its efforts to consolidate Japanese and Western European capitalism. Schlesinger also remarks that the Pentagon Papers seem to record "no instances of business intervention in American Vietnam policy." The relevance of this observation is not apparent, given the fact that the state executive is largely staffed by representatives of corporate interests, as has often been noted (see note 114). It is hardly necessary for business to "intervene" in an enterprise that it largely controls. Schlesinger also urges that "stupidity" should not be underestimated as a factor in shaping policy.

87 Derek Davies, "The Region," *Far Eastern Economic Review Yearbook*, 1971, p. 38; 1972, pp. 37–40. Although Davies refers to the domino theory as "a flight of fantasy," he unwittingly expresses a moderate version of it in such assessments as these. The economic and strategic significance of Southeast Asia is stressed by many observers. Few would go so far as Peter Lyon, who argues that if some enemy monopolized the region and exploited its resources fully (as Japan could not, in World War II), "then plainly the world balance of power very probably would have swung already in favour of South-east Asia's new hegemon" (*War and Peace in South-east*

Asia, p. 106). But, with qualifications, the point of view is not uncommon.

[88] On the British precedent, see Michael Barratt Brown, *After Imperialism*; Eric Hobsbawm, *Industry and Empire*.

[89] Leslie H. Gelb, "Vietnam: The System Worked," *Foreign Policy*, vol. 1, no. 3 (1971). See also his comments in "On Schlesinger and Ellsberg: A Reply," *New York Review of Books*, December 2, 1971, and in "Lessons of the Pentagon Papers," *Life*, September 17, 1971.

[90] Daniel Ellsberg explores in detail the hypothesis that domestic factors, in particular the effect of anticommunism on electoral success, predominated in decision making. "The Quagmire Myth and the Stalemate Machine," *Public Policy*, spring 1971. See his *Papers on the War*, for an extended version. Emphasis on these factors is not inconsistent with the imperialist interpretation, if we inquire further into the origins of domestic anticommunism, though an important question of emphasis remains (see note 102). Notice also that by 1965, questions of long-term motive were of diminished importance. We were there. Period. See the remarks of John McNaughton (IV, 47).

[91] Hannah Arendt, "Lying in Politics: Reflections on the Pentagon Papers," *New York Review of Books*, November 18, 1971.

[92] Similarly, the analyst, discussing the origins of the insurgency, notes that no direct links had been established between Hanoi and the Southern insurgents in the 1956–1959 period. Still he tends, rather cautiously, towards the view that "some form of DRV apparatus" may have "originated and controlled the insurgency" in those years (though "it can only be inferred"—the reader is invited to sample the evidence presented for the inference; I, 243).

[93] Senate Concurrent Resolution 91 of June 25, 1954, found "strong evidence of intervention by the international Communist movement in the State of Guatemala, whereby government institutions have been infiltrated by Communist agents, weapons of war have been secretly shipped into that country, and the pattern of Communist conquest has become manifest" (cited by Franck and Weisband, *Word Politics*, p. 52).

[94] It is sometimes argued that United States policy revealed its freedom from counterrevolutionary imperatives in Bolivia and Yugoslavia. In Bolivia, Eisenhower supported the most right-wing group that had any base of power—successfully, as it turned out, from the viewpoint of American economic interests. For a succinct review, see Rebecca Scott, "Economic Aid and Imperialism in Bolivia," *Monthly Review*, May 1972. As for Tito, Acheson explained in connection with the possibility of a "Titoist outcome" in Indochina that "U.S. attitude [could] take [account] such possibility only if every other possible avenue closed to preservation area from Kremlin control" (*DOD*, bk. 8, p. 197; May 1949). Recall that Acheson had no evidence of Kremlin control in Indochina, nicely illustrating the point at issue. In general, United States policy towards Yugoslavia in the context of the cold war hardly serves as a counterexample to the thesis that it is guided by the principle of maintaining a "stable" system of societies open to American economic penetration.

[95] On this matter, see John Gittings, "The Great Asian Conspiracy," in

Friedman and Selden, *America's Asia*. He shows how easily China replaced Russia as the master plotter in official and academic interpretation of Far Eastern affairs, when reliance on the alleged Russian role became too far-fetched. It now appears that the official demonology is being reconstructed once again, with the Soviet Union as the chief villain, surely a wise move by state propagandists. It would, for example, be difficult in the long run to gain taxpayer support for an immense military budget on the basis of the "Chinese threat," but it is considerably easier to whip up hysteria over the alleged Soviet menace, along the lines of the "bomber gap" and "missile gap" of earlier years. Precisely what we see today. The United States lead in deliverable warheads and strategic weapons technology (e.g., MIRV) notwithstanding, the Alsop brothers and the like would have us believe that we are now virtually at the mercy of the Kremlin.

96 Peter Wiles, "The Declining Self-confidence of the Super-powers," *International Affairs*, vol. 47, no. 2 (1971).

97 William Pfaff, *Condemned to Freedom*, p. 80. A variant is the view expressed by Michael Howard: "The suspicion, clumsiness, and brutality of the Russians; the inexperience and confusion of the Americans; the weariness, impotence and nostalgia of the British"—these were the major factors in preventing a postwar settlement. "The Americans, bless them, still found it hard to believe that natural processes would not everywhere throw up regimes which would docilely accept their leadership" ("Realists and Romantics: On Maintaining an International Order," *Encounter*, April 1972). This particular form of sentimentality finds little support in the historical record, which reveals fairly systematic policies designed to take over British positions of power and influence and to create a global capitalist order in which the United States, given its enormous advantages, would be likely to predominate. The United States did not believe that "natural processes" would lead to subservient regimes in Southern Europe, France, East Asia, and the Caribbean, nor did it await such processes; rather, it acted directly and forcefully to undermine popular forces it opposed or to institute regimes of the sort it preferred. While not uniformly successful, these policies and their execution revealed no more inexperience or confusion than might be expected, given the unavoidable uncertainties of global planning. See Kolko and Kolko, *Limits of Power*.

98 On Italy, see Gabriel Kolko, *The Politics of War*. On Greece, see the references of note 192. On Korea, see Jon Halliday, "The Korean Revolution," *Socialist Revolution*, vol. 1, no. 6 (1970); also Soon Sung Cho, *Korea in World Politics, 1940–1950*, and Gregory Henderson, *Korea: The Politics of the Vortex*, chaps. 5–6. Though Cho and Henderson do not accept Halliday's interpretation of these events, what they describe is the destruction of indigenous Korean political and social structures by force and terror and the imposition of a right-wing regime. Their explanation in terms of "blunders," "ignorance and policy weakness," and so on becomes much less persuasive if we consider United States Korean policy, not in isolation, as in common academic practice, but rather in its global context, where remarkable similarities appear to American intervention and its effects elsewhere, as in Greece at exactly the same time.

Halliday's openly and clearly expressed sympathies for socialist revolution may be compared with the conservative bias implicit—but, typically, never explicitly recognized—in Henderson and Cho. Consider such observations as these: Though under the People's Republic that the United States destroyed in South Korea there were occasional acts such as "interventions, usually against landlords in landlord-tenant disputes," nevertheless "people were generally well-behaved" (Henderson, p. 119); ". . . the Americans in the South took steps to encourage democratization by establishing an effective Korean administration under the military government, and by stamping out what they felt were irresponsible leftist political movements" (Cho, p. 131), beginning with the outright suppression of the Communist party in late 1946.

In fact, the Korean policy of the United States from 1945 presents suggestive analogies, in some interesting respects, to its policy in Vietnam, a matter that might be further explored.

[99] Arthur M. Schlesinger, Jr., *A Thousand Days*, p. 769.

[100] Tucker, *The Radical Left*, p. 112; *Nation or Empire?* p. 117.

[101] This is admitted even by those who deny that "Castro was unwillingly pushed into the Soviet camp by American blunders or malevolence" (Ernst Halperin, characterizing the position of Andrés Suárez, *Cuba: Castroism and Communism*, in the foreword). Thus Suárez points out that Cuba was attacked "by airplanes based along the U.S. coastline" at the time when the United States was using its influence to prevent the Cubans from buying jets in Great Britain (October 1959), and adds, "I think this makes it sufficiently clear why, and for what, Soviet aid was sought" (p. 74). Though the matter is not relevant to refuting Tucker's contention, a good case can be made that American hostility was a factor of some importance in Castro's shift to the Soviet camp. See Maurice Zeitlin and Robert Scheer, *Cuba: Tragedy in Our Hemisphere*. For a general discussion of the background, see Gordon Connel-Smith, *The Inter-American System*. He draws the quite reasonable conclusion that "the Cuban government's intention to implement a policy aimed at ending the privileged position hitherto enjoyed by the United States in the island's affairs" made the clash as inevitable as "the growing links between Cuba and international communism" (p. 170); and this intention also lies behind the fact that "the United States infinitely preferred Trujillo to Castro" (p. 169). Given the vagueness of his discussion, it is unclear whether Tucker would agree with this conclusion. If he would, then his objection to the "radical critique" is of vanishing empirical content.

[102] Tucker, *The Radical Left*, pp. 111–12. Emphasis mine. Tucker refers to a third consideration underlying Kennedy's observation on supporting a Trujillo as long as there is a risk of a Castro, namely, concern for domestic anticommunism. This overlooks the crucial question of the origins and function of this domestic anticommunism, in particular the role and purpose of state propaganda. On this matter see Richard M. Freeland, *The Truman Doctrine and the Origins of McCarthyism*, and several essays in David Horowitz, ed., *Corporations and the Cold War*.

[103] On certain similarities, see *American Power and the New Mandarins*,

chap. 2; also Hilary Conroy, "Japan's War in China: Historical Parallel to Vietnam?" *Pacific Affairs*, vol. 43, no. 2 (1970).

104 Supporting what might misleadingly be called a United States security interest. On the relation between Greece and American interests in the Middle East, see Kolko and Kolko, *Limits of Power*, chap. 8.

105 M. S. Modiano, "Stans, in Athens, Hails the Regime," *New York Times*, April 24, 1971. It may be recalled that the Truman Doctrine was, in the first instance, specifically directed to Greece and Turkey. Greece required United States assistance "to become a self-supporting and self-respecting democracy" and "the future of Turkey as an independent and economically sound state is clearly no less important to the freedom-loving peoples of the world than the future of Greece" (Harry S. Truman, March 12, 1947). A look at the state of freedom in Greece and Turkey twenty-five years later gives a certain insight into the "policy of the United States," as formulated by President Truman on that occasion: "to support free peoples who are resisting attempted subjugation by armed minorities or by outside pressures."

106 William Y. Elliot, ed., *The Political Economy of American Foreign Policy*, p. 42. For quotations from this interesting document, and some discussion, see my *At War with Asia*, pp. 5, 17, 35–8. See Brown, *After Imperialism*, for a historical discussion of this matter.

107 Raymond Vernon (*Sovereignty at Bay*) concludes that the multinational corporations are "seen as posing a threat [in the host countries] for government leaders bent on control, for local businessmen who aspire to compete, and for intellectuals who are hoping to challenge the status quo" (pp. 249, 265). But he makes no mention of workers who are concerned, say, that management can break a strike by threatening to transfer operations to another country. Unions and others concerned with workers' interests take a different view. See, e.g., Hugh Scanlon, "International Combines Versus the Unions," *Bulletin of the Institute for Workers' Control*, vol. 1, no. 4 (1969); and several articles in the preceding special issue on the motor industry. These articles, incidentally, deal with concrete examples, not merely hypothetical concerns. See also John Gennard, *Multinational Corporations and British Labour*, again with several concrete examples. Vernon's failure to consider this matter cannot be attributed to his (likely) belief that the concern is irrational, since he does not seem overly impressed with the "psychic needs" of the "élite groups" he does consider.

It is, furthermore, disturbing to see how myths are perpetuated in such work. Consider Vernon's reference to the "extraordinary concept of aid to less-developed countries"—a look at the facts would show that this concept is something less than extraordinary; see, e.g., Michael Hudson, "The Political Economy of Foreign Aid," in Denis Goulet and Michael Hudson, *The Myth of Aid*—or his speculation that nations will "continue to emphasize such goals as the redistribution of personal income" (pp. 213, 257). Which nations will "continue" to emphasize such goals? The United States?

108 Connell-Smith, *Inter-American System*, pp. 343–4.

109 Church Subcommittee Hearings, p. 165. See note 85 above.

[110] *Ibid.*, p. 208. See, in this connection, "The Hanna Industrial Complex, Part I," *NACLA Newsletter*, vol. 2, no. 3 (May 1968). Hanna was one of the major beneficiaries of the 1964 coup.

[111] *Washington Post*, December 6, 1971: some "awkward points" for visiting dictator Medici. Christopher Roper reports in the finance section of the *Manchester Guardian Weekly*, May 13, 1972: "Wages have been deliberately held down, and statistical evidence shows that real wages of factory workers in São Paulo—the largest industrial centre in the southern hemisphere of the world—have been almost halved over the past 10 years. Family incomes have only kept pace by workers working longer hours and wives going out to work." But, "foreign capital has been given a warm welcome"; "Volkswagen operates one of the largest integrated car manufacturing plants in the world; Ford is about to manufacture Pinto engines for Detroit in São Paulo [the ones Henry Ford decided not to make in Britain? cf. note 107]; and Nippon Steel from Japan is thinking about building one of the world's largest steel mills." Notice that while United States policy is quite clearly determined, as stated, by "the protection and expansion . . . of our economic interests," the rules of the international capitalist game, if more or less followed, lead to certain problems even for the strongest player.

[112] Marcio Moreira Alves, "Brazil: What Terror Is Like," *The Nation*, March 15, 1971. Alves is a former member of Parliament, a leader of the Catholic left, now in exile in Paris. He cites figures indicating that the average wage for 70 percent of workers has declined by almost 20 percent since 1964, while production has increased by more than 20 percent. He also describes the concentration of wealth, "the hunger and misery that drive millions of landless peasants to the cities," the destruction of peasant leagues by the army, the police and the private paramilitary forces of landlords, the banning in many places of the Catholic basic-education movement which promoted peasant organization, the destruction of schools for peasants established by foreign missionaries, "the incredible violence that the state itself must use to keep the masses quiet while the privileged squander the nation's riches," the torture and murder, the anti-Semitism of the military officers, and so on.

[113] Church Subcommittee Hearings, p. 149.

[114] On this matter, see Kolko, *Roots of American Foreign Policy*, chap. 1; Richard Barnet, *The Economy of Death*, pt. 2, and *Roots of War*, chap. 3 and pt. 2; G. William Domhoff, *The Higher Circles*, chap. 5; David Horowitz, "The Foundations," *Ramparts*, April 1969, and "The Making of America's China Policy," *Ramparts*, October 1971. See also Scott, *War Conspiracy*, introduction and chap. 8, on interconnections between the CIA and important business interests.

[115] See p. 43 above. This particular factor is explored by Seymour Melman in his *Pentagon Capitalism*.

[116] See *At War with Asia*, chap. 1, for some further discussion of the multiplicity of mutually supportive factors and the stable system they tend to produce.

[117] For instance, Herbert Feis ridicules the view, which he attributes without specific reference to Gar Alperovitz, that "the Soviet government . . . was merely the hapless object of our vicious diplo-

macy." The view that Alperovitz actually develops is that "the Cold War cannot be understood simply as an American response to a Soviet challenge, but rather as the insidious interaction of mutual suspicions, blame for which must be shared by all." Cf. Alperovitz, *Cold War Essays*, pp. 135, 31; also Christopher Lasch's comments, in the introduction, on "the general failure of orthodox historians to engage the revisionist argument."

118 On the substance of the "Nixon Doctrine," see John Dower's essay in Brodine *et al.*, *Open Secret*.

119 McGeorge Bundy, February 7, 1965; III, 687–91. The reprisals against North Vietnam are for "*any* VC act of violence to persons or property," as in the case of the Pleiku attack used as a pretext for initiating the bombing of the North, where there was not even a pretense that North Vietnamese were involved. This is quite in accord with NSC 5429/2, more than ten years before. Cf. p. 101 below.

120 April 6, 1964. The Security Council then proceeded to adopt a resolution condemning reprisals as "incompatible with the purposes and principles of the United Nations." For this and other references to the illegality of reprisal, see Lawyers Committee on American Policy Toward Vietnam, *Vietnam and International Law*, pp. 53–4, 98–101.

121 In the North, at least. In the South, and under Nixon-Kissinger in Laos and Cambodia, the question arises in a different form. With memories of gas chambers, some may be reluctant (as I have been personally) to use such terms as "genocide." The question whether the term is technically appropriate, in the light of the United Nations Convention of 1948, is a different matter. It was considered by the Russell Tribunal well before the significant escalation of the technological war in 1968 and on the basis of a small fraction of the evidence now available. See John Duffett, ed., *Against the Crime of Silence*, pp. 612–43.

122 IV, 71–4. Discussing the plans to destroy North Vietnamese petroleum reserves, the analyst notes that "neither in OSD nor the White House had anyone opposed these measures on other than prudential grounds—the risk of alienating allies or provoking Chinese or Russian intervention or uncertainty that results would justify either the risks or the costs" (IV, 74–5).

123 See Gabriel Kolko in Duffett, *Against the Crime of Silence*, p. 224.

124 See *Chronology of the Vietnam War*, bk. 1, distributed by Association d'Amitié Franco-Vietnamienne, 5, rue Las Cases, 75-Paris (7).

125 Note that RT in 1965 amounted to 33,000 tons of bombs, of a total of about 530,000 dropped on North Vietnam by end 1968. See Rafael Littauer *et al.*, *The Air War in Indochina*, p. SS-14.

126 See *American Power and the New Mandarins*, p. 15; chapter 3 below, pp. 225–6. See also Barry Weisberg, ed., *Ecocide in Indochina*, in particular the eyewitness report by Orville Schell and Barry Weisberg, p. 24. Attacks on the "dams and waterways in the crucial Red River Delta" were reported during the first monsoon season following the initiation of RT ("The 'Enemy': 20,000 Missions Later," *Newsweek*, October 11, 1965). The planes struck in August, according to this report. On the logic of such attacks, see the staff study "The Attack on the Irrigation Dams in North Korea," *Air Uni-*

versity Quarterly Review, Winter 1953–54. Gloating over the USAF attack on dams which caused a flash flood that "scooped clean 27 miles of valley below," constituting "one of the most significant air operations of the Korean War," the study explains that the smashing of the dams means "the destruction of their chief sustenance—rice": "The Westerner can little conceive the awesome meaning which the loss of this staple food commodity has for the Asian—starvation and slow death . . . more feared than the deadliest plague. Hence the show of rage, the flare of violent tempers. . . ."

127 Bernard Fall, "This Isn't Munich, It's Spain," *Ramparts*, December 1965; reprinted in *Last Reflections*, pp. 232–3.

128 The hospital compound that replaced it was bombed on December 26, 1971. See the eyewitness report by Banning Garrett, who visited a few days later, *The Guardian* (New York), February 16, 1972; *New York Times*, February 10, 1972, contains a briefer report. The hospital was visited by George Wald on February 19; see his "Our Bombs Fall on People," *Washington Monthly*, May 1972. See also the report of Joel Henri of AFP, *New York Times*, May 9, 1972: "In the bomb-scarred provinces of Thanhhoa and Namha, where no military target could be seen, this correspondent today visited a hospital and school struck by American bombs. . . . It was hard for the visitors to believe that the destruction [of the Thanh Hoa hospital], which was considerable, could have been the result of a mistake. The buildings, surrounded by rice fields, were also attacked last December, according to the North Vietnamese." Henri is describing the raid of April 27, 1972. This final destruction of the hospital caused it to be evacuated to the mountains. Henri also visited a village where the primary school was bombed during morning classes, leaving 20 dead and 25 wounded: "We looked for the military targets that might have justified the raid, but there was nothing—just mud and straw huts."

129 C. O. Holmquist, "Developments and Problems in Carrier-Based Attack Aircraft," *Naval Review*, 1969, p. 214. Laser-controlled bombs and other innovations now give pinpoint accuracy, it is claimed. Therefore, the extensive destruction of civilian targets cannot be attributed to "error." Cf. Claude Julien, reporting from Hanoi on the "remarkable precision of American bombings" of "hospitals, dikes, villages," *Le Monde*, May 20, 1972. See introduction, pp. x–xi above.

130 Stavins *et al.*, *Washington Plans an Aggressive War*, pp. 182–3. Stavins' analysis is also interesting with regard to the "conspiracy" in the field against Washington. Pilots have complained that inter-service rivalries led to dangerous missions with high loss rate. See also Colonel James Donovan, *Militarism, U.S.A.*, pp. 180–1.

131 IV, 408–9. Shortly after the Iron Triangle was "destroyed" in Operation CEDAR FALLS, "basically the same area" was invaded again in Operation JUNCTION CITY. The reader will find a brief description of the latter, but not the official map indicating the areas, including many villages, scheduled for destruction by preliminary air and artillery bombardment.

132 Griffiths, *Vietnam Inc.*, p. 89. Fall, *Last Reflections*, p. 248. See also Jonathan Schell, *The Village of Ben Suc: my American Power and the New Mandarins*, chap. 3, n. 19, pp. 276–8.

133 B-52 raids in 1965 in the densely populated Mekong Delta were reported by Bernard Fall, "Vietnam Blitz." Takashi Oka reported B-52 raids in "the populous delta" on December 4, 1965 (*Christian Science Monitor*; Melman, *In the Name of America* p. 248), noting the civilian casualties and the refugees fleeing to government-controlled areas "because they could no longer bear the continuous bombings." Fall also flew on bombing attacks on undefended villages, at about the same time ("This Isn't Munich, It's Spain"), as have many others. George Smith, a special forces sergeant captured by the NLF, reports B-52 raids (in Cambodia, he believes), along with constant and heavy bombing with napalm and high explosives in the free-fire zone where his camp was located, the latter from December 1964 (*P.O.W.: Two Years with the Vietcong*). Of course, the bombers were no more able to avoid villages than his POW camp. See also Russo, "Inside the RAND Corporation," on the effects of B-52 raids, as determined from refugee interviews. See also pp. 5–6 above.

134 Bernard Fall, "Vietcong—the Unseen Enemy in Vietnam," *New Society*, April 22, 1965, reprinted in Bernard Fall and Marcus G. Raskin, eds., *The Vietnam Reader*, p. 261.

135 T. D. Allman, "The Blind Bombers," *Far Eastern Economic Review*, January 29, 1972.

136 *New York Times*, letter, January 12, 1972.

137 Sidney Hook, "Lord Russell and the War Crimes 'Trial,'" *New Leader*, October 24, 1966. The reader who suspects that Hook may have learned something since may turn to *The Humanist*, January 1971, where he describes the destruction in Vietnam as "the unintended consequences of military action."

138 Rather consistently. In the same (1966) article, Hook refers to the United States' Dominican intervention of 1965 as an "error" traceable to "mistaken appraisal of the involvement of foreign Communist regimes."

139 McGeorge Bundy, "End of Either/Or," *Foreign Affairs*, vol. 45, no. 2 (1967). My reference is inexact, since Bundy seemed to regard anyone who disagreed on more than tactical matters as a wild man. Earlier, "the McGeorge Bundy group" (which included McNaughton, Cooper, and Unger) drafted a memorandum (February 7, 1965; III, 309) which "represents a highly personal Bundy assessment and point of view," and which notes that "none of the special solutions or criticisms put forward with zeal by individual reformers in government or in the press is of major importance." The Americans in Vietnam are the "first team," and though some of their tactical decisions may not have been perfect, clearly only a wild man in the wings would dare to question the first team in any more fundamental way.

140 A. J. Langguth, "Vietnam—1964: Exhilaration—1968: Frustration —1970: Hopelessness," *New York Times Magazine*, October 4, 1970, p. 89. Five years earlier he wrote in the same place: "I would say the war in South Vietnam changed irrevocably on Feb. 19, 1965 . . . [when] America began using its immense air power . . . [to] bomb South Vietnam" (Melman, *In the Name of America*, p. 174). The same source contains many other reports of American correspondents on the "hundreds of air strikes every day against villages and

other targets 'suspected' of harboring the Viet Cong in cases where there is no ground engagement" (Raymond Coffey, p. 181), the pattern of forced refugee generation by bombs and shells. Recall the claims of General Tidwell, p. 72 above.

141 Reuters, *New York Times*, March 18, 1965; Melman, *In the Name of America*, p. 185.

142 Stanley Karnow, *New York Herald Tribune*, December 28, 1964; Melman, *In the Name of America*, pp. 184–5. Karnow blames the Viet Cong, whose presence led to the attack and who within a week were "sanctimoniously denouncing 'this monstrous crime.' " Though convinced that the Viet Cong denunciation was "sanctimonious," Karnow does not address the more pertinent question: Was it correct?

It might incidentally be noted that ARVN reportedly used villagers, including children, specifically to draw enemy fire. See the August 1965 news report cited by Edward S. Herman, *Atrocities in Vietnam*, pp. 31–2. The United States has since refined this strategy. Local troops are used to establish contact with the enemy, then withdrawn (if possible) so that the area can be plastered with an air and artillery barrage (cf. Branfman, *Voices from the Plain of Jars*, p. 25). Sometimes, as in the Laos invasion of early 1971, the tactic partially backfires and the "friendly" forces are decimated as well. A related device is the use of civilians to compel soldiers to fight, as when Montagnard families were denied evacuation from Kontum (spring 1972) or when the remnants of the Meo in Laos were denied the opportunity to move to unsettled areas to the west and kept in the path of the Pathet Lao–NVA advance towards Vientiane, according to well-informed observers.

143 Alain C. Enthoven and K. Wayne Smith, *How Much Is Enough?* pp. 305–6, reporting a Systems Analysis study. "Unobserved strikes" are strikes against "places where the enemy might be." Civilians "might be" there as well; or to be more realistic, they are the true enemy. The study concludes that the effects of such strikes on civilians in Viet Cong and friendly areas were often "undesirable," probably creating more Viet Cong than they "eliminated." Unobserved strikes constituted about 65 percent of the tonnage of bombs and artillery rounds in 1966, and cost more than $2 billion. Despite the pretense of statistical evaluation, the fact surely is that the United States has no information about the effects of this indiscriminate and blind attack on "enemy" and "friendly" areas.

On the rise in Viet Cong recruitment, generally attributed to unrestricted bombardment, see references in *American Power and the New Mandarins*, chap. 3, n. 11, p. 276. Similar reports are common from Laos (see Fred Branfman, "Presidential War in Laos," in Adams and McCoy, *Laos*, p. 241) and Cambodia (see Richard Dudman, *Forty Days with the Enemy*; Boris Baczynskyj, "Bombing Turns Cambodian Villagers into Refugees," Dispatch News Service International, February 21, 1972, citing, for example, the case of a man who joined the Communists after an aerial attack left 50 dead in his native village). See chapter 2, section II, below.

144 Malcolm Browne, cited in *American Power and the New Mandarins*, p. 285, with further references from the same period (cf. pp. 335–6). More than half the total tonnage dropped on South Viet-

nam has been delivered by B-52s, much of it in settled areas. See Littauer *et al.*, *Air War*, pp. 4–8; also note 133, above. For details on bombing, see Jonathan Schell, *The Military Half*, and many other sources.

[145] Cf. the comments by George Carver of the CIA (IV, 82) cited above, p. 63. Perhaps it is such comments as these that Chester Cooper had in mind when he observed that the Pentagon Papers make the CIA "look good" ("The CIA and Decision-making," p. 228).

[146] Bernard Fall, "Vietnam Blitz." This, Fall suggests, is the reason why few weapons are found among the corpses. Note the early date of these comments. The author was very well informed, and no dove.

[147] IV, 360. Cf. IV, 487, 548. The date of the "first direct troop commitment to the Delta" is given as January 1967 (IV, 389). Jeffrey Race states that a battalion of the 25th Infantry Division arrived in Long An Province in September 1966, "the first deployment of an American combat unit into the Mekong Delta," though it was only in February 1967 that "more aggressive tactics were adopted" *Long An*, pp. 216–17). NLF losses were high "since the start of serious American combat operations in early 1967" (p. 270). The government "violence program" involved heavy use of air and artillery attacks, which "had a far more devastating impact on noncombatants than on combatants," according to defectors. During 1968 artillery bombardment became so intense that "large areas of the province looked (in words of one official) 'like the face of the moon' " (pp. 236–7).

Race explains in detail how the NLF defeated the United States–backed GVN in this crucial delta province by 1965. Infiltration was "negligible," and the first PAVN (North Vietnamese) main-force battalions entered the province between December 1967 and February 1968, for missions against Saigon (p. 211). On press reports of PAVN troops in the delta, see *At War with Asia*, pp. 99–100.

[148] January 9, 1967; Melman, *In the Name of America*, p. 98.

[149] Cf. *ibid.*, p. 384; *At War with Asia*, pp. 93–101; Ellsberg, "Bombing and Other Crimes," in *Papers on the War*. Ellsberg notes that General Ewell, commanding the 9th Division in the delta, "so completely freed his helicopter gunners from restraints against firing on sampans in canals lined on both sides with housing that the Division reported body-count ratios of 'friendly' to 'enemy' dead unmatched in the history of the war." Ewell was following the tactical principles laid down by the commanding general of the 1st Division, William DePuy, chief planner for Westmoreland, in the densely populated areas to the north. Kevin Buckley studied in detail one operation of Ewell's 9th Division in 1968, in the delta province of Kien Hoa. "The death toll there," he writes, "made the My Lai massacre look trifling by comparison." Official statistics cite nearly 11,000 killed, with 748 weapons found. An estimated 5,000 were noncombatant civilians ("at least"). The rest were combatants—that is, people defending their homes from the American aggressors. This operation was regarded as one of the most successful (and "most representative") "episodes in the history of pacification in Vietnam." As General Abrams later stated, "the performance of this division has been

magnificent." In this operation, "the fabric of society long established by the NLF was destroyed" (*Newsweek*, June 19, 1972).

150 Naturally, this does not prevent the State Department (or the press) from referring to this as "Hanoi's offensive" (IV, 581).

151 II, 517. Typically, the analyst does not notice the absurdity of this formulation, or what it implies as to who is "the enemy."

152 Littauer *et al.*, *Air War*, pp. 4–10 ff. See Schell, *Military Half*.

153 *Boston Globe*, December 10, 1971; reprinted from the *Washington Post*.

154 General DePuy; cf. Ellsberg, "Bombing and Other Crimes."

155 Komer, "Impact of Pacification on Insurgency in South Vietnam," *Journal of International Affairs*, vol. 25, no. 1 (1971). Cf. chapter 3.

156 Komer, "Epilogue," *ibid.*, no. 2; Eqbal Ahmad, "Revolutionary War and Counter-insurgency," *ibid.*, no. 1, pp. 44.

157 Robert Komer, "Pacification: A Look Back," *Army*, June 1970, p. 23.

158 Allan Goodman, "The Ending of the War as a Setting for the Future Development of South Vietnam," *Asian Survey*, vol. 11, no. 4 (1971), p. 342 n.

159 UPI, *Le Monde*, November 5, 1971. Quotes are retranslated, since I have not come across this UPI report in the American press, apart from a reference by Richard Ward in *The Guardian*, November 17, 1971. For information on Operation Phoenix in 1968–9, see *At War with Asia*, pp. 301–2, and Herman, *Atrocities in Vietnam*, p. 47. On American programs in earlier years to develop "assassination teams" and "prosecutors-executors," see William A. Nighswonger, *Rural Pacification in Vietnam*, pp. 136–7.

For more recent reports, see also Seymour Hersh, *Cover-up*; Race, *Long An*; Fitzgerald, *Fire in the Lake*. For a general review of the Phoenix program, see Jon Cooper, "Operation Phoenix," Department of History, Dartmouth College.

The official figures cited in the UPI report are far more conservative than those cited in other sources. An official publication of the Saigon Ministry of Information gives the figure 40,994 killed in the Phoenix program of a total of 81,039 convicted, killed, rallied. The period covered is August 1, 1968, given as the date of the launching of the Phoenix program, through mid-1971 (*Vietnam 1967–71*, p. 52). Senator Kennedy refers to "the estimated 48,000 civilians of the Vietcong infrastructure who have been killed by American-sponsored assassination teams" (*Problems of War Victims in Indochina*, Hearings before the [Kennedy] Subcommittee on Refugees and Escapees, U.S. Senate, May 9, 1972, p. 9). The killing of 40,000 of the "communist infrastructure" is reported by the Saigon Ministry of Information under the heading "Programme Defending People Against Terrorism."

160 Reported in Jon Cooper, "Operation Phoenix." The informant is Don Luce.

161 Tad Szulc, *New York Times*, April 7, 1971.

162 Frances Starner, "I'll Do It My Way," *Far Eastern Economic Review*, November 6, 1971.

163 Richard West, "Vietnam: The Year of the Rat," *New Statesman*, February 25, 1972. See also chapter 3, note 71.

164 Former American participants report that United States intelligence nets were also penetrated by right-wing Vietnamese groups who fed

reports to fuel the "bloodbath theory," knowing that these would be transmitted to Washington and would leak to industrious reporters. To explain the absence of predicted uprisings and bloodbaths, the same right-wing agents point to the success of the Phoenix program in weakening the NLF infrastructure. Thus while inciting bloodbath fears to gain United States support, these agents are also attempting to increase support for terror programs which may well succeed in providing such sects as the VNQDD with a degree of political control under the American aegis. See the report by Jeffrey Stein, an agent handler in 1968–1969, "Bloodbath over the Rainbow," *The Phoenix* [Boston], May 10, 1972. As he notes, the bloodbath argument conveniently overlooks the absence of a bloodbath in areas under long NLF control—apart from the bloodbath caused by United States air and artillery.

165 See Jon Cooper, "Operation Phoenix," for details. Also Kahin and Lewis, *The United States in Vietnam*, app. 15.

166 Pfaff, *Condemned to Freedom*, pp. 75–7, a close paraphrase (with no acknowledgment) of some remarkable passages in Townsend Hoopes's *Limits of Intervention*, on which I have commented elsewhere (*At War with Asia*, pp. 297–300). Since Hoopes mentions Pfaff in this earlier book, it is unclear who deserves the credit for these insights.

167 Pfaff adds at this point that "it is not clear that [the Chinese Communists] understand the significance of the claim which Mao Tse-tung has made that China can 'win' a nuclear war in which 300 million Chinese would die." This "claim" has been frequently attributed to Mao in anticommunist propaganda, but no source has been discovered. Chang Hsin-hai concludes that it is "an outrageous and unmitigated falsehood, which everybody has accepted as gospel truth" (*America and China*, p. 227).

168 On the welfare of the Vietnamese under French rule, see Ngo Vinh Long, *Before the August Revolution*.

169 On the earlier period, see Truong Buu Lam, *Patterns of Vietnamese Response to Foreign Intervention*; Tam Vu and Nguyen Khac Vien, *A Century of National Struggle*; David G. Marr, *Vietnamese Anti-colonialism*; Long, *August Revolution*.

170 Colin S. Gray, "What RAND Hath Wrought," *Foreign Policy*, vol. 1, no. 4 (1971).

171 "The lucrative US presence . . . created a virtual gold mine of wealth which is directly or indirectly syphoned off and pocketed by the officials." Compare the situation since. From 1966 through 1971, United States economic assistance to South Vietnam averaged over $600 million per year; the capital flow from South Vietnam is about one-third of this. The recent fiscal reforms (heralded as the "autumn revolution"—fall 1971) raised the price of rice, sugar, milk powder, and pharmaceuticals while lowering prices for refrigerators and air conditioners. Rotten rice still sells at black-market prices. Phi Bang, "South Vietnam: A Hand-to-Mouth Economy," *Far Eastern Economic Review*, January 15, 1972. For more examples, see *Thoi-Bao Ga*, December 1971. On corruption, see references of note 64.

172 Cited in Philippe Devillers and Jean Lacouture, *End of a War*, pp. 322–3. The authors note that Chauvel's report described America's

intentions "with great clarity." See *At War with Asia*, p. 33, for a longer excerpt.

173 For a discussion of the severe distortion of the crucial 1954–1960 period in the Pentagon history, see my essay in Chomsky and Zinn, *Critical Essays*, which also discusses covert activities that are reported in the Pentagon study, in particular the 34-A operations launched on February 1, 1964, and their bearing on the 1964 escalation of the war in Laos.

174 Bernard Fall, "Viet-Nam—the Agonizing Reappraisal," *Current History*, February 1965; reprinted in Fall and Raskin, *Vietnam Reader*, p. 339. See *American Power and the New Mandarins*, chap. 3, nn. 46, 47, for additional reports from the public record. A detailed account of these operations, which he dates from 1958, is given by Chaffard, *Les Deux Guerres*, pp. 366–75. See also Wilfred Burchett, "The Receiving End," in Chomsky and Zinn, *Critical Essays*, for reports from North Vietnam.

I have come across only one reference to Lansdale's missions in the Pentagon Papers per se, namely, DOD, bk. 2, tab 1, IV.A.5, p. 11: "Colonel Lansdale described a U.S. instigated black propaganda campaign of pamphlets and announcements, ostensibly Viet Minh in origin. . . ." This is from the material missing in the Gravel edition, I, 291.

175 For some amusing comments on the elections provision, see Dennis Duncanson, *Government and Revolution in Vietnam*, pp. 7–8. He regards it as a subsidiary detail, not a main feature, and claims that apart from the DRV, "everybody else" took the agreements to be merely "a deal to establish peace through territorial concessions." On what "everybody else" actually thought, there is an ample literature. See, e.g., S. R. SarDesai, *Indian Foreign Policy in Cambodia, Laos and Vietnam*, chap. 4.

176 Quotes and comment from SarDesai, *Indian Foreign Policy*. See also Mieczyslaw Maneli (the strongly anticommunist former legal and political adviser to the Polish delegation of the ICC), *War of the Vanquished*, chap. 2; Kahin and Lewis, *U.S. in Vietnam*; Marvin E. Gettleman, ed., *Vietnam: History, Documents and Opinions*, pt. 5; and many other sources. Bernard Fall expresses the view of serious anticommunist sources when he states that "South Viet-Nam refused to hold elections by July, 1956, since this would have meant handing over control of the South to Ho Chi Minh" (*Last Reflections*, p. 146). The problem was that Ho had created "the *one* effective political organization the country has ever had" and that he was fighting for "purely Vietnamese *national* objectives, and that fact is terribly important to this very day" (1967; *ibid.*, pp. 46, 87).

177 Gettleman, *Vietnam*, p. 172.

178 Cooper, *Lost Crusade*, p. 166.

179 Cf. Kahin and Lewis, *U.S. in Vietnam*. See also Kahin's comments on the history of American-promoted elections in *The New Republic*, February 12, 1972. Also Fall, "Vietnam's 12 Elections," in *Last Reflections*.

180 Thieu Son, in the Saigon newspaper *Dien Tin*, August 24, 1971; translated in part in *Thoi-Bao Ga*, October 1971.

181 May 1967; IV, 182. To realize this commitment, natives of South

Vietnam who had infiltrated back "should be expelled as a matter of principle," or permitted to remain if they are "prepared to accept peaceful political activity under the Constitution" (which prohibits communism). He does not add that they must be prepared to obey laws such as those described in the references of note 165, which make Communist or much neutralist activity a serious crime.

[182] Robert Thompson, "A Successful End to the War in Viet Nam," *Pacific Community*, vol. 2, no. 3 (1971).

[183] Roger Hilsman, "Two American Counterstrategies to Guerrilla Warfare," in Tang Tsou, *China in Crisis*, vol. 2, pp. 283, 291. Hilsman elaborates this concept of "free choice" further in his book *To Move a Nation*. For Thompson's own formulation, accurately presented by Hilsman, see his *Defeating Communist Insurgency*, pp. 141–3.

[184] Dean Rusk claimed in April 1963 that seven million Vietnamese—almost half the population—lived in strategic hamlets. Cited in Cooper, *Lost Crusade*, p. 201.

[185] See Austin, *President's War*; Scott, *War Conspiracy*, chap. 3; Stavins et al., *Washington Plans an Aggressive War*; Joseph C. Goulden, *Truth is the First Casualty*; E. G. Windchy, *Tonkin Gulf*. These studies raise serious doubts as to whether the August 4 incident in Tonkin Gulf, which led to the "retaliatory" bombing, ever occurred. They make it plain that whatever Washington may have chosen to believe, the evidence for the alleged attack was slight and contradictory, and that subsequent administration testimony demonstrated either astonishing ignorance or outright deception. Even if the attack did take place (with no damage to the American vessels), the retaliatory attack was indefensible, not only because of its scale but because of the extensive provocation: specifically, GVN naval attacks, with American vessels seeking to draw attention elsewhere. The Pentagon analyst concludes that the August 4 attack took place and was almost certainly deliberate (III, 186). His analysis, however, is superficial as compared with the studies cited. It generally follows the lines of McNamara's discredited Senate testimony.

[186] Not surprisingly, Sir Robert Thompson regards the 1964 election in exactly the same light. "Not until after the Tonkin Gulf incident in August, 1964, with its consequent Congress resolution and his own outstanding success against Senator Goldwater in the Presidential election at the end of the year was President Johnson in a position to take a major decision . . . the only option left was escalation" (*No Exit from Vietnam*, p. 16).

[187] Douglas Pike, *Vietcong*, p. 362.

[188] After the decision to bomb the North, the White House informed Taylor in Saigon that a presidential announcement was under consideration which would state that the bombing "will be reported to the United Nations Security Council under the Provisions of Article 51 of the United Nations Charter"—that is, as a measure of collective self-defense—but the analyst states that this "intention . . . was dropped several days later." There appears to be no other instance of any consideration of the legal obligations of the United States.

[189] Recall the wording of the State Department White Paper of 1961, explaining how "the authorities in South Viet-Nam refused to fall

into this well-laid trap"—namely, the 1956 elections agreed upon at Geneva. Cited in Kahin and Lewis, *U.S. in Vietnam*, p. 58. Throughout, the United States executive and its local subsidiaries had to keep stepping lively to avoid such traps laid by the wily Communists.

190 See, e.g., Franz Schurmann *et al.*, *The Politics of Escalation in Vietnam*; Scott, *War Conspiracy*. Compare also Scott's discussion of the bombing of the Soviet ship *Turkestan* in Haiphong harbor, with the analyst's reference to "an unfortunate case of bad aiming" (IV, 187)—possibly the case, though a serious analysis would hardly rest merely with repeating the government's excuses.

191 See Cooper, *Lost Crusade*, pp. 327–8. Also Draper, *Abuse of Power*, pp. 167–8; Chaffard, *Les Deux Guerres*, pp. 382–8, 393–4.

192 For example, Walt Rostow has claimed that the Indochinese Communists were "enflamed" by Stalin after World War II and that Stalin was also responsible for the Greek rebellion. He cites no evidence. For some quotes, see my *American Power and the New Mandarins*, pp. 327–8, 360. For discussion of the facts with regard to Greece, see Gabriel Kolko, *Politics of War*; Kolko and Kolko, *Limits of Power*; Richard Barnet, *Intervention and Revolution*. For some parallels between Greece and Vietnam, see Todd Gitlin, "Counter-insurgency: Myth and Reality in Greece," in David Horowitz, ed., *Containment and Revolution*; and L. S. Stavrianos, "Greece's Other History," *New York Review of Books*, June 17, 1971. The beliefs of Rostow and others with regard to Greece can perhaps be attributed to ignorance. With regard to Indochina, the assumption is unlikely. See also note 95. As part of the "many good suggestions and wise counsel" given him by Truman, Lyndon Johnson cites Truman's experience in facing "problems of aggression" in Greece and Turkey (*Vantage Point*, p. 31).

193 As compared with the "democratically-elected Government of the Republic of Korea" (NSC memorandum, March 1949, *DOD*, bk. 8, p. 269). For an example of the persistence of such astonishing illusions, see the secret memorandum to the president by George Ball, October 5, 1964, *Atlantic Monthly*, July 1972. Distinguishing the case of Korea from Vietnam, he writes: "In 1950 the *Korean Government* under Syngman Rhee was stable. It had the general support of principal elements in the country. . . . The Korean people were still excited by their newfound freedom; they were fresh for the war." On the facts, see the references of note 98. In *American Power and the New Mandarins*, I discussed many similar examples of historical fantasies at high levels of decision making (cf. chap. 3, pp. 262–6, and chap. 6, pp. 364–5, n. 29, on Hilsman's and Stevenson's "proofs" of Chinese aggressiveness). Unfortunately, these absurdities must be taken seriously, given the vast resources of terror in the hands of those whose decisions are guided (or justified) by them.

194 Cited by Cooper, *Lost Crusade*, p. 171. See p. 56 above. Cooper wonders only why he didn't mention the North Vietnamese, "who, even more than the Chinese Communists, were causing the mischief in Laos and Vietnam." On events in Laos at the time, see notes 198–201, 216, 225; chapter 2, section I; and references cited there. See also introduction, note 24.

195 This objective was assigned 20 percent importance, as compared with 70 percent importance to the objective: "To avoid a humiliating U.S. defeat (to our reputation as a guarantor)" (III, 349). The welfare of the Vietnamese was granted a 10 percent share.

196 See also the curious conclusions of William Bundy in 1971, discussed in my *Problems of Knowledge and Freedom*, pp. 82–3.

197 On the character and significance of the May 1959 meeting in Hanoi, as discussed in the Pentagon Papers and by independent scholars, see my essay in Chomsky and Zinn, *Critical Essays*.

198 See Gareth Porter, "After Geneva: Subverting Laotian Neutrality," in Adams and McCoy, *Laos*; Scott, *War Conspiracy*; C. A. Stevenson, *The End of Nowhere*; and references cited in chapter 2, section I. It is possible that there was North Vietnamese support for the Pathet Lao, as Arthur Dommen asserts, on evidence that hardly seems compelling. Thai pilots were sent to Laos for counterinsurgency missions in March 1964. The role of Thai rangers in covert operations in Laos (Operation Hardnose) remains obscure (see III, 578, 610). Fred Branfman estimates that by 1970 the United States had brought in at least 10,000 Asians into Laos as mercenaries, in comparison with the perhaps 5,000 North Vietnamese engaged in combat ("Presidential War in Laos," pp. 266, 278–9). Lansdale's report of July 1961 (II, 643–4) describes some of the early stages of these operations. The White Star Mobile Training Teams consisting of United States Special Forces personnel, introduced into Laos covertly in the last few weeks of the Eisenhower administration (Stevenson, *End of Nowhere*, p. 185) or perhaps in 1959 (Porter, "After Geneva," p. 183), "had the purpose and effect of establishing U.S. control over foreign forces" (II, 464). Laos was serving as a model for Vietnam, in this and other instances. See the references cited for further evidence. On the contribution of the Pentagon history see Stevenson, *End of Nowhere*, postscript; Walter Haney, "The Pentagon Papers and U.S. involvement in Laos," in Chomsky and Zinn, *Critical Essays*; Jonathan Mirsky, "High Drama on Foggy Bottom," *Saturday Review*, January 1, 1972.

By 1964, United States involvement was extensive. Refugees report bombing from May 1964. For refugee reports, see chapter 2, section I.

199 Hugh Toye, *Laos: Buffer State or Battleground*, p. 154. On the training of commandos abroad for covert operations in North Vietnam, see Chaffard, *Les Deux Guerres*, p. 368.

200 Jim Lucas of Scripps-Howard, cited in Stevenson, *End of Nowhere*, p. 89; Denis Warner, July 1961, cited in *At War with Asia*, p. 203.

201 The interpretation of events in Laos in this period is particularly distorted in the Pentagon Papers. See my essay in Chomsky and Zinn, *Critical Essays*.

202 On the scale and character of this infiltration, United States government estimates must be taken with a grain of salt. Chaffard reports that French intelligence gives far lower estimates (*Les Deux Guerres*, p. 359). This is a more neutral and probably more accurate source, given the long years of contact. The Pentagon analyst remarks that the judgments of a "rise and change in the nature of infiltration" in August 1964 may have been influenced by the fact

that this was expected in reaction to the "Tonkin reprisals," and that evidence of greatly increased infiltration was an explicit condition for "systematic military action against DRV," which top officials were beginning to regard as "inevitable" (III, 192). A former DIA analyst reports that from 1964–1965 until 1967, "the generals in Saigon worked to build up U.S. troop strength" and therefore "wanted every bit of evidence brought to the fore that could show that infiltration was increasing. DIA obliged" (also emphasizing the enemy's ability to recruit locally). Patrick McGarvey, cited by Graham T. Allison and Morton H. Halperin, "Bureaucratic Politics," *World Politics*, vol. 24, no. 3 (1972), p. 74. Cf. also Allen S. Whiting, "Scholar and Policy-maker," *ibid.*, p. 233, on the crucial role of "insight and intuition" rather than " 'hard' evidence clandestinely acquired" in intelligence estimates. The author, to mid-1966, was Director, Office of Research and Analysis for Far East, Bureau of Intelligence and Research, Department of State, from the evidence in the Pentagon Papers, the most successful of the intelligence agencies in analysis and evaluation.

203 The image of "Indian fighting" was much on the minds of the American military. See *American Power and the New Mandarins*, chap. 3, n. 42, for references. See also Michael Rogin, "Liberal Society and the Indian Question," *Politics and Society*, May 1971, for some interesting background.

204 II, 693; Bureau of Intelligence and Research, State Department, December 3, 1962.

205 Schlesinger, *Thousand Days*, p. 759.

206 See note 4. For some references from the public record, see chapter 3.

207 Draper, *Abuse of Power*.

208 See my essay in Chomsky and Zinn, *Critical Essays*, for details on United States government beliefs with regard to PAVN units in the South, as revealed by the Pentagon history.

209 See p. 103, above, and the references of note 198. In July 1967 it was discovered that Chinese Nationalists, "disguised so as to appear to be South Vietnamese with Nung ancestry," were being used on covert operations by the GVN, apparently the result of a secret agreement of 1966. The JCS disapproved, "despite appeals from COMUSMACV." MACV "advised against US cooperation" in the occupation by the GVN of an island claimed by Communist and Nationalist China, with the intention of constructing an airfield (II, 402). Americans who have been engaged in clandestine operations in Indochina report the presence of CIA-trained Chinese Nationalists, but I have no way of verifying these reports. Many Chinese (up to 50,000) were reported in North Vietnam in construction and repair operations during the bombing of the North in 1965–1968; these reports rarely note that the United States was bombing an internal Chinese railway, the only rail connection between southwestern China and the rest of the country, which happened to pass near Hanoi. I noted no reference to this fact in the Pentagon study, but it is mentioned by George Ball (see note 192 above) as a possible reason why China might intervene.

210 See Hearings Before the [Symington] Subcommittee on United States Security Agreements and Commitments Abroad, U.S. Senate, 1969, pt. 3: "Kingdom of Thailand," pp. 646–7, 753–4, 851–3,

discussed in my "Revolt in the Academy." The testimony here might be usefully contrasted with the remarks by Senator Gordon Allott, who claims that "Red Chinese troops were [in 1962] roaming at will through a good portion of northern Thailand" and "still are, except that now they are actually engaging in acts of war" (August 12, 1969, reprinted in *Congressional Record*, August 3, 1971, p. S12948).

211 See chapter 2, section I, and references cited there, particularly note 12.

212 Cooper, *Lost Crusade*, pp. 264-5. See chapter 3 below.

213 For a discussion of such evidence, see my chapter in Chomsky and Zinn, *Critical Essays*.

214 Jean-Claude Pomonti and Serge Thion, *Des courtisans aux partisans*, p. 209. Bernard Fall also questioned—in fact ridiculed—the "American official view" ("Viet-Cong—the Unseen Enemy in Viet-Nam") as have other noncommunist observers. Cf. Chaffard, *Les Deux Guerres*, for extensive discussion. Cf. also Richard West's report from Phu Quoc island, thirty miles west of the mainland and remote from infiltration but largely under NLF control (*Sketches from Vietnam*). Since United States intelligence sources are unavailable, it is impossible to evaluate them (see notes 164, 202). However, occasional comments raise questions as to how well they support the "American official view" that Fall and others reject. Allan Goodman reports that "Vietcong who defected in 1961–1962, in part, gave as their reason for changing sides the reluctance of Hanoi to authorize anything beyond political action among the population" ("Diplomatic and Strategic Outcomes of the Conflict," in Walter Isard, ed., *Vietnam: Issues and Alternatives*). A survey of Viet Cong prisoners and defectors just prior to the American escalation of early 1965 found "most native South Vietnamese guerrillas unaware of any North Vietnamese role in the war, except as a valued ally" (*New York Times*, June 7, 1965; cited in *American Power and the New Mandarins*, pp. 243, 282–3).

215 Cf. Race, *Long An*; Fitzgerald, *Fire in the Lake*, Chaffard, *Les Deux Guerres*; Robert Sansom, *The Economics of Insurgency in the Mekong Delta of Vietnam*. For some discussion of Race's valuable study in this context, see my essay in Chomsky and Zinn, *Critical Essays*. Also very useful is the documentation in Pike, *Viet Cong*.

216 In January 1962, Viet Cong forces were estimated at 16,500, as compared to "South Vietnamese" forces of more than 175,000, with additional paramilitary forces of 110,000 (II, 656). The United States government assessment of the situation in Laos in the same year (1961) is not very different: "By the spring of 1961 the NLHS [political arm of the Pathet Lao] appeared to be in a position to take over the entire country" (State Department *Background Notes*, March 1969), despite vast U.S. efforts in support of the extreme right.

217 Note the analogy to the Nixon-Kissinger diplomacy today: China and the Soviet Union are to impose constraints on the DRV-PRG and influence them to call off the struggle against the United States–imposed regime in the South. It is natural that Kissinger, who fancies himself a geopolitician, should generalize the strategy of an earlier period to a global scale.

218 See note 47, and pp. 133–4 below.

219 Cooper, *Lost Crusade*, p. 256; cf. also pp. 313–4, 430. Cf. also the analysis of the situation of 1965 by John Paul Vann, discussed below in chapter 3, pp. 232–3. American officials in Saigon estimated in 1962 that half the population supported the NLF (Robert Scigliano, *South Vietnam: Nation Under Stress*, p. 145). A similar estimate is repeated even by Douglas Pike (*War, Peace and the Viet Cong*, p. 6). It is doubtful that George Washington could have claimed as much.

220 Cf. Jean Lacouture, *Vietnam: Between Two Truces*, p. 188.

221 For details, from an interesting document of December 1963, see my essay in Chomsky and Zinn, *Critical Essays*.

222 John T. McAlister, Jr., and Paul Mus, *The Vietnamese and their Revolution*, p. 160. For a particularly forceful statement to this effect, see Bernard Fall, cited in chapter 3, pp. 221–2. It should be recalled that Fall was bitterly anticommunist and strongly in support of United States aims in Vietnam, though appalled at the means by which they were being carried out, and concerned in the end that "Viet-Nam as a cultural and historic entity . . . is threatened with extinction" under the blows of the American war machine (*Last Reflections*, pp. 33–4).

223 Maneli, *War of the Vanquished*, pp. 214, 216. See note 176. The book is interesting for a number of revelations, in particular, in the support it gives to persistent rumors of a Diem-Nhu rapprochement with Hanoi that was under consideration in 1963, just prior to the coup that overthrew Diem. Cf. also Chaffard, *Les Deux Guerres*, chap. 8. If this was indeed a factor in the coup, then the United States role was even more cynical than the record in the Pentagon Papers indicates. John P. Roche claims that the Kennedy administration had made a "decision" that Diem and Nhu "must not be permitted to make a private deal with Ho Chi Minh" and that Washington regarded the prospect of "an American departure from the premises" (an expected consequence of a "private deal," that is, a political settlement) as "unthinkable." He also asserts that the Pentagon historians ignored evidence he had given them to this effect. "The Pentagon Papers," *Political Science Quarterly*, vol. 87, no. 2 1972). If he is correct, then the example stands as another case where the historians distorted the record in an effort to present United States actions in a less unfavorable light (to be sure, this is not Roche's point).

224 Chaffard, *Les Deux Guerres*, p. 288.

225 It is commonly asserted in American studies that the North Vietnamese are responsible for the breakdown of the Geneva Agreements of 1962, beginning with their refusal to withdraw the extensive military forces that the United States government claims they had deployed in Laos. Stevenson, in one of the more serious works, asserts that "only forty of the estimated 10,000 North Vietnamese in Laos left through ICC checkpoints" (*End of Nowhere*, p. 179). His source is Arthur Dommen, *Conflict in Laos*, p. 240. Dommen's source is an unidentified spokesman of the British Foreign Office. As to Dommen's reliability, see chapter 2, section I, and my essay in Chomsky and Zinn, *Critical Essays*. Evidently, on such evidence as this one can conclude virtually nothing, and it is ir-

responsible merely to cite these unsubstantiated claims by deeply committed commentators as proof that North Vietnam was responsible for the breakdown of the Geneva Agreements. For further discussion, see *At War with Asia*, chap. 4; section I of chapter 2 below, and references cited there; Chaffard, *Les Deux Guerres*. Dommen concedes that CIA-supported Meo guerrillas, "sitting astride the natural communication route between Vientiane and the NLHS base area in Sam Neua," may have hampered communication sufficiently to have caused deterioration of the well-developed NLHS infrastructure (see above, notes 200, 216) in Vientiane Province (Dommen, p. 308); but he does not go on to point out that United States support for the guerrillas constituted a serious violation of the 1962 agreements from the outset and was a factor in the renewal of conflict.

226 This was, of course, the reason for the United States terror program then intensified in the delta (cf. note 149), where, it will be recalled, few NVA troops were present.

227 King, "Political Balance," p. 405. He quotes (p. 417) the Saigon newspaper *Dien Tin*, March 30, 1971: in any place "in which our magnificent allies the Americans are present, at that place Vietnamese lives weigh no more than those of earthworms or crickets," a painfully accurate description.

228 Averell Harriman, "Missed Opportunities: How We Got Where We Are," *Washington Post*, May 9, 1972. Harriman also points out that when the negotiations began, North Vietnam withdrew 90 percent of its troops from the northern two provinces, half of them over 200 miles into North Vietnam. "The United States was then in a favorable bargaining position since it had over half a million men in South Vietnam," not to speak of more than 50,000 Korean mercenaries. For references from the press at the time, see *At War with Asia*, pp. 43ff. From January to September 1969 there was a sharp decline in bombing of the infiltration routes in southern Laos, probably related to the same DRV withdrawal of military force in expectation of some results from the negotiations in Paris. The planes available were simply shifted to northern Laos, where they turned to the enterprise described in chapter 2, section I, below. Cf. Hearings before the [Symington] Subcommittee on United States Security Agreements and Commitments Abroad, U.S. Senate, October 1969, pt. 2: "Kingdom of Laos," p. 464.

229 Roche, "Pentagon Papers."

230 Johnson, *Vantage Point*, p. 63.

231 On August 29, 1963, the French government announced its support for a policy in Vietnam based on "independence vis-à-vis the outside, in peace and unity at home, and in concord with their neighbors." Kennedy's comment, cited below, was a response to this statement (cf. Fall, *Two Viet-Nams*, p. 392; for Fall's reservations, see pp. 400ff.). On July 23, 1964, General de Gaulle recommended a conference aiming at establishing the neutrality of all Indochina. President Johnson responded, "We do not believe in conferences called to ratify terror; so our policy is unchanged." Cf. Chaffard, *Les Deux Guerres*, pp. 362ff.

232 Robert Shaplen, "Letter from Vietnam," *New Yorker*, June 24, 1972.

233 *Wall Street Journal*, June 16, 1972.

234 One of the highest interagency priorities recommended in April 1966; II, 582.

235 See, for example, Vietnam Veterans Against the War, eds., *Winter Soldier Investigation*; James S. Kunen, *Standard Operating Procedure*; D. Thorne and G. Butler, eds., *The New Soldier*; Citizens' Commission of Inquiry, *The Dellums Committee Hearings on War Crimes in Vietnam*.

236 Described, perhaps, as "the familiar Communist-neutralist bray" (III, 621).

237 Robert Drinan, *Boston Globe*, February 7, 1972.

CHAPTER 2

The Wider War

I. LAOS

The Pentagon Papers, discussed in chapter 1, provide only limited information with regard to the war in Laos. They do, however, exhibit clearly the general framework within which this war was pursued. In Laos as in Vietnam, the guiding principle for tactical decisions was the Tanham-Duncanson doctrine, "All the dilemmas are practical and as neutral in an ethical sense as the laws of physics" (see chapter 1, section I). The problems, in short, are technical ones. The goal is to establish the rule of selected social groups in the society that is subject to the experiment in counterinsurgency. A number of methods are available, ranging from rural development and commodity import programs to B-52s, cluster bombs, and crop destruction, and the task facing the technician is to combine these methods in such a manner as to maximize the probability that the approved social order will be maintained and all modes of existence that depart from this pattern will be impeded or terminated. The only constraint is cost: cost to the planners and to the interests they represent. Where the cost is slight, the destruction will correspondingly be vast. Since the peasant society of Laos was weak and defenseless and the war was conducted in virtual secrecy, the costs were minimal. The predictable result is the Plain of Jars, once a thriving, largely rural community and now a blackened wasteland.

Air Force Secretary Robert Seamans states that he has visited northern Laos—where, he reports, "I have seen no evidence of indiscriminate bombing."[1] It is the North Vietnamese who are "rough," and the people are not "against the

United States—just the opposite." Ambassador William Sullivan has testified before Congress that only military targets are attacked, that "villages or any inhabited places [are] out of bounds to the US air activities," and that "the North Vietnamese are pushing the population out ahead of them."[2] No refugees write letters to American newspapers or appear at senatorial hearings to contest such claims. Nevertheless, documentation on the American war in Laos is gradually accumulating, and it reveals these claims to be a shameless lie.

The statement of the air force secretary that he has seen no signs of indiscriminate bombing may be usefully compared with the eyewitness report of T. D. Allman, who flew over the Plain of Jars at about the same time.

> Now it is empty and ravaged, a striking example of what less than three years of intensive U.S. bombing can do to a rural area.
>
> In large areas the original bright green has been destroyed and replaced by an abstract pattern of black and bright metallic colours. Much of the remaining foliage is stunted and dull from the use of defoliants. Black is now the main colour of the northern and eastern reaches of the plain. Napalm is dropped regularly to burn off vegetation, and fires burn constantly, creating giant rectangles of black. During the flight plumes of smoke could be seen rising from freshly bombed areas.
>
> The main routes into the plain are mercilessly bombed, apparently on a non-stop basis. There, and along the rim of the plain, the dominant colour is yellow. All vegetation has been destroyed and the craters, literally, are countless. . . . In many places it is impossible to distinguish individual craters; there are just endless patches of churned earth, repeatedly bombed. . . . Further to the south-east, Xieng Khouangville, once a French-style market town and the most populous in Communist Laos, lies empty and totally destroyed. . . .
>
> Along the main Communist access routes leading into the plain, the innumerable pockmarks of 500 lb bombs give way to the giant crater patterns created by the B52s. The saturation bombings are used in an attempt to extinguish all human life in the target area, and to create landslides to block roads. . . .
>
> Both the Pathet Lao leader, Prince Souphanouvong, and the US aid mission once had plans for developing the

plain into the economic centre of the north Laotian hills. Now, even if the war ended tomorrow, it might take years for the ecological balance to restore itself, and just as long to rebuild towns and villages, and recover fields.

Even then the plain would for decades, if not longer, present the peril of hundreds of thousands of unexploded bombs, mines, and booby traps.[3]

Even in government-controlled areas, fields and villages are littered with unexploded antipersonnel weapons. Michael Morrow visited a village four miles from Luang Prabang, the royal capital. It was temporarily occupied by Communist troops who attacked a nearby air base. "When the counter-attack came all but one of the thatch and bamboo houses of the village were burnt down or blown up by bombs of marauding planes. . . . Trekking through a bamboo thicket which, according to the villagers, had previously been checked by American demolition experts, this reporter came across two unexploded CBUs [cluster bomb units] in fifteen minutes searching." In other nearby areas Morrow "saw at least twenty-five CBUs plus one unexploded artillery shell, one live mortar round and one undetonated M-79 grenade round," all discovered by villagers in the course of their normal work routine. "Most dramatically, on a brush and banana covered hill directly behind the village a 'mother' bomb of CBUs rests undetonated with its yellow 'baby' bombs, some in and some out, like the roe of a stuck sturgeon," with the markings of the United States Air Force clearly visible. Villagers cannot tend their fields nor let their children play freely. "And it is unlikely that Americans are or will ever be around to pick up the unexploded pieces of the most extensive bombing campaign in history."[4]

But Robert Seamans has seen no evidence of indiscriminate bombing.

A number of air force personnel who have taken part in the bombing have reported the bombing of villages. An air force major who directed high-altitude bombing from a spotter plane told reporter Joe Nicholson, Jr.: "I would be given flights of fighter-bombers by the aerial command post and occasionally I would guide the fighter-bombers into villages."

A marine pilot stated: "To the extent that I knew, we were bombing villages all the time. Our bombing was generally just a matter of releasing bombs at certain coordinates." A photo-interpreter at Udorn Air Force Base in Thailand reported:

> I saw photographs of between 10 and 25 villages destroyed—all with bomb craters. There were a lot of vehicles destroyed in the villages, indicating they were live villages, inhabited. The only place people could exist up there on the Plain of Jars would be either in a dense jungle or in a cave. And we were bombing caves. A single human path was enough for us to bomb. All human activity was considered enemy activity.[5]

Photo-intelligence expert James Walkley, who was a CINCPAC (Commander in Chief, Pacific) briefer for Laos, reports having seen about 150 photographs of over a hundred bombed villages. But, he reports, photos of bombed villages were never picked for the briefings, but only photos of destroyed trucks, burning supplies, and so on. As to the southern sections of North Vietnam, they were "pretty well devoid of any villages that might have existed at one time." He also reports the bombing of a hospital in a cave with CBUs and Rockeye missiles, and the bombing of a village near Xieng Khouangville by B-52s.[6]

Testimony from refugees is also accumulating.[7] The person primarily responsible for public awareness of the American war in Laos and its consequences is Fred Branfman, a Lao-speaking American who spent four years in Laos in the International Voluntary Services (IVS), as an educational consultant for USAID, and as a journalist. Some of the documentation he has collected appears in Senate hearings.[8] See also his *Voices from the Plain of Jars*, a collection of essays and drawings by Laotian refugees, with discussion and analysis, the only extensive public record to date from the victims in Indochina.

Another Lao-speaking American, Walter Haney, has compiled a detailed collection of refugee interviews: "A Survey of Civilian War Casualties Among Refugees from the Plain of Jars."[9] Haney became concerned about the bombing in the

Plain of Jars when some of his Lao students began to transmit reports from refugees in 1970. One wrote:

> During the bombing, if the planes couldn't select a place to bomb, but they saw some animals or people, they would simply drop the bombs on them. This was the primary reason why the refugees fled from the homes of their birth and came here. . . . The most important reason why the refugees had to come here from their villages must be the bombing.

The refugees Haney interviewed describe not only a wide range of bombs and antipersonnel weapons but also what appear to be several types of poison. They tell of indiscriminate bombing of villages and fields, entirely unrelated to any ground combat. One reports (secondhand) the dropping of exploding pens and watches. Some of the deaths reported are from late 1964 and 1965, but the bombing did not reach the level of true annihilation until 1968 and 1969.

Ambassador Sullivan, in accompanying comments, agrees that Haney's is "a serious and carefully prepared piece of work," and cannot contest his conclusions, though he denies the use of poison. Sullivan suggests that Haney's interviews, though accurate, are atypical, since these refugees were caught up in the fighting that "raged back and forth over the Plain of Jars." He also states that the 189 deaths in a population of 8,500 refugees, while "too many," are still a small number "given the intensity of the fighting that took place."

The explanation will not do. The evidence from other sources (specifically, those cited above and the further references they contain) indicates that Haney's interviews are quite typical, except for the report of poisons from three refugee camps. Furthermore, as the reader can easily ascertain, the interviews reveal that there was no fighting nearby in most instances, and in fact no soldiers were present, or had been present, in many cases. In general, refugees, defectors, and prisoners report that the bombing had little military significance in the narrow sense, quite understandably. PAVN (North Vietnamese) and Pathet Lao soldiers naturally remain hidden in the forests, far from visible targets, as the United States Air Force and civilian officials in Vientiane understand perfectly well. The purposes of the bombardment, assuming rationality, were quite different. As for the reference to 189 deaths in a population of 8,500, this is a minor fib; Haney did not conduct 8,500 interviews, but sampled from a population of 8,500. As noted, Sullivan and others have repeatedly testified before Congress that United States planes did not attack villages or populated areas. These interviews are a significant contribution to the growing mass of evidence to the contrary. Only someone whose mind is closed to empirical evidence can retain his faith in what the administration has reported to Congress and the public. It may be recalled that false, fictitious, or fraudulent statements and representations by government officials in the area of their concern are not only morally grotesque, in such matters as these, but also technically criminal (see chapter 1, note 41).

The best-known American writer on contemporary Laos, Arthur Dommen, speaks of "the continual disruptions caused by American bombings" which "inconvenienced the Pathet Lao."[10] Such terms as "disruption" and "inconvenience" somehow do not quite convey the essence of the experiences recounted by the refugees. Dommen writes with much scorn about reporters who file their stories from the swimming pool of the Lane Xang Hotel in Vientiane (p. 302), but he was apparently unable to discover (or unwilling to report) what can be learned from the refugees in miserable camps a few miles away. He also gives only an oblique reference to the eyewitness testimony of Jacques Decornoy from Sam Neua Province in 1968,[11] unreported in the American press, to my knowledge, despite considerable efforts to obtain press coverage. Dommen is much more concerned with the North Vietnamese, who come down the Ho Chi Minh Trail like "a column of ants," "a living, organic monster"; "one brings one's shoe down in their path, crushing a few of them and temporarily sowing confusion," and "then the whole column pushes forward once more, trampling over the bodies of their slain comrades" (p. 357: "The shoe represents the sudden appearance of a flight of American bombing planes overhead," in case the reader didn't get the point). As for the "U.S. policy makers," they are purehearted Eagle Scouts who are "of one mind in regarding Hanoi's behavior as a direct challenge to the traditional American belief that justice will prevail in the world" (p. 381). "It is only against this background of a tradition of fair play and justice that the American commitment of half a million men to the Vietnam war can be understood."

The implicit ideological premises that underlie such judgments are revealed elsewhere, as when Dommen notes that "North Vietnamese" goals in Laos include progressive taxation, moves towards economic equality, and discouraging the conspicuous consumption that establishes a villager's status. These are part of "the price to be paid for liberation" at the hands of the North Vietnamese or the Pathet Lao, in Dommen's view (p. 361). In such passages, he expresses openly his quite dogmatic faith in the purity of American goals and in the principles of inegalitarian ideology, which could only be challenged by vicious Communists. Characteristically, writers who approach contemporary affairs from such assumptions think of themselves as neutral and value-free, as compared with "committed scholars," who make explicit their values and social beliefs.

The official position of the United States government is that it was drawn into the war in Laos in response to North Vietnamese aggression. Government sources seek to demonstrate that the Pathet Lao are entirely controlled by the DRV, while the press tends to overlook their existence altogether. Evidence in support of the government's case is meager and unconvincing.[12] The bombardment of southern Laos is of course related to the American effort in South Vietnam, and now Cambodia, but as already noted, the administration concedes that the bombing of northern Laos is not related to operations in South Vietnam and Cambodia.[13] The question of DRV participation, military or otherwise, is interesting and important. It must again be emphasized that the available evidence is sketchy, the original sources on all sides are partisan and untrustworthy, and the conclusions stated often go far beyond the evidence and are then repeated uncritically elsewhere. The literature must be treated with caution when specific claims are made. Tracing references, one often discovers that the original source was an obviously interested party who supplied no evidence, the alleged statement of an unidentified official of some government, or an intelligence report that is unavailable, so that its basis and possible qualifications are unknown. (See, for example, chapter 1, note 225; introduction, note 24.)

As an example, consider the unqualified statement by Langer and Zasloff that "an estimated 67,000 North Vietnamese military personnel now serve in Laos."[14] Their sole source is a statement to this effect by President Nixon on March 6, 1970. But the speech in which this statement appears was full of errors of fact,[15] and the particular figure cited is highly questionable if only because United States military attachés in Vientiane were giving a figure of 50,000 or less at exactly the same time,[16] and appeared unaware of the new North Vietnamese invasion reported by the president in that speech.

Using Langer and Zasloff's figures, Arthur Dommen gives the remarkably low estimate of about one combat regiment of PAVN available in northern Laos as of 1968.[17] It must of course be borne in mind that the figures of "North Vietnamese military personnel" reported in United States government statements include every old man carrying a bag of rice on his back. The intensive bombing must have increased the supply problems for the Pathet Lao and the North Vietnamese in Laos, and therefore increased the proportion of "military personnel" of this order, one would suppose.

According to a recent report, the Royal Lao Government was holding 92 North Vietnamese prisoners; 73 North Vietnamese had been captured since 1968, as compared with 2,494 Pathet Lao.[18] Carl Strock reports that the Red Cross lists the Vietnamese prisoners merely as "ethnic Vietnamese," "leaving open the possibility that they come from Laos' own large Vietnamese community." Such numbers hardly confirm United States government claims, or the press reporting, which generally refers to all actions in Laos as "North Vietnamese." Strock also reports at least 1,500 United States casualties, including 400 killed and more than 200 missing in Laos.[19]

Like France before it, the United States mobilized hill tribesmen to block the Lao resistance forces (Lao Issara, Pathet Lao). By 1961, about 9,000 Meo tribesmen were engaged in guerrilla operations in "Communist-dominated territory in Laos" under the political leadership of Touby

Lyfoung, who had sided with the French against the Lao Issara, and under the military direction of Vang Pao, with command control "exercised by the chief CIA Vientiane with the advice of Chief MAAG Laos."[20] Ronald J. Rickenbach, former refugee relief officer, AID/Laos, testified that "after the restrictions placed on overt U.S. military involvement in Laos by the Geneva Accords of 1962, the role of advising the guerrilla forces fell under the operational wing of the CIA," adding that "at this time . . . AID became directly and officially involved with the paramilitary aspects of the program."[21] As noted earlier, the CIA-directed guerrilla actions were a significant factor in upsetting the rather tenuous agreements of 1962 (see chapter 1, note 225). The consequences have been disastrous, and reports indicate that the hill tribesmen are facing extinction as an organized society.

One of the few Westerners not connected with the CIA or USAID to have traveled in Meo areas in Laos is John Everingham, a Lao-speaking Australian who has visited these areas several times since February 1968. He describes vividly what has happened to those Meo "naive enough to trust the CIA," who promised to establish a "Meo nation" if they would fight the Pathet Lao. He found few boys over the age of twelve as he wandered in September 1970 "through dying village after dying village." The "CIA clandestine army is a one-way 'copter ride to death," he reports. "None, but none, of those conscripted since 1966 has ever come back." Eleven- and twelve-year-old boys are being taken by CIA recruiters for the helicopter ride to death. "American bombing policy has also turned more than half the total area of Laos to a land of charred ruins where people fear the sky,"[22] so that "nothing be left standing or alive for the communists to inherit." The many Meo deserters cannot flee to the Pathet Lao zones, or they too will be subjected to the merciless bombardment. "Like desperate dogs they are trapped, and the CIA holds the leash, and is not about to let it go as long as the Meo army can hold back the Pathet Lao a little longer, giving the Americans and their allies a little more security 100 miles south at the Thailand border."[23]

A USIS survey of refugees from the Plain of Jars conducted in June and July of 1970 concluded that "the bombing is clearly the most compelling reason for moving." Half of the refugees surveyed said that fear of the bombing was the reason for their flight; 20 percent gave dislike of the Pathet Lao as the reason. Eight months later the United States Embassy in Laos published a book called *Facts on Foreign Aid*, with a section on "Causes and Motives in Refugee Movements":

> The motives that prompt a people to choose between two kinds of rule are not always clear, but three conditions of life under the Pathet Lao appear to have prompted the choice of evacuation: the rice tax, portage, and the draft. The people grew more rice than they had ever grown before, but they had less for themselves. They paid it out in the form of taxes—rice to help the state, trading rice, and rice from the heart. The Pathet Lao devised an elaborate labor system of convoys and work crews. They drafted all the young men for the army. The refugees from the Plain of Jars say that primarily for these reasons they choose to leave their home.[24]

Nothing here about what was "clearly the most compelling reason for moving," or even about the "disruptions" or "inconvenience" caused by the United States air war in Laos.

A staff report of the Kennedy Subcommittee (September 28, 1970)[25] concludes that the purpose of the bombardment was "to destroy the physical and social infrastructure" in areas held by the Pathet Lao and "to interdict North Vietnamese infiltration." The available evidence indicates that the first of these aims has been substantially accomplished. Thus the secret executive war in Laos has succeeded in two respects: first, in destroying the physical and social infrastructure of Pathet Lao-held areas, which still contain about one-third of the population; and second, in achieving this goal in relative secrecy.

In other respects, too, the American war in Laos has been a partial success. The cost has not been high by the standards of Vietnam. The Kennedy Subcommittee staff report estimates that "the military was spending, at peak periods, upwards of $4,680,000 a day on bombing sorties over Laos." Direct military assistance is classified, but it would appear to be on the order of $500 million since 1962, reaching over $90 million in 1969 and more in 1970.[26] CIA expenditures are of course unknown. The USAID "refugee relief program" of several million dollars a year must also be counted as a direct military expenditure, since it was largely "a program to support anti-Communist guerrillas in areas which, under the Geneva Accords, were Pathet Lao controlled."[27] Nevertheless, military expenditures are nothing like those in Vietnam.

The Kennedy Subcommittee staff report cites three "major operational programs in Laos" in addition to the bombardment: (1) "The creation of an American-directed civil administration that parallels the structure" of the Royal Lao Government; (2) "The support and supervision of a ground war fought principally by paramilitary groups drawn from highland tribes, such as the Meo"; (3) "The conducting and support of massive evacuations of local villagers from Pathet Lao regions in order to deny the enemy population resources."[28] Again, the similarities to Vietnam are evident (see chapter 1).

These programs, like the massive bombardment, have had a certain success. The staff report concludes that the American-directed civil administration has managed "to keep the government afloat" and "to preserve the shell, if not the substance, of a neutralist government in Vientiane" with nominal authority "at least in the strategic Mekong Valley region bordering Thailand." This serves longer-range American purposes, buying time for the Thai elite, the main support for American aims in Southeast Asia, and helping to secure the "second line of defense" in Southeast Asia. As to the ground war, this has been only a partial success. Communist forces seem stronger on the ground than ever before, and the Meo have been decimated.

What possibilities there may be for reconciliation between the remnants of the Meo and the Lao one can only guess. Refugees from the Plain of Jars speak constantly of the savagery of the CIA clandestine army of Meo and other tribesmen. To cite one of many examples, a refugee whose younger brother was killed by Meo soldiers in 1964 while searching in the forest for food and something he could sell says that the Meo soldiers "shoot anyone they see in the forest."[29] Drawing PAVN forces into the war in Laos also serves American purposes in a certain sense. It further reduces the possibility of independent Lao nationalism combined with social and economic development under the Pathet Lao, and sets the stage for a Thai-Vietnamese rivalry that may weaken and fragment mainland Southeast Asia for many years to come. Since American casualties have been light, there is little reaction or concern at home—a necessary ingredient of successful counterinsurgency.

The third major operational program, massive evacuation of civilians, has contributed to "generating" hundreds of thousands of refugees, many of whom barely subsist in government-controlled areas. But this program has, no doubt, denied "population resources" to the enemy, although some men and women who are capable of bearing arms appear to have chosen to remain with the Pathet Lao.

In short, though the war may not have been quite as successful as Senator Javits and others believe,[30] nevertheless the combination of secrecy and raw power applied against a weak and largely defenseless society has achieved results that have eluded the American forces in Vietnam.

Evidence concerning the Pathet Lao and its programs is scanty, and must for the moment be derived largely from the reports of refugees.[31] In April 1970 I interviewed refugees who had recently been brought from the Plain of Jars, and several urban intellectuals who had lived in that area,[32] and obtained many detailed transcriptions of interviews with refugees from both southern and northern Laos. Information derived from such sources must be treated with caution. Some informants are openly sympathetic to the Pathet Lao. They naturally insist upon anonymity, and there is no way to obtain independent verification of their reports except from other refugees. Most refugees tend to give rather stereotyped responses and are reluctant to speak openly to people whom they assume to be representatives of the American government (or, as one commented, American soldiers in civilian dress). On several occasions, discussions in a refugee camp were terminated by bystanders when sensitive issues arose—particularly when some informants were giving reports that appeared favorable to the Pathet Lao. Nevertheless, the accounts of personal experience give a fairly consistent picture of life in the Pathet Lao zones. On the basis of what information I have been able to obtain from other sources, I believe this picture to be plausible.

The programs described by the refugees were rather moderate and low-keyed. In 1965 a mild land reform was carried out in the Plain of Jars, a land-rich area. It was followed by efforts to encourage some cooperation among peasants, leading to mixed collective-private farming, which seems to have been widely practiced by 1967. There were significant educational reforms. A literacy campaign appears to have been quite successful, and an adult-education program was undertaken that included arithmetic and other skills as well as reading and writing. The language of instruction in the schools was changed from French to Lao. Teachers were instructed to introduce what was called "a liberated style of education" that would "teach people to love their country." A USAID worker reports that peasants regard the Pathet Lao as "traditionalists," and the emphasis on "the national culture," folk culture, and so on was stressed by many informants. Teachers report that the level of instruction was raised in language and mathematics, and that four grades were introduced for everyone, in principle. A plan to extend education to seven years could not be implemented because of the bombardment, which emptied towns and villages by 1968–1969. Mechanical teaching of reading was replaced by instruction with content, dealing primarily with agriculture and practical matters, and an emphasis on "building our own country and not working for foreign people."

Some men and women were taken to the nearby town of Phonesavan (first bombed in 1965 and completely destroyed in January 1969) for training as teachers, civil administrators, and health workers. Opinions vary as to the efficacy of the training. American sources (see note 31 below) report that Lao and mountain tribesmen were brought to North Vietnam for technical and medical training.

At the same time, peasants were urged to improve production. A wealthy peasant, rather unsympathetic to the Pathet Lao, said that they were always made to study.

They taught us mainly agriculture. One must produce more. Build the economy. One man should do the work of ten.

> If you produce more, you can exchange it for clothes and money. Then we can exchange the produce with other countries.

Another wealthy peasant complained that "they only respect you if you have torn clothing." And indeed, the Pathet Lao reforms seem to have primarily benefitted the poor. Peasants were urged to abandon the use of honorific phrases and to act, and treat each other, as equals. Women were to be treated equally, and many were trained as nurses and soldiers. Money seems to have been largely eliminated. Cadres who returned to the village after training were supported by taxation. All sources agreed that the Pathet Lao administration was honest, even those who complained of the taxation, study, and other changes. Refugees commonly referred to the incessant efforts of cadres to persuade, and their avoidance of force or coercion. The major complaint voiced by refugees against the Pathet Lao concerned the compulsory porterage, which became an onerous burden on the peasants after the bombing drove the soldiers to remote areas where they could not be supplied by trucks.

Refugees generally reported little contact with North Vietnamese, soldiers or civilians, or even with Pathet Lao soldiers. In 1967, outsiders were replaced in the Phonesavan area by local cadres drawn from "awakening groups" in the villages, which were responsible for local implementation of Pathet Lao programs.

Villages had a multitude of organizations: for administration, defense, youth, women, education, irrigation, agriculture, and so on. These elected their own leaders, and chose representatives to deal with outside experts on such matters as irrigation.

Apart from Pathet Lao textbooks, which seem rather impressive, I have seen no documentary evidence concerning Pathet Lao programs. From the evidence available to me, it seems a fair judgment that the Pathet Lao are the only organized indigenous force in Laos that has any realistic or comprehensive plan for social and economic development, any program that might mobilize the mass of the peasantry or provide them with a means for participation in social and political institutions. One can only speculate as to how successful these programs might have been had it not been for the relentless American attack.

Pathet Lao programs, as described by refugees, may be usefully compared with the programs of the National Liberation Front as these are revealed in investigations cited above (see chapter 1, note 215). In the case of Pathet Lao programs, the conclusions of government-sponsored research betray some remarkable attitudes, rather like Dommen's reaction (cited above, p. 178) to steps towards economic equality.[33] It is interesting, in the same connection, to contrast factual studies of the NLF with the pronouncements of some of the more committed ideologists, such as Dennis Duncanson, who asserts —with no pretense of evidence—that the "technique of revolutionary warfare" starts from "the harnessing to an external political cause of organized crime" in countries lacking sufficient police; the "fundamental problem" facing Vietnam is "the protection of the individual villager from the intimidation, immediate or in prospect, of revolutionaries" (and "there should be no mistake," he chides the skeptical, about the "unprecedentedly altruistic" motives of the United States).[34] This, incidentally, is the same author who warns elsewhere of those "who repudiate the thorny quest for objectivity, substituting a predetermined Truth of their own choosing."[35]

Similarly, Ithiel Pool sees only "village thugs" who "line up with major powers."[36] With astounding cynicism, he adds:

> Under present circumstances the Viet Cong cannot even offer security in exchange for their ruthlessness. As a result it is a standard phenomenon that wherever the Viet Cong is in control, the population declines fairly rapidly as people move out.

The "ruthlessness" that he alleges to exist is, by his own account, the "exploitative and violent" Viet Cong behavior as their "situation . . . has become worse," that is, after the American invasion of South Vietnam. If, in response to a devastating attack by a superpower, resistance forces are driven to become exploitative and violent, it is solely the resistance that is culpable, in his view. As to the population decline, though Pool refers to "refugees fleeing the war," he makes no mention of just what they were fleeing: B-52 raids in settled areas, for example, or the practices that destroyed 70 percent of the villages in Quang Ngai Province by 1967. The implication that somehow the Viet Cong were to blame for the population decline is too grotesque for comment. Perhaps one should expect no more from a political theorist who concludes, finally, that "what we mean by modernization and political development" is that "the organization that exerts the monopoly of force" extends from the great society to the village level, where it can operate efficiently. This is the sole criterion. Applying it, we conclude that the most efficient totalitarian society will—by definition—achieve the peak of modernization and political development.

In Laos as in South Vietnam, the United States has been bringing modernization and social and political development with cluster bombs and napalm and bribes for the rich. In Laos as in South Vietnam, it has been forced to combat the best-organized and most effective popular indigenous movements, and failing in this effort, to destroy the political and social fabric of the rural society. It has been able to forestall the victory of indigenous popular forces, and has labored mightily to convert its imperial aggression in Indochina into a regional conflict, along the Korean model. In Laos, massive bombardment proved to be the only available device to resolve the ethically neutral dilemmas of counterinsurgency. The cost to the United States has not been great, although the cost to the people of Laos is incalculable. Furthermore, American policy makers may well conclude that such "executive wars," carried out in secrecy, with mercenary troops, CIA subversion, and massive bombardment from impregnable sanctuaries, constitute a successful technique of counterrevolutionary intervention. This appears to be the meaning of the "Nixon Doctrine." If so, the potential cost to developing countries elsewhere may be immense.

II. CAMBODIA

Though information is not extensive, it appears that the tragedy of Laos is being re-enacted in Cambodia. An investigating team of the GAO (General Accounting Office) concluded that United States and South Vietnamese bombing in Cambodia is "a very significant cause of refugees and civilian casualties," and estimated that almost a third of the seven million population may be refugees. Discussing the investigation, undertaken at his request, Senator Kennedy quoted an intelligence memorandum reporting from one area that "what the villagers feared most was the possibility of indiscriminate artillery and air strikes." Captured American correspondents have given similar accounts, some still unpublished. The story is by now familiar, including the United States government denials and claims that it is the North Vietnamese invasion that is the cause, and the assessment by reporters that bombing and artillery are a major, perhaps the primary, factor, with the savagery of the Saigon Army, another carryover from the days of French imperialism, adding its contribution. And a final note from the GAO report: "The policy of the United States is not to become involved with the problems of civilian war victims in Cambodia."[37]

In other respects also the story is familiar, and is illuminated significantly by several recent publications.[38] Pomonti and Thion note that "the mechanism by which American bombs create resistance is too well known for us to describe here" (p. 288). They cite reports by captured correspondents and others who give some details, and also discuss peasant loyalty to Sihanouk and the success of the Khmer guerrillas, backed and advised by Vietnamese Communists, in creating the basis for a long-term popular struggle against the Phnom Penh regime, increasingly an instrument of foreign power. The US-ARVN military intervention in March–April 1970, and the direct invasion at the end of April, had the effect of extending the guerrilla movement throughout Cambodia. While Sihanouk's appeals from Peking gave a certain legitimacy to the insurrection, "it was surely the sudden and appalling reality of the war brought about by the Saigon military forces that set the process in motion," along with the extension of American bombardment which "dismantled" the rural society "under conditions more brutal than those of South Vietnam in 1965" (pp. 261 ff., 274).

Charles Meyer, who also writes from an intimate knowledge of Cambodia, describes how the Vietnamese Communists, on leaving the border regions after the coup of March 18, 1970, and the subsequent US-ARVN incursions, proceeded, in accordance with the classic Asian guerrilla strategy, to construct a massive peasant organization and a popular army on the Vietnamese model. According to his account, authentically Cambodian popular structures are being created in the two-thirds of the country controlled by the revolutionary forces, basing themselves on the methods of the Khmer maquis of earlier years, in particular those who fled the repression of 1967. He estimates that the Vietnamese constitute about 90 percent of the military forces in the frontier regions where they face the US-ARVN forces, and about 20 to 50 percent in other regions where they confront the forces of the Cambodian government and its Saigon allies (pp. 390–1). He foresees a long-term civil war, the urban "army of the privileged, supported by the richest power in the world, against the army of the poor, the army of the interior, the true army of the Khmer people," "a revolutionary army of peasants" (pp. 401, 398). Little propaganda is needed to enlist peasants in the revolutionary cause. "The peasants have seen the soldiers who observe revolutionary discipline, then those who followed them behaving like highwaymen. Having suffered the misdeeds of the army of the rich, they naturally rally to the guerrilla forces of the poor" (p. 344). What is more:

> Cambodia has been subjected in its turn to the destruction of American air power. The methodical destruction of economic resources, of rubber plantations and factories, of rice fields and forests, of peaceful and delightful villages which disappeared one after another beneath the bombs and napalm, has no military justification and serves essentially to starve the population. . . . it is difficult to imagine the intensity of their hatred for those who have destroyed their villages and their possessions. [p. 405]

The Americans, he predicts, must continue to Americanize and Vietnamize the war to prop up the government that they know to have little popular support: "it is evident that the fate of Cambodia [i.e., the Phnom Penh regime] is tied to that of the extremist governments of fascist tendency whose survival depends exclusively on the continuance of American protection" (pp. 363–5). Pomonti and Thion give a similar picture, in their very informative study (see pt. 3). Meyer, incidentally, is regarded by the left as a hostile observer.

Recently, Serge Thion spent two weeks in regions immediately to the west and northwest of Phnom Penh. His reports in *Le Monde* (April 26–28, 1972) are the most recent and most detailed description of the situation in the zones under the control of the Cambodian maquis, the Cambodian united national front (FUNC). These zones, he reports, begin at the very outskirts of Phnom Penh. Thion attended a meeting of three to four thousand people, many of whom were living in areas under Phnom Penh control. To him it appeared that political and military control by the front was total. After the withdrawal of the forces of the Lon Nol regime, "insecurity comes principally from the sky." Every village that he visited had been subjected to aerial attack with bombs and napalm, apparently at random. Many of the villages have been evacuated and elaborate precautions limit the number of casualties: "victims are chiefly the aged, the deaf or ill, or children, killed by surprise," very much as refugees report from Laos. The destructive aerial attacks and the pillage and violence of the Lon Nol forces—particularly the CIA-trained former Khmer Serei—have, as elsewhere, served to solidify peasant support for the resistance. The superior of a pagoda destroyed by a napalm attack, which also burned all of the quarters of the bonzes, described the destruction of religious structures by air attack and by the Lon Nol troops, who then accused the North Vietnamese of these acts. Others gave similar reports. While such accusations may achieve some credibility in the West and perhaps even in Phnom Penh, the villagers can see with their own eyes what is happening.

After the March 1970 coup that overthrew the Sihanouk regime, Marshal Lon Nol attempted to arouse religious fanaticism as a support for the regime, calling for a holy war against the atheist Viet Cong and Pathet Lao (he also tried to stir ethnic hatreds, even initiating a massacre of thousands of Vietnamese in which, it appears, Cambodian peasants generally refused to take part). Thion's impression is that this effort was a total failure, and that in the end it will "turn against its authors," as the Buddhist clergy experience directly the contrasting behavior of the Lon Nol army and its American and GVN backers, and on the other hand, that of the guerrillas with their appeal to traditional peasant sentiments and their simplicity and restraint. He cautions that this can only be an impression, based on partial information.

Thion saw "no trace of foreign aid," either Vietnamese advisers or military forces or even supplies. Rather, what he observed was the "progressive construction of an entirely autonomous force." The Vietnamese forces, he concludes, have largely returned to their former border "sanctuaries," though they may still defend certain strategic sectors elsewhere. "The presence of NLF troops or military advisers is much reduced since March–April 1970, as FUNC develops its own politico-military structure." Many cadres are being trained, among them some urban intellectuals. The Front appears to have the support of the bonzes, who retain their traditional authority in rural Cambodia. He suspects that a good proportion of the leading cadres are from the small Cambodian left, which had taken to the countryside following the 1967 repression. Many people, he reports, say that they have seen Hou Yuon, the leftist parliamentary delegate who disappeared in 1967 and was widely assumed to have been assassinated by the government.[39] Popular committees administer the villages, organized by the Front, though "their composition reflects the general will of the inhabitants."

Peasants whom Thion interviewed confirmed that the massacre of pro-Sihanouk peasants by the army shortly after the March 1970 coup had aroused great indignation and contributed to the Front's success. Peasant loyalty to Sihanouk is apparent. Thion reports that if the prince had not called for an insurrection and supported the Front in his radio messages from Peking, the guerrillas would have had much greater difficulty in establishing themselves in the rural heartland of Cambodia. While the bombing has been "a decisive argument" animating the Khmer opposition to the American-backed Phnom Penh regime, a major factor in the Front success, Thion concludes, has been the contrast between the urban corruption of Phnom Penh and the traditionalism and morality of the maquis. The guerrillas are "asphyxiating the cities," and the dominant impression is rather like that of

South Vietnam in 1964. Thion believes that only massive American intervention can prevent the victory of the indigenous resistance forces based on the peasantry.

Thion's direct observations seem to me to confirm the earlier analysis and expectations of Meyer and Pomonti-Thion, and to confirm and significantly extend as well the general impressions of captured correspondents. The similarity to earlier stages of the Vietnamese and Laotian revolutionary movements is also striking. While the limitations of available information must again be stressed, nevertheless there seems a good deal of plausibility to the general picture that emerges.

President Nixon has described Cambodia as "the Nixon doctrine in its purest form."[40] For once, he may have spoken the exact truth.

Cambodia was plunged into the Indochina war as an immediate consequence of the coup of March 18, 1970, in which Sihanouk was overthrown. The immediate background to the coup has been explored recently by T. D. Allman, through interviews with members of the Cambodian elite.[41] His evidence suggests that "the most striking elements of the anti-Sihanouk conspiracy—for such it seems to have been—were its total lack of spontaneity, and the plotters' easy sacrifice of good relations with the all-powerful Vietnamese Communists in the interests of domestic and political expediency." The allegedly spontaneous anti-Vietnamese demonstrations and the sacking of the North Vietnamese and Provisional Revolutionary Government embassies were, he concludes, organized by the plotters. Elsewhere, Allman and others have pointed out that prior to the coup, Vietnamese Communist forces kept close to the border and—despite some claims to the contrary—are not known to have intervened further in Cambodian affairs. Allman's conclusion that the coup was well prepared and served selfish interests of a segment of the elite also coincides with the general observations of others.

In a subsequent interview with Son Ngoc Thanh, now prime minister of the Phnom Penh regime and for many years associated with the CIA and the American Special Forces while leading guerrilla operations against Sihanouk, Allman presents "indications of indirect U.S. support for Prince Sihanouk's ouster" in the March 18 coup. Thanh "indicated that at least some Americans, in an official capacity, supported plots to overthrow Sihanouk" in late 1969 and 1970. Thanh gives details of contacts between Lon Nol's agents and Cambodian army officers involved in the coup planning, United States government agents, and his own headquarters, and describes assurances of support by United States government agents "for anti-Sihanouk moves in Cambodia, including a two-pronged invasion of the country."[42] These revelations lend substance to the report by former Special Forces Captain Robert Marasco that he is "certain" that the CIA and South Vietnamese intelligence had agents in Cambodia prior to the coup.[43]

In a recent interview, Marasco told reporter Richard A. Fineberg that he ran intelligence nets in Cambodia during 1968 and 1969, hiring and training Khmer Serei agents as well as other Cambodians for his mission.[44] Further information bearing on this matter appears in the heavily censored trial record of John J. McCarthy, Jr., formerly a Special Forces captain and "commanding officer of a top-secret Cambodian operation known as Project Cherry,"[45] phased out, apparently, in 1967. McCarthy served two years of a twenty-year sentence (overturned on appeal) for the murder of a Cambodian interpreter who was a Khmer Serei member and was suspected of being a Communist-trained double agent. In the trial, McCarthy identified the Khmer Serei as "an organization which in effect plans the political overthrow of the Cambodian government." McCarthy now states that Thanh was a key figure in his January 1968 court-martial at Longbinh, South Vietnam. His attorneys requested Thanh's appearance, but the army said that it could not compel foreign nationals to testify (Thanh was then living in South Vietnam). The trial record refers to a man named Tan Son Hai, identified by one member of the Cherry team as "the leader or high priest of the Khmer Serei." McCarthy informed Fineberg that he believed that Thanh and Tan Son Hai were "one and the same person." Prior to the trial, the Khmer Serei presented McCarthy with a gold medallion for killing the agent, with a citation signed by Son Ngoc Thanh as "leader of the Khmer Serei."

Senator Mike Gravel has stated: "It is incredible to take the position—as the White House has done—that the U.S. conducted continuous clandestine incursions into Cambodia, hired and trained members of a sect avowedly dedicated to Sihanouk's overthrow, and still did not know that a coup was being planned."[46] The position always was incredible. In the light of Allman's interview with Prime Minister Son Ngoc Thanh, perhaps even those who have heretofore ridiculed the idea of a CIA role in the coup may have second thoughts.[47]

Charles Meyer concludes that "it is evident that the CIA played a role in the course of events that led to the March 18 coup," and raises some questions about Indonesian and particularly Japanese involvement, and about the possible involvement of oil interests.[48] Meyer regards the coup group as essentially pro-Japanese in their orientation, and describes Japanese efforts to take over a dominant position in Cambodia (p. 253). Pomonti and Thion discuss the same developments (p. 259), noting that Japanese participation in the May 1970 meeting in Jakarta signaled Japan's "political re-entry in Southeast Asia," following the recovery of positions of economic strength. They note correctly that this is an essential component of the Nixon Doctrine (see chapter 4 below). They also note the long-standing Japanese connections of many of the current leaders of the coup regime, in particular Son Ngoc Thanh, and their relations with the "Black Dragon" secret society that involves captains of Japanese industry and military leaders. They report the return to Cambodia, after the coup, of a Japanese diplomat, well known in Cambodian circles since the Japanese occupation, who is an "important member" of the Black Dragon society. Meyer also reports the earlier efforts of Japanese secret societies, blocked in the 1950s by Sihanouk, though Japanese influence in Cambodian economic affairs nevertheless inevitably proceeded.

A few days after the March 18 coup, US-ARVN military activities began in conjunction with the Cambodian army. Pomonti and Thion report that "on March 20, that is only two days after the overthrow of Prince Sihanouk, General Do Cao Tri, commander of the South Vietnamese Third Military Region, sent several regiments into Parrot's Beak [Svay Rieng Province of Cambodia]" (p. 151). Ground and air operations continued, including a combined operation of the Cambodian and Saigon armies on April 14. Finally the outright invasion took place on April 29.[49] Until mid-April the NLF-NVA units seem to have remained in the border areas to which they had been driven by American air and ground attacks in Vietnam. According to Meyer, the attack on the frontier sanctuaries had been planned for several months by the American command. The result was a "cataclysm" for the civilian population. The NLF and NVA troops left the border areas to escape aerial attack and then encirclement, but "hundreds of Cambodian peasants were crushed by aerial bombardment, their habitations burned, cultivated land and rubber plantations destroyed." The American operation was "carried out brutally" and the South Vietnamese operation immediately became "an enterprise of pillage and sacking accompanied by torture and murder," confirming the "sinister reputation" acquired by the elite units of General Tri "in the villages of their own country" (Meyer, pp. 340–1). The further developments are as indicated above.

As already noted, what information exists indicates that the developments in Cambodia are remarkably similar to those in Laos and South Vietnam earlier. Meyer observes that the origins of the Cambodian revolution in the late 1960s were in many respects similar to the early stages of the NLF: peasant revolts in reaction to the corruption and tyranny of provincial authorities, followed by a witch-hunt and extensive repression. In response, a low-keyed resistance developed. Pomonti and Thion report that well-known left-wing intellectuals joined the maquis in 1963, but that the situation changed significantly with the peasant insurrection of 1967, near the Thai border. Sihanouk, according to Meyer, had in his hands a very detailed report showing that the peasants were driven to rebellion by the corrupt provincial authorities, but nevertheless undertook a general repression of the left, blaming it (and later, foreign Communist influences) for the indigenous rebellion. In fact, an early official statement on the crisis reported that "the chief of state has clearly proclaimed that the local rebellion was a strictly internal affair with no foreign support or encouragement," blaming CIA agents and others for spreading false rumors in an effort "to divide the Khmer nation in two parts, irreconcilably hostile, in order to prepare the pretext for a

direct intervention."[50] But after demonstrations by students
and other signs of unrest, including the mysterious disappearance of several left-wing delegates who were either murdered
by the government or joined the maquis,[51] Sihanouk changed
his position and declared that the rebellion was the work of
foreign-instigated left-wing activists.

Neither Meyer nor Pomonti and Thion see any evidence for
Sihanouk's claim that the revolutionaries were agents of Sino-
Vietnamese communism. Meyer concludes that "it seems that
the armed struggle of the Khmers rouges [Sihanouk's term]
was undertaken not only without the support of the Chinese
and Vietnamese, but against their will" (p. 201). Pomonti
and Thion confirm this conclusion, pointing out that as far as
is known the Vietnamese Communists avoided interfering in
Cambodian affairs, and though they may have maintained
contacts with the Cambodian guerrillas, they did little to
encourage or support them prior to the March 18 coup and its
aftermath. "The slow but sure progress of the partisans," they
believe, "is easily explained by the burdensome conditions of
the peasantry," intensified by police repression. Sihanouk and
the right-wing groups on which he increasingly depended
sought to conceal the existence of the rebellion by a "xeno-
phobic campaign" and propaganda with regard to "external
intervention" which apparently did not really exist (pp.
124–5).

At the same time, particularly from 1966, the economic
situation was deteriorating. A small segment of urban society
was becoming richer and richer while the peasant masses were
becoming impoverished, a fact discussed by left-wing intellectuals who joined the maquis (Meyer, pp. 205, 195, 42). By
1969 it appeared that there was no way to escape the economic
decline except through "liberalization of the economy and the
return of American aid, handing over the administration of
the country to the extreme right with results that are now
known" (p. 215). Meyer suggests that it was in this context
that Sihanouk launched his campaign against the Vietnamese
Communists in the border areas, in an effort to convince the
White House of his "good intentions" (p. 287). He further
suggests that much of this was "playing to the gallery," for
American ears, and that Sihanouk so informed the NLF and

Hanoi. Nevertheless, Sihanouk undoubtedly feared Vietnamese socialism, as he would have feared any dynamic form of Vietnamese nationalism. "Within the logic of their choice of a politics of rapprochement with the United States," Sihanouk and the Cambodian right could no longer maintain their material assistance and support for the Vietnamese Communists, and relations worsened (p. 295). Allying himself with the right to crush the left opposition, Sihanouk found himself with no room to maneuver. By January 1969, the CIA-trained and CIA-financed Khmer Serei, who had been engaged in military operations against Cambodia since the late 1950s, particularly since 1963, began to "rally" to the Cambodian army (pp. 274, 240, 300). Like many other commentators, Meyer sees in this a CIA initiative that was part of the planning for the March 18 coup, which followed in due course.

In outline, these appear to be the major developments that led to the coup that plunged Cambodia into the terror of the Indochina war. Prior to the coup, Cambodia had been subjected to attempts at subversion and direct aggression by its American–backed neighbors, Thailand and South Vietnam. Diem's troops had attacked the Parrot's Beak area in May 1957. A CIA-backed plot to dismember Cambodia in 1958–1960 was blocked, on information supplied by the French and Chinese embassies (Meyer, pp. 146–7; Pomonti and Thion, p. 56). While there were provocations from CIA-backed groups in Thailand, the situation on the Vietnamese frontier was much more serious. "From 1957, but particularly from 1964, American–South Vietnamese forces attacked posts and villages, bombed rice fields, machine-gunned trucks, napalmed or defoliated the Cambodian side of the frontier," causing hundreds of casualties each year (Pomonti and Thion, p. 132). Meyer reports that "at the end of 1963, the 'Khmers Serei,' equipped and trained by the CIA, made more frequent incursions into Cambodian territory from bases in South Vietnam and Thailand" (cf. pp. 10–11 above).[52] The dates are suggestive. At exactly this time the United States was intensifying its clandestine operations elsewhere in Indochina in an effort to bolster the collapsing South Vietnamese regime, laying the groundwork for the vast expansion of the war in 1965.

"Each day," Meyer continues, "Khmer peasants fell under

American bombs and bullets," as "the American-South Vietnamese attacks, ever more murderous, multiplied against the frontier villages of Cambodia" (pp. 241, 243). By April 1969, rubber plantations were subjected to defoliation by air attack in Kompong Cham Province (p. 243). The reasons for this are not entirely clear. It is possible that these attacks were undertaken in preparation for military strikes that were to follow the coup then being planned. Another possibility is that the attack was aimed at the largely Vietnamese labor force, who "had always actively supported the struggle for national liberation" (Pomonti and Thion, p. 207). All of this, however, was nothing as compared with what was to come, after the coup and the subsequent events. "The population of inner Cambodia—rural Cambodia—is today in danger of death, victims of the power of American destruction at the service of the new directors of Phnom Penh" (Meyer, pp. 41–2).

Until the very end of this period, there is little evidence of military conflict between Vietnamese Communist forces and Cambodians. Pomonti and Thion report that provocations by the Cambodian army, sometimes collaborating with the United States military, led to "a very restricted number of really bloody incidents" with Vietnamese Communist forces by 1969 (p. 135). It is known "with certainty," they say, "that in the wake of the anti-Vietnamese political line launched by Sihanouk in 1968, Khmer officers occasionally cooperated at the frontier with American and South Vietnamese forces against the NLF guerrillas." As far as is known, it was the American invasion of Vietnam in the mid-1960s that was responsible for the stationing of guerrilla forces in the border areas. The Vietnamese migration into Cambodia, terminated in 1954, began again ten years later, according to Meyer, "with the exodus of South Vietnamese who were subjected to the bombardment and 'defoliation' of American air power" (p. 258). The first evidence of Vietnamese encampments on the Cambodian side of the border was discovered in late 1967. There is no doubt that after massive air and ground operations such as JUNCTION CITY in 1967, Vietnamese peasants and guerrillas took refuge along these border areas.

According to a map in Meyer's book, by March 1970, Vietnamese were scattered along border areas to a maximum depth of perhaps 25 kilometers in the extreme northeast provinces, which were to a considerable extent under the control of indigenous guerrillas. Pomonti and Thion agree. They assert, citing official Cambodian sources, that apart from the sparsely populated region of the extreme northeast, where Laos, Vietnam, and Cambodia meet, the "Viet Cong zones" never reached more than 10 kilometers from the border (p. 205). Throughout the region, they report, "the intervention of a powerful American expeditionary corps in Vietnam forced the local insurgents to progressively construct a network of bases in a zone which occasionally reached 20 kilometers into the Cambodian side of the border" (p. 179). The reason why the American command could not find the "red Pentagon," COSVN, during the Cambodian invasion was that it was not there; the Vietnamese partisans controlled enough "sanctuaries" in their own country to maintain their internal command (p. 209–10). Relations between the Vietnamese guerrillas and the Cambodians in the border areas were friendly, they report. There were economic advantages for the Cambodian peasants, and the NLF also provided administrative and health services. They believe that the amicable relations between the Vietnamese Communists and the Cambodian peasantry explain in part the peasant response to Sihanouk's appeal for antigovernment demonstrations after the coup, from his exile in Peking (pp. 175–80). It is also possible that the US-ARVN military attacks for many years, including B-52 raids and rocket attacks from helicopters (p. 206), may have reinforced the opposition of the Cambodian peasants in the border regions to a central government that was clearly destined to be an appendage to the Saigon ally of the United States.

In *At War with Asia*, chapter 3, I discussed the background of the March 18, 1970 coup and subsequent events, giving many details concerning the events just outlined, on the basis of the information then available to me (June 1970). Milton Osborne has criticized this account,[53] suggesting that the comments I quoted with regard to Sihanouk written during the 1960s "need substantial qualification" and that the evidence I cited on Vietnamese Communist use of Cambodian territory in the middle 1960s is more ambiguous than I indicated. He also questions my reliance on French sources. I think that Osborne is correct in his observation about the comments I quoted on peasant support for Sihanouk and on his unique role as a representative of Cambodian nationalism. The most extreme examples, however, came not from French sources but from T. D. Allman and other English-speaking observers. In this case, closer reliance on the reports of Jacques Decornoy, in particular, would have restored the balance. Decornoy had been reporting, both in print and privately, that peasant support for Sihanouk was not so firm as most observers claimed and that the peasant revolts of 1967 were a serious matter, reflecting peasant discontent. While agreeing with Osborne's criticism on this point (apart from the remark about French sources), I think it only proper to add that the comments I quoted were quite representative of the available literature.[54] Meyer points out—to my knowledge quite accurately—that all diplomats and observers were misled by "a cult of personality lacking ideological support and overestimated the power of the prince over the peasant masses who acclaimed him" (p. 377). The sources cited here, considerably more detailed than anything available in mid-1970 on the recent period, are an important corrective. A precise estimate of Sihanouk's support among the peasantry is of course quite impossible. Pomonti and Thion cite evidence that it remains considerable (cf. pp. 178–9, 274 ff.). The reports of captured correspondents tend to confirm this judgment, as do Thion's recent observations, noted above.

As to my conclusions about Vietnamese Communist use of Cambodian territory, these were derived almost exclusively from English sources (such as Michael Leifer, *Current History*, February 1969, and several articles of Allman's). Though Osborne's caution is no doubt in order, still I know of no serious evidence that calls these judgments into question. They are confirmed by the far more detailed and informed studies cited here.

Curiously, excerpts from the same chapter of *At War with Asia* were reviewed again in some detail in *Pacific Affairs* two issues later, by Michael Leifer.[55] He criticizes several omissions, some of which are specifically discussed in the fuller original from which the excerpts were taken. There are points of disagreement, however. Leifer regards Sihanouk's "policy of assiduous accommodation towards the Vietnamese Communists" as a major factor in his deposition, and notes that Sihanouk himself was moving towards a breach with the Vietnamese Communists and had denounced them. I had given little attention to these factors, relying rather on Leifer's earlier observations (*Current History*, February 1969) and others that indicated that the Vietnamese Communists were keeping strictly to border areas after having been driven from Vietnamese soil by American ground and air operations from 1967, and were rather careful to avoid interfering in internal Cambodian affairs. I also discounted Sihanouk's denunciations, which were not supported by the kind of evidence that his government and independent observers presented concerning US-ARVN military actions (such as the Cambodian White Book of January 1970), and which might well be explicable on other grounds, in particular, as an effort to explain away the rising rural unrest in Cambodia. While much remains obscure and conclusions can only be tentative, the evidence now available—some of it discussed above—does not seem to me to justify any revision of my earlier conclusions, with the exceptions noted: domestic unrest and the deteriorating economic situation in Cambodia should have been given much greater emphasis, and the comments quoted on Sihanouk's popularity should perhaps have been further qualified. It might be noted that Meyer believes that "Sihanouk was convinced [wrongly, in Meyer's judgment] that his internal problems depended exclusively on the Vietcong and 'their infiltrations in Cambodian territory and their interference in the internal affairs of our country'" (p. 310). But the observations and evidence cited earlier suggest that this "conviction" might have been somewhat artificial, an outgrowth of his association with the right-wing forces after 1966, his efforts to play down the rural insurgency, and the moves towards closer association with the United States, in an effort to overcome the deteriorating economic situation. Real or not, the conviction appears baseless.

Allman, in his recent investigations,[56] comments: "Interestingly enough, my informants, in the course of half a dozen interviews, never named Sihanouk's foreign policy of maintaining good relations with the Vietnamese Communists as a reason for ousting him." One said: "He had power too long. We wanted it. The only way to get at him was by attacking the Vietcong." The main fear of the coup plotters, according to Allman, was that Sihanouk would return, rally the country behind him, and hold elections which he would win—according to Allman's informants, "because he was so popular with the peasants." In essentials, these conclusions conform to those I drew on earlier and much more spotty evidence.

It would be interesting to inquire further into NLF-DRV intervention in Cambodia, to see whether any evidence can be obtained to substantiate claims that are now current. Naturally, a serious study of this matter will not overlook the relation between DRV-NLF use of Cambodian territory and the United States military operations in Vietnam that were designed to destroy indigenous Vietnamese forces and to drive them into Cambodia. Once again, it is hardly surprising that, say, after Operation JUNCTION CITY in 1967, Vietnamese were to be found in neighboring areas of Cambodia—after their villages had been wiped out by United States air and artillery strikes and subsequent ground sweeps. On this matter, I will simply refer to the remarks in At War with Asia (particularly pp. 127-9, chap. 3, sec. 1), which I believe to be entirely appropriate.

One might hope to learn something about these matters from the Pentagon Papers, but unfortunately that is not the case. As pointed out in chapter 1, the Pentagon Papers are rather narrowly focused, and generally avoid discussion of clandestine activities. There are a few references to Cambodia, but they are not very illuminating. Subversion and direct aggression by the Diem regime and the Thai in the late 1950s, very probably backed by United States intelligence, are not mentioned at all. There is only a passing remark that "in 1958, a crisis between South Vietnam and Cambodia erupted over boundary disputes and border violations."[57] The renewed escalation of clandestine activities from late 1963 is also unnoticed. US-ARVN military activities against Cambodia from 1964, though reasonably well documented,[58] also escaped the attention of the Pentagon historians.

In October 1961, commenting on a plan to send a SEATO

force to mount some sort of border guard, intelligence observed that if this action appeared to be effective in reducing infiltration, the Communists would probably increase the use of the mountain-trail system through Cambodia (II, 78).[59] The reference indicates that intelligence believed that such a system was being used at the time, no doubt marginally, as other comments on infiltration make clear. Intelligence made the obvious point that adoption of the "Concept of Intervention in Vietnam" then being considered would lead to an expansion of the war, as the Vietnamese resistance would respond. At the same time, intelligence reported that 80 to 90 percent of the estimated 17,000 Viet Cong were locally recruited and relied on supplies obtained locally, and that the infiltrators were returning to "territory long familiar to them," that is, their homes (II, 72, 75, 77).

On March 16, 1964, the secretary of defense reported to the president that "serious thought" was being given to "direct military action against North Vietnam," including such border control actions as "hot pursuit of VC forces moving across the Cambodian border and destruction of VC bases on the Vietnam/Cambodian line." He recommended that these operations be put on seventy-two-hour notice (III, 503; II, 195). In December 1964, the Saigon leadership noted that current plans presented to them said nothing about Viet Cong use of Cambodia (II, 345). A year later, in December 1965, Prime Minister Ky pressed for action against Cambodian sanctuaries, including cross-border attacks and a Khmer Serei expedition. According to the Pentagon historian, "State directed Lodge to keep him on a tight leash" (II, 368).

In 1967, concern over the Cambodian sanctuaries increases, quite naturally, since they were becoming real as a consequence of the United States military actions in Vietnam. In January CINCPAC expressed his concern to the Joint Chiefs of Staff over the infiltration through Cambodia and the importance of the "sanctuary" as a source of supplies, particularly rice. He noted that infiltration through Cambodia of both men and supplies was a direct consequence of the "success" of United States military operations in North Vietnam and Laos, and, "after pleading for a more 'balanced' program," recommended that "we must be prepared in all respects to use the necessary degree of force to attain our objectives" (IV, 410–12). Reporting to the president in April, General Westmoreland discussed the use of Cambodia as a supply base "in the DRV's grand design," first for rice and later for ammunition. He also described his contingency plans to send South Vietnamese troops with United States advisers into Cambodia (II, 443).

John McNaughton noted in May that Cambodia was "becoming more and more important as a supply base—now of food and medicines, perhaps ammunition later" (IV, 479). This was after the massive United States military operations along the borders in February, March, and April (see chapter 1, section VI, subsections 6, 7). That Cambodia was a source of food for the NLF is of course not in question. From the point of view of the United States government, this was aggression, just as the very existence of NLF cadres and units in their home villages was always regarded as aggression (see chapter 1, section VI, subsection 6).

The following day a memorandum of the Joint Chiefs stated: "It may ultimately become necessary to conduct military operations into Cambodia to deny the Viet Cong/North Vietnamese Army forces the psychological, military, and logistical advantages of this sanctuary" (IV, 492). The same memorandum went on to warn that nuclear weapons might be necessary in the event of Chinese Communist intervention anywhere in Indochina, the general assumption throughout.

An intelligence briefing for McNamara in Saigon in July stated that the enemy's military region 10 in South Vietnam extends into Cambodia: "He has stated that MR 10 is to become the biggest base area of the war." In the Fishhook area, the report continued, the enemy "has formed a replacement and refitting center reported to be 8,000 strong," for units "badly mauled in SVN." An agent reported a Viet Cong arsenal in the Parrot's Beak area, which is also used by the Viet Cong in transit between Tay Ninh and the delta (IV, 519).

In October the Joint Chiefs presented the president with a "summary of actions within present guidelines," which included expansion of "current DANIEL BOONE reconnaissance program by extending the area of operations for the full length of the SVN/Cambodia border; authorize use of helicopters; remove limitations on number of missions." Also: "Authorize DANIEL BOONE forces to conduct limited sabotage/destruction activity; authorize calling in tactical airstrikes on enemy targets near the border" (IV, 535). Among the "risks" of such a program were the "adverse political reaction" and the possibility that Cambodia "might seek to defend its territory."

It is interesting that these recommendations that the "reconnaissance program" be extended and that use of helicopters and airstrikes be authorized follows long after the actual use of helicopters and airstrikes, exactly as was the case in South Vietnam prior to 1965. Thus in July 1966, an American study team happened to be present immediately after an American helicopter attack on a Cambodian village. The attack was first denied, then conceded; eyewitnesses, including a CBS television team, were present. The Cambodian government submitted to the United Nations a detailed report of a combined US-ARVN–South Korean ground attack along with an air attack on a Cambodian village that was then burned down by the invading forces who occupied the area for two weeks.[60] Yet these and other such operations have entirely escaped the notice of the Pentagon historians; and a more interesting fact, long after they occurred the military command was discovered to be seeking authorization for strikes against "military targets" in areas where civilians have long been subjected to exactly such attacks. Evidently, there was considerable deception within the civilian and military-intelligence structures of the government, and—once again—remarkable ignorance of facts that could have been ascertained from the public record.

In the fall of 1967 the RVN chief of staff stated that "we have to solve the problem of Laos and Cambodia and the sanctuaries or the war might last 30 years" (IV, 527). At latest report, the "problem" has not been solved. In fact, it has been seriously exacerbated by the genius of the Nixon-Kissinger plan for Vietnam.

A final remark on Cambodia appears in a memorandum of the secretary of defense of March 1968. He suggests that in a United Nations appeal, Sihanouk might "highlight his internal Chinese-backed threat" (IV, 582). As usual (see chapter 1), the highest authorities in the United States, along with the intelligence agencies, accepted without serious question the principle that China was backing subversion and aggression everywhere in Indochina. Absence of evidence has never shaken this belief, always retained for its utility rather than on grounds of factual support. As already noted, Charles Meyer, who spent many years in close association with ruling circles in Cambodia, found no substance to this belief, and in fact remarks that China was the one country to give constructive aid to Cambodia, and also that it followed throughout "a very flexible policy, very respectful of the sovereignty of the country."[61] The same can hardly be said of those who speak so easily of Chinese-backed internal threats to Cambodia.

Notes

Section I of this essay is drawn in part from my article "Une guerre américaine 'camouflée,'" *Le Monde diplomatique*, December 1970, reprinted in *Journal of Contemporary Asia*, vol. 1, No. 3 (1971).

1 George Wilson, *Washington Post–Boston Globe*, January 17, 1972.

2 Hearings Before the [Kennedy] Subcommittee on Refugees and Escapees, U.S. Senate, May 7, 1970, pp. 54, 57. For many similar statements, see Hearings Before the [Symington] Subcommittee on United States Security Agreements and Commitments Abroad, U.S. Senate, October–November 1969, pts. 2 and 3.

    Elsewhere Sullivan has testified that the war in northern Laos has nothing to do with operations in South Vietnam or Cambodia. *War-Related Civilian Problems in Indochina*, Hearings Before the [Kennedy] Subcommittee on Refugees and Escapees, U.S. Senate, April 21–22, 1971, pt. 3: "Laos and Cambodia," pp. 43, 45.

3 T. D. Allman, "Landscape Without Figures," *Manchester Guardian Weekly*, January 1, 1972; *Far Eastern Economic Review*, January 8, 1972.

4 Michael Morrow, "Unexploded Bombs Threat to Laotian Villagers," Dispatch News Service International, bi-weekly Asian releases, January 10, 1972.

5 Joe Nicholson, Jr., "Bombing of Laotian Villages Revealed," *ibid*.

6 Interview with Fred Branfman, March 19, 1972; Jack Anderson, "U.S. Bombings of Laos Villages," *Washington Post*, April 9, 1972. Walkley also testified about these matters before Judge John Lanham, Circuit Court of the First Circuit, Hawaii, October 5–8, 1971, after a demonstration at a Honeywell plant. Honeywell is one of the major manufacturers of antipersonnel weapons used in these and other operations.

[7] For such information as was available by mid-1970, see several articles in Nina S. Adams and Alfred W. McCoy, eds., *Laos: War and Revolution;* and my *At War with Asia,* chap. 4.

[8] *War-Related Civilian Problems in Indochina,* Kennedy Subcommittee Hearings, April 1971, app. 2.

[9] It appears in app. 2 in Kennedy Subcommittee Hearings, July 22, 1971. See also his study "A Survey of Civilian Fatalities Among Refugees from Xieng Khouang Province, Laos," in *Problems of War Victims in Indochina,* Hearings Before the [Kennedy] Subcommittee on Refugees and Escapees, U.S. Senate, May 9, 1972, pt. 2: "Laos and Cambodia," app. 2.

[10] Arthur Dommen, *Conflict in Laos,* pp. 308, 311.

[11] *Ibid.* p. 311, without explicit mention. This is the only reference to the impact on civilians of the bombing in Laos, in this case in Sam Neua Province. Decornoy's reports appear in Adams and McCoy, *Laos.*

[12] I have reviewed what there is in *At War with Asia,* chap. 4. The Langer and Zasloff RAND study reviewed there has since appeared as a book: Paul F. Langer and Joseph J. Zasloff, *North Vietnam and the Pathet Lao.* For a further effort to determine the facts, see Fred Branfman's important article "Presidential War in Laos," in Adams and McCoy, *Laos.* On American involvement in earlier years, see several other articles in that collection, particularly Gareth Porter, "After Geneva: Subverting Laotian Neutrality," which deals with the crucial 1962–1964 period. See also the references cited in Chapter 1.

[13] See note 2 above.

[14] Langer and Zasloff, *North Vietnam and the Pathet Lao,* p. 151.

[15] Cf. Branfman, "Presidential War in Laos"; Peter Dale Scott, *The War Conspiracy,* chap. 2.

[16] Cf. Branfman, "Presidential War in Laos," p. 269; *At War with Asia,* p. 214, citing D. S. Greenway of *Time–Life.* Carl Strock reports that United States military attachés were still giving the figure of 48,000 North Vietnamese in January 1971; "No News from Laos," *Far Eastern Economic Review,* January 30, 1971.

[17] Dommen, *Conflict in Laos,* p. 386.

[18] *Laos: April 1971,* Staff Report of the [Symington] Subcommittee on United States Security Agreements and Commitments Abroad, U.S. Senate, April 1971, p. 20.

[19] Strock, "No News from Laos."

[20] General Lansdale's memo for Ambassador Taylor, July 1961, "Resources for Unconventional Warfare, S.E. Asia," in Gerald Gold *et al.,* eds., *The Pentagon Papers,* pp. 131ff.; *The Pentagon Papers,* Senator Gravel Edition, II, 643ff. See also Branfman, *Voices from the Plain of Jars,* p. 13. It is generally estimated that about two-thirds of the Meo were associated with the CIA operations, the remaining one-third joining with the Pathet Lao. For background, see Alfred W. McCoy *et al., The Politics of Heroin in Southeast Asia.* Vang Pao was a company commander of a Meo irregular unit fighting with the French forces.

[21] Kennedy Subcommittee Hearings, May 7, 1970, p. 24. Rickenbach accepts the government claim, for which no serious evidence so far

exists, that the Meo were organized to block a North Vietnamese invasion in the late 1950s. The Meo, he believes, were exploited by the United States government for their regional usefulness, destroyed in the process, and abandoned.

22 Rickenbach also reports "indiscriminate bombing of civilian population centers" which has wrought "havoc and meaningless destruction (rather than military advantage)." He gives several examples.

23 John Everingham, "Decimation of the Meo," National Anti-war Conference, Sydney, Australia, February 1971.

In February 1972, Everingham was captured by the Pathet Lao and released after a month in the Plain of Jars area. Throughout, the Pathet Lao were in charge, as far as he could determine. He saw few Vietnamese—none after the first day in captivity. The areas through which he passed were subjected to constant bombing, primarily antipersonnel CBUs which, he observed, are "dump[ed] randomly . . . in the forested gullies between the mountains where both military camps and, separately, civilian villages were hidden." See *American Report*, April 21, April 28, and May 5, 1972; all three reports appear in *Win*, May 1, 1972.

24 Both the USIS and the embassy reports are cited by Walter Haney, "The Pentagon Papers and United States Involvement in Laos," in *The Pentagon Papers*, Senator Gravel Edition, vol. 5, *Critical Essays*, eds. Noam Chomsky and Howard Zinn.

25 *Refugee and Civilian War Casualty Problems in Indochina*, Staff Report for the Kennedy Subcommittee on Refugees and Escapees, U.S. Senate, September 28, 1970.

26 Hearings Before the [Symington] Subcommittee on United States Security Agreements and Commitments Abroad, U.S. Senate, October 1969, pt. 2: "Kingdom of Laos, pp. 526, 553. Henceforth cited as Symington Subcommittee Hearings, 1970.

27 Kennedy Subcommittee staff report, p. 23. John Hannah, the director of USAID, has conceded publicly that USAID serves as a CIA "cover" in Laos (June 7, 1970). See Adams and McCoy, *Laos*.

28 Kennedy Subcommittee staff report, p. 19.

29 Haney, "Pentagon Papers," p. 70. See references cited earlier for description of the behavior of the CIA army when it briefly conquered the Plain of Jars in late 1969.

30 Symington Subcommittee Hearings, 1970, pt. 3, pp. 792, 780–1, 790.

31 There are several American government reports: Edward T. McKeithen, *Life under the P.L.* and *The Role of North Vietnamese Cadres*; Langer and Zasloff, *North Vietnam and Pathet Lao*. These reports, which as expected are quite hostile to the Pathet Lao, present considerable data not inconsistent with the reports of refugees that were available to me. See *At War with Asia* for some discussion of this material. See also the important study by G. Chapelier and J. Van Malderghem, "Plain of Jars, Social Changes Under Five Years of Pathet-Lao Administration," *Asia Quarterly* [Brussels], 1971/1. On certain specific matters—such as the role of "awakening groups"—their conclusions differ from the reports I obtained from refugees who were clearly Pathet Lao sympathizers. See also the reports in *Voices from the Plain of Jars*, which seem to corroborate the picture I obtained.

32 A verbatim interview that seemed to me particularly interesting appears in Adams and McCoy, *Laos*, chap. 29.

33 For some discussion, see *At War with Asia*, pp. 222–23.

34 Dennis Duncanson, *Government and Revolution in Vietnam*, pp. 6, 21.

In *War Comes to Long An*, Jeffrey Race notes reports that criminals constituted "one small but important source of recruits" for the NLF, revealing "how little [the party] were hobbled by any narrow doctrinaire outlook"(p. 173). In general, "priority in recruitment and promotion was given to the lowest economic strata," former Viet Minh being the first group of post-Geneva recruits (pp. 168, 172). This was consistent with the strategy of "developing policies more congenial to the interests of [the great majority of the country's population] than were the policies of the government" (p. 150), the key to the NLF victory by 1965. He gives details to show how "the absence of popular recourse against criminal behavior by government officials" provided "fertile ground for Party propaganda" (pp. 88–9) and discusses at length the role of government terror. As to "organized crime," it has deeply penetrated Southeast Asia through the medium of the ruling groups established by the United States. See references of chapter 4, note 15.

35 Book reviews, *Pacific Affairs*, vol. 44, no. 4 (1971–2).

36 Ithiel de Sola Pool, "Village Violence and International Violence," Peace Research Society Papers, no. 9, Cambridge Conference, 1968. Reprinted in Pool, ed., *Reprints of Publications on Vietnam, 1966–1970*, May 1971, privately printed.

37 See Terence Smith, *New York Times*, December 5, 1971; Iver Peterson, *New York Times*, December 2, 1971; Darius Jhabvala, *Boston Globe*, February 6, 1972. On the behavior of ARVN, see *New York Times*, December 6, 1970; Iver Peterson, *New York Times*, December 10, 1970; Henry Kamm, *New York Times*, March 21, 1971; July 2, 1971; Sydney Schanberg, *New York Times*, September 9, 1971; and the books cited in note 38 below.

38 Jean-Claude Pomonti and Serge Thion, *Des courtisans aux partisans*; Charles Meyer, *Derrière le sourire khmer*.

39 Cf. *At War with Asia*, p. 142 n.

40 Press conference, November 12, 1971; *U.S. State Department Bulletin*, December 6, 1971, p. 646.

41 T. D. Allman, "Who Killed Sihanouk?" *Manchester Guardian*, September 18, 1971.

42 "U.S. Indirectly Supported Sihanouk's Ouster," Dispatch News Service International, bi-weekly Asian releases, October 11, 1971.

43 Pomonti and Thion, *Des courtisans aux partisans*, p. 222, citing a report in *Le Monde* of a BBC interview. Marasco was a Special Forces captain who was accused of having assassinated a Vietnamese spy, Thai Khac Chuyen.

44 "Ex-Beret Links New Cambodia Prime Minister to Murder Trial," Dispatch News Service International, April 5, 1972; parts appear in *Chicago Sun-Times*, April 9, 1972.

45 *Ibid.*

46 Richard A. Fineberg, "Cambodian Premier Links CIA to Sihanouk Ouster," *St. Louis Post-Dispatch*, April 6, 1972. Fineberg discusses

Allman's interview with Thanh, and also reports that Milton Osborne in early 1971 had given a similar account, based on interviews with Thanh's brother.

47 For example, Professors Edwin Reischauer and Milton Sacks, at a public meeting in Cambridge, Mass., in the summer of 1970, on recent events in Cambodia.

48 Meyer, *Derrière le sourire khmer*, pp. 321–4. Cf. also Pomonti and Thion, *Des courtisans aux partisans*, chaps. 10 and 11 and pp. 221–2.

49 For a detailed account of US–ARVN military actions from mid-March, at times in coordination with the Cambodian military, see Jeff Pearson and Jessica Smilowitz, "Biting the Fishhook," *Bulletin of Concerned Asian Scholars*, vol. 2, no. 4 (Fall 1970).

50 *Etudes cambodgiennes*, April–June 1967, p. 4, cited by Pomonti and Thion, pp. 113–4.

51 *At War with Asia*, p. 142 n.

52 Several American veterans have reported frequent incursions into Cambodian border areas in 1967–1968, up to 20 kilometers. See the testimony of Larry Rottmann, information officer of the 25th Infantry Division, National Veterans Inquiry, Washington, D.C., December 1970, in James S. Kunen, *Standard Operating Procedures*, p. 56.

On the American-backed military offensive in northern and central Laos in the fall of 1963, shortly after the increasing CIA infiltration into Laos, see Gareth Porter, "After Geneva," pp. 198–9. Peter Dale Scott has discussed the escalation of United States clandestine activities in Indochina in the fall of 1963 ("Vietnamization and the Drama of the Pentagon Papers," in Chomsky and Zinn, *Critical Essays*). He points out that the autumn military offensive in Laos coincided with an escalation of the CIA-supported Khmer Serei activities against Sihanouk that were noted also by Meyer and Pomonti-Thion. He also cites a *New York Times* report of November 20, 1963, on two captured Khmer Serei infiltrators who described their activities against the Cambodian government from a fortified hamlet in South Vietnam under the control of United States military advisers.

53 Milton Osborne, review of *At War with Asia* by Noam Chomsky, *Pacific Affairs*, vol. 44, no. 2 (1971).

54 Many others could be cited. For example, Robert Shaplen wrote that the Khmer people "cherished and revered [Sihanouk], but in a wider sense the relationship went far beyond that of parent and offspring, to that of a Superman-style hero and his audience" ("Cambodia Is Sihanouk," in Jonathan S. Grant *et al.*, eds., *Cambodia: the Widening War in Indochina*, p. 79). I should add that in my discussion several *caveats* were entered, such as note 12, p. 124: "Those familiar with internal Cambodian politics regard the information that is available to Westerners as being of highly uncertain quality, and any effort at detailed interpretation must surely be taken with caution."

On these matters, in addition to the sources cited above, see also William Rosoff, "Dissension in the Kingdom," in Grant *et al.*, *Cambodia*.

55 Michael Leifer, review of *Cambodia*, by Jonathan S. Grant *et al.*, eds., *Pacific Affairs*, vol. 44, no. 4 (1971–72).

56 Allman, "Who Killed Sihanouk?"

57 Department of Defense, *United States–Vietnam Relations, 1945–67*, bk. 2, IV. A.5, tab. 3, p. 64. This is the government offset edition of the Pentagon Papers.

58 See *At War with Asia*, chap. 3, for examples and further references. Some eases has been reported in the American press (see note 52 above).

59 References are to the Senator Gravel Edition of *The Pentagon Papers*, by volume and page.

60 See *At War with Asia*, pp. 121–2.

61 Meyer, *Derrière le sourire khmer*, p. 219.

CHAPTER 3

The Rule of Force in International Affairs

Two different issues arise when the American experience in Vietnam is considered in the context of the Nuremberg trials and related international conventions: the issue of "legality" and the issue of justice. The first is a technical question of law and history—by the standards of international law as formally accepted by the great powers, how is the American war in Indochina to be judged? The second question is more elusive. It is the question of proper standards. Are the principles of Nuremberg and related international law satisfactory and appropriate in the case of great-power intervention, as in Vietnam and Czechoslovakia, for example? The recent study of Nuremberg and Vietnam by Telford Taylor—the chief counsel for the prosecution at Nuremberg, a historian, professor of law, and retired brigadier general—is devoted to the first of these topics, but occasional remarks bear on the second as well. It is possible that Taylor's brief but informative study will set the framework for much of the subsequent debate over war crimes and broader questions of proper international conduct. Though conservative in assumptions and narrow in compass—overly so, in my opinion—Taylor's investigation leads to strong conclusions. He comes close to suggesting that the military and civilian leadership of the United States from 1965 to the present are liable to prosecution as war criminals under the standards of Nuremberg. No less controversial are the self-imposed limitations of his study. In many respects, Taylor's book offers a convenient point of departure for an investigation of the issues of legality and justice.

I. "WAR CRIMES" AND "JUSTICE"

The issue of justice is not to be discounted. International law is in effect a body of moral principles accepted as valid by those who ratify treaties and other agreements. Furthermore, as Taylor emphasizes, treaties and manuals "are only partial embodiments of the laws of war." The preamble of the 1907 Hague Convention, for example, states that questions not covered should be resolved by "the principles of the law of nations, as they result from the usages established among civilized peoples, from the laws of humanity, and from the dictates of the public conscience."[1] It therefore makes sense to inquire into the *acceptability* as well as the political and social *content* of such principles as have been codified and generally adopted, and to consider them in the light of the dictates of public conscience and the laws of humanity, unclear as these may be. As to "usages established among civilized peoples," Justice Jackson, in an interim report to the president in 1945, wrote that "we are put under a heavy responsibility to see that our behavior during this unsettled period will direct the world's thought toward a firmer enforcement of the laws of international conduct, so as to make war less attractive to those who have governments and the destinies of peoples in their power" (p. 77). How have we met this responsibility in the postwar era? The question touches not only on the legality of American conduct in the light of Nuremberg and related principles, but also on the character of these principles themselves.

Taylor's discussion of the Nuremberg judgments reveals a fundamental moral flaw in the principles that emerged from those trials. Rejecting the argument that the bombing of North Vietnam constitutes a war crime, Taylor observes that "whatever the laws of war in this field *ought* to be, certainly Nuremberg furnishes no basis for these accusations" (p. 142). Yet this bombing has laid waste most of North Vietnam, including large cities with the exceptions of Hanoi and Haiphong.[2] The reason the law of war crimes does not reach American bombing is straightforward:

> Since both sides [in World War II] had played the terrible
> game of urban destruction—the Allies far more success-
> fully—there was no basis for criminal charges against Ger-
> mans or Japanese, and in fact no such charges were
> brought. [Pp. 140–1]

> Aerial bombardment had been used so extensively and
> ruthlessly on the Allied side as well as the Axis side that
> neither at Nuremberg nor Tokyo was the issue made a part
> of the trials. [P. 89]

Similarly, charges against German admirals for violating the
London Naval Treaty of 1930 were dismissed after testimony
by Admiral Nimitz, which "established that in this regard the
Germans had done nothing that the British and Americans
had not also done" (p. 37). The Nuremberg Tribunal ruled
that the German admirals should be subjected to no criminal
penalties for their violation of international law, because the
laws in question "had been abrogated by the practice of the
belligerents on both sides under the stress of military necessity" (p. 38). Taylor concludes that "to punish the foe—especially the vanquished foe—for conduct in which the enforcing
nation has engaged, would be so grossly inequitable as to
discredit the laws themselves" (p. 39).

From such comments we can derive the operational definition of "crime of war" as conceived at Nuremberg. Criminal
acts were to be treated as crimes only if the defeated enemy,
but not the victors, had engaged in them. No doubt it would
be "grossly inequitable" to punish the vanquished foe for
conduct in which the enforcing nation had engaged. It would,
however, be just and equitable to punish both victor and
vanquished for their criminal acts. This option, which Taylor
does not mention, was not adopted by the postwar tribunals.
They chose instead "to discredit the laws themselves" by restricting their definition of criminal conduct so as to exclude
punishment of the victors.[3]

The conclusion that Nuremberg is to be understood as the
judgment of victors, rather than as the achievement of a new
level of international morality, is reinforced by Taylor's discussion of aggressive war. The distinctive contribution of
Nuremberg, he points out, was to establish the category of
crimes against peace: "Planning, preparation, initiation or

waging of a war of aggression or a war in violation of international treaties, agreements or assurances," or "participation in a common plan or conspiracy" to this end.[4] "In terms of substantive international law," Taylor writes, "and in the mind of the general public, the salient feature of the Nuremberg trials was the decision that individuals could be held guilty for participation in the planning and waging of 'a war of aggression'" (p. 84). "Indisputably it was a cardinal part of the postwar policy of the United States Government to establish the criminality under international law of aggressive warfare . . . " (p. 76).

But, Taylor argues, a court could hardly decide the question of whether the United States has violated the antiaggression provisions of the Nuremberg or United Nations charters.[5] For one reason, "the evidentiary problems would be well-nigh insuperable." At Nuremberg and Tokyo, the Allies had access to secret diplomatic and military document files, which would not be made available by the United States and South Vietnamese governments. "Total military victories such as those that ended the Second World War are comparatively rare in modern history, and it is difficult to envisage other circumstances that would unlock the secret files" (pp. 118–19). But if only access to the secret files can provide proof that aggressive war has been waged, then it follows that the "salient feature of the Nuremberg trials" will normally be relevant only to the case of an enemy that has suffered total military defeat.

Actually, Taylor vacillates somewhat on the matter of proof of aggression, in that he seems to trust the executive branch to make unilateral judgments regarding aggression by other states, despite the "insuperable" evidentiary problems. He writes that "until 1965 [he] supported American intervention in Vietnam as an aggression-checking undertaking in the spirit of the United Nations Charter" (p. 206).[6] It was permissible in Taylor's opinion for the American executive to determine unilaterally that North Vietnam was engaged in aggressive war prior to 1965, and to join South Vietnam in collective self-defense against the armed attack from the North, under article 51 of the United Nations Charter. So uniquely competent is the United States to exercise this judgment, he seems to believe, that it was unnecessary even to adhere to the provision in article 51 that measures taken in the exercise of the right of self-defense be immediately reported to the Security Council,[7] or to the provision in article 39 that "the Security Council shall determine the existence of any threat to the peace, breach of the peace, or act of aggression" and shall determine what measures shall be taken.

In fact, I think that Taylor exaggerates the "evidentiary problems" of determining whether the United States is engaged in aggression in Southeast Asia, just as he underestimates the difficulty of establishing that it was engaged in collective self-defense against armed attack. His discussion of aggressive war seems to me inadequate in other respects as well.

There is still more serious issue at stake when we consider the acceptability of the principles of international law as codified in the Charter of Nuremberg and elsewhere. These principles were formulated by representatives of established governments, without the participation of representatives of mass-based popular movements that seek to overthrow recognized governments or that establish revolutionary governments. Richard Falk holds that "from the perspective of international order the capacity to govern is certainly an element in claiming political legitimacy,"[8] and Thomas J. Farer speaks of "the dangerous ambiguity of just when the insurgency has achieved sufficient status to require equal treatment."[9] This point is crucial in assessing Taylor's belief that the United States was engaged in an "aggression-checking" undertaking in Vietnam in, say, 1962. In that year American officials in Saigon estimated that half the population supported the National Liberation Front.[10] Furthermore, there was no evidence of North Vietnamese participation in any combat, and 10,000 American troops were in South Vietnam, many directly engaged in military actions.[11] Bernard Fall noted that "since 1961 Americans die in Viet-Nam, and in American uniforms. And they die fighting."[12] In March of 1962, United States officials admitted that American pilots were flying combat missions (bombing and strafing). By October, it was reported that 30 percent of all air missions in South Vietnam had American Air Force pilots at their controls.[13] By late 1962 the United States was directly involved in large military actions in the Mekong Delta and the Camau Peninsula.[14] In a book published in 1963, Richard Tregaskis reported interviews with American helicopter pilots who describe how the "wild men" of the 362nd Squadron used to shoot civilians for sport in "solid VC areas."[15] It has also been reported that in 1962, air commandos of the Special Operations Force, "wearing civilian clothes and flying planes with the markings of the South Vietnamese Air Force . . . attacked Vietcong concentrations in the jungles."[16]

There is, in short, a good case that the United States was involved in direct military attacks against indigenous popular forces in South Vietnam as early as 1962. It would be fair to call this "aggressive war" if, indeed, the capacity to govern is an element in claiming political legitimacy. Suppose that one were to hold, on the contrary, that governments recognized by the major powers are legally permitted to call in outside force to put down a domestic insurgency, while insurgents are not entitled to seek outside help. Suppose further that this rule applies even where the insurgents consitute the only effective government in large areas and the only mass-based political organization,[17] and where these insurgents are asking support from a state from which they have been arbitrarily separated by great-power intervention and subversion.[18] If this hypothesized rule is an accurate interpretation of the currently prevailing system of international law, then the only appropriate conclusion is that this system of law is to be disregarded as without moral force. Or, to be more precise, the conclusion must be that this system of law is simply a device for ratifying imperial practice.

These questions do not arise in any direct way in Taylor's discussion, in part because he scarcely touches on the pre-1965 period to which they are directly relevant. Similar problems, however, are implicit in his discussion of the legality of various modes of warfare. As already noted, Taylor argues that aerial warfare is not intrinsically unlawful, although the "silence of Nuremberg" on this matter raises questions "especially relevant to American bombing policies . . . in South Vietnam" (p. 142). The routine destruction of villages by American firepower and ground sweeps and the forced evacuation of population are, he argues, of doubtful legality, and reprisal attacks against villages harboring Viet Cong—official policy, as he notes—are a "flagrant violation" of the Geneva Conventions (p. 145). What is more, Taylor believes the establishment of free-fire zones to be illegal (p. 147). But he emphasizes the great problems in determining how legal principles should apply under the circumstances of Vietnam, where a superpower is using its technological resources to destroy guerrilla forces that conceal themselves among the population. The basic problem is this:

> The enemy does not respect those laws, the terrain lends itself to clandestine operations in which women and children frequently participate, the hostile and the friendly do not label themselves as such, and individuals of the yellow race are hard for our soldiers to identify. As in the Philippines 65 years ago, our troops are thousands of miles from home in uncomfortable, dangerous and unfamiliar surroundings. No one not utterly blind to the realities can fail to acknowledge and make allowance for the difficulties and uncertainties they face in distinguishing inoffensive noncombatants from hostile partisans. [P. 152]

The enemy "is undeniably in violation of the traditional laws of war and the Geneva Conventions, based as they are on the distinction between combatants and noncombatants" in two specific respects: the enemy does not wear "a fixed distinctive emblem recognizable at a distance" or "carry arms openly," as American soldiers do. The law, as reaffirmed at Nuremberg, states that "a civilian who aids, abets, or participates in the fighting is liable to punishment as a war criminal." This may seem harsh, Taylor writes, but "it is certainly the law" (pp. 136-7),[19] just as the law may not apply to aerial bombardment of towns and villages in an effort to break the enemy's will or to deny him material or human resources.

These observations come very close to branding "people's war" illegal, while permitting the use of the technology of the industrial powers to suppress it. An essential feature of revolutionary people's war, Vietnamese style, is that it combines political and military action, thus blurring the distinction between combatants and noncombatants. The Vietnamese revolutionaries in general attempted to follow the Maoist injunction that "a bloodless transition is what we would like and we should strive for it."[20] Even Douglas Pike concedes that the NLF "maintained that its contest with the GVN and the United States should be fought out at the political level and that the use of massed military might was in itself illegitimate," until forced by the United States and the GVN "to use counterforce to survive."[21] When the NLF resorted to counterforce to survive, it exploited its natural advantage, the ability of the guerrillas to blend into the sympathetic local population, just as the United States exploited its natural advantage in the technology of surveillance and destruction.

These characteristics of people's war were outlined years ago by the leading Vietnamese Communist ideologist Truong Chinh:

> [There are] those who have a tendency only to rely on military action. . . . They tend to believe that everything can be settled by armed force; they do not apply political mobilization, are unwilling to give explanations and to convince people; . . . . fighting spiritedly, they neglect political cal work; they do not . . . act in such a way that the army and the people can wholeheartedly help one another.[22]

Citing this passage, Bernard Fall noted that "once more, the enemy has been kind enough to give us the recipe of his victory."[23] The recipe is to gain political support among the people and to engage the population as a whole in the struggle against the central government backed—in this case imposed —by foreign military force. The participation of civilians in the revolutionary war reflects its political and social character, just as saturation bombing by B-52s based in sanctuaries in Guam and Thailand reveals the essential political and social character of American "counterinsurgency." The laws of war rule the former illegal, while the silence of Nuremberg falls over American practice. These laws, Taylor maintains, condemn as war criminals the civilians who take up arms against a foreign enemy or its local protégés; such civilians are "undeniably in violation" of the laws of war. But with regard to the American pilots who have destroyed towns and villages and devastated farmland and forest, driving millions from their homes and killing unknown numbers throughout Indochina, or to those who planned this policy, the laws of war have little to say. At most "the silence of Nuremberg . . . asks [questions] . . . relevant to American bombing policies . . . in South Vietnam" (p. 142), and presumably in Laos and Cambodia as well (but see above, p. 218).

These laws, so understood, are the weapon of the strong, and are of no moral force or validity. It is a political decision to accept an interpretation of the law that holds that a government installed and maintained by a foreign power (as in South Vietnam or Hungary) has the right to call upon this foreign power to suppress an insurgency that has gained such extensive political support that insurgents are indistinguishable from the population, and holds that civilian participants in the insurgency are war criminals. It is a political decision to accept as valid the law that combatants must identify themselves as such to the soldiers of the foreign army, while that same law raises no objection to the dispatch of soldiers "thousands of miles from home" to "unlovely circumstances" in which they cannot distinguish noncombatants from partisans.

Though Taylor is quite right to insist on the difficulties and uncertainties faced by these troops, there is no reason to withhold condemnation from the political leaders who sent them there, or to grant any validity to the legal system that permits this while condemning the enemy's recipe for victory: winning popular support and using this support in the only way a popular movement can to overthrow the local representatives of a foreign superpower. No reason, that is, apart from the political judgment that a great power has the right to impose a regime of its choice, by force, in some foreign land. The system of law, so interpreted, is merely a ratification of imperialist practice.

Though Taylor is not entirely explicit, it seems that he accepts the political judgment that the United States has the right to impose the regime of its choice in South Vietnam. In his discussion of war aims, he refers to "our stated policy," namely, "to gain and hold the political allegiance of the South Vietnamese to a non-communist government, while giving them defensive assistance against any military means used by the North" (p. 189). His only stated objection to this policy is that it was unlikely to work, under the circumstances of Vietnam. As to the "defensive assistance" against the North, surely he is aware that the main NLF fighting units were indigenous from the start, and remained so until the United States internationalized the war. He apparently believes that it was legitimate for the United States to introduce its military forces, as it did in the early 1960s, to gain and hold the political allegiance of the South Vietnamese to the noncommunist government installed by the United States in 1954. Taylor refers to the "deeply idealistic strain in the American interventionist tradition" (p. 186), as when McKinley justified the war against Spain in 1898. This is a very superficial historical judgment. Virtually every imperial power has justified its actions on "idealistic" grounds. This was true of the British and French empires, the Japanese in East Asia,[24] and the Russians in Eastern Europe. That the leaders and populations of the imperial powers may even succumb to these delusions is hardly significant. It is remarkable that the standards by which we would judge other cases of imperial intervention seem so difficult to comprehend when applied to our own actions.[25]

Taylor asks whether the American conduct of the war, with forced resettlement, complicity in the torture of prisoners, enthusiasm for body counts, devastation of large areas to expose the insurgents, free-fire zones, and the Son My massacre, was merely "a terrible, mad aberration" (p. 152). He answers correctly that in part it was a consequence of the specific features of the Vietnam war cited above, which make the laws of war so difficult to apply. In fact, the policy of forced resettlement and devastation of large areas of the country was a rational, perhaps even a necessary, response to the specific circumstances of the Vietnam war. Bernard Fall, bitterly anticommunist and a strong supporter of the American war before it reached its full fury, explained this fact very well in the early 1960s.

> Why is it that we must use top-notch elite forces, the cream of the crop of American, British, French, or Australian commando and special warfare schools; armed with the very best that advanced technology can provide; to defeat Viet-Minh, Algerians, or Malay "CT's" [Chinese terrorists], almost none of whom can lay claim to similar expert training and only in the rarest of cases to equality in fire power?

The answer is very simple: It takes all the technical

proficiency our system can provide to make up for the woeful lack of popular support and political savvy of most of the regimes that the West has thus far sought to prop up. The Americans who are now fighting in South Viet-Nam have come to appreciate this fact out of first-hand experience.[26]

Today, there is vastly more evidence to support Fall's conclusion. "The element of real popular support is vital," he wrote.[27] And it was exactly this "real popular support" that led Washington to adopt the policy of forced population removal that has reduced the peasantry from about 85 percent to about half of the population, while laying waste the countryside. If international law has nothing to say about this except that civilians aiding the resistance are war criminals), then its moral bankruptcy is revealed with stark clarity.

II. "WAR CRIMES" IN VIETNAM

The major topic that Taylor considers, however, is the more narrow question of the legality of American actions in Vietnam when measured against the framework of Nuremberg and related conventions. In his analysis of the American intervention after 1965, Taylor concludes that there is definite evidence that war crimes have been committed and that culpability for these crimes extends to high levels of military command and civilian leadership. The evidence in this regard is extensive.

The primary example that Taylor considers is the My Lai massacre. Dr. Alje Vennema, director of a Canadian hospital near the site of the massacre, reports that he knew of it at once but did nothing because it was not at all out of the ordinary. His patients were constantly reporting such incidents to him. The province of Quang Ngai, in which My Lai is located, had been virtually destroyed. Half the population had been forced into refugee camps, and children were starving and wounded.[28] Colonel Oran Henderson, the highest ranking officer to have faced court-martial charges for the My Lai massacre, states that "every unit of brigade size has its Mylai hidden some place," though "every unit doesn't have a Ridenhour."[29]

This observation is borne out by direct testimony of veterans throughout the country. To cite just a few random examples, a highly decorated helicopter gunner testified in El Paso, Texas, on May 5, 1971, that of the thirty-nine Vietnamese he had killed, one was an old man riding a bicycle and ten were a group of unarmed civilians. In each case, he claims to have acted on direct order from his commanding officer. A former member of the Coast Guard testified that his orders were to pilot a small motorboat through delta canals shooting randomly into every village to see if there were inhabitants. In hearings conducted by the Citizens' Commission of Inquiry on United States War Crimes, in Washington, D.C., December 1–3, 1970, a medic in the 101st Airborne Division testified that approximately twenty-seven civilians in a peaceful meeting were killed in an unprovoked attack by American tanks firing a barrage of tiny arrowlike nails. A marine forward observer testified that he counted twenty dead civilians after an unprovoked artillery strike on two villages. Another marine corporal testified that his unit was ordered to fire on starving civilians scavenging in a garbage dump after their food supplies had been destroyed in 1966 (rice fields had been napalmed to destroy food in this free-fire zone). A former army sergeant testified before an unofficial House committee headed by Representative Ronald Dellums that he took part in killing about thirty unresisting Vietnamese civilians in the village of Truong Khanh, near My Lai, in April 1969. This testimony was confirmed to reporters by Vietnamese women in a refugee camp.[30] The Winter Soldier Investigation in Detroit produced voluminous testimony on atrocities,[31] as have other inquiries.

A former helicopter gunner with 176 confirmed "kills" told reporter Joseph Lelyveld that his gunship was ordered to halt a flight of peasants. When the pilot reported that he had no way to do so, he received orders to "shoot them." Thirty or forty unarmed villagers were then killed by the gunship. Trainees said that their instructor had written President Nixon after the Calley verdict about his own involvement in an incident in which six gunships attacked a village, killing 350 villagers,[32] after a helicopter crew member had been shot.

Refugees, reporters, and other observers have presented

voluminous substantiating evidence. What is particularly important is that these episodes appear to be quite routine.

> I have personally accompanied a routine operation in which U.S. Cobra helicopters fired 20mm. cannons into the houses of a typical village in territory controlled by the National Liberation Front. They also shot the villagers who ran out of the houses. This was termed "prepping the area" by the American lieutenant colonel who directed the operation. "We sort of shoot it up to see if anything moves," he explained, and he added by way of reassurance that this treatment was perfectly routine.[33]

An official map of the 25th Infantry Division delineates large areas subjected to artillery and air bombardment prior to the ground sweeps of Operation Junction City in 1967. Within these areas there were over twenty identifiable villages with populations of 5,000, according to earlier census figures.

New York Times correspondent R. W. Apple writes that he heard the "mere gook rule," according to which "anything that moves and has a yellow skin is an enemy, unless there is incontrovertible evidence to the contrary," repeated "100 times by majors and sergeants and privates." This, he writes, is "official policy, a part of everyday life." He goes on:

> Not so evident to the average rifleman, but clear enough to those of us who have had an opportunity to travel about the country, is a deliberate policy of creating refugees wherever possible. An Army general . . . explained the idea to me as follows: "You've got to dry up the sea the guerrillas swim in—that's the peasants—and the best way to do that is blast the hell out of their villages so they'll come into our refugee camps. No villages, no guerrillas: simple.[34]

He adds further that Generals Westmoreland and Abrams, as well as Presidents Johnson and Nixon, surely knew this.[35]

It is this policy of "no villages, no guerrillas"—the policy of destroying the rural society—that is referred to as "forced-draft urbanization and modernization" by some of the more cynical academic technocrats who deal with Vietnam; "a euphemism to end all euphemisms" (p. 202), as Taylor appropriately comments. Apple's account indicates that this policy was not inadvertent, something that the United States command "stumbled upon" in an "absent-minded way,"[36] but rather was planned and understood in advance.

Neil Sheehan's widely discussed article on war crimes[37] makes the same point. Sheehan claims that "classified military documents specifically talk about bombing villages in communist-held areas 'to deprive the enemy of the population resource.' " He refers to a secret study in the summer of 1966 which proposed reconsideration of the policy of unrestricted bombing and shelling which was "urbanizing" the population.[38] This proposal was vetoed at the highest level of American authority in Saigon, he writes. It was decided instead to continue to employ "air and artillery to terrorize the peasantry and raze the countryside." One of the basic American tactics was "unrestricted air and artillery bombardments of peasant hamlets"—"devastation had become a fundamental element in [the American] strategy to win the war." The rural civilian population was the target of the American attack "because it was believed that their existence was important to the enemy." The idea was to defeat the Vietnamese Communists "by obliterating their strategic base, the rural population."[39]

The United States authorities have a point when they argue that My Lai is not the typical incident of the Vietnam war. More typical, almost the war in microcosm, is the story of the village of Phuqui on the Batangan Peninsula, 130 miles southeast of Hue. In January 1969, 12,000 peasants in this region were forced from their homes in an American ground sweep, loaded on helicopters, and shipped to interrogation centers and a waterless camp near Quang Ngai over which floated a banner saying, "We thank you for liberating us from communist terror." According to official military statistics, there were 158 NVA and Viet Cong dead and 268 wounded in the six-month campaign of which this was a part. These refugees (who incidentally seem to have included the remnants of My Lai) had lived in caves and bunkers for months before the forced evacuation because of the heavy American bombing and artillery and naval shelling. A dike was "blasted by American jets to deprive the North Vietnamese of a food supply."[40] As of April 1971, the dike had not been repaired: "As a result, the salt water of the South China Sea continues to submerge the fields where rice once grew." About 4,000 refugees, including 1,500 in Phuqui, have since returned. Phuqui is now surrounded by ten-foot rows of bamboo. It is under guard, and no one may enter or leave between 6:00 P.M. and 5:00 A.M. "The hills that overlook the flooded paddies, once scattered with huts, are 'ironed'—a word used by the peasants to mean filled with bomb fragments, mines and unexploded artillery shells. B-52 bomb craters nearly 20 feet deep pock the hills." One reason why the dike has not been rebuilt may be that—in the words of an American official—"two years ago the people on the peninsula were written off as communists. It would not be surprising if the attitudes still linger among the Vietnamese today." Most of the population go without basic food. "Province officials neither affirm nor deny police action to limit the peasants' rice. . . . It has long been a practice to control the supply of South Vietnam's food, however, to insure that the Vietcong cannot eat excess peasant food." An American working in the province said, "You might say that Phuqui has been forgotten."

Forgotten it has been, along with hundreds of other villages like it.

The American war in Indochina is a record of war crimes and crimes against humanity, a record of mounting horror. For the reasons noted by Bernard Fall in the early stages of the war,[41] there may well have been no alternative.[42] The war has been directed against the rural population and the land that sustains them. Since 1961–1962 American forces have been directly involved in bombing, strafing, forced population removal of millions of peasants, crop destruction and defoliation, and destruction of agricultural lands and the irrigation system. The land is pock-marked with millions of bomb craters. Lumber operations are impossible in forests where trees are riddled with shell fragments. Some six and a half million acres have been defoliated with chemical poisons, often applied at tremendous concentrations. Included are perhaps a half-million acres of crop-growing land. South Vietnam, once a major rice exporter, is now importing enormous quantities of food, according to Vietnamese sources.[43] About one acre in six has been sprayed by defoliants. In many areas, there are no signs of recovery. Crop destruction is done largely with an arsenical compound which may remain in the soil for years and is not cleared for use on crops in the United States. A contaminant in the herbicides, dioxin, is known to be a highly potent agent causing birth defects in mammals. Through 1969, a half-million acres of forest had been destroyed by giant tractors with Rome plow blades, widely used in other areas as well. These areas are scraped bare. Nothing may grow again. Arthur Westing, a biologist, former marine officer, and director of the Herbicide Assessment Commission of the American Association for the Advancement of Science, writes that "we may well be altering drastically and detrimentally the ecology of vast acreages of South Vietnam."[44] "These vegetational wastelands will remain one of the legacies of our presence for decades to come"[45]—perhaps permanently.

The effects of these policies on the population can be easily imagined. Hunger and starvation from crop destruction and forced population removal have been noted since 1961.[46] Millions of people had been removed—often by force—into controlled areas, by the early 1960s. After 1965, air and artillery bombardment and ground sweeps accounted for the overwhelming majority of the refugees.

In South Vietnam, perhaps half the population has been killed, maimed, or driven from their homes. In Laos, perhaps a quarter of the population of about three million are refugees. Another third live under some of the most intense bombardment in history. Refugees report that they lived in caves and tunnels, under bombing so intensive that not even a dog could cross a path without being attacked by an American jet. Whole villages were moved repeatedly into tunnels deeper and deeper in the forest as the scope of the bombing was extended. The fertile Plain of Jars in northern Laos was finally cleared and turned into a free-fire zone. These refugees, incidentally, report that they rarely saw NVA troops and that Pathet Lao soldiers were rarely to be found in the villages. The areas in question are far from South Vietnam or the "Ho Chi Minh Trail." In Cambodia, the Kennedy subcommittee estimated that by September 1970—after four months of regular bombardment—there were about a million refugees out of a population of about six million. The intensive bombardment also has been reported by captured correspondents. According to Richard Dudman's direct observations in captivity, "the bombing and shooting was radicalizing the people of rural Cambodia and was turning the countryside into a massive, dedicated, and effective revolutionary base."[47] As elsewhere in Indochina, this is both a consequence and a cause of the American bombardment.

On April 21, 1971, Representative Paul McCloskey, just returned from Indochina, testified before the Kennedy subcommittee that an air force lieutenant colonel at Udorn Air Force Base in Thailand said that "there just aren't any villages in Northern Laos anymore, or in southern North Viet Nam either, for that matter." Government reports, secret until unearthed with great effort by McCloskey, confirm the overwhelming evidence of refugee reports concerning the virtual destruction of large areas of rural Laos controlled by the Pathet Lao.[48]

Much the same is true in Vietnam. McCloskey quotes a top Civil Operations and Revolutionary Development Support (CORDS) official who informed him, in Vietnam a year ago, "that in a single province, Quang Nam, American and allied forces had destroyed and razed 307 of the original 555 hamlets of the province." He adds, "I was flown over square mile after square mile where every village, home, and treeline had been burned to the ground; this was part of a rice denial and search and destroy program admittedly based on the need to deny the Vietcong the ability to obtain food, hospitalization, cover and concealment which the villages would otherwise afford."[49]

The *United States Army Field Manual* permits measures to "destroy, through chemical or bacterial agents harmless to man, crops intended solely for consumption by the armed forces (if that fact can be determined)."[50] Yet the descriptions of crop destruction cited above, and those of the AAAS Herbicide Assessment Commission, suggest that nearly all the food destroyed would have been consumed by civilians. It should be remembered that Goering was convicted at Nuremberg for crimes against humanity in part because of orders requiring diversion of food from occupied territories to German needs, and that the United States in Tokyo also supported prosecution of Japanese military officials for crop destruction in China.[51]

The province that McCloskey described, Quang Nam, is the subject of a book by the former senior AID official there, William Nighswonger.[52] He explains that "the battle for Quang Nam was lost by the government to Viet-Cong forces recruited for the most part from within the province." A major reason for their success was "the progressive social and economic results" shown by their programs. As elsewhere in Indochina, it was the success of the Communist-led forces in gaining popular support through successful programs[53] that led to the American effort to destroy the rural society in which the revolution was rooted.

Robert Shaplen concludes that "the war's overall effects on the Vietnamese have been cataclysmically destructive, not only in physical terms but psychologically and socially."[54] Furthermore, these effects are overwhelmingly attributable to American firepower and tactics. Unless one assumes a high degree of idiocy on the part of the American command and the civilian leadership in Washington, it is necessary to suppose that something of the sort was anticipated when these tactics were designed. Furthermore, there is mounting evidence, some of it just cited, that the probable effects were understood in advance, and were even intended. Finally, it is important to bear in mind that these tactics, though sharply intensified in 1965 and again in 1968, can be traced back to the early 1960s. In fact the Diem regime, installed and kept in power by the United States, initiated a virtual war on peasant supporters of the Viet Minh in the mid-1950s.[55]

In the face of such evidence, which has by now been recorded at great length in many easily accessible sources, it requires a real act of faith to doubt that the American command and the civilian authorities are responsible for war crimes and crimes against humanity in the sense of Nuremberg. In fact, it is difficult to understand the surprise or concern over My Lai, considering the relative triviality of this incident in the context of the over-all American policies in Indochina.

Taylor observes, correctly and appropriately, that "the war, in the massive, lethal dimensions it acquired after 1964, was

the work of highly educated academics and administrators"—
the Kennedy advisers, Rusk, McNamara, Bundy, Rostow, who
stayed on with President Johnson and "who must bear major
responsibility for the war and the course it took" (p. 205).
The same is true of the war in the years 1961–1964, with its
lethal effects—small, to be sure, compared with what was to
come, but nonetheless hardly acceptable by civilized standards.

Discussion of American war crimes in Vietnam is often
sharply criticized as dishonest, or even as a form of self-hatred,
if not "balanced" by an account of the crimes of the "enemy."
Such criticism is at best thoughtless and at worst hypocritical.
Not only has the criminal violence of the United States in
Vietnam (and throughout Indochina) been far greater in
scale than anything attributable to any Indochinese forces, but
it is also in an entirely different category from a moral as well
as legal point of view for the obvious reason that it is foreign
in origin. How would we respond to the claim that discussion
of the acts of the fascist aggressors in World War II must be
"balanced" by an account of the terrorism of the resistance in
occupied countries?[56] Furthermore, such critics rarely note
that if the crimes of all participants are to be discussed in a
balanced manner, then it is also necessary to detail the crimes
of the Korean and other Asian mercenaries employed by the
United States and, more important still, the criminal violence
of the regime instituted and protected by United States force.
Its terroristic attack on the people of South Vietnam long
preceded and also always outweighed by a considerable margin the terrorism of its Vietnamese antagonists.[57] Equally
thoughtless, or hypocritical, is the opinion commonly expressed by critics of the United States intervention who say
that the American command has descended to the level of the
Communists. There can be no doubt that the savagery and
barbarism of the American attack on the population of South
Vietnam is entirely without parallel in this miserable conflict.[58]

The one example that is repeatedly cited in an effort to
prove the contrary is the massacre that took place in Hue
during the Tet offensive of February 1968. Let us put aside
the fact that it occurred in a region that had already been
devastated by United States military force, from early 1965,
and consider the massacre itself, which in the United States

and England has become notorious as the classic example of a Communist bloodbath. Don Oberdorfer describes this as "the most extensive political slaughter of the war."[59] Estimates of the scale of the Communist massacre range from 200 (police chief of Hue) to 2,800 (Oberdorfer, based on data from Douglas Pike whom he regards, surprisingly, as a reliable source). Len Ackland, an IVS worker in Hue in 1967 who returned in April 1968 to investigate, was informed by American and Vietnamese officials that about 700 Vietnamese were killed by the Viet Cong, an estimate generally supported by his detailed investigations, which also indicate that the killings were by local NLF forces and primarily during the last days of the bloody month-long battle as these forces were retreating.[60] Whatever the exact numbers may be, there is no doubt that a brutal massacre took place.

There was also another slaughter in Hue at the same time, scarcely mentioned by Oberdorfer[61] and forgotten or passed over in silence by most others. The same officials who reported 700 killed by the Viet Cong estimated that 3,000 to 4,000 civilians had been killed in the United States–GVN bombing and shelling. Undersecretary of the Air Force Townsend Hoopes reports that 2,000 civilians were buried in the rubble of the bombardment. The NLF reported that 2,000 victims of the bombardment were buried in mass graves. (Oberdorfer reports that "2800 victims of the occupation" were discovered in mass graves—it may, perhaps, be doubted that when these graves were discovered many months later it was determined by careful autopsy that these were victims of the Communist "political slaughter.") The marines, according to Oberdorfer, list "Communist losses" at more than 5,000, while Hoopes states that a "sizable part" of the Communist force of 1,000 men who had captured the city escaped. A French priest from Hue estimates that about 1,100, mostly students, teachers, and priests, were killed by the GVN after the United States Marines had recaptured the city.[62] Richard West, who was in Hue shortly after the battle, estimates "several hundred Vietnamese and a handful of foreigners" killed by Communists and suggests that victims of My Lai–style massacres may be among those buried in the mass graves.[63] British photographer-journalist Philip Jones Griffiths concludes that most of the victims "were killed by the most hysterical use of American firepower ever seen," and then designated "as the victims of a Communist massacre."[64]

Even if the United States government propaganda that is widely accepted as fact in the English-speaking countries were true and told the whole story, the Communist massacre at Hue would be a minor event in the context of the American slaughter of the people of South Vietnam. When the full range of facts is considered, however, it appears that the Hue massacre is attributable in large part, and perhaps predominantly, to the American military. This is not surprising, in view of the relative scale of the means of violence available to the contending forces.

It remains to discuss two essential points: first, the argument that the American actions were permitted by "military necessity," and second, the claim that United States intervention was justified in collective self-defense against armed attack, under article 51 of the United Nations Charter. Taylor discusses both of these matters, but in what seems to me an unsatisfactory way.

III. MILITARY NECESSITY

In a sense, it is correct that the American policy of "no villages, no guerrillas" was based on military necessity. American planners were well aware of the enormous popular support for the Communist-led resistance forces, the so-called "Viet Cong," and the lack of any significant popular base for the government (see p. 216 above). Furthermore, there is no great secret as to why the Viet Cong were so successful in gaining popular support.[65]

The field operations coordinator of the United States Operations Mission, John Paul Vann, circulated a report[66] in 1965 on how the war should be fought. His premises were that a social revolution was in process in South Vietnam, "primarily identified with the National Liberation Front," and that "a popular political base for the Government of South Vietnam does not now exist." "The dissatisfaction of the agrarian population . . . today is largely expressed through alliance with the NLF," he wrote. "The existing government is oriented toward the exploitation of the rural and lower class urban populations." Since it is "naive," he explained, to expect that "an unsophisticated, relatively illiterate, rural population [will] recognize and oppose the evils of Communism," the United States must institute "effective political indoctrination of the population" under an American-maintained "autocratic government." The document opposes mere reliance on gadgetry, air power, and artillery, and rejects the expressed view of a United States officer who stated that "if these people want to stay there and support the Communists, then they can expect to be bombed." The report is based on the further assumption that the social revolution is "not incompatible" with United States aims, but that "the aspirations of the majority" can only be realized "through a non-Communist government." According to Vann, the United States should be the judge of what would be "best" for the unsophisticated peasants of Vietnam. The United States, he argued, must impose "a benevolently inclined autocracy or dictatorship . . . while laying the foundation for a democratically oriented [government]." Vann's report expresses the benevolent face of imperialism. It is outspoken in its colonialist assumptions. From Taylor's few remarks on the subject, one might surmise that he would agree with Vann's proposals and leading assumptions.

As already noted, Taylor accepts the legitimacy of the effort to "gain and hold the political allegiance of the South Vietnamese to a non-Communist government" (p. 189), while doubting the possibility of doing so. He regards faulty judgment and overreliance on military means as the primary defects of American policy (pp. 188–9). He accuses United States authorities of "under-maintenance": too much bombing and not enough concentration on the "civil half" (pp. 196–202). He raises no objection to the direct use of force in the early 1960s or to the support of large-scale terror in the late 1950s in the interest of maintaining the regime that the United States had installed.[67] Nowhere does he raise the fundamental question: Is it legitimate for the United States to use its power to impose a particular social and political order on some foreign land, supposing that it can do so within the limits of "proportionality" of force applied?

Failure to raise this question makes Taylor's discussion of "causation" quite unsatisfactory. He rejects the view, attributed to unnamed critics, that "things [went] so wrong . . . because our leaders were war criminals." This "is an unsatisfactory answer in terms of causation, for it assumes that the leaders wanted things to turn out as they have, whereas in fact it is plain that those responsible are exceedingly dissatisfied with the present consequences of their policies." Both the criticism and Taylor's rejection of it are intelligible only on the assumption that questions of legitimacy of intent do not arise in the case of the American leadership. If we regard the intentions of the American leadership as criminal, then it would be correct—indeed, virtually tautological—to say that things went wrong (that is, criminal acts were undertaken) because our leaders were war criminals. On this assumption, it would be irrelevant to remark that things did not turn out as they hoped. Thus no one would argue that the defendants at Nuremberg should have been acquitted merely because they too were "dissatisfied with the consequences of their policies."

In referring to "things go[ing] so wrong," Taylor seems to have in mind "the avalanche of death and destruction" that destroyed the credibility of "whatever peace-keeping and protective intentions may have governed our initial involvement in Vietnam." In Taylor's view, the evidence "strongly indicate[s] that there was a misfit between ends and means; that the military leaders never grasped the essentially political aims of intervention, and the political leaders neglected or were unable to police the means that the military adopted to fulfill what they conceived to be their mission." Instead of pursuing "our stated policy," namely, "to gain and hold the political allegiance of the South Vietnamese to a non-Communist government, while giving them defensive assistance against any military means used by the North," our leaders chose to "ignore the South Vietnamese people, treat South Vietnam as a battlefield, and kill all the North Vietnamese or Vietcong found on or moving toward the battlefield"—and in fact, to treat the rural population of South Vietnam in much the same way. "The sad story of America's venture in Vietnam is that the military means rapidly submerged the political ends.

. . . " We were "prone to shatter what we try to save" (pp. 188–9, 207).

Whether "our stated policy" could have been successfully followed "is and will remain an unanswered question," Taylor observes. Whether "our stated policy" was legitimate in the first place and should have been undertaken at all is a question that is not only unanswered but unasked. But surely this is the fundamental question.

Taylor expresses a very common view when he criticizes American policy because we destroyed the country in order to save it, in the phrase of the unhappy American air force major who was responsible for the destruction of Ben Tre during the Tet offensive. The true "American tragedy"—a potential tragedy for many others, in a far more real sense—is, in my opinion, our continued inability to apply to ourselves the standards that we properly use in evaluating the behavior of other powers. If Americans had the moral courage to do so, they would ask themselves for whom they were "saving" Vietnam, and whether they had a right to intervene to "save" it. They would perceive that the American intervention should be described as a war against the rural society of South Vietnam, not an effort to save it for anyone except collaborationist leaders and such marginal political forces as they could rally. Ultimately, the American leadership was saving Vietnam for its own global interests. The interests of the Vietnamese people amounted to 10 percent of the American objective, in the calculation of Assistant Secretary of Defense John McNaughton, as revealed in the Pentagon Papers (the other 90 percent is an amalgam of fantasy and self-delusion, as he expresses American aims—cf. chapter 1, note 195). What American aims really were is a matter of legitimate debate (for my views, see chapter 1, section V). But it is hardly a matter of debate that the needs and interests of the Vietnamese people counted for as little as the legal prohibition against the threat or use of force in international affairs.

Had the American political leadership been concerned with the needs and interests of the people of South Vietnam or with the solemn treaty obligations of the United States, they would not have undertaken the "stated policy" of imposing a noncommunist government and defending it from its own population through 1964, and invading South Vietnam to destroy the indigenous resistance in later years. The Pentagon Papers make it quite clear that the American political leadership undertook its attack on the rural society of South Vietnam with eyes open. The Vann memorandum cited above, and much other evidence, reveals that the same was true of those who were implementing the policy laid down in Washington.

Taylor believes that some of the American failures in Vietnam can be traced to the fact that "the armed services no longer possess leaders of stature and influence comparable to the heroes of the Second World War" (p. 201). This is an unfair criticism. The difference between World War II and Vietnam has to do with the character of the wars, not the character of the military commanders. The military in both wars was entrusted with implementation of the policies laid down by the civilian leadership. In the case of Vietnam, this was the policy of "gain[ing] and hold[ing] the political allegiance of the South Vietnamese to a non-Communist government." To implement this policy effectively, the military command was compelled to abandon the benevolent imperialist pose and to destroy the rural society, the social base of the revolution. The civilian leadership was well aware of what was taking place and made no effort to change policy.

Ambassador Robert W. Komer, chief pacification adviser to the GVN in 1967–1968, explains that "U.S. military intervention had averted final collapse of the coup-ridden GVN and had created a favorable military environment in which the largely political competition for control and support of the key rural population could begin again."[68] The United States escalation overcame the difficulty that there was "little GVN administration . . . outside Saigon," and made it possible ultimately to initiate the "comprehensive" and "massive" 1967–1970 pacification program in an effort to cope with what was clearly "a revolutionary, largely political conflict."[69] Despite the qualms of the benevolent imperialists such as Vann, it is difficult to see how this aim could have been achieved except through the means employed, namely, what Komer describes as "massive U.S. military intervention at horrendous cost."[70]

In this sense, it can be argued that the horrendous cost of the American military intervention—including defoliation, forced population removal, bombing, harassment and interdiction, free-fire zones, antipersonnel weapons, the Phoenix program of assassination and terror,[71] the torture of prisoners to gain information—was a military necessity, and thus no crime if military necessity justifies departure from the language of international agreements. All of this is arguable given the essential premise that the United States was justified in intervening by force in this "revolutionary, largely political conflict" to guarantee the rule of the regime it had originally imposed in 1954 and its successors—the rule of the landholding and urban elite, the military officers, and the Northern Catholics who provided the social base for a regime that was clearly incapable of holding out on its own against a domestic insurgency.

The question whether this premise is valid arises in its sharpest form in the pre-1965 period with which Taylor does not concern himself. By 1965, as Vann noted,[72] these questions of principle were largely irrelevant. After the "large scale participation by U.S. ground forces," he wrote, "it is almost inconceivable that the United States will withdraw from Vietnam short of a military victory or a negotiated settlement that assures the autonomy of South Vietnam."[73] The same view was held by civilians close to the administration, including some who were later to become outspoken doves. Thus Richard Goodwin wrote in 1966 that continued American combat was justified by "the bedrock vital interest of the United States" which must serve as the "single standard" for policy formation, namely, "to establish that American military power, once committed to defend another nation,[74] cannot be driven from the field."[75]

Even today, it is well understood by the American command that military force must be used to destroy the political movement that the Saigon regime has never been able to defeat politically. A special intelligence survey ordered by General John H. Cushman, the top American official in the

Mekong Delta, warns that the enemy is expanding his political network and "reverting to a political-struggle phase."[76] William Colby adds that "we need to prevent the enemy from putting in this network, because that will permit the Communists to revive later on."[77] Once again, given the premise that the United States has the right to intervene to impose the regime of its choice, "military necessity" could justify the continued use of overwhelming military force against the Vietnamese, the Laotians, and the rural Cambodians as well.

It should be added that the premise that American military intervention in other nations' affairs is justified is solidly enshrined in American history. Taylor refers to the American conquest of the Philippines at the turn of the century. Whatever "idealistic" motives McKinley may have professed, the fact is that the United States overcame a domestic popular movement by force and terror, at tremendous cost to the native inhabitants. Seventy years later, the peasantry—three-quarters of the population—still lives under material conditions not very different from those of the Spanish occupation.[78] In Thailand, a postwar effort at parliamentary democracy led by the liberal democrat Pridi Phanomyong was overthrown by a military coup that reinstituted the Japanese collaborator who had declared war on the United States. Substantial and continuing American assistance has supported a terroristic regime that has willingly integrated itself into the American-Japanese Pacific system. Pridi, who had fought with the American OSS against the Japanese during World War II, found his way to China. In Korea in 1945, the United States overthrew an already established popular regime, making use of Japanese troops and collaborators. By 1949 the American command had succeeded in destroying the existing unions, the popular local councils, and all popular indigenous groups, and had instituted a right-wing dictatorship of the wealthy elite and military-police forces—employing ample terror in the process.

Vietnam is exceptional only because these familiar objectives have been so difficult to achieve. The goal in Vietnam remains: to concentrate and control the population, separating it from main force guerrilla units, and to create a dependent economy that adapts itself to the needs and capacities of the industrialized societies of the West (and Japan), under the rule of wealthy collaborators, with a mere pretense of democracy. As to the peasants, one can recall the words of a South Vietnamese writer speaking of the period of French domination: "the peasants [can] grit their teeth and nurse their hatred amidst the paddy fields."[79] And the residents of the miserable urban slums can do the same.

This is in fact the model of national and social development that the benevolent imperialists such as Vann offer to underdeveloped societies, whether they are aware of it or not. It is to achieve such magnificent results as these that they are willing to subject the population of Indochina, allegedly for their own good, to the benefits of American technology, as has been done in Vietnam for the past decade.

IV. AGGRESSION AND COLLECTIVE SELF-DEFENSE

The final matter to be considered is what Taylor describes as the "salient feature" of Nuremberg, namely, the issue of crimes against peace. As Taylor observes, the justification for the American intervention in Vietnam can only be article 51 of the United Nations Charter. Invocation of this article assumes that the United States is engaged in collective self-defense against an armed attack from North Vietnam. There has been extensive discussion of this matter. It is curious that Taylor barely alludes to it and makes no effort to deal with arguments that have been presented repeatedly in legal and historical literature.[80] The fundamental problem in establishing the United States' case is that American military intervention preceded and has always been far more extensive than North Vietnamese involvement. (There is, in addition, a question as to the relative rights of North Vietnamese and Americans to be fighting in South Vietnam, after the unification provisions of the Geneva Agreements were subverted.) To cite one crucial moment, consider early 1965, the point at which Taylor begins to have doubts about the legitimacy of the American involvement. Chester Cooper, who had been directly involved in Southeast Asian affairs since 1954 and was in charge of Asian affairs for the White House under the Johnson administration, wrote:

> Communist strength had increased substantially during the first few months of 1965. By the end of April it was believed that 100,000 Viet Cong irregulars and between 38,-000 and 46,000 main-force enemy troops, including *a full battalion of regular North Vietnamese troops,* were in South Vietnam. Meanwhile American combat forces were moving into South Vietnam at a rapid rate; in late April more than 35,000 American troops had been deployed and by early May the number had increased to 45,000.[81]

The single North Vietnamese battalion of 400 to 500 men was tentatively identified in late April.[82]

In February 1965, the Johnson administration attempted to justify the new escalation with a White Paper, which, Cooper notes, "proved to be a dismal disappointment." The problem was that "the actual findings [regarding North Vietnamese involvement] seemed pretty frail." No regular troops could be identified. As for infiltrators, even if allegedly "known" and "probable" infiltrators were combined, the average southward movement beginning in 1959, when the insurrection was already solidly in progress, was "little more than 9000 per year," which did not "loom very large" as compared with the half-million-man Saigon army and the 23,000 regular American troops deployed. "The information on enemy weapons," he observed, "was even less earth-shaking." The three 75-millimeter recoilless rifles of Chinese Communist origin, forty-six Soviet-made rifles, forty submachine guns, and one automatic pistol of Czech origin that had been captured (and that might have been bought on the open market) did not seem too impressive as compared with over $860 million in military assistance given by the United States to the Saigon government since 1961.[83] In fact, the weapons of Communist origin constituted less than 2½ percent of the captured weapons, as I. F. Stone noted at the time.[84]

As to the infiltrators, the figures seem even less impressive when we recall that so far as is known, these were overwhelmingly South Vietnamese returning to their homes. It is difficult to see why this should be impermissible, after the subversion of the Geneva Agreements and the American and Saigon violations of the Geneva Accords,[85] the Diemist repression, and the renewal of guerrilla war in the South in 1957. Furthermore, Cooper makes no mention of the "infiltration" by the United States into South Vietnam of South Vietnamese trained at American military bases; nor, for that matter, of the saboteur groups and guerrilla teams of South Vietnamese infiltrated to the North since 1956, according to Bernard Fall.[86] Nor, finally, does Cooper mention that American troops had been directly involved in military operations since 1961–1962.

All in all, the case that the United States was merely exercising the inherent right of collective self-defense against an armed attack from North Vietnam is frail indeed. Yet one who defends the legitimacy of the American involvement must go beyond even this and claim that the United States had the right to determine unilaterally that there had been "aggression from the North" and to escalate its already substantial military involvement in South Vietnam, bypassing the stipulations in the United Nations Charter concerning the role of the Security Council in determining the existence of a threat to peace. Unless all of this is accepted, one must conclude that the American military actions are illegal, and themselves constitute aggression—that there was aggression, not from the north, but from the east.

Unfortunately, Taylor has virtually nothing to say about these frequently debated questions. His treatment of the matter of aggression is, in general, unsatisfying. In discussing the allegation that North Vietnam is guilty of aggression in South Vietnam, Taylor points to "strong evidence." "Indisputably, the ground fighting has all taken place in South Vietnam," not in North Vietnam. But, he argues, the case is not clear, since the Geneva Agreements merely established two "zones" and explicitly declared the military demarcation line to be "provisional" and not "a political or territorial boundary" (pp. 101–2). Furthermore, South Vietnam, with United States support, declined to proceed with the scheduled elections. Of course, if it is unclear whether North Vietnam is guilty of aggression, it is correspondingly unclear whether

American military action is justified by article 51, which in fact speaks not of "aggression," but of "armed attack," a narrower category.[87]

Furthermore, the "strong evidence" that Taylor cites and questions cuts other ways as well. Thus, for example, ground fighting has taken place in South Vietnam, not the United States. By Taylor's standards, there is thus "strong evidence" that the United States is guilty of aggression in South Vietnam, particularly since American authorities have admitted that the GVN had little administrative authority outside of Saigon by 1965 (see pp. 232, 236 above). Taylor never considers this question in his discussion of aggressive war.[88] Rather, he states the case for possible American aggression as follows:

> . . . the case . . . is based on the conclusions that both South Vietnam and the United States violated the Geneva Declaration of 1954 by hostile acts against the North, unlawful rearmament, and refusal to carry out the 1956 national elections provided for in the Declaration, and that the United States likewise violated the United Nations Charter by bombing North Vietnam. [Pp. 96–7]

But these charges constitute only part of the case. A much more serious charge is that the United States has engaged in aggressive warfare in South Vietnam in violation of the provisions of the United Nations Charter concerning the use of force. These charges are based on military actions taken against an insurgency that the United States recognized to be popular and successful—far more popular than the government it had installed and maintained, which had lost the war by 1965 despite the absence of any regular North Vietnamese troops. Taylor does not mention these matters, I presume, because of his tacit assumption that the United States had the right to intervene with its ground, helicopter, and air forces in what some American authorities have recognized to be a "revolutionary, largely political conflict" (see p. 236 above).

It might be argued that the stipulations of the United Nations Charter regarding the threat or use of force (specifically, article 2[4]) have been so eroded as to be effectively inoperative. The issue is discussed by Thomas M. Franck in a recent study.[89] He discusses "the changed realities of the postwar quarter-century" that have so shattered the precepts of article 2(4) that "only the words remain." Franck is surely right in arguing that "both super-Powers have succeeded in establishing norms of conduct within their regional organizations which have effectively undermined Article 2(4)," beginning with the insistence by the United States "that a state's sovereignty is subject to the overriding right of a region to demand conformity to regional standards." An example is the United States condemnation of "not intervention by foreign troops but of a 'foreign' ideology," as in the Guatemalan affair of 1954. This was the direct precursor of the Brezhnev doctrine. Franck is also correct in observing that "national self-interest, particularly the national self-interest of the super-Powers, has usually won out over treaty obligations." It might be added that the United States has developed a concept of "regional organization" that incorporates large parts of Southeast Asia in a "regional organization" where it assumes the right to operate freely, and that the violations of article 2(4) can arguably be traced back to the immediate postwar activities of the great powers in securing their spheres of influence. The British and then American interventions in Greece, beginning in 1944, would be particularly significant examples.

Despite his important observations on the behavior of the great powers, Franck's discussion seems to me to be flawed, in several instances, by an implicit bias in favor of these powers. In discussing the "changing nature of warfare" he cites two categories: "wars of agitation, infiltration, and subversion carried on by proxy through national liberation movements," and nuclear wars. With respect to direct violations of article 2(4), it is of course the first category that is of primary concern, notwithstanding the great powers' attempts to disguise their interventions on grounds of a presumed relation to great-power conflict. But Franck's discussion of this category begs the basic question. As he points out later in the same article, "One man's war of national liberation is another's aggression or subversion, and vice versa." A bias is revealed in that he generally takes the position of the second man: the new kinds of warfare which, he argues, have led to the erosion of article 2(4) are characterized as wars of infiltration and subversion carried on by proxy. If, taking the contrary view, these should be characterized as imperial interventions to repress movements of national liberation, then it follows that the erosion of article 2(4) has not been caused by the "changing realities of the postwar quarter-century," but primarily by the postwar forms of the traditional behavior of great powers. By begging the question in the particular way he does, Franck seems to take his stand, without argument or even explicit assertion, on the side of the great powers. This bias is only partially mitigated by his later references to a third factor in the erosion of article 2(4), namely, "the increased authoritarianism of regional systems dominated by a super-Power," and by his extensive discussion of the role of the great powers in undermining article 2(4) by continual intervention within their respective "regional organizations."

A similar bias appears when Franck refers to the "significant support" given to indigenous Communist insurgents by China in Laos and South Vietnam, for example. As his further comments indicate, the available evidence suggests that Chinese aid has always been small as compared with that given by the United States and its allies to the right-wing forces. Franck's reference to propaganda as a form of intervention hardly applies in this case. China's position has generally been that wars of national liberation must be indigenous and cannot rely on China for substantive material support. Incidentally, so far as is known, the only Chinese troops fighting in the Indochina war are the Chinese Nationalist troops employed by the United States, particularly in clandestine operations in Laos.

The same questions are begged when Franck asserts that "the small-scale and diffuse but significant and frequent new wars of insurgency have, by their nature, made clearcut distinctions between aggression and self-defense . . . exceedingly difficult." Thus he points out that it strains credulity "to be told that Poland had attacked Germany or South Korea the North," but in the case of wars of national liberation, "it is often difficult even to establish convincingly" who is the aggressor. He might have used a different analogy. It would strain credulity to be told that Hungary attacked the Soviet Union in 1956, or that the Philippines attacked the United States at the turn of the century, or that the American colonies attacked England in 1776. If one takes the view that wars of national liberation and great-power interventions constitute a continuation of the classic pattern, to be sure with certain modifications, then these are more appropriate analogies, and there is nothing strikingly new about the postwar period.

As to the outside support for wars of national liberation, recall the vast support given by the French to the American colonies in the Revolutionary War.

> There is no question but that the American Revolutionary War, when considered as a "normal" insurgency, entirely fits the bill of the many revolutionary wars which afflict the middle of the twentieth century. Shorn of almost two centuries of 4th-of-July oratory, it was a military operation fought by a very small armed minority—at almost no time did Washington's forces exceed 8,000 men in a country which had at least 300,000 able-bodied males—and backed by a force of 31,897 French ground troops, and 12,660 sailors and Marines manning sixty-one major vessels.[90]

Even compensating for the effect of Fourth-of-July oratory, we would have no difficulty in evaluating the bias of a contemporary British writer who referred to the American Revolution, in Franck's terms, as a war of agitation, infiltration, and subversion carried on by proxy through a national liberation movement. Taking Fall's point of view, which I believe to be much closer to accuracy than the position implicit in the parts of Franck's discussion cited here, we must conclude that there is no strikingly new factor in the postwar era that led to the erosion of article 2(4). Rather, one must agree with U Thant, I believe, when he says, in words that Franck quotes: "In the final analysis there can be no solid foundation for peace in the world so long as the super-Powers insist on taking unilateral military action whenever they claim to see a threat to their security"[91]—or, we may add, a threat to the perceived self-interest of dominant social groups.

While it is beyond question that what remains of article 2(4) is "only the words," there seems no reason to suppose that this is any change from earlier norms or that it is a consequence of changes in world affairs that could not have been foreseen by the framers of the United Nations Charter. There is, furthermore, no reason to conclude that the precepts of article 2(4) should not be considered applicable. Of course, these precepts suffer from the absence of an enforcing authority, which is a general defect of international law.

The question of the right of intervention and the threat or use of force by the great powers to impose social and political arrangements in developing countries should be at the forefront of any investigation of Vietnam, whether in the light of Nuremberg or in a broader historical context. By failing even to raise such questions, Taylor considerably reduces the significance of his discussion, it seems to me. For future policy decisions, these are surely the major issues. In a dozen places in the world the United States is providing military support to regimes that are attempting to suppress internal insurgency, in ways that might lead to direct military intervention.[92] It can be plausibly argued that in Greece it is the American military support for the colonels that prevents a popular insurgency. In much of Latin America, the same is true.

> Almost all Latin American regimes can now suppress rural insurrections of willful foes. Because of a number of factors, none is as weak as Fulgencio Batista's government of the 1950s. U.S. AID's Public Safety Division has trained police as a first line of defense against terrorism in at least 14 republics; armies are better equipped as $1.75 billion in U.S. military aid has poured into the Americas; upward of 20,000 latino officers and enlisted men have trained at Ft. Gulick in the Canal Zone, and now available are new antiguerrilla weapons developed in Vietnam, which run the gamut from specially designed helicopters to body smellers.[93]

These remarks recall the observation of General Maxwell Taylor in 1963 that in Vietnam "we have a going laboratory where we see subversive insurgency . . . being applied in all its forms." The Pentagon, recognizing "the importance of the area as a laboratory," had already sent "teams out there looking at the equipment requirements of this kind of guerrilla warfare."[94] There is considerable evidence, in fact, that the United States has exploited Vietnam as a laboratory for counterinsurgency, testing weapons and tactics for the wars it anticipates in much the same way that other powers used Spain in 1936–1939.[95]

Among the Latin American regimes that are using the

technology designed in the Vietnam laboratory for countering insurgency, there are several that owe their existence to interference from the United States. In Guatemala, a promising reform-minded regime was overthrown by United States subversion in 1954. For the past several years, in the course of an anticommunist extermination campaign, there has been a virtual bloodbath, as some 4,000 peasants were killed indiscriminately with weapons supplied by the American military aid program.[96] Donald Robinson reports that he observed a Special Operations Force team training Guatemalan Air Force men to use newly designed Bell helicopters to pursue guerrillas.[97] It is even possible that there was still more direct United States military involvement. Vice President Marroquin Rojas claimed several years ago that American planes based in Panama were conducting raids in Guatemala, using napalm in areas suspected of harboring guerrillas,[98] and returning to their Panamanian bases. Missionaries working in Guatemala report that they have seen the results of napalm raids.

The extent of American involvement in counterrevolutionary warfare in the postwar period cannot be realistically estimated. There is enough information available to indicate that it is very great. While the United States is surely not alone in undertaking forceful intervention in the internal affairs of other nations, no other power in the postwar period has employed even a fraction of the military force used by the United States in its efforts to destroy indigenous forces to which it has been opposed in other lands.

It is this general policy of counterrevolutionary intervention, raised almost to the level of a national ideology during the Kennedy administration and inherent in Henry Kissinger's doctrine of "limited wars,"[99] which must be reconsidered if we are to be serious about an inquiry into national policy or into the general issues of legality and justice raised and sometimes skirted at Nuremberg, approached but rarely faced directly in treaties and international agreements, and forced upon the consciousness of any civilized person by the tragedy of Vietnam.

Notes

This essay is a revised version of a contribution to a symposium on war
crimes, based on Telford Taylor, *Nuremberg and Vietnam: An
American Tragedy.* The original version was published in the *Yale
Law Journal,* vol. 80, no. 7 (June 1971).

1 Telford Taylor, *Nuremberg and Vietnam: An American Tragedy,* p. 29.
Subsequent references to this book will be by page number only.

2 Whether Taylor is aware of the extent of American bombing in North
Vietnam is unclear. Other commentators are not. For example, Neil
Sheehan wrote: "Although the North Vietnamese may not believe
it, in the North a conscious effort was made to bomb only military,
and what limited industrial targets were available, and to weigh
probable civilian casualties against the military advantages to be
gained . . ." ("Should We Have War Crimes Trials?" *New York
Times,* March 28, 1971). The thirty-three books which Sheehan
reviews in this piece contain much evidence to the contrary, and
Sheehan does not explain why he discounts that evidence. From my
own limited observations in the neighborhood of Hanoi, I join the
North Vietnamese in "not believing it." Nor do I think that
Sheehan would "believe it" if he were to walk through the ruins of
Phu Ly or Thanh Hoa, let alone the much more heavily bombed
areas farther from Hanoi. Nevertheless, the bombing of North Viet-
nam, despite its enormous scale, has been well below that of South
Vietnam and Laos in intensity and destructiveness.

3 Justice Radhabinod Pal, dissenting at Tokyo, argued that the dropping
of the atom bomb was a criminal act exceeding any charged against
those accused at the Tokyo trials. *International Military Tribunal
for the Far East* (Calcutta: Sanyal & Co., 1953), p. 621. The
relevant passages are cited in my *American Power and the New
Mandarins,* pp. 168–9. Pal did not, however, suggest prosecution for
the decision to use the atom bombs. Taylor believes that the Naga-
saki bombing, at least, can be considered a war crime (p. 143).

4 P. 79; United Nations, General Assembly, *Report of the International
Law Commission,* Suppl. 12 (A/1316), 1950, p. 11, reprinted in
Herbert W. Briggs, ed., *The Law of Nations: Cases, Documents
and Notes,* 2nd ed. (New York: Appleton-Century-Crofts, 1952).

5 One might raise the question whether the Nuremberg and United
Nations charters are equivalent in status. I will not pursue the
question here. But it does seem to me, as argued below, that there is
a powerful case that the United States has grossly violated both in
Indochina.

The recent release of the Pentagon Papers would appear to go a
long way towards overcoming the difficulty regarding "evidentiary
problems" that Taylor cites and, in my opinion, greatly overesti-
mates. One of the interesting features of these documents is how
well they corroborate the interpretations of American policy in

Indochina that appear, for example, in Franz Schurmann *et al., The Politics of Escalation in Vietnam.* The documentary record shows that the publicly available evidence was sufficient to determine the main lines of American policy. These documents would appear to provide direct evidence of a conspiracy to wage an expanding war of aggression and to violate the provisions of the United Nations Charter regarding pacific settlement of disputes. See chapter 1.

6 Whether Taylor still accepts this assessment is not entirely clear.

7 The United States formally submitted the Vietnam question to the Security Council only in January 1966 (United Nations, Security Council, *Official Records,* vol. 21, suppl. January–March [S/7105], 1966, p. 105). Prior to that, the United States asked the council to consider the (alleged) Tonkin Gulf incident in August 1964 (*Official Records,* vol. 19, suppl. July–September [S/5849], 1964, p. 135), and submitted reports in February 1965 (*Official Records,* vol. 20, suppl. January–March [S/6174], 1965, p. 43) after the sharp escalation of American bombing in South and North Vietnam. See "The Legality of U.S. Participation in the Defense of Viet-Nam," *U.S. Department of State Bulletin,* vol. 54 (1966), reprinted in Richard A. Falk, ed., *The Vietnam War and International Law,* pp. 583, 590 (henceforth cited as *Falk—Vietnam*). Direct United States military engagement began in 1961–1962.

8 Richard A. Falk, "International Law and the United States Role in Viet Nam: A Response to Professor Moore," *Yale Law Journal,* vol. 76 (1967), pp. 1051, 1130 n. 80, reprinted in *Falk—Vietnam,* pp. 445, 480 n. 80.

9 Thomas J. Farer, "Intervention in Civil Wars: A Modest Proposal," *Columbia Law Review,* vol. 67 (1967), pp. 266, 271, reprinted in *Falk—Vietnam,* pp. 509, 514.

10 Robert Scigliano, *South Vietnam,* p. 145. Scigliano was a member of the Michigan State University Vietnam Advisory Group.

11 See, for example, George McT. Kahin and John W. Lewis, *The United States in Vietnam,* p. 137.

12 Bernard Fall, *Street Without Joy,* p. 346.

13 *New York Times,* March 10, 1962; October 17, 1962. The 30 percent figure excludes helicopter flights. By the beginning of 1964, the United States had 248 helicopters in Vietnam; by the end of the year, there were 327. See V. S. G. Sharp and W. C. Westmoreland, *Report on the War in Vietnam (As of 30 June 1968),* p. 85 (1968). By comparison, the French never had more than ten operational helicopters in Indochina until April 1954 (Fall, *Street Without Joy,* p. 242).

14 Robert Shaplen, *The Lost Revolution,* pp. 170 ff. No North Vietnamese were discovered in the delta until 1968. American bombing of civilians in the Camau Peninsula in the early 1960s has been confirmed by Colonel Fletcher Prouty (retired), who served at the time in liaison between the CIA and the air force ("Review of the War," WNET-TV, Channel 13, New York, February 15, 1971). American airstrikes on villages in the early 1960s have been confirmed by reporters. Malcolm Browne (AP correspondent in Vietnam from 1961) described visits to hamlets that had been hit by napalm and heavy bombs in American airstrikes; "there is no question that the results are revolting. Unfortunately, the Viet Cong

builds bunkers so skillfully it is rarely touched by aerial bombs or napalm, except in cases of direct hits. But huts are flattened, and civilian loss of life is generally high. In some, the charred bodies of children and babies have made pathetic piles in the middle of the remains of market places" (*The New Face of War*, p. 118). Obviously, this was known to the American command and civilian leadership. To cite only the most obvious evidence, the introduction to Browne's book is written by Henry Cabot Lodge, then between two terms as United States Ambassador to Vietnam. It should be noted that the Tokyo Tribunal judged cabinet members responsible for war crimes in connection with the treatment of prisoners if, having knowledge of them, they did not resign. See Erwin Knoll and Judith N. McFadden, eds., *War Crimes and the American Conscience*, p. 195, for relevant excerpts from the tribunal.

15 Richard Tregaskis, *Vietnam Diary*, p. 108.

16 Donald Robinson, "America's Air Guerrillas—Will They Stop Future Vietnams?" *Parade*, supplement to *Boston Sunday Globe*, January 31, 1971. It was the SOF, according to this account, that conducted the raid against an abandoned prisoner-of-war camp near Son Tay in North Vietnam, in November 1970.

17 Even Douglas Pike, who is often hardly more than a propagandist for the American government, admits that the NLF constituted the only "mass-based political party in South Vietnam" and that in late 1964, it was impossible for the American-supported government to consider a coalition with the NLF, for fear that "the whale would swallow the minnow" (*Viet Cong*, pp. 110, 361–2). Elsewhere, Pike has estimated that in 1963, "perhaps half the population of South Vietnam at least tacitly supported the NLF" (*War, Peace, and the Viet Cong*, p. 6). See also p. 216 above. It is, of course, not very difficult for a great power to establish a government that will applaud its intervention. For example, the 14th Congress of the Czechoslovak Communist Party, the first "officially recognized" Congress since 1966, opened with "applause and cheers" for the Russian invasion of 1968 (*Boston Globe*, Reuters, May 26, 1971).

18 I refer, in this instance, to the United States–supported refusal of the regime it had instituted in South Vietnam to adhere to the election provision of the Geneva Agreements of 1954. Similarly, in Laos, when the Pathet Lao won an unexpected victory in the election of 1958 (after substantial American efforts to buy the election for the right), the United States played a major role in the overthrow of the coalition government. See Len Ackland, "No Place for Neutralism: The Eisenhower Administration and Laos," in Nina S. Adams and Alfred W. McCoy, eds., *Laos: War and Revolution*; Jonathan Mirsky and Stephen Stonefield, "The United States in Laos," in Edward Friedman and Mark Selden, eds., *America's Asia*, pp. 253–323. See also chapter 2, section I.

19 Whether it is "certainly the law" is open to question.

20 Cited by Leo Goodstadt, "Might and Right," *Far Eastern Economic Review*, April 10, 1971, p. 22. Goodstadt observes that "physical force was always a second-best choice for Mao."

21 Pike, *Viet Cong*, pp. 91–2. Pike later observed that "armed combat was a GVN-imposed requirement; the NLF was obliged to use counterforce to survive" (p. 101).

22 Truong Chinh, *La résistance vaincra*, cited in Fall, *Street Without Joy*, pp. 372–3 (excerpt translated by Fall).

23 Fall, *Street Without Joy*, pp. 372–3.

24 On Japan's professedly defensive and idealistic motivations in the 1930s, see the references in chap. 2 of *American Power and the New Mandarins*, pp. 176–7, 179–84, 189–90, 193–202.

25 American innocence in this regard is if anything surpassed by that of our British allies. For example, the anonymous weekly columnist (presumably the editor) of the *Far Eastern Economic Review*, generally a sober journal, writes that "it must be evident to any openminded person that, whatever the effects of America's intervention in Vietnam, the action was taken with the most idealistic of motives and with the best of intentions. . . . [To] claim that the United States is in Vietnam for imperialist reasons . . . is manifest nonsense" (column "Traveller's Tales," *Far Eastern Economic Review*, February 20, 1971). Conceivably one might argue that despite ample evidence to the contrary, the United States is thus unique in world history, but to insist on the certainty of this most dubious judgment is merely a form of hysteria. The columnist also demonstrates the neutrality of the *Review*, as contrasted with "committed" scholars: thus the *Review*, he writes, does not hesitate to "criticize what it regards as mistakes in [American] strategy or policy," or to publish "bitter attacks on Vietcong atrocities." True objectivity. The columnist also prides himself on his "sophistication" for "printing one of the few editorials which attempted to establish a sympathetic understanding for the troops who took part in the massacre at My Lai," failing to note that the American peace movement, which he denounces, had almost universally taken the same position, but without glorying in its sophistication for its ability to distinguish the acts of soldiers in the field from the calculated decisions of planners who are remote from any threat.

26 Fall, *Street Without Joy*, p. 373. Note that this was written in the early 1960s, at a time when Taylor "supported American intervention in Vietnam as an aggression-checking undertaking in the spirit of the United Nations Charter" (p. 206). Three years after this work appeared, Secretary of Defense McNamara testified before Congress that the Viet Cong and the North Vietnamese were "operating . . . without, for all practical purposes, a single wheeled vehicle in all of South Vietnam." See the statement by Senator Proxmire, *Congressional Record*, vol. 177 (April 5, 1971), p. S4585.

27 Fall, *Street Without Joy*, p. 378.

28 Interview in the *Ottawa Citizen*, January 12, 1970. An American working in Quang Ngai hospital estimated in 1967, a year before My Lai, that about 70 percent of the civilian war casualties there were caused by American and allied bombardment—that is, in an area more or less under American control, where victims could reach the town hospital. For quotations and references, see my *American Power and the New Mandarins*, p. 284, and *At War with Asia*, pp. 270–1.

29 *New York Times*, May 25, 1971. The reference is to Ronald L. Ridenhour, the Vietnam veteran who disclosed the incident to the secretary of defense a year after it occurred. The incident has been noted at once by the NLF, along with many other incidents that are

still not acknowledged or discussed. Details were disclosed in Paris on June 15, 1968, but were neglected by the Western media. For a justifiably bitter account, see Erich Wulff, "Le Crime de Song My: Avec les félicitations du commandant en chef," *Africasia* [Paris], April 26–May 9, 1971. Wulff is a West German physician who spent six years in Vietnam and who testified concerning the "new 'Ouradours and Lidices' " before the Russell Tribunal in 1967. His testimony is recorded in "A Doctor Reports from South Vietnam—Testimony by Erich Wulff," in John Duffett, ed., *Against the Crime of Silence*.

30 *New York Times*, April 29, 1971; *Boston Globe*, May 10, 1971. The Dellums Committee Hearings have since been published (1972) by Vintage Books (Citizens' Commission of Inquiry, *The Dellums Committee Hearings on War Crimes in Vietnam*).

31 *Congressional Record*, vol. 177 (1971), pp. E2826–2900. Published by Beacon Press in 1972 (Vietnam Veterans Against the War, eds., *The Winter Soldier Investigation*).

32 *New York Times*, April 26, 1972.

33 Statement of E. Opton, in Knoll and McFadden, *War Crimes*, p. 114.

34 R. W. Apple, "Calley: The Real Guilt," *New Statesman*, April 2, 1971, p. 449. The coercive character of earlier population removal was also well understood by the American command. Sharp and Westmoreland wrote that the first Strategic Hamlet Program in March 1962 "involved forced relocation of rural peasants, notwithstanding their strong attachment to their ancestral plots of land" (*Report on the War in Vietnam*, p. 79). This report consists largely of apologetics and is not, in my opinion, to be taken seriously, unless independently confirmed, except with regard to the details of the American military engagement.

35 Apple, "Calley: The Real Guilt," p. 34.

36 This occasionally heard explanation is plainly absurd, even if we believe its original formulation by Samuel P. Huntington, "The Bases of Accommodation," *Foreign Affairs*, vol. 46, no. 4 (1968). The Huntington article appeared prior to the massive escalation of the American bombing in the countryside of Indochina. But if the effects of millions of tons of bombs and thousands of square miles of defoliation could not have been predicted beforehand, which is difficult enough to believe, it was surely known by mid-1968. The same cynical pretense is maintained by Lieutenant Colonel John Paul Vann (retired), senior United States adviser for "pacification" in South Vietnam (see below, pp. 232–3). He is quoted in *Newsweek* (January 20, 1969) as stating that "we inadvertently stumbled on the solution to guerrilla warfare—urbanization" (cited by L. A. G. Moss and Z. M. Shalizi, "War and Urbanization in Indochina," in Jonathan S. Grant *et al.*, eds., *Cambodia: The Widening War in Indochina*, p. 192).

37 Sheehan, "Should We Have War Crimes Trials?"

38 Cf. note 36 above.

39 Sheehan, "Should We Have War Crimes Trials?"

40 *New York Times*, April 6, 1971. The quotations and most of the cited material comes from this report. The rest is taken from an earlier report by Henry Kamm in the *New York Times*, November 15,

1969, and from a White Paper of the American Friends Service Committee (May 5, 1969), which gives the reports of Vietnamese-speaking field workers on the scene.

41 Fall, *Street Without Joy*.

42 It might be argued that domestic political considerations made it impossible for the president to saturate Vietnam with enough American troops to obviate the need for destructive firepower. Recall, however, that the French never sent conscripts to Vietnam and probably deployed no more than about 70,000 native French troops in all of Indochina. For references on French military strength, see chapter 1, note 4. The American war in Vietnam is unusual, if not unique, in that the public was willing to tolerate, for a time, the deployment of an enormous conscript army to fight what was in essence a colonial war.

43 See note 46 below.

44 Arthur Westing, "Poisoning Plants for Peace," *Friends Journal*, vol. 16 (1970). Figures cited in text come from this article and that cited in note 45 below.

45 Arthur Westing, "Ecocide in Indochina," *Natural History*, March 1971.

46 Ngo Vinh Long, "Leaf Abscission," in Barry Weisberg, ed., *Ecocide in Indochina*, p. 54. Long mentions that crop destruction was used at that time to force the population into strategic hamlets.

In *Thoi-Bao Ga* (a Vietnamese student journal published in Cambridge, Mass.) Long writes that according to the Saigon newspaper *Tin Sang*, November 12, 1970, the chairman of the Committee on Agriculture of the GVN declared that American chemical defoliants had destroyed approximately 60 percent of all crops in South Vietnam. The March 9, 1971 issue of the Saigon daily *Duoc Nha Nam* reports that South Vietnam imported one-half million metric tons of rice from the United States in 1970, enough, in Long's estimate, to feed five million persons. Nevertheless, journalists and others report widespread hunger, even starvation (*Thoi-Bao Ga*, March–April 1971, p. 6).

Bryce Nelson, a *Los Angeles Times* reporter who was formerly a reporter for *Science*, writes that an unreleased report of the AAAS Herbicide Assessment Commission notes the death of ninety people within a four-month period (September to December 1970) from exposure to spraying and drinking water contaminated with herbicides (*Village Voice*, January 28, 1971). A former IVS worker with four years experience in South Vietnam reports "numerous encounters" with farmers in Can Tho and Tay Ninh provinces whose crops were destroyed. He also reports seeing patients in Tay Ninh hospital "with limbs and faces burned mercilessly by phosphorus" and "child after child scarred or disfigured in some hideous way" in hospitals in the Mekong Delta (Letter to the editor from Roger Montgomery, *New York Times*, January 22, 1971). See chapter 1, note 10.

47 Richard Dudman, *Forty Days with the Enemy*, p. 69.

48 See *New York Times*, April 22, 1971; *Boston Globe*, April 16, 1971; *Boston Globe*, April 23, 1971. See also *Congressional Record*, vol. 117 (February 18, 1971), formal testimony of Representative McCloskey, pp. H794–800. See also chapter 2, section I.

[49] *Congressional Record*, vol. 117 (1971), p. H796. Similar reports on Quang Ngai and Quang Tin provinces were given in 1967 before the massive escalation of the air war in 1968 (Jonathan Schell, *The Military Half*).

[50] *The Law of Land Warfare*, Department of the Army Field Manual FM 27–10 (1956), p. 18, par. 37.

[51] Statement by George Bunn, professor of law at the University of Wisconsin and formerly General Counsel, U.S. Arms Control and Disarmament Agency, "The Broad Implications of the Continued Use of Herbicides in Southeast Asia," AAAS Annual Meeting, December 29, 1970. Mimeographed.

[52] William A. Nighswonger, *Rural Pacification in Vietnam*.

[53] For discussion, see Jeffrey Race, "How They Won," *Asian Survey*, August 1970; Robert L. Sansom, *The Economics of Insurgency in the Mekong Delta of Vietnam*. Race was an adviser to a district chief in Long An Province, south of Saigon, while in the United States Army. Sansom is an air force captain and a member of the staff of the National Security Council. Noncommunist reporters who have visited NLF-controlled areas give substantiating evidence. See the report by Jacques Doyon cited in Committee of Concerned Asian Scholars, *The Indochina Story*, p. 36. See also Katsuichi Honda, *The National Liberation Front* and *Vietnam: A Voice from the Villages* (collections of articles by Honda, privately translated and reprinted from the Japanese journal *Asahi Shimbun* in 1967). See also chapter 1, references of note 215. Regarding Pathet Lao programs as seen by refugees, see the verbatim interview in Adams and McCoy, *Laos*, pp. 451–9, and my *At War with Asia*, p. 239. See also Mark Selden, "People's War and the Transformation of Peasant Society," in Selden and Friedman, *America's Asia*; chapter 2, section I, above.

[54] Robert Shaplen, "The Challenge Ahead," *Columbia Journalism Review*, vol. 9, no. 4, 1970–71.

[55] For some discussion and further references, see Edward S. Herman, *Atrocities in Vietnam*, chap. 2. All of this was well understood at the time. See, for example, R. W. Lindholm, ed., *Vietnam: The First Five Years*.

[56] See, for example, the remarks on Chinese nationalist terrorism against collaborators with the Japanese cited in my *Problems of Knowledge and Freedom*, p. 95.

[57] On the resort to violence by the NLF see the comments by Douglas Pike, p. 219 above, and the far more detailed analysis by Jeffrey Race, *War Comes to Long An*.

[58] See Herman, *Atrocities in Vietnam*, for an effort to estimate relative scale.

[59] Don Oberdorfer, *Tet*, p. 201.

[60] Len Ackland, "Hue," unpublished, one of the sources used by Oberdorfer. Predictably, others play the numbers game quite fast and loose. Donald Kirk, a very well informed correspondent, reports that "about 4000 citizens were massacred then before U.S. forces drove the North Vietnamese from the citadel . . . after 28 days of house-to-house fighting," implying that the 4,000 were massacred by the North Vietnamese (*Chicago Tribune*, May 4, 1972). Sir Robert Thompson claims that the Communists executed 5,700 people and

that "in captured documents they gloated over those figures and only complained that they had not killed enough" (*New York Times*, June 15, 1972). No such document has ever been produced, even including the "captured documents" that were mysteriously discovered immediately after the publicity over the My Lai incidents in November 1969, allegedly "mislaid" for a year and a half. Senator William Saxbe will settle for no less than 7,000 murdered by the "North Vietnamese," considerably more than the total number killed from all causes during the fighting (*Congressional Record*, May 3, 1972).

61 Oberdorfer, incidentally, reports "something over a hundred civilians" killed at My Lai, referring as a source to Seymour Hersh, *My Lai 4*, where the number is estimated at about 400 to 500.

62 Oriana Fallaci, "Working Up to Killing," *Washington Monthly*, February 1972.

63 Richard West, *New Statesman*, January 28, 1972.

64 Philip Jones Griffiths, *Vietnam Inc.*, p. 137. Griffiths' book contains pictures of the ongoing fighting in Hue. See my *At War with Asia*, pp. 295–6, and Herman, *Atrocities in Vietnam*, for some discussion and references concerning both massacres, including references not identified above.

65 See note 53 above.

66 This report, untitled in my copy, was given personally by Vann in 1971 to the Australian social psychologist Alex Carey, who has studied in particular the Australian role in Vietnam. See Carey's carefully documented pamphlet, *Australian Atrocities in Vietnam 1–19* (undated pamphlet), which describes what he refers to as "our drift towards the standards of Hitler and the Gestapo."

67 See note 55 above.

68 Robert W. Komer, "Impact of Pacification on Insurgency in South Vietnam," *Journal of International Affairs*, vol. 25, no. 1 (1971). He is referring to the outright American invasion and bombing escalation in the South in February 1965.

69 *Ibid.* Recall the remarks by Richard Falk, p. 216 above, on capacity to govern as an element in claiming political legitimacy.

70 Komer, "Impact of Pacification." These benevolent imperialists, it should be noted, did not dissociate themselves from United States policies despite their reservations even after the grim effects were obvious. See note 14 above.

71 The Phoenix program is "aimed at neutralizing the clandestine Vietcong politico-administrative apparatus, which many regard as the key to their insurgent capabilities" (Komer, "Impact of Pacification"). "Neutralization" is Bureaucratese for "assassination or capture." Estimates as to the numbers "neutralized" vary. Deputy United States Ambassador William E. Colby, principal United States official in charge of pacification, testified before the Senate Foreign Relations Committee that close to 20,000 were "neutralized" in 1969, of whom 6,187 were killed. For comparison, the Saigon government claims that 4,619 civilians were killed by "the enemy" in 1969. The Phoenix program of course accounts for only a small fraction of the civilians killed by combined American-GVN forces. Len Ackland, a former IVS worker in South Vietnam and then a team leader and analyst for RAND, points out that the

Phoenix program is designed to capture or murder civilians: "people who serve the political party, the National Liberation Front, as tax collectors, clerks, postmen, etc." For references and further documentation, see my *At War with Asia*, pp. 301–2; Herman, *Atrocities in Vietnam*, pp. 46–7. See also pp. 91–3, 161 above.

[72] See note 66 above.

[73] The latter phrase is a code term in American political terminology, for rule of South Vietnam by a noncommunist government. The NLF political program of 1962, largely ignored—even suppressed—in the United States, called for the neutralization of South Vietnam, Laos, and Cambodia. One might argue that this was a deception, but it is unclear that the United States has unilateral authority to use military force in acting on its skepticism.

[74] This is another formulation of the inexpressible statement that South Vietnam must be ruled by the American-imposed noncommunist government. Goodwin was well aware, and explains in this book, that the insurgency even at that time was overwhelmingly domestic.

[75] Richard Goodwin, *Triumph or Tragedy*, p. 38. For many other expressions of related views, see the citations and references in my *American Power and the New Mandarins*, particularly chap. 3, "The Logic of Withdrawal," pp. 221–94.

[76] *New York Times*, May 24, 1971.

[77] *Ibid.* See note 71 above (identifying William Colby).

[78] In October 1937 President Manuel Quezon pointed out that while "the rich can live in extravagant luxury . . . the men and women who till the soil or work in the factories are hardly better off now than they were during the Spanish regime. . . . thirty-five years of American regime has brought him only disappointments and sometimes despair . . ." (G. E. Taylor, *The Philippines and the United States*, p. 21). Taylor adds much information to confirm this judgment and concludes that by the late 1930s, "the mass of the people may have been worse off than before" the American occupation (p. 85). The Bell report of 1950 revealed that inequalities of income had become even more marked while the average standard of living had not reached prewar levels (p. 137).

The director of the USAID Mission in the Philippines, Wesley D. Haraldson, testified before a House subcommittee on April 25, 1967, that the condition of the average farmer "has not changed in the last fifty years. . . . In the past ten years the rich have become richer and the poor have become poorer" (Haraldson cited in Hernando J. Abaya, *The Untold Philippine Story*, p. 360).

[79] Phi-Van, "The Peasants (Dan Que)," appendix to Ngo Vinh Long, *Before the August Revolution*.

[80] See, for example, Lawyers Committee on American Policy Towards Vietnam, *Vietnam and International Law*. See also several papers in *Falk—Vietnam*. The most recent study, which appeared after Taylor's book, is William L. Standard, *Aggression: Our Asian Disaster*. See also chapter 1, sections III, VI (subsections 5, 6).

[81] Chester Cooper, *The Lost Crusade*, pp. 276–7. Emphasis added.

[82] For details see Theodore Draper, *Abuse of Power*, pp. 73–82. There has been no attempt to respond to Draper's devastating critique of administration claims regarding the North Vietnamese troop involvement in the South. The astonishing internal contradictions

suffice in themselves to make the government case unbelievable. See also the references in note 80 above. Recall that this North Vietnamese battalion was allegedly detected in the South two and a half months after the regular bombing of North Vietnam had been initiated, eight and a half months after the first bombing of strategic targets in North Vietnam in a "reprisal" for an incident which probably never occurred. The government claims regarding North Vietnamese aggression in Laos and Cambodia are no more compelling. See chapter 2.

83 Cooper, *Lost Crusade*, pp. 264–5.

84 I. F. Stone, "A Reply to the White Paper," *I. F. Stone's Weekly*, March 8, 1965.

85 "It appears from the International Control Commission's reports that through February 28, 1961, about 154 violations had been registered against the South and only one violation against the North" (Scigliano, *South Vietnam*, p. 154). Scigliano argues that the North has the advantage of being "more acute, or devious" and that the "inability of ICC teams to perform their duties . . . is much greater in North than South Vietnam" (p. 155). However, one ICC report states: "As has been revealed in the preceding paragraphs, the degree of co-operation given to the Commission by the two parties has not been the same. While the Commission has experienced difficulties in North Vietnam, the major part of its difficulties has arisen in South Vietnam" (International Control Commission, *Sixth Interim Report of the International Commission for Supervision and Control in Vietnam*, Cmnd. No. 31, pp. 26–31, reprinted in Marvin E. Gettleman, ed., *Viet Nam: History, Documents and Opinions*, pp. 170–2. On the matter of the obligations of North and South Vietnam with regard to the Geneva Agreements, see Daniel G. Partan, "Legal Aspects of the Vietnam Conflict," in *Falk—Vietnam*, pp. 201, 209–16.

86 Bernard Fall, "Vietnam: The Agonizing Reappraisal," *Current History*, February 1965. For further references see my *American Power and the New Mandarins*, pp. 242–3, 281–2. For further confirmation, see Joseph Zasloff, *Political Motivation of the Viet Cong* RAND Memorandum RM-4703-2—ISA/ARPA (May 1968), p. 124. From the Pentagon Papers, we now know that these actions began in 1954.

87 See note 80 above.

88 Taylor's only reference to the issue is the following, in a different context: "When we sent hundreds of thousands of troops to South Vietnam, bombed North Vietnam, and moved into Cambodia, were our national leaders as guilty of launching a war of aggression as were Hitler and his generals . . . ?" (p. 13). The question is not taken up again.

89 Thomas M. Franck, "Who Killed Article 2(4)? or: Changing Norms Governing the Use of Force by States," *American Journal of International Law*, vol. 64, no. 4 (1970).

90 Bernard Fall, *Last Reflections on a War*, p. 276.

91 Franck, "Who Killed Article 2(4)?"

92 For recent discussion of this possibility, see Walter Goldstein, "The American Political System and the Next Vietnam," *Journal of International Affairs*, vol. 25, no. 1 (1971).

[93] George W. Grayson, Jr., *Washington Post*, January 10, 1971. Grayson is associate professor of government at William and Mary College, a specialist in Latin American politics and the theory of revolution.

[94] Hearings on Defense Department Appropriations Before a Subcommittee of the House Committee on Appropriations, 1963, cited in M. Klare, "The Pentagon's Counterinsurgency Research Infrastructure," *NACLA Newsletter*, vol. 4, no. 9 (1971).

[95] Exactly the same point was made by Malcolm Browne as early as 1964 (*The New Face of War*, p. xi).

[96] Gall, "Guerrilla Movements in Latin America," *New York Times*, March 28, 1971. The leader of the campaign, he points out, is now the elected president of Guatemala; his regime is the most brutal in the country's history, with large numbers killed in early 1971, including members of the legal noncommunist opposition.

[97] *Ibid*. See also note 16 above. These operations, incidentally, are worldwide. According to the same report, Colonel Fletcher Prouty states that air force–CIA units that preceded the formation of SOF flew Tibetan tribesmen to Colorado for combat training and then returned them to Tibet; a resistance force of up to 42,000 was organized, he claims. Robinson also reports that they form part of the American counterinsurgency operations in Thailand and that they have conducted missions in Saudi Arabia and even North Korea.

[98] Marcel Neidergang, "Violence et terreur," *Le Monde*, January 19, 1968.

[99] See particularly Henry Kissinger, *Nuclear Weapons and American Foreign Policy*, pp. 132–233; *The Necessity for Choice*, pp. 57–98. Kissinger discusses "limited war strategy" within the framework of great-power conflict. If we ask ourselves where these "limited wars" will be fought, however, a different interpretation suggests itself. In fact, each of the superpowers regularly interprets its efforts to maintain its hegemony within its own empire as a defense of some principle (freedom, socialism) from the encroachments of its rival. In this respect, the cold war has served the leadership of the superpowers as an admirable propaganda device for mobilizing their respective populations behind expensive and dangerous efforts to maintain imperial dominions. See, for example, Franck, "Who Killed Article 2(4)?"; and chapter 1, section V.

CHAPTER 4

Indochina: The Next Phase

The most striking feature of the American war in Indochina is undoubtedly its savagery, but no less remarkable is the continuity of policy and the persistence of basic assumptions over a quarter-century. The Pentagon Papers, discussed in chapter 1, now provide us with a revealing record of how Washington perceived the war—not to be confused with a record of the facts, an interesting point in itself. They demonstrate the unwavering commitment to a policy of destroying the Communist-led national movement of Indochina, and absorbing Indochina, so far as possible, within the domain of Western influence, regardless of popular will as expressed in indigenous movements. The means were available to demolish the society in which the nationalist movement was rooted, and these means were employed, out of "military necessity." The savagery of the war does not reflect some peculiar streak of barbarism in the United States command. Rather, there was no other way to solve the problem presented to it by the civilian leadership, the problem of destroying the nationalist movement that the Communists had "captured"—illegitimately, Washington being the judge of what is legitimate in Vietnam.

I will make no attempt to predict the final outcome of this struggle. There are a number of critical factors that I do not know how to assess. How long can the Vietnamese resistance continue to withstand the terroristic assault of the world's most advanced technology? What is the strength of the resistance in the urban concentrations created by a policy that was succinctly described by an American general: "No villages, no guerrillas, simple"? Will the people of the United States be willing to stand by, in relative passivity, while the government continues its grim work? A Harris poll of October 1971 showed that 57 percent of the population was opposed to air and helicopter support for the Saigon Army, and that 65 percent regard the American involvement as immoral (up from 47 percent in January). Will these feelings be translated into action, or will they simply be expressed to pollsters and thus remain virtually irrelevant to policy formation? These factors are decisive, and unpredictable, though we must bear in mind that one of them is subject to our influence.

I want to consider here a different question, namely, What does the Nixon administration plan? Since the public clearly wants peace, the rhetoric of the administration naturally will promise peace and American withdrawal. Some choose to believe it, while to other close observers "it now appears that President Nixon wants to end the war by winning it."[1]

The Nixon "peace plan" of January 1972 signals clearly the intention to pursue the war to victory, if this proves possible.[2] To impose a noncommunist regime in South Vietnam, it is necessary to separate the areas of population concentration from the main-force guerrilla units and the North Vietnamese forces, while preventing any organized social life in the areas ceded to the resistance. The technology of terror is assigned these tasks. At the same time, it is necessary to control the concentrated population and to "root out the infrastructure" of the enemy by the Phoenix program and other measures of repression. If the political structure of the opposition can be destroyed and the rule of the military and police forces successfully imposed, then the population can be granted a "free choice" under the Constitution (which outlaws communism). As the "nation builders" have always insisted, a "free choice" between the government and the Viet Cong will be possible only when the latter have been destroyed.

It is not irrational for the planners in Washington to regard their objectives as perhaps attainable, despite years of failure. The costs of the war, of course, are borne by the Vietnamese: their land and bodies and villages are destroyed, while the United States suffers polarization or inflation or a balance-of-payments problem. It is, furthermore, unclear whether a revolutionary movement that achieved its success because its programs were meaningful for the overwhelmingly rural society of Vietnam can also organize successfully among the slum dwellers of Saigon, for whom no domestically based program may be meaningful. No Vietnamese can be unaware of the awesome destructive power of American terror. Peasants in Phuyen Province who fought with the Viet Minh against the French, winning "independence of half of our country," in their accurate phrase, report that "a new generation of guerrillas is having a much worse war" because of the "American firepower, tremendous firepower—such as we never dreamed of in those days." One peasant, who had abandoned the life of resistance, said, "There is one thing I have—my patriotism—and all those Government officials can never be as proud of this as I am."[3] But the United States will cheerfully concede patriotic sentiments to the remnants of those who captured the nationalist movement, if only it can demolish this movement while imposing the rule of the local associates of Western imperialism. If this can be done by a "democratic election," once the conditions for a "free choice" are established, so much the better.

In more general terms, it would be accurate to describe the Vietnam war as a struggle between human will and advanced technology. Human will, however, has its limits, though they are far beyond what one could have imagined, as the Vietnamese revolutionaries have shown. The technology of destruction and repression can continue slowly to progress without practical limit. Antipersonnel weapons can be improved, from pellets, to metal flechettes that cannot be extracted without grave injury, to plastic fragments that cannot even be detected by X-ray, and who knows what tomorrow. The accuracy of bombing can be continually improved, so that 50,000 tons of bombs next month is the equivalent of considerably more than that today. It is not irrational to suppose that if the war goes on indefinitely, technology will ultimately prove victorious.

An additional factor that United States planners no doubt find encouraging is that the annihilation strategy in South Vietnam, directed against what they always knew to be an indigenous resistance movement based on the peasantry, had the consequence of drawing North Vietnamese forces into the war. (See chapter 1, pp. 125–7.) By destroying much of the rural society and concentrating the population into urban slums and in the Saigon Army, United States strategy had the consequence (and assuming minimal intelligence, the intended consequence) of creating the basis for a North-South conflict of the sort that American propaganda, with the cooperation of the mass media, had always claimed to exist. The United States did not originate the strategy of exacerbating ethnic, religious, and regional rivalries, but merely adopted it, as a matter of course, from its imperial predecessors. The analogy to Korea is suggestive, though not exact. It took several years for American forces to eradicate the indigenous social and political structures that were functioning when they landed in September 1945, and it was not until the Korean War (initiated and fought under circumstances much more ambiguous than the official ideology proclaims) that the internal civil struggle in the South was converted into a regional conflict more tolerable to the imperial power.

Assuming that the objectives outlined above can be achieved, and that the revolutionary forces in Vietnam can be prevented from operating effectively amidst the ruins of Vietnamese society, the "nation builders" face the next task: to create some sort of viable social structure out of the wreckage. How do they hope to accomplish this task? From the public record and from secret reports that have surfaced, we can gain some understanding of how American social scientists are hoping to deal with the latest phase in the dilemma of twenty-five years.

A confidential report to the Asian Development Bank by Columbia economist Emile Benoit takes as its working hypothesis that Saigon will have won a military victory by 1973, with 25,000 United States troops remaining after 1975 and the Viet Cong reduced to a low-level insurgency. The report notes that the Vietnamese labor force is more highly skilled than the prewar agricultural labor force, and can probably be directed to the production of components of assembled goods that will be marketed by multinational corporations. South Vietnam, and Southeast Asia in general, should serve primarily as a source of raw materials, complementing the Japan-based industrial economy of noncommunist East Asia; while producing some finished or semifinished manufactured goods for domestic use and export. State intervention in the economy should be avoided except for the financing of structural changes that will make private investment profitable. Small-scale private farming should be encouraged (but with no limit on the size of holdings) because "a farmer is willing to work his own land for a much smaller income than he would expect if he were a laborer on someone else's estate."[4] Wage costs should be kept down and local capitalism encouraged, but on a small scale. Decornoy writes that in the view of this report, "the Southeast Asia of the future appears as a kind of paradise for international bankers and investors, besides providing an inexhaustible supply of wood, petroleum and minerals for Japan's expanding economy." It might be added that this approach fits rather well into the general framework of Nixon administration policy, which "proposes to make private direct investment by multinational corporations the centre of American foreign aid in the 1970s," with the primary United States government role being to issue "political risk insurance" for private investment.[5]

Similar themes are taken up by Harvard economist Arthur Smithies in a number of studies. One, entitled "Economic Development in Vietnam: The Need for External Resources," is discussed by Jacques Decornoy in *Le Monde*, September 1, 1971. In addition, there is a series of papers "relating to the transition to economic development in Vietnam," dated August 1971 and stamped IDA, probably a part of a "Columbia University Research Project on the Problems and Possibilities of an International Organizational Role in the Economic Recovery and Development of North and South Vietnam," financed by the State Department. Smithies has been a consultant to the CIA, IDA (Institute of Defense Analysis), RAND, AID, and the National Security Council at various times since 1952, and more recently a consultant to ARPA (Advanced Research Project Agency of the Department of Defense) in Saigon. Since the papers are not publicly available, I will give some quotes and paraphrase to indicate the general flavor.

Smithies foresees "military stalemate and withering away of

the war, a process that can last for a decade or more." It is, he believes, "feasible" that "military security may be sufficient to permit the economy to operate under market forces and to be oriented toward the world economy with respect both to trade and the use of foreign capital." This possibility "offers far better prospects for development than any alternative."

Smithies' analysis of the prospects consists largely of conventional ideology, based on the general thesis that "it is hard to think of any interference with the market system in Vietnam that cannot be regarded as an impediment to development." As to the effects of the war, "at fantastic cost, it has fulfilled some of the necessary 'preconditions' for development." It would be more accurate to say that the traditional society and culture have been substantially demolished and a mass of rootless individuals created—a classical, virtually ideal labor market—along with "spectacular harbors," airfields, a communications system, and so on. The million men who have served in the Saigon Army and the additional quarter-million who have worked for the United States as civilians "provide the base for an industrial labor force with modern skills and attitudes." "As a new generation grows up, the horrors of war will fade, as they have in Japan and Korea," while "the profound changes in the economic life of the country, wrought by the war, will remain." With a "substantial infusion of external resources" through aid and foreign investment, and "sound domestic policies," the prospects are encouraging.

For the next decade, foreign aid of about $0.5 billion annually will be needed, but "if development succeeds and national security increases, private capital inflows can be expected to contribute an increased share of the total." The adjustment process might be a matter of one or two decades. "Private direct [foreign] investment has a vital role to play" and "may well have to be the most dynamic factor in Vietnamese development."

"Sound domestic policies" are those that integrate South Vietnam into the free-world economy, resisting "economic parochialism" and state interference (apart from fiscal policy, urban reconditioning, construction of large infrastructure projects, public health and education, including "conversion of skills acquired in the army to economic purposes"). There is a plentiful labor supply, but it is important to resist the pressure of labor to establish real wages that are too high. Social welfare policies (such as minimum wages or encouragement of trade unions) may also raise labor costs, thus losing for the country its cheap labor advantage. "Too much emphasis on equality can reduce savings and incentives to invest" and "the government should recognize that premature establishment of a welfare state can seriously impede development."

Not all Vietnamese, however, need subordinate their aspirations to the requirements of development within the free-world economy. It is "of prime importance for Vietnam to acquire entrepreneurs," as in Korea, "who know the ways of the world market" (and who, as in the model societies, live accordingly, one must assume). Anglo-American concepts of business organization should be fostered, displacing Vietnamese, French, or Chinese traditions. Private enterprise should be "strongly encouraged" and most controls abolished in agriculture and other sectors. "Foreign trade should be the focus of policy formation." Smithies investigates in detail ways in which the United States can influence the Saigon government "to create a good environment for effective performance of the private sector." The suggested models are Taiwan, Korea, Singapore, Hong Kong, and Pakistan (which "has done significantly better than India with an open economy"—and has done particularly well for the twenty-odd families who own and control most of the "open economy"). Cam Ranh Bay might become the center of labor-intensive industry.

In general, "development can best be achieved in the context of private enterprise market economy" and "there should be a strong preference for private enterprise," which should, furthermore, be "subject to the tests of [international] competition," with the inevitable (though unstated) result that it will be subordinated to foreign capital.

Given its critical role, foreign investment "must be liberated from the uncertainties and obstacles that beset it." Needless to say, this is the only form of liberation that Smithies contemplates.

One might take note of some possible objections to the thesis that full integration into the capitalist world system with a private-enterprise market economy is the best imaginable mode of development. In this connection Smithies merely comments that if it is to compete in international markets, Vietnam must imitate its successful Asian neighbors, such as South Korea, "just as Japan imitated the West in the last century." Japan, of course, did not follow Smithies' prescriptions for development. It did not rely primarily on foreign investment or merely integrate itself into the global capitalist market, avoiding central planning or state interference in economic affairs. The Japanese model hardly supports the belief that virtually any interference with the market system (internal or global) will prove an impediment to development. But the counterexample is irrelevant: "Lacking the genius of Japan, [South Vietnam] must probably accomplish this [imitating its market-oriented neighbors] by inviting them [foreign investors] to bring their business within its borders." Good, hard, nonideological economic analysis.

The consequences of the liberation of foreign investment can easily be foreseen, say, by considering the example of Latin America, where in 1966 more than 40 percent of manufactured exports were from United States firms, as compared with less than 12 percent in 1957.[6] The most recent country liberated, the Dominican Republic, serves as a useful example. Elena de la Souchère describes the effective return of Santo Domingo to the Trujillo era—but with a difference. In the first place, though the terror and violence are familiar, the new "Trujillism without Trujillo" imposes virtually no limits on "Praetorian corruption." The "Benefactor" who was the gift of the United States Marines two generations ago was the true chief of the armed forces, and was therefore able to impose at least some limits on their demands. But the present pale copy of the "Benefactor" is more "their deputy at the National Palace." Furthermore, as distinct from the original version, Balaguer has created no domestic capitalism to compete with American corporations, but is rather "the docile instrument of American interests." The door has been opened wide to American capital, which has been liberated from earlier impediments. While the gross national product has risen along with the vast increase in American investment, so have debt, balance-of-payments deficits, and a dangerous dependency. The expansion of the economy "is oriented towards the interests of foreign corporations and the Dominican privileged classes, with no concern for the real needs of the country." Salaries remain low, the agrarian reform has been arrested, and a surplus peasant population flows into the cities, where there is no work. Strikes are on the increase and the social situation is explosive. In the face of American-backed military power, no political change seems possible. The natural result is terror, social demoralization, and for the American investor and the local elite, profits.[7]

Another example, Brazil, was liberated a year earlier (see chapter 1, section VI, pp. 62, 155).

It is also possible to raise various questions about the "success stories" of Asia that Smithies cites, and about the alternative model for development offered by China, North Korea, and North Vietnam (or others that might be imagined). One might, say, inquire into the vast contribution of America's Asian wars to Japanese and Korean development,[8] or into the consequences for the Korean people of the heavy dependence on the United States and Japan, the widening trade gap, increasing indebtedness, extensive unemployment, stagnation of agricultural production, and so on.[9] And it might be worthwhile to consider the conclusion of a knowledgeable observer that "in almost all respects, surprisingly, the living standard of the Taiwanese seems to come off second-best" in a comparison with Canton.[10] Smithies' ode to the free-market model for development might also have included a glance at the details of the Pakistani "open economy" that so impresses him, for example, at the evidence that more than three-quarters of the population are no better off than twenty years ago, and that perhaps 15 or 20 percent may actually be poorer in real terms despite an estimated 25 percent increase of real output per capita[11]; or at the fact that more time, money, and effort "have been expended in providing Karachi with popular brands of fizzy drinks than in providing it with a hygienic milk supply."[12] His recommendations for Vietnam are perhaps not based on quite so unchallengeable a body of fact as he seems to believe.

Smithies points out that if oil is discovered in Vietnam, the whole situation will be transformed. Rumors abound on this matter, ranging from skepticism to reports that "South Vietnam's potential production is larger than that of Indonesia—possibly comparable with leading producing areas in the Middle East."[13] It need hardly be stressed that these prospects will reinforce the commitment of the United States government to maintain control of the coastal areas of Indochina. T. D. Allman reports that the search for oil in South Vietnam may have been planned for about ten years, but was delayed until actual strikes had been made in Indonesia, and because of a ten-year-old oil glut, now ending: "Investors apparently now feel that the war in Vietnam, and the American presence in Indochina, will drag on at least long enough for them to get their money back."[14] It should be noted that apart from the importance of maintaining control of Southeast Asian oil, there is here a potentially rich source of capital for reconstructing South Vietnam on the approved free-world model, and enhancing the power of the local entrepreneurs who know the ways of the free-world economy and are committed to integrating South Vietnam within it. As Gabriel Kolko has pointed out, the recent flurry of activity concerning oil investment should probably be seen in the light of the need for "economic Vietnamization," a growing problem if the artificial economy of South Vietnam can no longer be sustained by American military expenditures and a dole from the American taxpayer.[15]

Ideas rather like those of Benoit and Smithies are developed in the public record as well, for example, in several of the papers of a symposium organized by the Council on Vietnamese Studies of SEADAG on Vietnam's development in the postwar era, held in October 1970. The council is financed by AID to give the government advice "which we are trying to convert into program operation."[16] To be sure, it affects a rather different public pose, not unlike much academic scholarship in the social sciences. The former head of the council, Professor Samuel Huntington of Harvard, has stated publicly that the council has never to his knowledge undertaken any task for the State Department and that its primary concern is "to raise funds from public and private sources to support scholarly research on Vietnam."[17] The little that is known of its activities, however, indicates that this statement is rather disingenuous, and confirms the conclusions of those who pay the piper. For example, the May 1969 meeting was devoted to a discussion of a paper by Huntington entitled "Getting Ready for Political Competition in South Vietnam." The paper tries to develop a strategy for overcoming the political advantages of the National Liberation Front in South Vietnam, given the possibility that events will force the United States to enter into the political competition that it has always, for obvious reasons, sought to avoid. Huntington's paper and the ensuing discussion (according to minutes which have been privately circulated) wrestled inconclusively with the problem that the NLF is admittedly "the most powerful purely political national organization." Huntington suggested various techniques that might be used to overcome the political advantages of the NLF: pork-barrel projects, electoral manipulations of various kinds, "inducements and coercions to foster alliances or mergers among political actors," control of media, various covert means. The participants discussed and explored these possibilities, rather pessimistically.[18] Perhaps this is an example of what the chairman of the Department of Government at Harvard regards as "scholarly research on Vietnam." The symposium on postwar development—in this case, made public—is a comparable example of neutral, balanced scholarship.

In conformity with the public image, the symposium was introduced with a statement that the council "has been concerned since its founding with advancing knowledge about Viet-Nam," promoting "scholarly research on Vietnamese society and politics," and providing "a forum for the interchange of ideas among specialists," principally through meetings "in which a wide range of viewpoints is represented."[19] In keeping with this objective, the symposium contains one contribution that considers the possibility that the Communists will win in Vietnam. The author, Hans Heymann, Jr., is identified as an economist at RAND. Presumably, this is the same Hans Heymann who was on the staff of Robert Komer in the White House when Komer was chief adviser to President Johnson on pacification, and who wrote memos on the most effective ways for the United States to "exercise leverage with the Vietnamese government," for example, with "credible sanctions" but

with care not to "undermine the self-respect of the Vietnamese government in its own eyes and in the eyes of the South
Vietnamese people."[20] Heymann's contribution to the symposium is entitled "Imposing Communism on the Economy
of South Vietnam: A Conjectural View." As the title suggests,
the contents are at the level of scholarly neutrality, objectivity,
and insight that one would expect from a colonial administrator concerned with pacification. He assumes, without argument, that the South will be subordinated to the North and
that the pattern of its development will be set by the "mistakes as well as 'successes'" of the North. As an objective
scholar, Heymann comprehends that there will be mistakes
but no successes in the North—at best "successes." The discussion continues in this vein.

Apart from this gesture towards "a wide range of viewpoints," the symposium operates on the assumption that
communism will not be "imposed" on the people of South
Vietnam, who will therefore freely choose to accept more
civilized Western ways, after having been gently nudged
towards this free choice by several million tons of bombs and
artillery and the depredations of hundreds of thousands of
American and mercenary troops. The papers appear in *Asian
Survey*, April 1971. A firm advocate of "truth-in-packaging"
might look askance at the publication in a scholarly journal of
a symposium of a group organized and financed by AID to
give the government advice which can be converted into program operation, but the papers nevertheless (or better, therefore) repay careful reading.

The symposiasts are, for the most part, enthusiastic about
the prospects for noncommunist Pacific Asia (christened
NOCPA), which the chairman of the Council on Foreign
Relations, summarizing, expects to be "the fastest growing and
most dynamic economic region in the world in the 1970s." As
several participants observe, this region is of particular importance to Japan, and may be its second most important market,
after the United States, as well as a major source of raw materials for Japan and the United States, where the demand for
minerals will grow "extremely rapidly." By 1980, some predict,
NOCPA may account for 40 to 50 percent of Japanese
imports and exports. Japan has a labor shortage and a need to

place labor-intensive manufacturing facilities elsewhere, as well as to export pollution, and NOCPA may be just the answer. In fact, it might be recalled that in an earlier period Japan imported a Korean labor force into Japan,[21] but it is preferable to export Japanese-owned productive facilities instead, thus avoiding the social problems and other unpleasant by-products of industrialization.

More generally, "producers, and retail merchandising operations in the Western World will increasingly look to this area for their supplies, even of products they once produced themselves," while "this area is becoming an enormous market for the commercial exports of the West." "Today, there is rapidly increasing exploitation of the internationalization of the production base itself," and Eastern Asia "seems especially well suited to internationalization of production." For example, television sets can be made in part in Hong Kong, in part in Korea, assembled in Japan, and exported to the United States and Europe. A reasonable share in the profits will return to the United States, through the dominant United States share in ownership of multinational corporations.

South Vietnam has a significant role to play in the system that is envisioned. The Mekong region might become the major source of food for NOCPA; Vietnam could be the "Imperial Valley of East Asia . . . but on a far larger scale." Furthermore, the "supply of human skills," as well as the infrastructure, has been much improved by the war, and there has been a vast flow of manpower to the urban areas. As a representative of the United States Department of Agriculture puts it, "Saigon's population swelled phenomenally in response to efforts to attract manpower away from VC areas." None of the scholars is so indelicate as to describe the methods by which manpower was "attracted" to urban areas, though one does note that the GVN has neither sought to improve the quality of urban life nor is likely to do so in the immediate future. Saigon's population has indeed swelled phenomenally.

Saigon's population density averages about seventy-five thousand per square mile, but there are some blocks where nearly two thousand people are crowded into three or four acres [and not in high-rise apartment houses]. An American official who has acted as an adviser to the Vietnamese on municipal problems for several years has estimated that ten per cent of the city's population live in splendor and comfort, forty per cent live a lower-middle class life of survival, and fifty per cent live in abject squalor. . . . There is no doubt that the Americans have altered the entire fabric of Saigon life, and one feels that a new breakdown is inevitable unless something drastic is done. What we have done is to create a social spectrum with a *nouveau riche* class at one end, a new class of poor people, largely refugees, at the other, and in the middle a classless majority, who have lived off the American presence.

Flying across the city by helicopter, one can see "growing patches of slums in most of the districts" and "the pattern of destruction wrought by the war—mostly by the 1968 Tet offensive," in which the worst damage was "caused mostly by American planes bombing entrenched Communist attackers."[22]

The official who writes of "efforts to attract manpower away from VC areas" is surely not ignorant of the nature of those efforts in rural Vietnam. The casual phrase strikes a note of savagery, of cold and mindless brutality, not untypical of "scholarly research on Vietnamese society and politics" as conducted by those who provide the government with advice "which we are trying to convert into program operation," or by those who try to mask the horror with scholarly detachment.

Whatever the means for attracting it may have been, the manpower is now there, in the decaying urban slums. Furthermore, army discipline "should facilitate transition from the ways of a traditional society to the needs of industrial discipline in the postwar period," that is, if it proves possible to resist the pressure for social welfare policies of which Smithies warned. It will also be necessary to overcome the artificial nature of Vietnam's economy, with wealth and employment concentrated in the supply of goods and services to United States personnel, and to modify the practices of the absentee landlords, importers, and wealthy businessmen who squander their incomes on conspicuous consumption and transfer abroad the capital provided by the American taxpayer.

Japanese support is necessary if the hopes of the United States government to control South Vietnam and integrate it into the free-world economy are to be realized. This is only fair. As Smithies explains, Japan has been "a main beneficiary of the operation" of the United States in Vietnam, and therefore it "should carry a major share of the aid burden in the future." There has been some increase in Japanese aid and investment, though its scale is still small. "The United States Government, in the Sato-Nixon meeting on Oct. 24 [1970], requested that Japan give $150 million in aid to South Vietnam as part of the overall aid program for Indo-China, and Prime Minister Eisaku Sato answered that Japan would duly consider the matter, according to Government spokesmen who were close to the summit meeting." It was also indicated "that Japan will take a forward-looking stand on the request." Yen credits on a smaller scale have since been offered for a thermal powerhouse and other projects.[23]

Japanese aid is not, of course, an exercise in altruism and humanitarian concern. Rather, "foreign aid is a most stable and profit-assured business," and "the slogan today is 'no business like the foreign aid business'"[24]—an attitude not unique to Japan, of course. Japanese government economic experts have been studying potential development projects in South Vietnam to supplement already established Japanese plants. President Thieu, at the opening of one of these, praised it as a first step towards "a solid national economy"[25] —as solid as the economies of the Philippines, Thailand, and South Korea, if all works out for the best. Present plans include Japanese-backed factories, the development of the greater Cam Ranh Bay area (which has substantial deposits of first-grade silica and limestone) as an integrated industrial-port complex, and so on. A Japanese investment team estimated that "it would take two years to repair war damage and build up resources, from four to six years to develop a self-supporting economy and eight years before South Vietnam could participate productively in the overall development of Southeast Asia,"[26] in the manner of the model societies of the region. There are now joint Japanese-Vietnamese ventures for production of agricultural machinery and diesel engines, stamped (and presumably marketed from) Osaka, and the major Japanese television and radio manufacturers are beginning to produce appliances in South Vietnam.[27] The Vietnam National Company, a joint venture of Japan's Matsushita and Vietnamese interests, has been manufacturing radios in South Vietnam since early 1971, and is now introducing assembly lines for television sets, refrigerators, and electric and gas stoves, just what is needed by the peasants of Vietnam and the residents of the urban slums. "Praising the intelligence and dexterity of young Vietnamese workers, the Japanese parent also announced its ultimate intention to use the Saigon venture as an export processing plant," using workers trained in various skills in connection with United States military activities.[28]

> In the field of investment in South Vietnam, the Japanese are streets ahead of other foreign investors. What appears to have attracted the Japanese has been a specific offer by the Saigon Government: any foreign firm willing to establish an assembly plant in Vietnam will automatically be granted the monopoly to export to South Vietnam the readymade products until the plant is ready to operate. . . .

South Vietnam's regulations governing imports, an effort to save foreign exchange, caused a reduction in imports from Japan in 1970 and 1971. "To offset the decline in trade with South Vietnam and secure a head start in the postwar era, many Japanese firms established themselves in South Vietnam in 1971 and set up joint ventures with local interests."[29] Ever cautious, the Japanese are thinking of postwar development, after proper conditions for investment have been established.[30] The more ambitious and imaginative proposals of the scholars of the Council on Vietnamese Studies remain, for the time being, only projections, as foreign capital awaits the outcome of the preliminary steps that are required to liberate it from the uncertainties and obstacles that beset it.

A supplement to the *Mainichi Daily News*, November 1, 1971, supplied to the newspaper by a quasi-governmental news service in Saigon through the Saigon embassy in Tokyo, announces that "the nightmare of conflict in South Vietnam has yielded unexpected dividends in the development of human and material resources that will be of vital importance to future economic growth" and that "the postwar industrial potential of South Vietnam offers a fertile new field for investment." It refers hopefully to the new industrial complex near Bien Hoa, the home of "the first Japanese companies with a real stake in South Vietnam's economic future" (namely, the Japanese-backed agricultural-machinery factory established in March 1971). "The people of Vietnam view the post-war era of this country as an exciting time of rising expectations," the supplement continues. It is hoped that the free-trade center being planned at Cam Ranh Bay will attract considerable foreign investment. A fairly detailed Japanese study of "post-war economic development in Viet Nam" concludes that Cam Ranh is without doubt "the best site for a free port in Southeast Asia." "From the viewpoint of labor quality, the South Vietnamese people are deemed superior to the inhabitants of adjacent nations," and there is a great mass of potential workers, including those who "have been compelled to evacuate to urban areas as their homes have been burned down and their land laid waste by military operations." Thus the prospects for investors at Cam Ranh and elsewhere are not unfavorable.[31]

Ambassador Bunker has called for

> . . . an effective strategy . . . to further participation in foreign trade and to attract private investment from abroad. . . . The recent petroleum law and the new investment law now before the upper House indicate the Government's desire to create a flexible long-term investment policy which will serve Vietnam's interests while at the same time it creates an economic climate foreign investors will find attractive.[32]

Needless to say, his notion of "Vietnam's interests" is a very special one, just as Japanese investment teams have a particular interpretation of "participating productively in the overall development of Southeast Asia."

United States investment is also proceeding, in a rather gingerly fashion. The Ford Motor Company submitted a proposal for an assembly plant, part of its long-term program to create—and if possible dominate—a potential Asian market, and American Motors followed shortly after.[33] Ford proposes to set up a wholly owned subsidiary with capital investment of about $2.5 million and a projected capacity of about 3,000 utility trucks per year in the first phase. American Motors has a 10 percent interest in Nam Viet Motor Corporation, with 30 percent held by the Panama-registered holding company of the "Eisenberg industrial and development empire" which announces that it is set to "go into Vietnam in a big way, without any reservations," and 60 percent held by "Vietnamese interests of American-Chinese background." The company is to assemble jeeps, beginning by May 1973. The "Eisenberg empire" is also planning to become involved in a cement plant and a pulp and paper factory. Singer Sewing Machines, First National City Bank of New York (joining Chase Manhattan and Bank of America), a "top-flight" chemical firm, and a leading American cigarette company ("US-quality cigarettes have become well known country-wide during years of black market trading"), and others are planning to open branches or subsidiaries.[34]

> South Vietnam, heir to a colossal armory of infrastructure facilities as the war grinds down, is showing signs of becoming a potentially attractive investment site to a number of companies. . . . While a flood of investment is unlikely here before the war is finished, investors should get a considerable fillip as soon as (a) the World Bank extends its first loan to Vietnam, and (b) US investment guarantees are made available.[35]

There's the rub, of course. The difficulty is that foreign investment is still not liberated from a number of uncertainties and obstacles, in particular, the uncertainty as to whether the United States can maintain military control. The United States government needs the investment to enable it to reconstitute an obedient society, but the investors would prefer that the obedience come first. Though they support the government's aims and indeed provide much of the personnel to formulate and conduct state policy, nevertheless they will not cooperate at the risk of their private interests. Exactly as in the case of research and development for advanced technology, they want the state to mobilize the resources of the whole society to prepare the ground for corporate profit. The Vietnamese have been a hard nut to crack, and the costs of dominating Indochina are far greater than anticipated— though it must be recalled that the costs, so called, are in part profits for selected elements in the American economy. As a result, many of the more far-sighted representatives of the corporate elite that largely manages state policy have strongly urged that this enterprise be liquidated. Whether their views will prevail remains to be seen.

In the meantime, those who await proof of obedience are, in their own way, trying to help with this aspect of the problem as well. The Philco subdivision of Ford is a major supplier for the electronic battlefield in Vietnam, and is involved in the development of military communications systems elsewhere in Southeast Asia, particularly in Thailand, for many years the base for United States operations in the region and now threatened by a rising insurgency of its own.[36] A recent review summarizes the Ford contribution aptly:

> The "Better Idea People" at Ford are engaged in a worldwide auto strategy. As a multinational corporation, the company has the resources to act as a stabilizing economic force in the third world and, should that prove insufficient, the international firm can supply the Pentagon with the means of stabilizing the third world's markets by force.[37]

It should be noted that hesitations with regard to investment are limited to Vietnam. Elsewhere in NOCPA, as one observer puts it, "US business and financial giants seem to be making plans for transforming the 'Pacific Basin' countries including Oceania into a Japanese-American Co-prosperity Sphere that will outshine the original version."[38] As noted by the editor of the *Far Eastern Economic Review*, among others, all of this takes place behind the shield provided by American military intervention in Vietnam. (See chapter 1, section VI, pp. 48–9.)

T. D. Allman writes that "the Vietnam war will undoubtedly end up as a textbook study of imperialism, but the economic element, on the face of it, seems to have manifested itself rather late."[39] He is thinking primarily of oil, but a broader view with greater historical depth would reveal that the Vietnam war began as a "study of imperialism," with a significant economic element, and though other factors entered in along the way, has fundamentally remained so throughout. Contrary to what a superficial view might suggest, the fact that the United States is now calling upon Japan to help rescue its Vietnamese enterprise in no way contradicts the thesis that an explicit and early motive of United States policy in Indochina was to offer inducements to Japan to refrain from "accommodating" to the so-called Communist powers. (See chapter 1, section V, for further discussion.)

To achieve a Korea-type solution in Vietnam, the United States has been forced to destroy the society of Vietnam and the land itself on a scale with few precedents. As noted earlier, it must now proceed to separate the areas in which the population has been concentrated from main-force guerrilla units and the North Vietnamese forces that have been drawn into the war by the American intervention. It must also somehow construct a viable society in the regions to which the population has been driven (or "attracted," in the terminology its spokesmen favor). It must ensure that there do not exist feasible prospects for social and economic development that are rooted in the domestic society itself, for if such prospects exist, they will be pursued and exploited by indigenous social and political forces, and the United States will lose control. United States policy must therefore ensure that the only hope for survival lies in a foreign-based economy, dominated by those who know the ways of the world market, with social and cultural patterns oriented towards the needs and interests of the industrial societies.

For quite similar reasons, as Joseph Buttinger has pointed out, the Diem regime was unable to tolerate democratic, representative structures: "Local elections [in 1954] would have given the Vietminh control of most of the rural communities," since the Vietminh "was not only popular and in effective political control of large regions, but it alone had people with the requisite organizational skills to exploit whatever opportunities for democratic self-expression the regime opened up," and would therefore have "captured" any "freely constituted organizations."[40] For the same reasons, the United States has remained unable to offer a "free choice" to the peasants of Indochina, and continues today to resist any political accommodation among Vietnamese, and to demand, rather, that the insurgents lay down their arms and, in effect, surrender to the Saigon regime of French collaborators, trusting their fate to its tender mercies, after which "elections" will be held along the lines outlined by Huntington and others (see references of note 18).

This is the essential meaning of the Nixon "peace plan" presented on January 25, 1972, with its call for a cease-fire, that is, a settlement which would permit the Saigon Army and the extensive police apparatus to continue to function freely, while the opposition places its fate in the hands of the Saigon authorities and their American backers. The plans for integrating the "protected" regions of South Vietnam into the United States-Japanese Pacific system are part and parcel of this long-term effort.

The plan to convert the Pacific Basin into a Japanese-American co-prosperity sphere that will outshine the original version has important implications for the United States and for the countries of the region. United States direct overseas investment has risen rapidly since World War II, most dramatically during the 1960s. United States investment in the Pacific Basin is not enormous today, but it should be recalled it was not enormous in Canada in 1950.[41] Overseas operations are now a major source of profit for many multinational corporations.[42] Some economists believe that the United States is becoming a "mature creditor country," producing services more than goods, exporting its productive capacity, and using the profits from its foreign investments to purchase manufactured imports[43] produced by cheap and disciplined labor abroad. However one interprets current trends, there is no doubt that the production of American companies abroad is vast in scale—according to some estimates, it is about equivalent to the gross national product of Japan. This fact alone gives the United States an important stake in maintaining "stability" abroad. There is some debate as to whether the exporting of productive capacity does or does not carry with it ultimately the loss of jobs at home.[44] The unions seem convinced that it does.[45] A United Electrical Workers Union pamphlet entitled *How Foreign Is "Foreign" Competition?* cites many examples of investment abroad for sale in the United States, such as a Motorola plant in South Korea with production costs one-tenth those of a similar plant in Arizona, with a labor force that works six days a week, ten or eleven hours a day, for 11 to 17 cents an hour. The president of Mitsubishi Motor Corporation notes that Japanese wages are one-quarter those of the United States, though skill and technological competence are quite high. "Would it not be more profitable," he asks, "for an American manufacturer to import compacts instead of spending vast sums on developing its own models in this low-price field?"[46]

In the natural course of events, one would expect production for profit to shift to the exploitation of cheaper labor, and the concentration of United States productive capacity and technological skill on the production of waste for the Pentagon can only accelerate this tendency, as intellectual resources, technical skills, and capital are diverted from useful production. It is possible that there will be an increasing surplus population at home that has to be "controlled" just as the foreign domains to which American productive capacity shifts will have to be kept "stable." These tendencies, in short, suggest an intensification of both the imperialist drive and domestic controls in a tightly managed society.

But the implications for NOCPA are clearer still. The SEADAG symposiasts see a bright future for Vietnam as the Imperial Valley of East Asia. The farm workers in the Imperial Valley might tell them what that implies for the mass of the population. The analogy, to be sure, is misleading. The farm workers of Imperial Valley, Vietnam, will lack even that degree of political support and economic power available to American farm workers. There will be no grape or lettuce boycott to help them organize, and no votes to be won by supporting their efforts. But for the absentee landlords, importers, entrepeneurs serving foreign investors and the foreign market, and other local associates of the imperial powers and their international economic institutions, the prospects are no doubt more cheerful, at least in material terms.

There are several difficulties in this projection, specifically those unpredictable factors mentioned at the outset. If imperialism is far from a spent force, the same is true of resistance to imperial aggression and control. While some economists may regard this reaction as irrational, there is no reason to expect that the people of NOCPA will necessarily adopt the value system and ideological standards of American social scientists. As for the American people, with regard to Indochina many are either hawks or doves in the conventional sense of these terms, concerned merely with the costs of forceful intervention and differing only in their estimates of such costs. There are, however, others who are committed to self-determination and human rights and willing to act on their principles.

A Pentagon working group in March 1968 argued that further escalation would lead to "growing disaffection accompanied, as it certainly will be, by increased defiance of the draft and growing unrest in the cities," running "risks of provoking a domestic crisis of unprecedented proportions."[47] Many of those whose actions led to the tactical modifications in United States policy of spring 1968 have spent years in prison for their decency and courage. The state, naturally, does not look kindly upon efforts to restrain its criminal violence.

Many others seem discouraged at the failure of their efforts to end the war. Perhaps they do not appreciate the immense significance of their achievement in imposing at least some constraints on the violence of the state. We can be quite sure that as the dilemma of the United States government assumes new forms in the coming phase of the war, the domestic response will remain a factor of critical importance in determining the fate of the people of Indochina.

Notes

This essay is an expanded version of an article in *Ramparts*, May 1972.

[1] T. D. Allman, "Once More for Victory," *Far Eastern Economic Review*, February 19, 1972.

[2] See George McT. Kahin, "Nixon's Peace Plan," *New Republic*, February 12, 1972; I. F. Stone, "The Hidden Traps in Nixon's Peace Plan," *New York Review of Books*, March 9, 1972; my "Nixon's Peace Offer," *Ramparts*, April 1972.

[3] Gloria Emerson, *New York Times*, October 10, 1971.

[4] Jacques Decornoy, *Le Monde Weekly* (English), February 24, 1971; *Le Monde*, February 9. See Michael Morrow, Dispatch News Service International, May 4, 1971. Presumably, the Benoit report is the one discussed by David Francis, *Christian Science Monitor*, January 12, 1971.

[5] Bruce Nussbaum, "Aid Watershed in 1972," *Far Eastern Economic Review*, July 3, 1971.

[6] Figures cited in *NACLA Newsletter*, vol. 5, no. 6 (1971), from Herbert K. May, *The Effects of United States and Other Foreign Investment in Latin America*.

7 Elena de la Souchère, "République dominicaine: le néo-trujillisme s'appuie sur le terrorisme militaire," Le Monde diplomatique, March 1972. The situation is not dissimilar in Guatemala, liberated a decade earlier. See Susanne Bodenheimer, "Inside a State of Siege: Legalized Murder in Guatemala," Ramparts, June 1971.

8 On this and related matters discussed here, see Jon Halliday and Gavan McCormack, Japanese Imperialism Today.

9 See, for example, Jean Egan, "South Korea: Time to Face Facts," Far Eastern Economic Review, January 15, 1972.

10 Jon Unger, "Life in Canton," Dispatch News Service International, January 10, 1972.

11 Timothy and Leslie Nulty, "Pakistan: The Busy Bee Route to Development," Trans-action, February 1971.

12 Herbert Feldman, "Aid as Imperialism?" International Affairs, vol. 43, no. 2 (1967). See, in this connection, "Southeast Asia in Turmoil," Bulletin of Concerned Asian Scholars, vol. 4, no. 1 (1972).

13 An American oil geologist, cited by Ralph Lombardi, "Let Bidding Commence," Far Eastern Economic Review, February 5, 1972. He states that offshore surveys began in 1966. See Malcolm Caldwell's important essay, "Oil and Imperialism in East Asia," Journal of Contemporary Asia, vol. 1, no. 3 (1971), for background.

14 T. D. Allman, "Search in Earnest," Far Eastern Economic Review, July 24, 1971.

15 It has been argued that the United States government involvement in opium traffic can be understood in the same context. See Frank Browning and Banning Garrett, "The New Opium War," Ramparts, May 1971; David Feingold, "Opium and Politics in Laos," in Nina S. Adams and Alfred W. McCoy, eds., Laos: War and Revolution. See also Peter Dale Scott, The War Conspiracy, chap. 8. For an extensive study of this entire question, see Alfred W. McCoy, The Politics of Heroin in Southeast Asia.

16 Rutherford Poats, Assistant Administrator for the Far East, AID, Hearings before the Committee on Foreign Affairs on H.R. 12169, 1966, cited by Ronald A. Witton, "Ideology and Utopia in Development," Journal of Contemporary Asia, vol. 1, no. 2 (1970).

17 Letter, New York Review of Books, February 26, 1970.

18 Cf. my At War with Asia, chap. 1, p. 59, n. 99; chap. 3, p. 156, n. 65; Banning Garrett, "Vietnam: How Nixon Plans to Win," Ramparts, February 1971. To make myself clear, the immediate issue is not the particular prejudices and ideological commitments of one or another group of scholars or even the services they render to state power, but rather the effort to mask these prejudices and services as disinterested scholarly research. The general practice of young radical Asian scholars in recent years offers a refreshing contrast. They have not, in general, concealed their commitments, but have stated them openly and plainly. Such work is often characterized as "committed scholarship," a genre presumably distinct from "objective disinterested scholarship." This is utter nonsense. Anyone who goes beyond listing of names and dates works within a framework of beliefs and commitments. Some have the candor to make this clear, putting the reader on notice, while others prefer to delude themselves and others.

[19] James P. Grant, President of the Overseas Development Council, Assistant Administrator for Vietnam of AID, 1967–1969.

[20] *The Pentagon Papers*, Senator Gravel Edition, II, 503.

[21] For some data, see AMPO, nos. 9–10 (AMPO Collective, Tokyo).

[22] Robert Shaplen, "We Have Always Survived," *New Yorker*, April 15, 1972.

[23] Yasushi Hara, "Nixon Asks Sato to Give Aid to Saigon," *Asahi Evening News*, October 26, 1970; "S. Vietnam to Receive Yen Credit," *Japan Times*, June 20, 1971. Reprinted in *Looking Back*, July 1971.

[24] Koji Nakamura, "The Okinawa Payoff," *Far Eastern Economic Review*, August 21, 1971.

[25] AP, *Christian Science Monitor*, March 30, 1971.

[26] Phi Bang, "Screws on Thieu," *Far Eastern Economic Review*.

[27] *New York Times*, October 12, 1971; Phi Bang, "Leading the Field," *Far Eastern Economic Review*, March 4, 1972.

[28] *Business Asia*, February 25, 1972.

[29] Phi Bang, "Leading the Field."

[30] See François Nivolon, "Profit and Honour," *Far Eastern Economic Review*, April 24, 1971.

[31] Several sections of this study are reprinted in *Looking Back*, July 1971. The material from the supplement to the *Mainichi Daily News* is reprinted in *Looking Back*, November 1971.

[32] Speech to (Saigon) American Chamber of Commerce, *Department of State Bulletin*, February 15, 1971.

[33] *Christian Science Monitor*, November 18, 1971; Craig Whitney, *New York Times*, January 24, 1972.

[34] *Business Asia:* "A Host of Firms Express Confidence in Vietnam's Future with Investments of Money and Know-how," November 12, 1971; "First Fruits Are Reaped from Vietnam Measures," December 10, 1971.

[35] *Business International*, December 3, 1971.

[36] For some recent discussion, see Daniel Lee, "Blank Coup in Thailand," *New Left Review*, January–February 1972.

[37] Michigan Brain Mistrust Collective, "Southeast Asia: American Power versus Regionalism," *American Report*, December 10, 1971.

[38] John G. Roberts, "The American Zaibatsu," *Far Eastern Economic Review*, July 24, 1971, with further comments on the role of Japan in helping "US investments to pay off handsomely."

[39] Allman, "Search in Earnest."

[40] Joseph Buttinger, *Vietnam: A Dragon Embattled*, vol. 2, p. 856. Jeffrey Race quotes Mai Ngoc Duoc, province chief of Long An Province from 1957 to 1961:

> Naturally, if one wants real democracy, one should organize elections, and I agree with this idea for other countries that are not harassed by communists. It is difficult to have this kind of democracy in Vietnam, because the communists operate everywhere, and it would be difficult to control the elections to prevent them from getting their people in.

Duoc himself did not hesitate to fix national election returns, Race points out, *War Comes to Long An*, pp. 51–2. Duoc's views are essentially those of the United States government. See chapter 1, section VI, subsection 5.2. Elections are fine, particularly for domestic United States consumption, but only when the outcome is certain to be in accord with the perceived interests of the imperial power.

[41] For data with regard to manufacturing industries, see Raymond Vernon, *Sovereignty at Bay*, p. 65.

[42] For a review of the 1970 record and some projections, see Brendan Jones, "Overseas Earnings Bolster U.S. Companies," *New York Times*, June 6, 1971.

[43] See Lawrence B. Krause, "Why Exports Are Becoming Irrelevant," *Foreign Policy*, vol. 1, no. 3 (1971).

[44] See Vernon, *Sovereignty at Bay*, pp. 189–90, for a skeptical though largely speculative view.

[45] See, for example, the comments by labor participants in National Planning Association, *U.S. Foreign Economic Policy for the 1970s*, particularly, those of R. Faupl, T. Hannigan, and H. Samuel, pp. 44–7.

[46] Takashi Oka, "American Made—in Japan," *New York Times*, business and finance section, June 13, 1971.

[47] *Pentagon Papers*, IV, 564. See also above, introduction, p. vii, and chapter 1, section III, p. 25. Also pp. 291–4.

CHAPTER 5

On the Limits of Civil Disobedience

The Berrigans have a disturbing habit of posing hard questions, not only by what they write and say, but by what they do. A reasonable person will admit that there exist, in principle, circumstances under which civil disobedience, even sabotage, is legitimate. The Berrigans have argued, with care and patience, that such circumstances now exist: specifically, that nonviolent resistance to the Indochina war is a legitimate response to criminal acts of the American executive, and that a legitimate component of such nonviolent resistance is the destruction of property that has no right to exist in that its immediate function is to implement these criminal acts. They have suggested that such a response is not only legitimate in principle, but that it may also be efficacious in restricting, perhaps terminating, the criminal violence of the American war. They have not been content merely to present the argument, or—as many others have—to construct the case from which the conclusion follows, without explicitly drawing it. Rather, they have pursued the logic of the argument to its conclusion and have acted accordingly, destroying property that (they argue) has no right to exist. They have also denied that the state has the right to prosecute those who act to restrain its criminal violence; and again, they have acted accordingly, refusing to yield themselves voluntarily to state authorities.

Such actions challenge beliefs, attitudes, and assumptions that are rarely questioned, for one reason, because questioning them is quite uncomfortable. It is therefore not surprising that the unconventional thinking and actions of the Berrigans sometimes call forth irrational reactions. Consider, for example, the discussion by Andrew Greeley, director of the National Opinion Center, Chicago, in *Church World* (September 18, 1970). He claims that Daniel Berrigan is a totalitarian who would imprison those who do not accept his moral judgments, and charges him with advocating the destruction of American society, with preaching hatred for this society and its people. Such charges will astonish anyone who actually knows Daniel Berrigan, or who has any familiarity with his writings. Greeley's discussion, though in fact frivolous and irresponsible, should not merely be dismissed on these grounds, with no further comment. Rather, it should be interpreted as a testimony to the seriousness of the questions that the Berrigans pose. It is precisely because these are hard and serious questions that those who fear to face them are driven to outlandish distortion and fantastic accusations.

A serious reaction to the Berrigans' reasoning and actions will take account of the nature of the war in Southeast Asia, the functioning of American democracy, and the responsibilities of the citizen under such circumstances. One might, for example, reject their reasoning on the grounds that American intervention in Southeast Asia is legitimate (though perhaps no longer worth its cost and thus a mistake)—the dominant opinion in the United States today, I would guess; or that the intervention, though illegitimate, should not be opposed by civil disobedience, which is improper in a democracy; or that civil disobedience, though legitimate under the present circumstances, is still improper because it is ineffective (or even "counterproductive"), or because of its likely social consequences; or that civil disobedience, though legitimate and proper, should not include destruction of property and should be followed by willing submission to state authorities. These questions, and others like them, are the ones that should be raised concerning the Berrigans' choice of action—that is, their decision to act and their choice of means.

Because it is, I presume, the dominant opinion in the United States, the assumption that American intervention is legitimate (though perhaps unwise) can obviously not be ignored. There is a great deal of unchallenged documentary evidence that demonstrates, I believe conclusively, that the

United States has at no point been engaged in collective self-defense against an armed attack—the only legal basis for the use of force—but rather, that it extended its long-term armed intervention in Vietnam to a full-scale invasion of South Vietnam in early 1965 because the National Liberation Front had won the internal civil struggle, despite the extensive (and illegal) direct American intervention.

Defenders of American actions frequently argue that questions of law are too complex for the layman and should be left to experts. However, in this case a careful reading of the arguments, pro and con, reveals little divergence over questions of law. The issues debated are factual and historical: specifically, is the United States engaged in collective self-defense against armed attack from North Vietnam? This is an issue concerning which the layman is in a position to make a judgment, and the responsible citizen will not be frightened away from doing so by the claim that the matter is too esoteric for him to comprehend. Extensive documentation is available, and, I believe, it shows clearly that the American war is criminal, even in the narrowest technical sense.

When we turn to the character of the war, the issue of legalism fades. The belief that the war is legitimate, though perhaps unwise, is in my opinion scandalous by strictly intellectual as well as decent moral standards. And it is deeply disturbing that this view is dominant. From this fact, we can conclude that other interventions of a similar sort will follow, with little popular opposition, and that the Nixon administration may succeed in carrying out its intended "low-cost, long-haul" strategy in Indochina, maintaining the technological war at its present phenomenal level while relying, to the extent that it can, on native troops armed, led, supplied, trained, and backed by Americans. It is important to bear in mind that this is the general pattern of military conquest, colonial or otherwise. The Russians do not use the Soviet army directly to enforce order in Czechoslovakia, and even the Nazis relied largely on native forces to control the occupied territories of Europe. What is unusual about the American war is the inability to create a native structure that has sufficient legitimacy to control the domestic population. It is this deficiency that Nixon hopes to remedy, while maintaining the attack on Indochina at its present massive scale. And so long as the debate here turns solely on the question of "cost," this strategy may succeed in imposing the rule of the elites that the United States defends, a bitter tragedy for the peasant societies of Indochina. There is a great deal more to say about this matter, but this is not the place, and I will therefore drop the matter here, merely reiterating that I do not think one can object to the Berrigans' actions on the grounds that the American intervention is legitimate, though perhaps unwise.

One who agrees with this judgment will naturally turn to the question whether civil disobedience is an appropriate form of opposition to the war, in a democracy. Several issues are intermingled here. Suppose, for the sake of argument, that the United States was a perfectly functioning democracy, and that our policy in Indochina had been determined by an informed electorate, through the democratic process. Would it then follow that civil disobedience is illegitimate? The answer is, surely, that it would not follow from these assumptions alone. There is no principle that supports the conclusion that the people of Indochina must be subjected to a criminal attack if the American people so determine by exercise of their democratic rights. There is no principle from which it follows that a pure, unflawed democratic society must be permitted to continue tranquil and undisturbed while it carries out criminal actions. Rather, citizens of this society (under the circumstances we have postulated) are faced with a dilemma, a conflict of principles: on the one hand, there is the commitment to the democratic process; on the other, a commitment to save Vietnam (and Laos, and now Cambodia) from extinction as a cultural and historic entity—the fate predicted by Bernard Fall[1]—or simply to defend them from criminal attack. One has to weigh these conflicting principles and determine which is overriding under the circumstances. But this question leads us back immediately to the issue of the legitimacy and character of the American intervention. It seems to me that an objective and reasoned evaluation of the circumstances and historical facts leads to the conclusion that civil disobedience, if effective in curtailing the criminal aggression against Indochina, would be legitimate, even on the assumption that our policies in Indochina were the expression of the will of the people in a perfectly functioning democracy.

However, the assumption is quite unacceptable. I shall not discuss here the inevitable limitations on democracy under a highly centralized, militarized state capitalist system of the contemporary American variety. But consider the determination of policy in a narrower sense. In November 1964, the population voted overwhelmingly against the policies which were put into effect immediately after the election, policies which, it appears, had been proposed unanimously by the president's advisers even prior to the election, though the electorate was never so informed. Or consider American military action in Laos, discussed in chapter 2, section I. What does this have to do with the state of American democracy? A good deal, in fact. The destruction of the civilian society of rural Laos, in the areas under Pathet Lao administration, was carried out in secret. What is hidden from the Senate Foreign Relations Committee is, needless to say, hardly common knowledge in the population at large. It takes immense effort to discover what the United States is doing in Laos. Under these circumstances, it is rather pointless to talk about interfering with the democratic process through civil disobedience. The democratic process has been undermined, severely, by the executive branch of the government.

One of the most careful and informed students of executive decision making in Indochina, Daniel Ellsberg, testified before Congress in May 1970 that American policy "has, in fact, been far more knowing, and one would have to say cynical, to insiders, in its contravention of the [Geneva] accord and of our announced goals of self-determination, than an outsider would easily imagine." As an outsider, I can only report that the cynicism of the American executive in Indochina for the past twenty years has few historical parallels, the war in Laos being perhaps the most striking example. The fact that Congress has virtually abandoned its constitutional role is no reason for citizens to tolerate submissively the further erosion of democracy. If civil disobedience can effectively curb the lawless and largely secret actions of the executive, then it seems to me a proper course of action.

This leads us to the next and in my opinion most crucial issue. What has been the impact of various types of protest and resistance since 1965, when dissent rose beyond a murmur? Here we must separate two factors: the effect on decision making and the effect on public opinion. These do not necessarily correlate. For example, it is possible that some action might lead to a decision to restrict American military involvement, and at the same time to increased public support for this involvement. I doubt that this has happened, though a superficial interpretation of certain facts to which I will return might lead one to a different conclusion; but it is certainly a possibility. In any event, the two factors will obviously be kept separate by one who wishes to save Indochina from the fate of which Bernard Fall warned. Such a person will want to influence public attitudes to the war, and to persuade the public that the American intervention is illegitimate; but far more important, he will want to modify the decisions taken by the executive in its pursuit of the twenty-year goal of subjugating Indochina—a goal, incidentally, which seems to persist despite the public-relations efforts of the Nixon administration.

Judgments about the impact of dissent, in either respect, can only be tentative and impressionistic. Occasionally, someone close to the formation of policy gives a glimpse of what he believes to have been operative considerations. For the most part, one must try to reconstruct from very partial evidence. As far as public attitudes are concerned, even less is known. What evidence there is, is rather meaningless. For example, it appears that the short-term effect of mass demonstrations is to antagonize those segments of the population that would prefer not to be disturbed; hence the president's popularity is likely to rise after any action that increases the visibility of the war. The real question, however, is quite different: What would public attitudes be if the war in Vietnam were not continually forced to consciousness by such actions, if the war were as "invisible" to an apathetic public as the secret executive war in Laos of the past six years? What would have been the possibilities for persuasion, for debate, for discussion of the issues, had mass actions not focused attention on the war, while deepening the commitment of those who participated in them? There has been no systematic investigation of such questions—the only important ones. In fact, it is not at all clear how they could be systematically studied. My own impression, based largely on extensive speaking to quite a wide variety of audiences over the years, is that mass demonstrations have been a major factor in bringing the war to public attention, and that resistance, particularly draft resistance, has had an appreciable effect in bringing many people to examine their own complicity and to draw them to the kinds of actions that have influenced policy makers.

In some cases, it is clear that protest and resistance have had dramatic if small-scale effects. My own university, the Massachusetts Institute of Technology, can serve as an example. In 1965–1966, there was little interest in the war. Teach-ins drew small groups, often antagonistic. In fact, MIT students were prominently engaged in violent disruption of public meetings against the war. The mood slowly changed as the war continued, but a really dramatic change was caused by a sanctuary for an AWOL soldier in the fall of 1968. Not only did this draw great numbers of apathetic or hostile students into a serious consideration of the issues (hence, as usual, to strong and principled opposition to the war), but it also set the stage for the first, very belated critical inquiry, by the faculty and student body, into university complicity in the military enterprises of the state. Many similar examples can be cited.

Consider the question of the impact on policy. What, for example, was the effect of domestic protest on the rejection of Westmoreland's demand for 200,000 additional troops after the Tet offensive? Or on Nixon's turn to the strategy of a long-haul, low-cost war? Or on the extent of the Cambodian invasion? Or on the decision to refrain from bombing the center of Hanoi and Haiphong in 1965–1968, along with the rest of the country, which was devastated? We can make some educated guesses. Townsend Hoopes's interesting memoirs[2] indicate that one operative domestic factor in post-Tet planning was protest and resistance, the fear that American society would become ungovernable. (There were of course other factors, such as the international monetary crisis that threatened if the war were to be further escalated.)

Others who have been close to the formation of policy have

spoken in similar terms (see chapter 1, section II). This is important evidence; it supports the judgment that mass protest and resistance have been a major factor in bringing about the changes of tactics in executive policy in recent years. Thus the timing of Nixon's November 3, 1969 announcement of troop withdrawals, as well as its content and manner, strongly suggests that this was an effort to respond to (and defuse) the massive fall demonstrations; or in other words, that the fall actions were the immediate cause of this tactical adjustment. A comparison of Nixon's television performance announcing the Cambodian invasion with his second appearance, a week later, as he sought desperately to build bridges to the young, certainly suggests that the spontaneous student strike was a factor in limiting the plans for the invasion of Cambodia. (What they may have been, we can only guess and may never know.)

The secrecy and endless deception of the executive is itself a clear indication of its fear of public response to the actual facts of the war it is waging in Indochina. There is direct testimony, occasionally, that gives some insight into how the executive hopes to "pacify" the American population. Consider, for example, the testimony of Secretary of the Army Stanley Resor before the House Appropriations Committee, that time is "running on our side" in Vietnam and "therefore if we can just buy some time in the United States by these periodic progressive withdrawals and the American people can just shore up their patience and determination, I think we can bring this to a successful conclusion."[3]

No one would argue that every antiwar action has been effective in combatting the general passivity that permits the war makers to act freely, or in increasing the level of opposition to the war. However, it seems fairly clear that had it not been for the mass actions of protest and the determined resistance of a few, the scale and intensity of the American war in Southeast Asia would have been even more ferocious than what we have seen in the past years, and the general public (including, incidentally, the "academic community," which has generally been roused from quiescence only by student activism), though perhaps not enthusiastic, would have per-

sisted in what Hans Morgenthau calls "our conformist subservience to those in power."

Andrew Greeley, in the article cited earlier, reaches very
different conclusions. He claims that the war is ending "not
because of the Daniel Berrigans (quite the contrary, the research data suggest that the Berrigans and the rest of the
protesting rabble may have prolonged the war) but despite
them, because the members of a free and open society have,
however belatedly, made it impossible for the government to
continue to wage the war." He adds that "this is the first time
in the history of the human race that a major power has been
forced out of a war simply because its people do not approve
of it." The latter statement is clearly false. Consider only our
predecessors in the effort to maintain Western dominance in
Indochina. The French, as Bernard Fall pointed out, "never
dared to send conscripts to Viet-Nam, nor did they increase
the draft at home for fear of public opposition to the war"[4]—
despite their "historic interests" in Indochina. With the Nixon
doctrine, we are beginning to reduce the American commitment to victory to a level that the French government could
never achieve, because "its people did not approve of it." Had
the French approved of the war to the extent that Americans
still do, France could also have sent a massive conscript army,
though it obviously could not have matched the technological
resources with which we batter Indochina.

However, despite his carelessness and irresponsibility, it is
important to consider seriously the claim by the program
director of the National Opinion Center that the "protesting
rabble" may have prolonged the war. His claim that unspeci-
fied "research data" support this view is probably a reference
to the fact that polls generally indicate an increase in support
for the president after mass demonstrations. I have already
pointed out why this is quite meaningless. There are no further
"research data," to my knowledge, that suggest anything
significant about the effect of mass protest and resistance on
public attitudes, and as far as the effect on decision making is
concerned, what evidence there is suggests that mass protest
and resistance are precisely what has led to changes of tactics
over the years. But Greeley is on target, more or less, in assert-

ing that it is the public that has "made it impossible for the government to continue to wage the war." To be more accurate, it is certain segments of the public—largely the student movement—that have made it difficult for the government to wage the war with the freedom and abandon it would wish. And these segments of the public, Greeley's "protesting rabble," have been inspired, to a significant extent, by Dan and Phil Berrigan and a few others like them.

On the other hand, if the objects of Greeley's scorn had followed his example and advice over the past few years, then it is likely that Bernard Fall's warning would have come much closer to fulfillment. One can debate the exact degree of impact of the actions of the Berrigans and others like them, and the many thousands who have been influenced by their conscientious resistance to rouse themselves from apathy and involve themselves in visible opposition to the war. So far as I can see, there is no reasonable doubt that mass protest and resistance have been factors, perhaps major factors, in constraining the executive. And, though the evidence here is less compelling, it seems plausible that mass protest and resistance have, over the years, kept the war in the public eye and defeated the efforts to create the atmosphere of conformist subservience that would permit the free exercise of American military power. Whether this will continue to be the case, I cannot say. However, if the Greeleys have their way and the "protesting rabble" is silenced, then the Nixon strategy of an unending war of devastation may be pursued to the "successful conclusion" that Secretary Resor anticipates; and at best, the future prospects for the societies of Indochina are dim indeed. At worst, Resor's "successful conclusion" may be the genocide that Townsend Hoopes identifies as "the final conclusion" of our "strategic logic" in Vietnam.[5]

Such considerations still do not bear on the more specific question of the effects of actions such as the destruction of draft files at Catonsville. Suppose, for example, that one could show that such actions have helped create an atmosphere in which some people have been led to terrorist attacks that are deplorable in themselves, as well as useful only to the government, in its efforts to reinforce the conformist subservience to state power. Then one would have to conclude that the draft-file destruction was improper because of its social consequences, even if (as I believe) legitimate in principle. Again, judgments can only be tentative. However, from what information is available to me, I do not believe that actions such as those of the Catonsville Nine and the Milwaukee Fourteen have in any way contributed to terrorism. It might be argued that had there been a more extensive involvement in nonviolent actions such as those of the Berrigans, then perhaps the mood of desperation that leads some to terrorism might have been abated. I don't know how to evaluate this possibility.

Have the actions of the Berrigans and others led to a heightened consciousness and commitment to oppose the war? There is little doubt of this, though the circles may be small. Have they produced a negative reaction in wider circles, say a reversion to the kind of authoritarianism that benefits only state power? I know of no reason to believe this. My impression is that actions such as those in Catonsville and Milwaukee might receive broad support if the effort were made to explain and discuss them. If there has been a serious failing, I think it is in this indispensable second-order supporting effort.

I have not discussed the question of willing submission to arrest. It is often maintained that this is a necessary component of legitimate civil disobedience. I simply do not see the logic of this claim. There is no moral compulsion for one who seeks to prevent criminal actions of the state to submit voluntarily to punishment for his actions. Refusal to submit to punishment does not, in itself, imply a refusal to recognize the general legitimacy of the government (often proposed as the criterion to distinguish civil disobedience from rebellion), just as a refusal to contribute voluntarily to criminal acts by the payment of war taxes does not, in itself, challenge the legitimacy of the government. Rather, it is a challenge to the legitimacy of specific actions taken by what may or may not be a legitimate authority, on other grounds.

There is the more specific question: Is it proper to destroy draft files (granted, for the sake of discussion, that all other doubts about such actions have been allayed)? There is a coercive element in such actions, in that the rights of registrants and the demands on them are affected without their consent or choice. Furthermore, the effect is not to prevent recruitment for the armed forces but to redistribute it. One might say the same, in part, about draft resistance, although when the scale becomes significant—as in northern California, where extremely high rates of refusal to serve are reported, perhaps approaching two-thirds—there is a qualitative change in the political impact of the action. There has been a good deal of discussion of these matters, primarily among pacifists, and I have nothing to add. To me it seems that the crucial issue is the impact of such actions on ending the atrocity of the American war. If the contribution is significant, then this more than compensates for the element of coercion which, if we are to be honest, is rarely absent in nonviolent civil disobedience, much as one may and should try to diminish it.

In discussing the questions raised by the Berrigans' actions, I have tried to consider the issues dispassionately. Admittedly, this is difficult. We are not discussing abstract questions of logic but the fate of a people, the existence of a society. It is not necessary to visit Indochina to appreciate the horror of the American war. The point is that it is difficult, when one is willing to face the facts, to try to balance properly the legitimate types of disruption against the effects of our passivity on the people of Indochina.

At a lesser scale of intensity, it is difficult to be dispassionate about the Berrigans. No one who knows them can doubt that they are heroic individuals, willing to do what many realize should be done, regardless of the personal cost, with a simplicity of manner and a commitment to principle that can only inspire the deepest respect. There are not too many people of whom this can honestly be said. Andrew Greeley scoffs at the comparison of Dan Berrigan to Dietrich Bonhoeffer. The comparison, however, is quite appropriate.

In a recent statement, Richard Falk, Professor of International Law at Princeton, recalled Roosevelt's appeal to the German people:

> Hitler is committing these crimes against humanity in the name of the German people. I ask every German and every man everywhere under Nazi domination to show the world that he does not share these insane criminal desires.[6]

He adds, "A similar appeal to the American people by responsible leaders is long overdue." There has been and will be no such appeal. There have, however, been a few men and women who have shown that they will not be part of the criminal assault on the people of Indochina. The Berrigans are among those few.

Notes

This essay is a slightly abridged version of the article that originally appeared in the *Holy Cross Quarterly*, vol. 4, no. 1 (1971).

1 Bernard Fall, *Last Reflections on a War*, pp. 33–4.
2 Townsend Hoopes, *The Limits of Intervention*.
3 Stanley Resor, testimony of October 8, 1969, released December 2; quoted in *I. F. Stone's Weekly*, December 15, 1969. See also my article "Revolt in the Academy," *Modern Occasions*, vol. 1, no. 1 (1970). For further discussion of the topics mentioned here, see my "Mayday: The Case for Civil Disobedience," *New York Review of Books*, June 17, 1971.
4 Fall, *Last Reflections*, p. 231.
5 Hoopes, *Limits of Intervention*, p. 129.
6 Richard A. Falk, in Erwin Knoll and Judith N. McFadden, eds., *War Crimes and the American Conscience*, pp. 6–7.

CHAPTER 6

The Function of the University in a Time of Crisis

Writing 150 years ago, the great liberal reformer and humanist Wilhelm von Humboldt defined the university as "nothing other than the spiritual life of those human beings who are moved by external leisure or internal pressures toward learning and research." At every stage of his life, a free man will be driven, to a greater or lesser extent, by these "internal pressures." The society in which he lives may or may not provide him with the "external leisure" and the institutional forms in which he may realize this human need to discover and create, to explore and evaluate and come to understand, to refine and exercise his talents, to contemplate, to make his own individual contribution to contemporary culture, to analyze and criticize and transform this culture and the social structure in which it is rooted. Even if the university did not exist formally, Humboldt observes, "one person would privately reflect and collect, another join himself to men of his own age, a third find a circle of disciples. Such is the picture to which the state must remain faithful if it wishes to give an institutional form to such indefinite and rather accidental human operations."[1]

The extent to which existing institutional forms permit these human needs to be satisfied provides one measure of the level of civilization that a society has achieved. One element in the unending struggle to achieve a more just and humane social order will be the effort to remove the barriers—whether they be economic, ideological, or political—that stand in the way of the particular forms of individual self-fulfillment and collective action that the university should make possible.

It is the great merit of the student movement of the 1960s to have helped shatter the complacency that had settled over much of American intellectual life, with regard to both American society and the role of the universities within it. The renewed concern with university reform is in large measure a consequence of student activism. A great deal of energy has been directed to problems of "restructuring the university": democratizing it, redistributing "power" in it, reducing constraints on student freedom, as well as the dependence of the university on outside institutions. I suspect that little can be achieved of real substance along these lines. Formal changes in university structure will have little effect on what a student does with his life, or on the relation of the university to society. To the extent that reform does not reach the heart of the university—the content of the curriculum, the interaction between student and teacher, the nature of research, and in some fields, the practice that relates to theory—it will remain superficial. But it is doubtful that these matters will be significantly affected by the kinds of structural reform that are now being actively debated on many campuses.

It is pointless to discuss "the function of the university" in abstraction from concrete historical circumstances, as it would be a waste of effort to study any other social institution in this way. In a different society entirely different questions might arise as to the function of the university and the problems that are pressing. To one who believes, as I do, that our society must undergo drastic changes if civilization is to advance— perhaps even to survive—university reform will appear an insignificant matter except insofar as it contributes to social change. Apart from this question, improvements in the university can no doubt take place within the framework of the existing "institutional forms," and drastic revision of these forms will contribute little to it.

It is never an easy matter to determine to what extent deficiencies of a particular institution can actually be overcome through internal reform, and to what extent they reflect characteristics of society at large, or matters of individual psychology relatively independent of social forms. Consider, for example, the competitiveness fostered in the university, in fact, in the school system as a whole. It is difficult to convince oneself that this serves an educational purpose. Certainly, it does not prepare the student for the life of a scholar or scientist. It would be absurd to demand of the working scientist that he keep his work secret so that his colleagues will not know of his achievements, not be helped by his discoveries in pursuing their own studies and research. Yet this is what we often demand of the student in the classroom.

In later life, collective effort with sharing of discovery and mutual assistance is the ideal; if it is not the norm, we rightly interpret this as an inadequacy of those who cannot rise above personal aggrandizement and in this measure are incompetent as scholars, scientists, and teachers. Yet even at the most advanced level of graduate education, the student is discouraged by university regulations from working as any reasonable person would certainly choose to do: individually, where his interests lead him; collectively, when he can learn from and aid his fellows. Course projects and examinations are individual and competitive. Not only is the doctoral dissertation required to be a purely individual contribution; beyond this questionable requirement, there is a built-in bias towards insignificance in the demand that a finished piece of work be completed in a fixed time-span. The student is obliged to set himself a limited goal, and to avoid adventuresome, speculative investigation that may challenge the conventional framework of scholarship and, correspondingly, runs a high risk of failure. In this respect, the institutional forms of the university encourage mediocrity. Perhaps this is one reason why it is so common for a scholar to devote his career to trivial modifications of what he has already done. The patterns of thinking imposed in his early work, the poverty of conception that is fostered by too-rigid institutional forms, may limit his imagination and distort his vision. That many escape these limitations is a tribute to the human ability to resist pressures that tend to restrict the variety and creativity of life and thought. What is true even at the most advanced levels of graduate education is far more significant at earlier stages, as many critics have eloquently demonstrated. Still, it is not evident, even in this case, to what extent the fault is that of the universities and to what extent it is inherent in the role assigned them in a competitive society, where pursuit of self-interest is elevated to the highest goal.

Some of the pressures that impoverish the educational experience and distort the natural relation of student and teacher clearly have their origin in demands that are imposed on the school. Consider, for example, the problem defined by Daniel Bell: "higher education has been burdened with the task of becoming a gatekeeper—perhaps the only gatekeeper to significant place and privilege in society. . . . it means that the educational system is no longer geared to teaching but to judging."[2] Jencks and Riesman make a similar point: "college is a kind of protracted aptitude test for measuring certain aspects of intelligence and character." The result: "Reliance on colleges to preselect the upper-middle class obviously eliminates most youngsters born into lower-strata families, since they have 'the wrong attitudes' for academic success."[3] The effect is that the university serves as an instrument for ensuring the perpetuation of social privilege.

The same, incidentally, holds of later life. To achieve the Humboldtian ideal, a university should be open to any person, at any stage of life, who wishes to avail himself of this institutional form for enhancing his "spiritual life." In fact, there are programs for bringing corporate executives or engineers from industry to the university for specialized training or simply for broadening their cultural background, but none, to my knowledge, for shoemakers or industrial workers, who could in principle profit no less from these opportunities. Evidently, it would be misleading to describe these inequities merely as defects of the university.

In general, there is little if any educational function to the requirement that the university be concerned with certification as well as with education and research. On the contrary, this requirement interferes with its proper function. It is a demand imposed by a society that ensures, in many ways, the preservation of certain forms of privilege.

Or consider the often-voiced demand that the university serve the needs of the outside society—that its activities be "relevant" to general social concerns. Put in a very general way, this demand is justifiable. Translated into practice, however, it usually means that the universities provide a service to existing social institutions, those institutions that are in a position to articulate their needs and to subsidize the effort to meet them. It is not difficult for members of the "university community" to delude themselves into believing that they are maintaining a "neutral, value-free" position when they are simply responding to demands set elsewhere. In fact, to do so is to make a political decision, namely, to ratify the existing distribution of power, authority, and privilege in the society at large, and to take on a commitment to reinforce it. The Pentagon and the great corporations can formulate their needs and subsidize the kind of work that will answer to them. The peasants of Guatemala or the unemployed in Harlem are in no position to do so, obviously. A free society should encourage the development of a university that escapes the not-too-subtle compulsion to be "relevant" in this sense. The university will be able to make its contribution to a free society only to the extent that it overcomes the temptation to conform unthinkingly to the prevailing ideology and to the existing patterns of power and privilege.

In its relation to society, a free university should be expected to be, in a sense, "subversive." We take it for granted that creative work in any field will challenge prevailing orthodoxy. A physicist who refines yesterday's experiment, an engineer who merely seeks to improve existing devices, an artist who limits himself to styles and techniques that have been thoroughly explored, is rightly regarded as deficient in creative imagination. Exciting work in science, technology, scholarship, or the arts will probe the frontiers of understanding and try to create alternatives to the conventional assumptions. If, in some field of inquiry, this is no longer true, then the field will be abandoned by those who seek intellectual adventure.

These observations are clichés that few will question—except in the study of man and society. The social critic who seeks to formulate a vision of a more just and humane social order, and is concerned with the discrepancy—more often, the chasm—that separates this vision from the reality that confronts him, is a frightening creature who must "overcome his alienation" and become "responsible," "realistic," and "pragmatic." To decode these expressions: he must stop questioning our values and threatening our privilege. He may be concerned with technical modifications of existing society that improve its efficiency and blur its inequities, but he must not try to design a radically different alternative and involve himself in an attempt to bring about social change. He must, therefore, abandon the path of creative inquiry as it is conceived in other domains. It is hardly necessary to stress that this prejudice is even more rigidly institutionalized in the state socialist societies.

Obviously, a free mind may fall into error; the social critic is no less immune to this possibility than the inventive scientist or artist. It may be that at a given stage of technology, the most important activity is to improve the internal combustion engine, and that at a given stage of social evolution, primary attention should be given to the study of fiscal measures that will improve the operation of the state capitalism of the Western democracies. This is possible, but hardly obvious, in either case. The universities offer freedom and encouragement to those who question the first of these assumptions, but more rarely to those who question the second. The reasons are fairly clear. Since the dominant voice in any society is that of the beneficiaries of the status quo, the "alienated intellectual" who tries to pursue the normal path of honest inquiry—perhaps falling into error on the way—and thus often finds himself challenging the conventional wisdom, tends to be a lonely figure. The degree of protection and support afforded him by the university is, again, a measure of its success in fulfilling its proper function in a free society. It is, furthermore, a measure of the willingness of the society to submit its ideology and structure to critical analysis and evaluation, and of its willingness to overcome inequities and defects that will be revealed by such a critique.

Such problems as these—which will never cease to exist so long as human society continues—have become somewhat more critical in the last few years for a number of reasons. In an advanced industrial society, the link between the university and external social institutions tends to become more tight and intricate, because of the utility of the "knowledge that is produced" (to use a vulgar idiom) and the training that is provided. This is a familiar insight. Half a century ago,

Randolph Bourne noted that the World War had brought to leadership a liberal, technical intelligentsia, "immensely ready for the executive ordering of events, pitifully unprepared for the intellectual interpretation or the idealistic focussing of ends"; pragmatic intellectuals who "have absorbed the secret of scientific method as applied to political administration" and who readily "lined up in service of the war technique." Turning to the university, and taking Columbia University as the prototype, he described it as "a financial corporation, strictly analogous, in its motives and responses, to the corporation which is concerned in the production of industrial commodities. . . . The university produces learning instead of steel or rubber, but the nature of the academic commodity has become less and less potent in insuring for the academic workman a status materially different from that of any other kind of employee." The trustees, he claimed, define their obligation in this way: "to see that the quality of the commodity which the university produces is such as to seem reputable to the class which they represent." "Under trustee control," Bourne went on, "the American university has been degraded from its old, noble ideal of a community of scholarship to a private commercial corporation."[4]

Bourne's characterization of the university can be questioned in many respects, but it nevertheless has an unpleasant ring of authenticity, today even more than at the time when he wrote. It will not escape the reader that the student movement of the past few years has—quite independently—developed a very similar critique, often with the same rhetoric. Again, one can point to exaggerations and even flights of fancy, but it would be a mistake to overlook the kernel of truth within.

A further reason why the problems of the universities have become a more urgent concern than heretofore is that the universities have, on an unprecedented scale, come to be *the* center of intellectual life. Not only scientists and scholars but also writers and artists are drawn to the academic community. To the extent that this is true, to the extent that other independent intellectual communities disappear, the demands on the university increase. Probably this is a factor in the university crises of the past few years. With the depoliticization of American society in the 1950s and the narrowing of the range of social thought, the university seems to have become, for many students, almost the only center of intellectual stimulation. Lionel Trilling, in a recent interview, pointed out that he cannot draw on his own experience as a student to help him comprehend the motivation of the "militant students" at Columbia: "Like all my friends at college, I hadn't the slightest interest in the university as an institution: I thought of it, when I thought of it at all, as the inevitable philistine condition of one's being given leisure, a few interesting teachers and a library. I find it hard to believe that this isn't the natural attitude. . . ."[5] This is an apt comment. In the past, it was for the most part the football and fraternity crowd who had an interest in the university as such. But in this respect, there have been substantial changes. Now it is generally the most serious and thoughtful students who are concerned with the nature of the universities, and who feel hurt and deprived by its failings. Twenty years ago, these students—in an urban university, at least—would have looked elsewhere for the intellectual and social life that they now expect the university to provide.

Personally, I feel that the sharp challenges that have been raised by the student movement are among the few hopeful developments of these troubled years. It would be superficial, and in fact rather childish, to be so mesmerized by occasional absurdities of formulation or offensive acts as to fail to see the great significance of the issues that have been raised and that lie beneath the tumult. Only one totally lacking in judgment could find himself offended by "student extremism" and not, to an immensely greater extent, by the events and situations that motivate it. A person who can write such words as the following has, to put it as kindly as possible, lost his grasp of reality: "Quite a few of our universities have already decided that the only way to avoid on-campus riots is to give students academic credit for off-campus rioting ('fieldwork' in the ghettoes, among migrant workers, etc.)."[6] Consider the assumptions that would lead one to describe work in the ghettos or among migrant workers as a form of "rioting," or, for that matter, to regard work of this sort as necessarily inappropriate to a college program—as distinct from, say, work on biological warfare or counterinsurgency, which is not described in these terms.

Less extreme, but still seriously distorted, is the perception of the student movement expressed by George Kennan, who is concerned with what he sees as "the extremely disturbed and excited state of mind of a good portion of our student youth, floundering around as it is in its own terrifying wilderness of drugs, pornography, and political hysteria."[7] Again, it is striking that he is so much less concerned with the "extremely disturbed and excited state of mind" of those responsible for the fact that the tonnage of bombs dropped on South Vietnam exceeds the total expended by the United States Air Force in all theaters of World War II, or of those responsible for the anticommunist "political hysteria" of the 1950s, or, for that matter, of that great mass of students who are still "floundering around" in the traditional atmosphere of conformism and passivity of the colleges, and whose rioting is occasioned by football victories.

The irrationality which has been all too characteristic of the response to the student movement is itself a remarkable phenomenon, worthy of analysis. More important, however, is the effort to take the challenge presented by the student movement as a stimulus to critical thinking and social action, perhaps of a quite radical nature—a necessity in a society as troubled as ours, and as dangerous. Since World War II we have spent well over a trillion dollars on "defense," along with billions on an infantile competition to place a man on the moon. Scientists and technologists prepare to construct an antiballistic missile system at an ultimate cost of many billions of dollars though they know that it will contribute nothing to defense, that in fact it will raise a potentially suicidal arms race to new heights. At the same time, our cities crumble and millions suffer hunger and want, while those who try to publicize these conditions are investigated by the FBI. It is intolerable that our society should continue to arrogate to itself—in part for consumption, in part for unconscionable waste—almost half of the far from limitless material resources of the world. There are simply no words to describe our willingness to destroy, on a scale without parallel in the contemporary world, when our leaders detect a threat to the "national goals" that they formulate and that a passive and docile citizenry accepts. It may appear to be an extreme judgment when a social scientist from Pakistan asserts that "America has institutionalized even its genocide," referring to the fact that the extermination of the Indians "has become the object of public entertainment and children's games."[8] A look at school texts confirms his assessment, however. Consider the following description in a fourth-grade reader of the extermination of the Pequot tribe by Captain John Mason:

> "His little army attacked in the morning before it was light and took the Pequots by surprise. The soldiers broke down the stockade with their axes, rushed inside, and set fire to the wigwams. They killed nearly all the braves, squaws, and children, and burned their corn and other food. There were no Pequots left to make more trouble. When the other Indian tribes saw what good fighters the white men were, they kept the peace for many years."
> "I wish I were a man and had been there," thought Robert.[9]

A child who acquires such attitudes in the schools will become the man who can behave in the way described by a British eyewitness:

> I asked one American who had just ordered a strike on some huts and some sampans (blowing the latter to bits "with parts of the boat and bodies flying in all directions") if air attacks like this did not kill many harmless civilians. "But people shouldn't continue to live here," he said.[10]

It is hardly necessary to add that attitudes created in the schools are supported by the mass media, not only directly but by their encouragement of a general passivity. There is much truth in the observation of Paul Lazarsfeld and Robert Merton that:

> these media not only continue to affirm the *status quo* but, in the same measure, they fail to raise essential questions about the structure of society. Hence by leading toward conformism and by providing little basis for a critical appraisal of society, the commercially sponsored mass media indirectly but effectively restrain the cogent development of a genuinely critical outlook.[11]

This is not the place for an extended discussion; it is enough to point out that for reasons suggested by these few remarks, it is a matter of great urgency, for ourselves and for world society, that our institutions and ideology be subjected to serious critical analysis. The universities must be a primary object of such analysis, and at the same time might provide the "institutional form" within which it can be freely conducted. In these specific historical circumstances, it is useful to recall a remark of Bertrand Russell:

> Without rebellion, mankind would stagnate, and injustice would be irremediable. The man who refuses to obey authority has, therefore, in certain circumstances, a legitimate function, provided his disobedience has motives which are social rather than personal.[12]

It is these historical circumstances that define the context for a study of the function of the university and the current challenge to the university.

Reactions to the recent wave of student unrest throughout the world have varied widely. Nathan Glazer asks "whether the student radicals fundamentally represent a better world that can come into being, or whether they are not committed to outdated and romantic visions that cannot be realized, that contradict fundamentally other desires and hopes they themselves possess and that contradict even more the desires of most other people." He tends towards the latter view; the student radicals remind him "more of the Luddite machine smashers than the Socialist trade unionists who achieved citizenship and power for workers."[13] Consider, in contrast, the reaction of Paul Ricoeur to the massive rebellion of French students in May 1968:

> The signs are now eloquent. The West has entered into a cultural revolution which is distinctively its own, the revolution of the advanced industrial societies, even if it echoes or borrows from the Chinese revolution. It is a cultural revolution because it questions the world-vision, the conception of life, that underlie the economic and political structures and the totality of human relations. This revolution attacks capitalism not only because it fails to bring about social justice but also because it succeeds too well in deluding men by its own inhuman commitment to quantitative well-being. It attacks bureaucracy not only because it is burdensome and ineffectual, but because it places men in the role of slaves in relation to the totality of powers, of

structures and hierarchical relations from which they have become estranged. Finally, it attacks the nihilism of a society which, like a cancerous tissue, has no purpose beyond its own growth. Confronted with a senseless society, this cultural revolution tries to find the way to the creation of goods, of ideas, of values, in relation to their ends. The enterprise is gigantic; it will take years, decades, a century. . . .[14]

Glazer (like Brzezinski—see note 7) sees the student rebels as Luddites, displaced and unable to find their role in the new society of advanced technology and complex social management. They "come from the fields that have a restricted and ambiguous place in a contemporary society."[15] Ricoeur, on the other hand, expresses a very different perception: in the advanced industrial societies in the coming years there will be a sharp conflict between the centralizing force of a technical bureaucracy, managing society for dubious ends, and the forces that seek to reconstruct social life on a more human scale on the basis of "participation" and popular control. Both interpretations sense that a major historical process is under way. They differ in their judgment as to where they expect (and no doubt hope) it will end, and correspondingly, in the interpretation they give of student dissidence and rebellion. Both expect the university to be at the center of the conflict. Optimists may hope that it will be in the eye of the hurricane—but it is more realistic to expect that it will continue to be caught up in controversy and turmoil.

It is hardly in doubt that we are in the midst of a historical process of centralization and bureaucratization, not only in the economy but also in politics and social organization. The crisis of parliamentary institutions is a world-wide phenomenon.[16] Reactions can be seen not only in university rebellions but also in the search for forms of community organization and control—which have forced their way onto the front pages in recent months—and even, it seems, in tentative gropings towards more direct worker's control, often in opposition to the highly bureaucratized trade unions that are increasingly more remote from the day-to-day concerns of those whom the leadership claims to represent.[17] In Eastern Europe there are somewhat analogous developments. The student movement must, I believe, be understood in this more general context.

The universities will not be able to isolate themselves from the profound social conflict that appears likely, though its course can hardly be guessed. The linkage of the universities to other social institutions, noted earlier, guarantees this. In fact, there may be very serious questioning, in coming years, of the basic assumption of modern society that development of technology is inherently a desirable, inevitable process; and with it, a critique of the role of the university in advancing knowledge and technique and putting it to use. When students in Western Europe take as their war cry the chant "Ho, Ho, Ho Chi Minh," they are not merely protesting the Vietnam war and the crushing of the poor by the rich that it symbolizes; they are also reacting against the values of industrial society, protesting the role assigned to them as managers of this society, and rejecting the kind of rationality uninformed by any sense of justice, which—as they see it, with considerable accuracy—translates into practice as the knowledge how to preserve privilege and order but not to meet human needs. The American student movement is also animated in part by such concerns.

In many respects, the university is a legitimate target for protest. The unflattering portrait given by such critics as James Ridgeway[18] may be overdrawn, but it is basically realistic, and quite properly disturbing to the concerned student. Recognition of these characteristics of the university leads to revulsion and often militancy. Nevertheless, the problems brought to the surface may be irresoluble, within the framework of the university itself. Consider, for example, the matter of government contracts for research. It is a classical liberal ideal, echoed also by Marx, that "government and church should . . . be equally excluded from any influence on the school."[19] On the other hand, there is little doubt that government research contracts provide a hidden subsidy to the academic budget, by supporting faculty research which would otherwise have to be subsidized by the university. It is quite probable that the choice of research topics, in the natural sciences at least, is influenced very little by the source of funds, at least in the major universities. It is doubtful that scientific education can continue at a reasonable level without this kind of support. Furthermore, radical students will certainly ask themselves why support from the Defense Department is more objectionable than support from capitalist institutions—ultimately, from profits derived by exploitation—or support by tax-free gifts that in effect constitute a levy on the poor to support the education of the privileged.[20] It is impossible to escape the fact that the university is ultimately a parasitic institution, from an economic point of view. It cannot free itself from the inequities of the society in which it exists. At the same time, it is dependent for its existence as a relatively free institution on values that are upheld in the society at large. When, for example, Senator Fulbright criticizes the universities for having "betrayed a public trust" by associating themselves with the military-industrial complex instead of acting as an independent critical institution, he is expressing the values that permit the university to function as a free institution to the extent that it does. It is not impossible that these values will be a casualty of the domestic turmoil that is itself in part a consequence of American militarism. It would be foolish to remain blind to these dangers.

One legacy of classical liberalism that we must fight to uphold with unending vigilance, in the universities and without, is the commitment to a "free marketplace of ideas." To a certain extent, this commitment is merely verbal. The task, however, is to extend, not to limit, such freedom as exists—and it is not inconsiderable. Students are right to ask why faculty members should be permitted to contribute to the weapons cult or to work on counterinsurgency. They also point out, with much justice, that it is unreasonable to claim that this is simply a freely undertaken commitment. Access to funds, power, and influence is open to those who undertake this work, but not, say, to those who would prefer to study ways in which poorly armed guerrillas might combat an enemy with overwhelming technological superiority. Were the university truly "neutral" and "value-free," one kind of work would—as noted earlier—be as well supported as the other. The argument is valid, but does not change the fact that the commitment is nevertheless undertaken with eagerness and a belief that it is right. Only coercion could eliminate the freedom to undertake such work. Once the principle is established that coercion is legitimate, in this domain, it is rather clear against whom it will be used. And the principle of legitimacy of coercion would destroy the university as a serious institution; it would destroy its value to a free society. This must be recognized even in the light of the undeniable fact that the freedom falls far short of ideal.

In certain respects, the specific issue of Defense Department funding of research is a misleading one. Research on chemical and biological warfare or counterinsurgency would be no more benign if funded by the National Institutes of Health or the Social Science Research Council, just as work on high-energy physics is not corrupted if funding comes through the Department of Defense. The important question is the nature of the work and the uses to which it is likely to be put, not the bureaucratic issue of the source of funding. The latter is of some significance, insofar as one might argue that the Pentagon gains respectability and power by its support of serious research. For American society as a whole, this development is a very minor symptom of a real tragedy, the ongoing and perhaps irreversible militarization of American society. But in the particular case of the universities, these considerations seem to me marginal. Another side issue, in my opinion, is the question of a campus base for military research. In fact, the Vietnamese care very little whether the counterinsurgency technology that is used to destroy and repress them is developed in the halls of the university[21] or in private spin-offs on its periphery. And the victims of the endless arms race—the present victims of the waste of resources, material and intellectual, that are desperately needed elsewhere, or the possible future victims of a devastating catastrophe—to these unfortunates it is of little interest whether their fate is determined in a Department of Death on the university campus or in Los Alamos or Fort Detrick, hundreds of miles away. To move such work off campus is socially irrelevant. It might, in fact, even be a regressive step. It might be argued that as long as such work continues, it would be preferable for it to be done on campus, where it can become a focus for student activism and protest that may not only impede such work but also contribute to growing public awareness.

One of the most hopeful signs, in my opinion, is the increasing concern among students over the problem of the uses of research. There are few today who would agree with the judgment of Edward Teller that "we must trust our social processes" to make the best use of technological advance and "must not be deterred by arguments involving consequences or costs.²² The question of the uses of technology is multi-faceted: it involves complex historical and political judgments as well as technical issues. Properly, it should be faced by students at a time in life when they are relatively free from external pressures, free to explore the many dimensions of the problems and supported by a community with like concerns, rather than isolated in a competitive job market. For such reasons, the problems of campus-based military research seem to me rather complex.

Those who believe that radical social change is imperative in our society are faced with a dilemma when they consider university reform. They want the university to be a free institution, and they want the individuals in it to use this freedom in a civilized way. They observe that the university—or to be more precise, many of its members—are "lined up in the service of the war technique" and that it often functions in such a way as to entrench privilege and support repression. Given this largely correct observation, it is easy to move to some serious misconceptions. It is simply false to claim—as many now do—that the university exists only to provide manpower for the corporate system, or that the university (and the society) permit no meaningful work, or that the university merely serves to coerce and "channel" the student into a socially accepted life-style and ideology; even though it is true that the temptation to make choices that will lead in these directions is very great. To an overwhelming extent, the features of university life that rightly are offensive to many concerned students result not from trustee control, not from defense contracts, not from administrative decisions, but from the relatively free choices of faculty and students. Hence the dilemma noted above. "Restructuring of the university" is unlikely to be effective in eliminating the features of the institution that have sparked student criticism. In fact, many of the concrete proposals that I have seen are, I suspect, likely to have the opposite effect: namely, they may lead towards a system of enforceable regulations that may appear democratic on paper, but will limit the individual freedom that exists in an institution that is highly decentralized and rather loose in its structure of decision making and administration, hence fairly responsive to the wishes of its members.

It is possible to imagine useful reforms. I suspect, however, that they will have at best a small effect on the way the university functions. The real problem is a much deeper one: to change the choices and personal commitment of the individuals who make up the university. This is much harder than modification of formal structures, and is not likely to be effected by such restructuring in any very serious way.

More to the point, I believe, is the view expressed in the Port Huron statement of 1962, more or less the "founding document" of SDS:

> The university is located in a permanent position of social influence. Its educational function makes it indispensable and automatically makes it a crucial institution in the formation of social attitudes. In an unbelievably complicated world, it is the central institution for organizing, evaluating, and transmitting knowledge. . . . Social relevance, the accessibility to knowledge, and internal openness—these together make the university a potential base and agency in the movement of social change.
>
> Any new left in America must be, in large measure, a left with real intellectual skills, committed to deliberativeness, honesty, and reflection as working tools. The university permits the political life to be an adjunct to the academic one, and action to be informed by reason.[23]

University reform, in my opinion, should be directed towards such goals as these: not towards imposing constraints, but rather towards lessening them; not towards enjoining the work that now is often dominant—much of which I personally find detestable—but towards opening up alternatives. This can be done, I think, though it will require a degree of intellectual commitment that has, by and large, been lacking on the part of those concerned with university reform.

The university should compensate for the distorting factors introduced by external demands, which necessarily reflect the distribution of power in extra-university society, and by the dynamics of professionalization which, though not objectionable in itself, often tends to orient study towards problems that can be dealt with by existing technique and away from those that require new understanding. The university should be a center for radical social inquiry, as it is already a center for what might be called "radical inquiry" in the pure sciences. It should loosen its "institutional forms" even further, to permit a richer variety of work and study and experimentation, and should provide a home for the free intellectual, for the social critic, for the irreverent and radical thinking that is desperately needed if we are to escape from the dismal reality that threatens to overwhelm us. The primary barrier to such a development will not be the unwillingness of administrators or the stubbornness of trustees. It will be the unwillingness of students to do the difficult and serious work required, and the fear of the faculty that its security and authority, its guild structure, will be threatened.

These, I think, are the real barriers to serious reform and innovation in the universities, as matters now stand, though new barriers may arise if these are successfully overcome. These are the primary problems that should motivate and direct efforts to change the university. In general, I think that the so-called New Left has a task of historic importance; and I think that this task was formulated quite fittingly in the Port Huron statement, when it spoke of the necessity for "a left with real intellectual skills, committed to deliberativeness, honesty, and reflection as working tools," committed to a political life in which "action is informed by reason."

These are goals that can easily be forgotten in the heat of conflict, but they remain valid ones, and one can only hope that they will be continually resurrected as a guide to positive action.

Notes

This essay first appeared in Robert M. Hutchins and Mortimer J. Adler, eds., *The Great Ideas Today Nineteen Sixty-nine* (Chicago: Encyclopedia Britannica, 1969).

1 Wilhelm von Humboldt, "On the Inner and Outer Organization of the Higher Institutions of Learning in Berlin," parts translated in Marianne Cowan, ed., *Humanist Without Portfolio*.

2 Daniel Bell, "The Scholar Cornered," *American Scholar*, vol. 37, no. 3 (1968).

3 Christopher Jencks and David Riesman, *The Academic Revolution*, pp. 104, 100.

4 *The World of Randolph Bourne*, pp. 198, 85, 87. I do not intend my citation of these remarks to suggest approval of what is asserted or implied—as that universities were once a noble community of scholarship, or that the "academic workman" should have a status different from other employees. The "academic workman" is not the only one who should be freed from serving as a tool of production.

5 *Partisan Review*, vol. 35, no. 2 (1968).

6 Irving Kristol, "A Different Way to Restructure the University," *New York Times Magazine*, December 8, 1968. No less revealing is his next sentence: "And at Harvard—of all places!—there is now a course (Social Relations 148) which enrolls several hundred students and is given for credit, whose curriculum is devised by the S.D.S., whose classes are taught by S.D.S. sympathizers, and whose avowed aim is 'radicalization' of the students." Why, in fact, is it so scandalous that Harvard ("of all places!") should have a student-initiated course offering a radical critique of American society and its international behavior?

7 George Kennan, speech to the International Association for Cultural Freedom, Princeton, N.J., December 2; *New York Times*, December 4, 1968. Zbigniew Brzezinski, who interprets the student movement as basically "Luddite," describes Kennan as "in a mood of rage at the young."

8 Eqbal Ahmad, in Richard M. Pfeffer, ed. *No More Vietnams?* p. 18.

9 Harold B. Clifford, *Exploring New England*.

10 Richard West, *Sketches from Vietnam*, pp. 97–8.

11 Paul Lazarsfeld and Robert Merton, "Mass Communication, Popular Taste, and Organized Social Action," in Wilbur Schramm, ed., *Mass Communications*, quoted by D. W. Smythe and H. H. Wilson in a study in which they conclude that "the principal *function* of the commercially supported mass media in the United States is to market the output of the consumer goods industries and to train the population for loyalty to the American economic-political system" ("Cold War-mindedness and the Mass Media," in Neal D. Houghton, ed., *Struggle Against History*, pp. 71–2).

12 Bertrand Russell, *Power*, p. 252.

13 Nathan Glazer, " 'Student Power' in Berkeley," *Public Interest*, no. 13 (fall 1968).

14 Paul Ricoeur, *Le Monde*, June 9–10, 1968.

15 Glazer, " 'Student Power' in Berkeley."

16 For some illuminating discussion, see Michael Kidron, *Western Capitalism Since the War*.

17 *Ibid.*

18 James Ridgeway, *The Closed Corporation*.

19 Karl Marx, *Critique of the Gotha Programme*, 1875.

20 Cf. *ibid.* "If in some states of [the United States] the higher educational institutions are also 'free,' that only means in fact defraying the cost of the education of the upper classes from the general tax receipts."

21 As it continues to be. For example, one of the initiators of Project

Cambridge at MIT, Professor Ithiel Pool, states that this $7.6 million project will "strengthen" research in counterinsurgency (*Scientific Research*, September 15, 1969). At the same time, he characterizes student protests that this will be the case as "a lot of hogwash."

22 "Teller Urges Strong Nuclear Management," *Aviation Week and Space Technology*, April 22, 1963. We must "push scientific advancements to the limit," Teller urges: "the military requirements will soon follow." Concern over "the best human use of the advances already achieved" is in his view "an extremely grave symptom," which threatens the "whole dynamic civilization of the West, for which America is the spearhead."

23 Students for a Democratic Society, Port Huron Statement (1962), reprinted in Mitchell Cohen and Dennis Hale, eds., *The New Student Left*.

CHAPTER 7

Psychology and Ideology

I

A century ago, a voice of British liberalism described the "Chinaman" as "an inferior race of malleable orientals."[1] During the same years, anthropology became professionalized as a discipline, "intimately associated with the raise of raciology."[2] Presented with the claims of nineteenth-century racist anthropology, a rational person will ask two sorts of questions: What is the scientific status of the claims? and, What social or ideological needs do they serve? The questions are logically independent, but those of the second sort naturally come to the fore as scientific pretensions are undermined. In the case of nineteenth-century racist anthropology, the question of its scientific status is no longer seriously at issue, and it is not difficult to perceive its social function. If the Chinaman is malleable by nature, then what objection can there be to controls exercised by a superior race?

Consider now a generalization of the pseudoscience of the nineteenth century: It is not merely the heathen Chinese who are malleable by nature, but rather all people. Science has revealed that it is an illusion to speak of "freedom" and "dignity." What a person does is fully determined by his genetic endowment and history of reinforcement. Therefore we should make use of the best behavioral technology to shape and control behavior in the common interest.

Again, we may inquire into the exact meaning and scientific status of the claim, and the social functions it serves. Again, if the scientific status of whatever is clear is slight, then it is particularly interesting to consider the climate of opinion within which the claim is taken seriously.

II

In his speculations on human behavior, which are to be clearly distinguished from his experimental investigation of operant conditioning, B. F. Skinner offers a particular version of the theory of human malleability. The public reception is a matter of some interest. Skinner has been condemned as a trail blazer of totalitarian thinking and lauded for his advocacy of a tightly managed social environment. He is accused of immorality and praised as a spokesman for science and rationality in human affairs. He appears to be attacking fundamental human values, demanding control in place of the defense of freedom and dignity. There seems something scandalous in this, and since Skinner invokes the authority of science, some critics condemn science itself, or "the scientific view of man," for supporting such conclusions, while others assure us that science will "win out" over mysticism and irrational belief.

A close analysis shows that the appearance is misleading. Skinner is saying nothing about freedom and dignity, though he uses the words "freedom" and "dignity" in some odd and idiosyncratic sense. His speculations are devoid of scientific content and do not even hint at general outlines of a possible science of human behavior. Furthermore, Skinner imposes certain arbitrary limitations on scientific research which virtually guarantee continued failure.

As to its social implications, Skinner's science of human behavior, being quite vacuous, is as congenial to the libertarian as to the fascist. If certain of his remarks suggest one or another interpretation, it must be stressed that these do not follow from his "science" any more than their negations do. I think it would be more accurate to regard Skinner's *Beyond Freedom and Dignity* as a kind of Rorschach test. The fact that it is widely regarded as pointing the way to 1984 is, perhaps, a suggestive indication of certain tendencies in modern industrial society. There is little doubt that a theory of human malleability might be put to the service of totalitarian doctrine. If, indeed, freedom and dignity are merely the relics of outdated mystical beliefs, then what objection can there be to narrow and effective controls instituted to ensure "the survival of a culture"?

Given the prestige of science and the tendencies towards centralized authoritarian control that can easily be detected in modern industrial society, it is important to investigate seriously the claim that the science of behavior and a related technology provide the rationale and the means for control of behavior. What in fact has been demonstrated, or even plausibly suggested, in this regard?

Skinner assures us repeatedly that his science of behavior is advancing mightily and that there exists an effective technology of control. It is, he claims, a "fact that all control is exerted by the environment."[3] Consequently, "When we seem to turn control over to a person himself, we simply shift from one mode of control to another" (p. 97). The only serious task, then, is to design less "aversive" and more effective controls, an engineering problem. "The outlines of a technology are already clear" (p. 149). "We have the physical, biological, and behavioral technologies needed 'to save ourselves'; the problem is how to get people to use them" (p. 158).

It is a fact, Skinner maintains, that "behavior is shaped and maintained by its consequences" and that as the consequences contingent on behavior are investigated, more and more "they are taking over the explanatory functions previously assigned to personalities, states of mind, feelings, traits of character, purposes, and intentions" (p. 18).

> As a *science of behavior* adopts the strategy of physics and biology, the autonomous agent to which behavior has traditionally been attributed is replaced by the environment—the environment in which the species evolved and in which the behavior of the individual is shaped and maintained. [P. 184]

A "behavioral analysis" is thus replacing the "traditional appeal to states of mind, feelings, and other aspects of the autonomous man," and "is in fact much further advanced than its critics usually realize" (p. 160). Human behavior is a function of "conditions, environmental or genetic," and people should not object "when a scientific analysis traces their behavior to external conditions" (p. 75), or when a behavioral technology improves the system of control.

Not only has all of this been demonstrated; furthermore, it *must be* that as the science of behavior progresses, it will more fully establish these facts. "It is in the nature of scientific progress that the functions of autonomous man be taken over one by one as the role of the environment is better understood" (p. 58). This is the "scientific view," and "it is in the nature of scientific inquiry" that the evidence should shift in its favor (p. 101). "It is in the nature of an experimental analysis of human behavior that it should strip away the functions previously assigned to autonomous man and transfer them one by one to the controlling environment" (p. 198). Furthermore, physiology someday "will explain why behavior is indeed related to the antecedent events of which it can be shown to be a function" (p. 195).

These claims fall into two categories. In the first are claims about what has been discovered; in the second, assertions about what science must discover in its inexorable progress. It is likely that the hope or fear or resignation induced by Skinner's proclamations results, in part, from such assertions about the inevitability of scientific progress towards the demonstration that all control is exerted by the environment, that the ability of "autonomous man" to choose is an illusion.

Claims of the first sort must be evaluated in terms of the evidence presented for them. In the present instance, this is a simple task. No evidence is presented. In fact, as will become clear when we turn to more specific examples, the question of evidence is beside the point, since the claims dissolve into triviality or incoherence under analysis. Claims with regard to the inevitability of future discoveries are more ambiguous. Is Skinner saying that as a matter of necessity, science will show that behavior is completely determined by the environment? If so, his claim can be dismissed as pure dogmatism, foreign to the "nature of scientific inquiry." It is quite conceivable that as scientific understanding advances, it will reveal that even with full details about genetic endowment and personal history, a Laplacean omniscience could predict very little about what an organism will do. It is even possible that science may someday provide principled reasons for this conclusion (if indeed it is true). But perhaps Skinner is suggesting merely that the term "scientific understanding" be restricted to the prediction of behavior from environmental conditions. If so, then science may reveal, as it progresses, that "scientific understanding of human behavior," in this sense, is inherently limited. At the moment, we have virtually no scientific evidence and not the germs of an interesting hypothesis as to how human behavior is determined. Consequently, we can only express our hopes and guesses as to what some future science may demonstrate. In any event, the claims that Skinner puts forth in this category are either dogmatic or uninteresting, depending on which interpretation we give to them.

The dogmatic element in Skinner's thinking is further revealed when he states that "the task of a scientific analysis is to explain how the behavior of a person as a physical system is related to the conditions under which the human species evolved and the conditions under which the individual lives" (p. 14). Surely the task of a scientific analysis is to discover the facts and explain them. Suppose that in fact the human brain operates by physical principles (perhaps now unknown) that provide for free choice, appropriate to situations but only marginally affected by environmental contingencies. The task of scientific analysis is not—as Skinner believes—to demonstrate that the conditions to which he restricts his attention fully determine human behavior, but rather to discover whether in fact they do (or whether they are at all significant), a very different matter. If they do not, as seems quite plausible, the "task of a scientific analysis" will be to clarify the issues and discover an intelligible explanatory theory that will deal with the actual facts. Surely no scientist would follow Skinner in insisting on the a priori necessity that scientific investigation will lead to a particular conclusion, specified in advance.

In support of his belief that science will demonstrate that behavior is entirely a function of antecedent events, Skinner notes that physics advanced only when it "stopped personifying things" and attributing to them "wills, impulses, feelings, purposes," and so on (p. 8). Therefore, he concludes, the science of behavior will progress only when it stops personifying people and avoids reference to "internal states." No doubt physics advanced by rejecting the view that a rock's wish to fall is a factor in its "behavior," because in fact a rock has no such wish. For Skinner's argument to have any force, he must show that people have wills, impulses, feelings, purposes, and the like no more than rocks do. If people differ from rocks in this respect, then a science of human behavior will have to take account of this fact.

Similarly, Skinner is correct in asserting that "modern physics or most of biology" does not discuss such matters as "a crisis of belief" or "loss of confidence" (p. 10). Evidently, from this correct observation nothing follows with regard to the science of human behavior. Physics and biology, Skinner observes, "did not advance by looking more closely at the jubilance of a falling body, or . . . the nature of vital spirits, and we do not need to try to discover what personalities, states of mind, feelings, traits of character, plans, purposes, intentions, or the other perquisites of autonomous man really are in order to get on with a scientific analysis of behavior"; and we must neglect "supposed mediating states of mind" (p. 15). This is true enough, if indeed there are no mediating states that can be characterized by an abstract theory of mind, and if personalities, etc., are no more real than the jubilance of a falling body. But if the factual assumptions are false, then we certainly do need to try to discover what the "perquisites of autonomous man" really are and to determine the "mediating states of mind"—at least this is so if we wish to develop a science of human behavior with any intellectual content and explanatory force. Skinner might argue, more rationally, that his "science" does not overlook these "perquisites" and inner states but rather accounts in other ways for the phenomena discussed in these terms. We shall see directly what substance there is to such a claim.

It is hardly possible to argue that science has advanced only by repudiating hypotheses concerning "internal states." By rejecting the study of postulated inner states, Skinner reveals his hostility not only to "the nature of scientific inquiry" but even to common engineering practice. For example, Skinner believes that "information theory" ran into a "problem when an inner 'processor' had to be invented to convert input into output" (p. 18). This is a strange way of describing the matter; "information theory" ran into no such "problem." Rather, the consideration of "inner processors" in the mathematical theory of communication or its applications to psychology followed normal scientific and engineering practice. Suppose that an investigator is presented with a device whose functioning he does not understand, and suppose that through experiment he can obtain information about input-output relations for this device. He would not hesitate, if rational, to construct a theory of the internal states of the device and to test it against further evidence. He might also go on to try to determine the mechanisms that function in the ways described by his theory of internal states, and the physical principles at work—leaving open the possibility that new and unknown physical principles might be involved, a particularly important matter in the study of behavior of organisms. His theory of internal states might well be the only useful guide to further research. By objecting, *a priori*, to this commonplace research strategy, Skinner merely condemns his strange variety of "behavioral science" to continued ineptitude.

Skinner's antagonism to science is also revealed by his treatment of matters of fact. Psychologists concerned with the facts have argued that the child's acquisition of language and various concepts is in part a function of developmental age, that through maturational processes a child's language grows "like an embryo," and that isolation interferes with certain growth processes. Skinner rejects these hypotheses (pp. 139, 141, 221), and asserts rather that verbal and other environmental contingencies explain all of the observed phenomena. Neither here nor elsewhere does he provide any evidence or rational argument to this effect; nor does he show some other fault in the perfectly intelligible, though possibly incorrect, theories that he summarily rejects. (He does, however, give irrelevant objections that for some reason seem to him to be applicable —see pages cited above.) His dogmatism in this regard is particularly curious, since he would surely not deny that genetically determined maturational processes are involved in other aspects of development. But in this area he insists that the explanation must lie elsewhere. Though his conclusion might, by sheer accident, be correct, still it would be difficult to imagine an attitude more basically opposed to "the nature of scientific inquiry."

We cannot specify, *a priori*, what postulates and hypotheses are legitimate. Skinner's apriorism in this regard is no more legitimate than the claim that classical physics is not "science" because it appeals to the "occult force of gravity." If a concept or principle finds its place in an explanatory theory, it cannot be excluded on methodological grounds, as Skinner's discussion suggests. In general, Skinner's conception of science is very odd. Not only do his *a priori* methodological assumptions rule out all but the most trivial scientific theories; he is, furthermore, given to strange pronouncements such as the assertion that "the laws of science are descriptions of contingencies of reinforcement" (p. 189)—which I happily leave to others to decode.

It is important to bear in mind that Skinner's strictures do not define the practice of behavioral science. In fact, those who call themselves "behavioral scientists" or even "behaviorists" vary widely in the kinds of theoretical constructions that they are willing to admit. W. V. O. Quine, who on other occasions has attempted to work within the Skinnerian framework, goes so far as to define "behaviorism" simply as the insistence that conjectures and conclusions must eventually be verified in terms of observations.[4] As he points out, any reasonable person is a "behaviorist" in this sense. Quine's proposal signifies the demise of behaviorism as a substantive point of view, which is just as well. Whatever function "behaviorism" may have served in the past, it has become nothing more than a set of arbitrary restrictions on "legitimate" theory construction, and there is no reason why someone who investigates man and society should accept the kind of intellectual shackles that physical scientists would surely not tolerate and that condemn any intellectual pursuit to insignificance.

Notice that what is at issue here is not "philosophical behaviorism," a set of ideas about legitimate claims to knowledge, but rather behaviorism as a set of conditions imposed on legitimate theory construction in the study of mental abilities and achievements and human social organization. Thus a person might accept Quine's version of "behaviorism" for scientific theory construction, thus in effect abandoning the doctrine, while still maintaining that the scientific theories constructed in accordance with the condition that hypotheses must eventually be verified in terms of observations do not truly constitute "knowledge." If consistent, such a person will also reject the natural sciences as not constituting "true knowledge." It is, of course, possible to impose conditions of arbitrary severity on the concept "knowledge." Whatever the interest of this enterprise may be, it is not what I am discussing here. Nor am I discussing the question whether the system of unconscious rules and principles that the mind constructs, or the innate schematism that provides the basis for such constructions, should properly be called "knowledge," or perhaps be given some other name. In my opinion, no investigation of the concept of "knowledge" in ordinary usage will provide an answer to these questions, since it is too vague and unclear at precisely the critical points. This, however, is not the question at issue in the present discussion, and I will pursue it no further here.

Let us consider more carefully what Skinner means when he asserts that all behavior is externally controlled and that behavior is a function of genetic and environmental conditions. Does he mean that full knowledge of such conditions would permit, in principle, specific predictions as to what a person will do? Surely not. Skinner means that genetic and environmental conditions determine "probability of response." But he is so vague about this notion that it is unclear whether his claims about determinism amount to anything at all. No one would doubt that the likelihood of my going to the beach depends on the temperature, or that the likelihood of my producing a sentence of English rather than Chinese is "determined" by my past experience, or that the likelihood of my producing a sentence of a human language rather than of some imaginable but humanly inaccessible system is "determined" by my genetic constitution. We hardly need behavioral science to tell us this. When we look for more specific predictions, however, we find virtually nothing. Worse, we discover that Skinner's *a priori* limitations on "scientific" inquiry make it impossible for him even to formulate the relevant concepts, let alone investigate them.

Consider, for example, the notion "likelihood of producing

a sentence of English rather than Chinese." Given a characterization of "English" and "Chinese" by an abstract theory of
postulated internal states (mental states, if you like), it is
possible to give some meaning to this notion—though the
probabilities, being negligible under any known characterization of determining factors, will be of no interest for the
prediction of behavior.[5] But for Skinner, even this marginal
achievement is impossible. For Skinner, what we call "knowledge of French" is a "repertoire acquired as a person learns to
speak French" (p. 197). Therefore probabilities will be defined over such "repertoires." But what does it mean to say
that some utterance of English that I have never heard or
produced belongs to my "repertoire," but not any utterance of
Chinese (so that the former has a higher "probability")?
Skinnerians, at this point in the discussion, appeal to "similarity" or "generalization," always without characterizing the
ways in which a new expression is "similar" to familiar examples or "generalized" from them. The reason for this failure
is simple. So far as is known, the relevant properties can be
expressed only in terms of abstract theories which can be
taken as descriptions of postulated internal states of the
organism, and such theories are excluded, *a priori*, from
Skinner's "science." The immediate consequence is that the
Skinnerian must lapse into mysticism (unexplained "similarities" and "generalization" of a sort that cannot be specified)
as soon as the discussion touches the world of fact. While the
situation is perhaps clearer in the case of language, there is no
reason to suppose that other aspects of human behavior will
fall within the grasp of the "science" constrained by *a priori*
Skinnerian restrictions.

It is interesting, incidentally, to see how Skinner's defenders
respond to this inability to deal with concrete factual questions. Aubrey Yates, for example, refers to a criticism by
Breger and McGaugh,[6] who argue that the Skinnerian approach to language learning and usage cannot handle facts
that can be explained by postulating an abstract theory (a
grammar) that is learned and used. Yates presents the following rebuttal, which he regards as "devastating": "the assertion
that children learn and utilize a grammar is not . . . a 'fact'
which Skinner has to explain, if his theory is to remain viable,

but an *inference* or theoretical construct." "No one has ever observed a 'grammar' " and the child would be unable to specify it; "it is quite improper to set up a theoretical construct to account for complex verbal behavior and then demand that Skinner explain this theoretical construct by means of his own theory."[7]

But Breger and McGaugh do not insist that Skinner explain the theoretical construct "grammar" by means of his own theory (whatever this would mean); rather, they argue that by employing the theoretical construct "grammar" it is possible to account for important facts that escape the limits of Skinner's system. A proper answer would be that the proposed explanation fails, or that Skinner can explain these facts in some other way, or that the facts are not important for his particular purposes. But Yates's "devastating rebuttal," like Skinner's own refusal to face the problem, is merely an evasion. By similar logic a mystic could argue that his account of planetary motion is not to be rejected on grounds of its inability to deal with the phenomena explained by Newtonian physics, which is, after all, merely a theory designed to account for the facts. As to the remark that the grammar cannot be "observed" or specified by the child, of course no theoretical construct is "observed," and the insistence that abstract characterizations of internal mental states be accessible to introspection, by the child or anyone else, is again (despite its distinguished ancestry) mere dogmatism, to be dismissed in serious inquiry. The explanatory theory that Breger and McGaugh discuss may be quite wrong, but it is irrelevant to remark that it cannot be observed or described by the person whose behavior is allegedly explained by use of this theory. Unfortunately, this kind of maneuver is all too typical.

Skinner's own response to criticism is no less illuminating. He believes that people attack him and argue against his "scientific picture of man" because "the scientific formulation has destroyed accustomed reinforcers" and causes "behavior previously reinforced by credit or admiration [to] undergo extinction," since "a person can no longer take credit or be admired for what he does." And extinction, he asserts, "often leads to aggressive attack" (p. 212). Elsewhere, he accuses his critics of "emotional instability," citing comments of Arthur Koestler and Peter Gay to the effect that behaviorism is "a monumental triviality" marked by "innate naïveté" and "intellectual bankruptcy" (p. 165). Skinner does not attempt to meet this criticism by presenting some relevant results that are not a monumental triviality. He is quite unable to perceive that objection to his "scientific picture of man" derives, not from extinction of certain behavior or opposition to science, but from an ability to distinguish science from triviality and obvious error. Skinner does not comprehend the basic criticism: when his formulations are interpreted literally, they are trivially true, unsupported by evidence, or clearly false; and when these assertions are interpreted in his characteristically vague and metaphorical way, they are merely a poor substitute for ordinary usage. Such criticisms cannot be overcome by verbal magic, by mere reiteration that his approach is scientific and that those who do not see this are opposed to science or deranged.

Similarly, Skinner claims that Koestler's characterization of behaviorism is seventy years out of date, but does not indicate what great achievements of the past seventy years Koestler has neglected. In fact, the real achievements of behavioral science, so far as we know, in no way support Skinner's conclusions (insofar as these are nontrivial). It is for this reason, one must presume, that Skinner assures the reader that he has no "need to know the details of a scientific analysis of behavior" (p. 22), none of which are presented. It is not the depth or complexity of this theory that prevents Skinner from outlining it for the lay reader. For example, Jacques Monod, in his recent work on biology and human affairs,[8] gives a rather detailed presentation of achievements of modern biology that he believes to be relevant to his (clearly identified) speculations. I should add, to make myself clear, that I am not criticizing Skinner for the relative lack of significant achievement in the behavioral sciences as compared to, say, biology, but rather for his irresponsible claims regarding the "science of behavior" which the reader need not know but which has allegedly produced all sorts of remarkable results concerning the control of behavior.

III

Let us now turn to the evidence that Skinner provides for his extraordinary claims: as, that "an analysis of behavior" reveals that the achievements of artists, writers, statesmen, and scientists can be explained almost entirely in terms of environmental contingencies (p. 44); that it is the environment that makes a person wise or compassionate (p. 171); that "all these questions about purposes, feelings, knowledge, and so on, can be restated in terms of the environment to which a person has been exposed" and that "what a person 'intends to do' depends on what he has done in the past and what has then happened" (p. 72); and so on.

According to Skinner, apart from genetic endowment, behavior is determined entirely by reinforcement. To a hungry organism, food is a positive reinforcer. This means that "anything the organism does that is followed by the receipt of food is more likely to be done again whenever the organism is hungry" (p. 27); but "food is reinforcing only in a state of deprivation" (p. 37). A negative reinforcer is a stimulus that increases the probability of behavior that reduces the intensity of that stimulus; it is "aversive," and roughly speaking, constitutes a threat (p. 27). A stimulus can become a conditioned reinforcer by association with other reinforcers. Thus money is "reinforcing only after it has been exchanged for reinforcing things" (p. 33). The same is generally true of approval and affection. (The reader may attempt something that Skinner always avoids, namely, to characterize the "stimuli" that constitute "approval"—for example, why is the statement "this article ought to appear in journal such-and-such" an instance of "approval" when made by one person and of "disapproval" when made by another?) Behavior is shaped and maintained by the arrangement of such reinforcers. Thus, "We change the relative strengths of responses by differential reinforcement of alternative courses of action" (pp. 94–5); one's repertoire of behavior is determined by "the contingencies of reinforcement to which he is exposed as an individual" (p. 127); "an organism will range between vigorous activity and complete quiescence depending upon the schedules on which it has been reinforced" (p. 186). As Skinner realizes (though some of his defenders do not)[9] meticulous control is necessary to shape behavior in highly specific ways. Thus, "The culture . . . teaches a person to make fine discriminations by making differential reinforcement more precise" (p. 194), a fact which causes problems when "the verbal community cannot arrange the subtle contingencies necessary to teach fine distinctions among stimuli which are inaccessible to it"; "as a result the language of emotion is not precise" (p. 106).

The problem in "design of a culture" is to "make the social environment as free as possible of aversive stimuli" (p. 42), "to make life less punishing and in doing so to release for more reinforcing activities the time and energy consumed in the avoidance of punishment" (p. 81). It is an engineering problem, and we could get on with it if only we could overcome the irrational concern for freedom and dignity. What we require is the more effective use of the available technology, more and better controls. In fact, "A technology of behavior is available which would more successfully reduce the aversive consequences of behavior, proximate or deferred, and maximize the achievements of which the human organism is capable" (p. 125). But "the defenders of freedom oppose its use," thus contributing to social malaise and human suffering. It is this irrationality that Skinner hopes to persuade us to overcome.

At this point an annoying though obvious question intrudes. If Skinner's thesis is false, then there is no point in his having written the book or our reading it. But if his thesis is true, then there is also no point in his having written the book or our reading it. For the only point could be to modify behavior, and behavior, according to the thesis, is entirely controlled by arrangement of reinforcers. Therefore reading the book can modify behavior only if it is a reinforcer, that is, if reading the book increases the probability of the behavior which led to reading the book (assuming an appropriate state of deprivation). At this point, we seem to be reduced to gibberish.

As a counterargument it might be claimed that even if the thesis is false, there is a point to writing and reading the book, since certain false theses are illuminating and provocative. But this escape is hardly available. In this case, the thesis is elementary and not of much interest in itself. Its only value lies in its possible truth. But if the thesis is true, then reading or writing the book would appear to be an entire waste of time, since it reinforces no behavior.

Skinner would surely argue that reading the book, or perhaps the book itself, is a "reinforcer" in some other sense. He wants us to be persuaded by the book, and, not to our surprise, he refers to persuasion as a form of behavioral control, albeit a weak and ineffective form. Skinner hopes to persuade us to allow greater scope to the behavioral technologists, and apparently believes that reading this book will increase the probability of our behaving in such a way as to permit them greater scope (freedom?). Thus reading the book, he might claim, reinforces this behavior. It will change our behavior with respect to the "science of behavior" (p. 24).

Let us overlook the problem, insuperable in his terms, of specifying the notion "behavior that gives greater scope to behavioral technologists," and consider the claim that reading the book might reinforce such behavior. Unfortunately, the claim is clearly false, if we use the term "reinforce" with anything like its technical meaning. Recall that reading the book reinforces the desired behavior only if it is a consequence of the behavior, and obviously putting our fate in the hands of behavioral technologists is not behavior that led to (and hence can be reinforced by) reading Skinner's book. Therefore the claim can be true only if we deprive the term "reinforce" of its technical meaning. Combining these observations, we see that there can be some point to reading the book or to Skinner's having written it only if the thesis of the book is divorced from the "science of behavior" on which it allegedly rests.

Let us consider further the matter of "persuasion." According to Skinner, we persuade ("change minds") "by manipulating environmental contingencies," specifically, "by pointing to stimuli associated with positive consequences" and "making a situation more favorable for action, as by describing likely reinforcing consequences" (pp. 91–3). Even if we overlook that fact that persuasion, so characterized, is a form of control (a variety of "reinforcement") unknown to Skinner's science, his argument is in no way advanced. Suppose Skinner were to claim that his book might persuade us by pointing to positive consequences of behavioral technology. But this will not do at all. It is not enough for him to point to those consequences (for example, to draw pictures of happy people); rather he must show that these are indeed *consequences* of the recommended behavior. To persuade us, he must establish a connection between the recommended behavior and the pleasant situation he describes. The question is begged by use of the term "consequences."[10] It is not enough merely to conjoin a description of the desired behavior and a description of the "reinforcing" state of affairs (overlooking, again, that not even these notions are expressible in Skinner's terms). Were that sufficient for "persuasion," then we could "persuade" someone of the opposite by merely conjoining a description of an unpleasant state of affairs with a description of the behavior that Skinner hopes to produce.

If persuasion were merely a matter of pointing to reinforcing stimuli and the like, then any persuasive argument would retain its force if its steps were randomly interchanged, or if some of its steps were replaced by arbitrary descriptions of reinforcing stimuli. And the argument would lose its force if descriptions of unwelcome circumstances were randomly introduced. Of course, this is nonsense. For an argument to be persuasive, at least to a rational person, it must be coherent; its conclusions must follow from its premises. But these notions are entirely beyond the scope of Skinner's framework. When he states that "deriving new reasons from old, the process of deduction" merely "depends upon a much longer verbal history" (p. 96), he is indulging in hand waving of a most pathetic sort. Neither Skinner nor anyone else has offered the faintest hint that "the process of deduction" can be characterized in his terms on the basis of "verbal history," however long. An approach that cannot even formulate properly, let alone solve, the problem of why some new expression is intelligible, but not, say, a permutation of its component elements (see above, p. 327), cannot even begin to consider the notions "coherent argument" or "process of deduction."

Consider Skinner's claim that "we sample and change verbal behavior, not opinions" (so a behavioral analysis reveals) (p. 95). Taken literally, this means that if, under a credible threat of torture, I force someone to say, repeatedly, that the Earth stands still, then I have changed his opinion. Comment is unnecessary, and we perceive at once the significance of the "behavioral analysis" that yields this conclusion.

Skinner claims that persuasion is a weak method of control, and he asserts that "changing a mind is condoned by the defenders of freedom and dignity because it is an ineffective way of changing behavior, and the changer of minds can therefore escape from the charge that he is controlling people" (p. 97). Suppose that your doctor gives you a powerful and rational argument to the effect that if you continue to smoke, you will die a horrible death from lung cancer. Is it necessarily the case that this argument will be less effective in modifying your behavior than any arrangement of true reinforcers? In fact, whether persuasion is effective or not depends on the content of the argument (for a rational person), a factor that Skinner cannot begin to describe. The problem becomes still worse if we consider other forms of "changing minds." Suppose that a description of a napalm raid on a Vietnamese village induces someone in an American audience to carry out an act of sabotage. In this case, the effective stimulus is not a reinforcer, the mode of changing behavior may be quite effective, and the act that is performed (the behavior "reinforced") is entirely new (not in the "repertoire") and may not even have been hinted at in the "stimulus" that induced the change of behavior. In every possible respect, then, Skinner's account is simply incoherent.

Since his William James lectures of 1947,[11] Skinner has been sparring with these and related problems. The results are nil. It remains impossible for Skinner to formulate the relevant notions in his terms, let alone investigate them. What is more, no nontrivial scientific hypotheses with supporting evidence have been produced to substantiate the extravagant claims to which he is addicted.[12] Furthermore, this record of failure was predictable from the start, from an analysis of the problems and the means proposed to deal with them. It must be stressed that "verbal behavior" is the only aspect of human behavior that Skinner has attempted to investigate in any detail. To his credit, he recognized quite early that only through a successful analysis of language could he hope to come to terms with human behavior. By comparing the results that have been achieved in this twenty-five-year period with the claims that are still advanced, we gain a good insight into the nature of Skinner's science of behavior. My impression is, in fact, that the claims are becoming more extreme and more strident as the inability to support them and the reasons for this failure become increasingly obvious.

It is unnecessary to labor the point any further. Evidently, Skinner has no way of dealing with the factors that are involved in persuading someone or changing his mind. The attempt to invoke "reinforcement" merely leads to incoherence or pretense. The point is crucial. Skinner's discussion of persuasion and "changing minds" is one of the few instances in which he tries to come to terms with what he calls the "literature of freedom and dignity." The libertarian whom he condemns distinguishes between persuasion and certain forms of control. He advocates persuasion and objects to coercion. In response, Skinner claims that persuasion is itself a (weak) form of control and that by using weak methods of control we simply shift control to other environmental conditions, not to the person himself (pp. 97, 99). Thus, Skinner claims, the advocate of freedom and dignity is deluding himself in his belief that persuasion leaves the matter of choice to "autonomous man," and furthermore he poses a danger to society because he stands in the way of more effective controls. As we see, however, Skinner's argument against the "literature of freedom and dignity" is without force. Persuasion is no form of control at all, in Skinner's sense; in fact, he is quite unable to deal with the concept in his terms.

But there is little doubt that persuasion can "change minds" and affect behavior, on occasion, quite drastically. Since persuasion cannot be coherently described in terms of arrangement of reinforcers, it follows that behavior is not entirely determined by the specific contingencies to which Skinner arbitrarily restricts his attention, and that the major thesis of the book is false. Skinner can escape this conclusion only by claiming that persuasion *is* a matter of arranging reinforcing stimuli, but this claim is tenable only if the term "reinforcement" is deprived of its technical meaning and used as a mere substitute for the detailed and specific terminology of ordinary language (similarly, the notion of "arrangement or scheduling of reinforcement"). In any event, Skinner's "science of behavior" is irrelevant; the thesis of the book is either false (if we use terminology in its technical sense) or empty (if we do not). And the argument against the libertarian collapses entirely.

Not only is Skinner unable to uphold his claim that persuasion is a form of control, but he also offers not a particle of evidence to support his claim that the use of "weak methods of control" simply shifts the mode of control to some obscure environmental factor rather than to the mind of autonomous man. Of course, from the thesis that all behavior is controlled by the environment, it follows that reliance on weak rather than strong controls shifts control to other aspects of the environment. But the thesis, insofar as it is at all clear, is without empirical support, and in fact may even be quite empty, as we have seen in discussing "probability of response" and persuasion. Skinner is left with no coherent criticism of the "literature of freedom and dignity."

The emptiness of Skinner's system is nicely illustrated in his treatment of more peripheral matters. He claims (p. 112) that the statement "You should (you ought to) read *David Copperfield*" may be translated "You will be reinforced if you read *David Copperfield*." But what does this mean? Literally applying Skinner's definition (see above), it means that behavior that is followed by reading *David Copperfield* is more likely to be done again if you are in need of reading. Or perhaps it means that the act of reading *David Copperfield* will be followed by some stimulus that will increase the probability of this act. When I tell someone that he ought to read *David Copperfield*, then, I am telling him something of this sort. Suppose, say, I told you that you should read *David Copperfield* because this would disabuse you of the notion that Dickens is worth reading, or show you what true boredom really is. In fact, no matter how we try to interpret Skinner's suggestion, giving the term "reinforce" something like its literal sense, we fall into utter confusion.

Probably what Skinner has in mind in using the phrase "You will be reinforced if you read *David Copperfield*" is that you will like it, enjoy it, or learn something useful, and thus be "reinforced." But this gives the game away. We are now using "reinforce" in a sense quite different from that of the operant-conditioning paradigm. It would make no sense at all to try to apply results about scheduling of reinforcement, for example, to this situation. Furthermore, it is no wonder that we can "explain" behavior by using the nontechnical term "reinforce" with the full range of meaning of "like" or "enjoy" or "learn something from" or whatever. Similarly, when Skinner tells us that a fascinating hobby is "reinforcing" (p. 36), he is surely not claiming that the behavior that leads to indulging in this hobby will be increased in probability. Rather, he means that we enjoy the hobby. A literal interpretation of such remarks yields gibberish, and a metaphorical interpretation merely replaces an ordinary term by a homonym of a technical term, with no gain in precision.

The system of Skinnerian translation is quite readily available to anyone and can indeed be employed with no knowledge of the theory of operant conditioning and its results, and with no information, beyond normal observation, of the circumstances in which behavior takes place or the nature of the behavior itself. Recognizing this fact, we can appreciate the value of Skinner's "science of behavior" for the purposes at hand, and the insights it provides. But it is important to bear in mind that this system of translation leads to a significant loss of precision, for the simple reason that the full range of terms for the description and evaluation of behavior, attitude, opinion, and so on must be translated into the impoverished system of terminology borrowed from the laboratory (and deprived of its meaning in transition).[13] It is hardly surprising, then, that Skinnerian translation generally misses the point, even with the metaphorical use of such terms as "reinforce." Thus Skinner asserts that "a person wants something if he acts to get it when the occasion arises" (p. 37). It follows that it is impossible to act to get something, given the opportunity, but not to want it—say, to act thoughtlessly, or out of a sense of duty (we can, as usual, reduce Skinner's assertion to triviality by saying that what the person wants is to do his duty, and so on). It is clear from the context that Skinner means "if" as "if and only if." Thus it follows from his definition of "want" that it is impossible for a person to want something but not to act to get it when the occasion arises, say for reasons of conscience (again, we can escape to triviality by assigning such reasons to the "occasion"). Or consider the claim that "we are likely to admire behavior more as we understand it less" (p. 53). In a strong sense of "explain," it follows that we admire virtually all behavior, since we can explain virtually none. In a looser sense, Skinner is claiming that if Eichmann is incomprehensible to us but we understand why the Vietnamese fight on, then we are likely to admire Eichmann but not the Vietnamese resistance.

The real content of Skinner's system can be appreciated only by examining such cases, for example, as the following:

"Except when physically restrained, a person is least free or dignified when he is under threat of punishment" (p. 60). Thus someone who refuses to bend to authority in the face of severe threat has lost all dignity.

"We read books which help us say things we are on the verge of saying anyway but cannot quite say without help," and thus "we understand the author" (p. 86). Is the point supposed to be that we do not read books that we expect to disagree with, and would not be able to understand what they say? If not, the claim is empty. If so, it is absurd.

Things we call "good" are positive reinforcers and things we call "bad" are negative reinforcers (pp. 104, 107); we work to achieve positive reinforcers and avoid negative reinforcers (p. 107).[14] This explains why people, by definition, always seek good and avoid evil. Furthermore, "Behavior is called good or bad . . . according to the way it is usually reinforced by others" (p. 109). As long as Hitler was being "reinforced" by events and by those around him, his behavior was good. On the other hand, the behavior of Dietrich Bonhoeffer and Martin Niemoeller was, by definition, bad. In the Biblical tale, it was self-contradictory to seek ten good men in Sodom. Recall that the study of operant reinforcement, the conclusions of which we are now reviewing, is "a science of values" (p. 104).

"A person acts intentionally . . . in the sense that his behavior has been strengthened by consequences" (p. 108) — as in the case of a person who intentionally commits suicide.

The hero who has killed a monster is reinforced by praise "precisely to induce him to take on other monsters" (p.

111)—and thus is never praised on his deathbed or at his funeral.

The statement "You should (you ought to) tell the truth" means, in this science of value, "If you are reinforced by the approval of your fellow men, you will be reinforced when you tell the truth" (p. 112). In a subculture so cynical that telling the truth is regarded as absurd and not approved, one who is reinforced by approval ought not to tell the truth. Or to be more precise, the statement "You ought to tell the truth" is false. Similarly, it is wrong to tell someone not to steal if he is almost certain to get away with it, since "You ought not to steal" can be translated "If you tend to avoid punishment, avoid stealing" (p. 114).

"Scientific discoveries and inventions are improbable; that is what is meant by discovery and invention" (p. 155). Thus by arranging mathematical formulas in some novel and improbable way, I succeed (by definition) in making a mathematical discovery.

Stimuli attract attention because they have been associated with important things and have figured in contingencies of reinforcement (p. 187). Thus if a cat with two heads walked into a room, only those to whom cats were important would notice it; others would pay no attention. An entirely new stimulus—new to the species or the individual—would be entirely ignored.

A person may derive his rules of behavior "from an analysis of punitive contingencies" (p. 69), and a person may be reinforced "by the fact that the culture will long survive him" (p. 210). Thus something imagined can be a "reinforcing stimulus." (Try to apply to this example the fanciful discussion of "conditioned reinforcers" that "usurp" the reinforcing effort of deferred consequences—pp. 120–2.)

A person "behaves bravely when environmental circumstances induce him to do so" (p. 197). Since, as noted earlier, we act to achieve positive reinforcers, we can conclude that no one behaves bravely when punishment or death is a likely consequence (unless he is "reinforced" by "stimuli" that impinge on him after his death).

A young man who is dissatisfied, discouraged, frustrated, has no sense of purpose, and so on is simply one who is not properly reinforced (pp. 146–7). Therefore no one has such feelings if he can attain wealth and the positive reinforcers it can buy.

Notice that in most of these cases, perhaps all, we can convert error to tautology by relying on the vagueness of the Skinnerian terminology, for example, by using "reinforcement" as a cover term for whatever is liked, wanted, intended, and so on.

We can get a taste of the explanatory force of Skinner's theory from such (quite typical) examples as these: a pianist learns to play a scale smoothly because "smoothly played scales are reinforcing" (p. 204); "A person can know what it is to fight for a cause only after a long history during which he has learned to perceive and to know that state of affairs called fighting for a cause" (p. 190); and so on.

Similarly, we can perceive the power of Skinner's behavioral technology by considering the useful observations and advice he offers: "Punishable behavior can be minimized by creating circumstances in which it is not likely to occur" (p. 64); if a person "is strongly reinforced when he sees other people enjoying themselves . . . he will design an environment in which children are happy" (p. 150); if overpopulation, nuclear war, pollution, and depletion of resources are a problem, "we may then change practices to induce people to have fewer children, spend less on nuclear weapons, stop polluting the environment, and consume resources at a lower rate, respectively" (p. 152).

The reader may search for more profound thoughts than these. He may seek, but he will not find.

In this book, Skinner alludes more frequently to the role of genetic endowment than in his earlier speculations about human behavior and society. One would think that this would lead to some modification in his conclusions, or to new conclusions. It does not. The reason is that Skinner is as vague and uninformative about genetic endowment as he is about control by contingencies of reinforcement. Unfortunately, zero plus zero still equals zero.

According to Skinner, "The ease with which mentalistic explanations can be invented on the spot is perhaps the best gauge of how little attention we should pay to them" (p.

160). We can turn this into a true statement by replacing "mentalistic" with "Skinnerian." In fact, a Skinnerian translation is always available for any description of behavior—we can always say that an act is performed because it is "reinforcing" or "reinforced" or because the contingencies of reinforcement shaped behavior in this way, and so on. There is a handy explanation for any eventuality, and given the vacuity of the system, we can never be proved wrong.

But Skinner's comment on "mentalistic explanations" is surely incorrect, given his usage of this term. Consider, for example, the expressions (1)–(4):

(1) The two men promised their wives to kill each other
(2) The two men persuaded their wives to kill each other
(3) The two men promised me to kill each other
(4) The two men persuaded me to kill each other

We understand these sentences (even if they are new in our experience) in the following way: (1) is a close paraphrase of "Each of the two men promised his wife to kill the other" and means that the men are to kill each other; (2) is a close paraphrase of "The two men persuaded their wives each to kill the other" and means that the wives are to kill each other; (3) is a close paraphrase of "Each of the two men promised me to kill the other"; but (4) cannot be paraphrased in any of these ways, and in fact is not a sentence of our "repertoire" at all. One can propose an explanation for such facts as these within an abstract theory of language, a theory that Skinner would (quite legitimately) call "mentalistic." It is, however, not at all easy to invent a satisfactory "mentalistic explanation" for these and many related facts,[15] that is, a system of general principles that will explain these facts and will not be refuted by other facts. To construct a theory of "internal (mental) states" is no easy task, contrary to what Skinner believes; though in this case too a Skinnerian explanation, employing the mystical notions "similar" and "generalize," can of course be invented on the spot, no matter what the facts may be. Skinner's failure to understand this results from his unwillingness to attempt to construct explanatory theories that have empirical content in the domain of human thought and action. Because of this unwillingness, there is also no discernible progress—today's formulations in this domain are hardly different from those of fifteen or twenty years ago—and no convincing refutation, for those who are untroubled by the fact that explanations can be invented on the spot, whatever the facts may be, within a system that is devoid of substance.

IV

We have so far been considering the scientific status of Skinner's claims. Let us now turn to the matter of "design of a culture." The principles of Skinner's "science" tell us nothing about designing a culture (since they tell us virtually nothing), but that is not to say that Skinner leaves us completely in the dark as to what he has in mind. He believes that "the control of the population as a whole must be delegated to specialists—to police, priests, owners, teachers, therapists, and so on, with their specialized reinforcers and their codified contingencies" (p. 155). The controller and the designer of a culture should be members of the group that is controlled (p. 172). When the technology of behavior is "applied to the design of a culture, the survival of the culture functions as a value." If our culture "continues to take freedom or dignity, rather than its own survival, as its principal value, then it is possible that some other culture will make a greater contribution to the future." The refusal to exercise available controls may be "a lethal cultural mutation." "Life, liberty, and the pursuit of happiness are basic rights . . . [but] they have only a minor bearing on the survival of a culture" (pp. 180–3); one might wonder, then, what importance they have for the behavioral technologist who takes the survival of the culture as a value. These and similar observations, to which we turn directly, may be what lead some readers to suspect that Skinner is advocating a form of totalitarian control.

There is no doubt that in his specific recommendations, vague though they are, Skinner succeeds in differentiating his position from the "literature of freedom." Skinner claims that the latter has "overlooked . . . control which does not have aversive consequences at any time" (p. 41) and has encouraged opposition to all control, whereas he is proposing a much more extensive use of controls that have no aversive consequences. The most obvious form of control of this benign type is differential wages. It is, of course, incorrect to say that the "literature of freedom" has overlooked such controls. Since the industrial revolution, it has been much concerned with the problems of "wage slavery" and the "benign" forms of control that rely on deprivation and reward rather than direct punishment. This concern clearly distinguishes the literature of freedom from Skinner's social concepts. Or consider freedom of speech. Skinner's approach suggests that control of speech by direct punishment should be avoided, but that it is quite appropriate for speech to be controlled, say, by restricting good jobs to people who say what is approved by the designer of the culture. In accordance with Skinner's ideas, there would be no violation of academic freedom if promotions were granted only to those who conform, in their speech and writings, to the rules of the culture, though it would be wrong to go farther and punish those who deviate by saying what they believe to be true. Such deviants will simply remain in a state of deprivation. In fact, by giving people strict rules to follow, so that they know just what to say to be "reinforced" by promotion, we will be "making the world safer" and thus achieving the ends of behavioral technology (pp. 74, 81). The literature of freedom would, quite properly, reject and abhor such controls.

In fact, there is nothing in Skinner's approach that is incompatible with a police state in which rigid laws are enforced by people who are themselves subject to them and the threat of dire punishment hangs over all. Skinner argues that the goal of a behavioral technology is to "design a world in which behavior likely to be punished seldom or never occurs" —a world of "automatic goodness" (p. 66). The "real issue," he explains, "is the effectiveness of techniques of control" which will "make the world safer." We make the world safer for "babies, retardates, or psychotics" by arranging matters so that punishable behavior rarely occurs. If only all people could be treated in this way, "much time and energy would be saved" (pp. 66, 74). Skinner even offers, perhaps unintentionally, some indications as to how this benign environment might be brought into being:

> A state which converts all its citizens into spies or a religion which promotes the concept of an all-seeing God makes

escape from the punisher practically impossible, and punitive contingencies are then maximally effective. People behave well although there is no visible supervision. [Pp. 67–8]

Elsewhere, we learn that "of course" freedom "waxes as visible
control wanes" (p. 70). Therefore the situation just described
is one of maximal freedom, since there is no visible control; for
the same reason, it is a situation of maximal dignity. Furthermore, since "our task" is simply "to make life less punishing"
(p. 81), the situation just described would seem ideal. Since
people behave well, life will be minimally punishing. In this
way, we can progress "toward an environment in which men
are automatically good" (p. 73).

Extending these thoughts, consider a well-run concentration
camp with inmates spying on one another and the gas ovens
smoking in the distance, and perhaps an occasional verbal hint
as a reminder of the meaning of this reinforcer. It would
appear to be an almost perfect world. Skinner claims that a
totalitarian state is morally wrong because of its deferred
aversive consequences (p. 174). But in the delightful culture
we have just designed, there should be no aversive consequences, immediate or deferred. Unwanted behavior will be
eliminated from the start by the threat of the crematoria and
the all-seeing spies. Thus all behavior would be automatically
"good," as required. There would be no punishment. Everyone would be reinforced—differentially, of course, in accordance with ability to obey the rules. Within Skinner's scheme
there is no objection to this social order. Rather, it seems close
to ideal. Perhaps we could improve it still further by noting that
"the release from threat becomes more reinforcing the greater
the threat" (as in mountain climbing; p. 111). We can, then,
enhance the total reinforcement and improve the culture by
devising a still more intense threat, say, by introducing occasional screams, or by flashing pictures of hideous torture as we
describe the crematoria to our fellow citizens. The culture
might survive, perhaps for a thousand years.

Though Skinner's recommendations might be read in this
way, nevertheless it would be improper to conclude that
Skinner is advocating concentration camps and totalitarian
rule (though he also offers no objection). Such a conclusion
overlooks a fundamental property of Skinner's science,

namely, its vacuity. Though Skinner seems to believe that "survival of a culture" is an important value for the behavioral technologist, he fails to consider the questions that arise at once. When the culture changes, has it survived, or died? Suppose that it changes in such a way as to extend the basic individual rights that Skinner personally regards as outdated (pp. 180–3). Is this survival, or death? Do we want the thousand-year Reich to survive? Why not, if survival of the culture functions as a value for the behavioral technologist? Suppose that in fact people are "reinforced" by (that is, prefer) reduction of both sanctions and differential reinforcement. Do we then design the culture so as to lead to this result, thus diminishing effective controls rather than extending them, as Skinner urges? Suppose that humans happen to be so constructed that they desire the opportunity for freely undertaken productive work. Suppose that they want to be free from the meddling of technocrats and commissars, bankers and tycoons, mad bombers who engage in psychological tests of will with peasants defending their homes, behavioral scientists who can't tell a pigeon from a poet, or anyone else who tries to wish freedom and dignity out of existence or beat them into oblivion. Do we then "design our culture" to achieve these ends (which, of course, can be given an appropriate Skinnerian translation)? There are no answers to any of these questions in Skinner's science, despite his claim that it accommodates (fully, it seems) consideration of "values." It is for this reason that his approach is as congenial to an anarchist as to a Nazi, as already noted.[16]

V

Skinner's treatment of the notions "leisure" and "work" gives an interesting insight into the behaviorist system of beliefs (insofar as an identifiable doctrine still exists—see p. 325 above). Recall his assertion that the level of an organism's activity depends on its "environmental history of reinforcement" and that "an organism will range between vigorous activity and complete quiescence depending upon the schedules on which it has been reinforced" (p. 186). Weakening of controls, then, might induce passivity or random behavior, particularly under conditions of affluence (low deprivation). People are "at leisure," Skinner notes, if they "have little to do," for example, people who "have enough power to force or induce others to work for them," children, the retarded and mentally ill, members of affluent and welfare societies, and so on. Such people "appear to be able to 'do as they please.'" This, Skinner continues, "is a natural goal of the libertarian" (pp. 177–80). But leisure "is a condition for which the human species has been badly prepared," and therefore a dangerous condition.

Evidently, a distinction must be made between having nothing to do and being able to do as one pleases. Both states presuppose lack of compulsion, but being able to do as one pleases requires the availability of opportunities as well. Under Skinnerian assumptions, it is difficult to distinguish properly between having nothing to do and being able to do as one pleases, since there is no reason to expect anyone to take the opportunity to work without deprivation and reinforcement. Thus it is not surprising that Skinner slips easily from the definition of "leisure" as the state in which one appears to be able to do as one pleases, to the assertion that leisure (that is, having nothing to do) is a dangerous condition, as in the case of a caged lion or an institutionalized person.

Being able to do as one pleases is a natural goal of the libertarian, but having nothing to do is not. While it may be correct to say that the human species is badly prepared for having nothing to do, it is quite a different matter to say that it is badly prepared for the freedom to do as one pleases. People who are able to do as they please may work very hard, given the opportunity to do interesting work. Similarly a child who is "at leisure" in Skinner's sense may not have to be "reinforced" to expend energy in creative activities, but may eagerly exploit the opportunity to do so. Skinner's loose usage of the term "leisure," while understandable under his assumptions, nevertheless obscures the fundamental difference between freedom to do as one wishes (for Skinner, the appearance of this, since he believes there is no such thing) and having nothing to do, as in an institution or on welfare, when there is no interesting work available. Skinner's remarks thus convey the impression that it might be dangerous, perhaps another "lethal cultural mutation," to create social arrangements in which people are free to choose their work and to absorb themselves in satisfying work. A further comment that "specific cultural conditions" (not further specified) are necessary to enable those with leisure to engage in "artistic, literary, and scientific productivity" contributes as much to clarifying the issues as his other remarks about "contingencies of reinforcement."

Running through the discussion is a vague background assumption that unless "reinforcements" are provided, individuals will vegetate. That there may be an intrinsic human need to find productive work, that a free person may, given the opportunity, seek such work and pursue it with energy, is a possibility that is never faced—though of course the vacuous system of Skinnerian translation would permit us to say that such work is "reinforcing" (and undertaken for this reason), if we happen to enjoy tautologies.

The lingering background assumption in Skinner's discussion of leisure and liberty also arises in work that is somewhat more serious than his, in that it at least has the form of an argument and is based on some evidence. There is, at the moment, considerable controversy over a recent article by Harvard psychologist Richard Herrnstein[17] which purports to show that American society is drifting towards a stable hereditary meritocracy, with social stratification by inborn differences and a corresponding distribution of "rewards." The argument is based on the hypothesis that differences in mental abilities are inherited and that people close in mental ability are more likely to marry and reproduce,[18] so that there will be a tendency towards long-term stratification by mental ability, which Herrnstein takes to be measured by IQ. Secondly, Herrnstein argues that "success" requires mental ability and that social rewards "depend on success." This step in the argument embodies two assumptions: first, it is so in fact; and second, it must be so for society to function effectively. The conclusion is that there is a tendency towards hereditary meritocracy, with "social standing (which reflects earnings and prestige)" concentrated in groups with higher IQ. The tendency will be accelerated as society becomes more egalitarian, that is, as artificial social barriers are eliminated, defects in prenatal (e.g., nutritional) environment are overcome, and so on, so that natural ability can play a more direct role in attainment of social reward. Therefore, as society becomes more egalitarian, social rewards will be concentrated in a hereditary meritocratic elite.

Herrnstein has been widely denounced as a racist for this argument, a conclusion which seems to me unwarranted. There is, however, an ideological element in his argument that is absolutely critical to it. Consider the second step, that is, the claim that IQ is a factor in attaining reward and that this must be so for society to function effectively. Herrnstein recognizes that his argument will collapse if, indeed, society can be organized in accordance with the "socialist dictum, 'From each according to his ability, to each according to his needs.'" His argument would not apply in a society in which "income (economic, social, and political) is unaffected by success."

Actually, Herrnstein fails to point out that his argument not only requires the assumption that success must be rewarded, but that it must be rewarded in quite specific ways. If individuals are rewarded for success only by prestige, then no conclusions of any importance follow. It will only follow (granting his other assumptions) that children of people who are respected for their achievements will be more likely to be respected for their own achievements, an innocuous result even if true. It may be that the child of two Olympic swimmers has a greater than average chance of achieving the same success (and the acclaim for it), but no dire social consequences follow from this hypothesis.

Though the point seems obvious, it has been misunderstood (by Herrnstein, in particular) and therefore perhaps merits an additional comment. Assume, with Herrnstein, that ability "expresses itself in labor only for gain" and that such ability is partially heritable. Consider two parents with greater than average ability who attain thereby an increment R of reward beyond the average. By hypothesis, their child is likely to have higher than average ability, though less so than the parents, because of regression towards the mean, as Herrnstein notes. Thus the child will be expected to attain, by virtue of his own ability, an increment R' of reward beyond the average, where

R′ is less than R. Suppose that reward is wealth. Then the child's total increment, given the characteristics of this reward in our society, will be $R′+R_1+R_2+R_3$, where R_1 is that part of R transmitted to the child, R_2 is the increment resulting from the fact that R_1 itself generates additional wealth, and R_3 is the increment attained by the child beyond R′ by virtue of the initial advantages afforded him by R_1. In our society, R_1, R_2, and R_3 are substantial, and of course cumulative over generations. Thus if social reward is wealth, there may indeed be a significant tendency for reward to concentrate in family lines over time. If, on the other hand, social reward and its effects are nontransmittable, then the child's total increment is R′, in general less than R; there is nothing corresponding to the substantial and cumulative increment $R_1+R_2+R_3$. Thus if prestige and acclaim suffice as a motivating social reward, there will be no significant tendency for rewards to be concentrated in a "hereditary meritocracy" as Herrnstein predicts, and his "most troubling" conclusion vanishes. Whatever slight tendencies might exist in this direction are further diminished by the fact that matching in the kind of ability that brings "reward" is at best a partial factor in selecting mates. Finally, whatever tendency there might be for prestige to persist along family lines has none of the large-scale social effects of concentration of wealth.

Furthermore, prestige and acclaim differ from wealth in that by granting more of this "reward" to one individual, we do not correspondingly deprive another of it. Still accepting Herrnstein's assumption that individuals labor only for gain, if the reward is prestige, then performance can be assured generally by granting prestige to each individual to the extent that he achieves in accordance with his abilities, whatever his task. (Observe also that there is no reason to grant more prestige to those with more ability, so that from still another point of view Herrnstein's beliefs about the inevitability of a hereditary meritocracy are groundless, on the assumption that reward is prestige or acclaim). Of course, it is conceivable that some individual will work only if his reward in prestige is not only greater than what he would attain by not working or working less well, but also greater than the prestige given to others for their accomplishments. Such a person would also, presumably, feel deprived or punished if others are successful; say, if someone else writes an outstanding novel or makes a scientific discovery or does a fine job of carpentry, and is respected for his achievement. Rather than take pleasure in this fact, this unfortunate creature would be pained by it. For such a person, "differential prestige" would be a source of pain or pleasure and a necessary condition for undertaking any effort. There is, however, no reason to suppose that this form of psychic malady is characteristic of the human race.

It is interesting to note that Herrnstein does believe humans are so constituted by nature that this malady is characteristic of them. He argues that if prestige were sufficiently potent to "sustain work no less well than do the rewards in our society, including money and power," then lack of prestige would cause "sadness and regret" and society would be "stratified by a mortal competition for prestige" in the "hereditary meritocracy" he regards as unavoidable. As already noted, he is in error in assuming long-term stratification, even granting his assumptions, if reward is prestige. What of his further assumption that humans require "differential reward" in his special sense: that is, not merely more prestige than they would attain by not working or working less well, but more than their fellows? If it is true, then we can anticipate that people will suffer "painful psychic deprivations" if others achieve and are respected, and that they will find themselves in a "mortal competition for prestige." Though this is surely imaginable, the assumption seems to me even more curious and implausible than others that Herrnstein makes, to which we turn next. But whatever the status of this strange belief about human nature, it should be clear that it has no bearing on Herrnstein's central and "most troubling" conclusion. To repeat: If prestige and respect suffice to motivate labor (on Herrnstein's assumption that ability expresses itself in labor only for gain), there is no reason to expect a long-term tendency of any significance towards a stable hereditary "meritocracy," nor will such a tendency be enhanced by the realization of "contemporary political and social goals," nor is there any reason to accept Herrnstein's "extrapolation" that in any viable society a stable "hereditary meritocracy" will arise.

Nothing is left, in short, of his central and "most troubling" conclusion.

The conclusion that Herrnstein and others find disturbing is that wealth and power will tend to concentrate in a hereditary meritocracy. But this follows only on the assumption that wealth and power (not merely respect) must be the rewards of successful achievement and that these (or their effects) are transmitted from parents to children. The issue is confused by Herrnstein's failure to isolate the specific factors crucial to his argument, and his use of the phrase "income (economic, social, and political)" to cover "rewards" of all types, including respect as well as wealth. It is confused further by the fact that he continually slips into identifying "social standing" with wealth. Thus he writes that if the social ladder is tapered steeply, the obvious way to rescue the people at the bottom is "to increase the aggregate wealth of society so that there is more room at the top"—which is untrue, if "social standing" is a matter of acclaim and respect. (We overlook the fact that even on his tacit assumption, redistribution of income would appear to be an equally obvious strategy.)

Consider then the narrower assumption that is crucial to his argument: transmittable wealth and power accrue to mental ability, and must, for society to function effectively. If this assumption is false and society can be organized more or less in accordance with the "socialist dictum," then nothing is left of Herrnstein's argument (except that it will apply to a competitive society in which his other factual assumptions hold). But the assumption is true, Herrnstein claims. The reason is that ability "expresses itself in labor only for gain" and people "compete for gain—economic and otherwise." People will work only if they are rewarded in terms of "social and political influence or relief from threat." All of this is merely asserted; no justification is given for these assertions. Note again that the argument supports the disturbing conclusions he draws only if we identify the "gain" for which people allegedly compete as transmittable wealth and power.

What reason is there to believe the crucial assumption that people will work only for gain in (transmittable) wealth and power, so that society cannot be organized in accordance with the socialist dictum? In a decent society everyone would have the opportunity to find interesting work, and each person would be permitted the fullest possible scope for his talents. Would more be required, in particular, extrinsic reward in the form of wealth and power? Only if we assume that applying one's talents in interesting and socially useful work is not rewarding in itself, that there is no intrinsic satisfaction in creative and productive work, suited to one's abilities, or in helping others (say, one's family, friends, associates, or simply fellow members of society). Unless we suppose this, then even granting all of Herrnstein's other assumptions, it does not follow that there should be any concentration of wealth or power or influence in a hereditary elite.

The implicit assumption is the same as Skinner's, in effect. For Herrnstein's argument to have any force at all, we must assume that people labor only for gain, and that the satisfaction in interesting or socially beneficial work or in work well done or in the respect shown to such activities is not a sufficient "gain" to induce anyone to work. The assumption, in short, is that without material reward, people will vegetate. For this crucial assumption, no semblance of an argument is offered. Rather, Herrnstein merely asserts that if bakers and lumberjacks "got the top salaries and the top social approval,"[19] in place of those now at the top of the social ladder, then "the scale of I.Q.'s would also invert," and the most talented would strive to become bakers and lumberjacks. This, of course, is no argument, but merely a reiteration of the claim that, necessarily, individuals work only for extrinsic reward. Furthermore, it is an extremely implausible claim. I doubt very much that Herrnstein would become a baker or lumberjack if he could earn more money that way.

Similar points have been made in commentary on Herrnstein's article,[20] but in response he merely reiterates his belief that there is no way "to end the blight of differential rewards." Continued assertion, however, is not to be confused with argument. Herrnstein's further assertion that history shows . . . in effect concedes defeat. Of course, history shows concentration of wealth and power in the hands of those able to accumulate it. One thought Herrnstein was trying to do more than merely put forth this truism. By reducing his argument finally to this assertion, Herrnstein implicitly concedes that he has no justification for the crucial assumption on which his argument rests, the unargued and unsupported claim that the talented must receive higher rewards.

If we look more carefully at what history and experience show, we find that if free exercise is permitted to the combination of ruthlessness, cunning, obsequiousness, and whatever other qualities provide "success" in competitive societies, then those who have these qualities will rise to the top and will use their wealth and power to preserve and extend the privileges they attain. They will also construct ideologies to demonstrate that this result is only fair and just. We also find, contrary to capitalist ideology and behaviorist doctrine (of the nontautological variety), that many people often do not act solely, or even primarily, so as to achieve material gain, or even so as to maximize applause. As for the argument (if offered) that "history shows" the untenability of the "socialist dictum" that Herrnstein must reject for his argument to be valid, this may be assigned the same status as an eighteenth-century argument to the effect that capitalist democracy is impossible, as history shows.

One sometimes comes across arguments to the effect that people are "economic maximizers," as we can see from the fact that given the opportunity, some will accumulate material reward and power.[21] By similar logic we could prove that people are psychopathic criminals, since given social conditions under which those with violent criminal tendencies were free from all restraint, they might very well accumulate power and wealth while nonpsychopaths suffered in servitude. Evidently, from the lessons of history we can reach only the most tentative conclusions about basic human tendencies.

Suppose that Herrnstein's unargued and crucial claim is incorrect. Suppose that there is in fact some intrinsic satisfaction in employing one's talents in challenging and creative work. Then, one might argue, this should compensate even for a diminution of extrinsic reward; and "reinforcement" should be given for the performance of unpleasant and boring tasks. It follows, then, that there should be a concentration of wealth (and the power that comes from wealth) among the less talented. I do not urge this conclusion, but merely observe that it is more plausible than Herrnstein's if his fundamental and unsupported assumption is false.

The belief that people must be driven or drawn to work by "gain" is a curious one. Of course, it is true if we use the vacuous Skinnerian scheme and speak of the "reinforcing quality" of interesting or useful work; and it may be true, though irrelevant to Herrnstein's thesis, if the "gain" sought is merely general respect and prestige. The assumption necessary for Herrnstein's argument, namely, that people must be driven or drawn to work by reward of wealth or power, does not, obviously, derive from science, nor does it appear to be supported by personal experience. I suspect that Herrnstein would exclude himself from the generalization, as already noted. Thus I am not convinced that he would at once apply for a job as a garbage collector if this were to pay more than his present position as a teacher and research psychologist. He would say, I am sure, that he does his work not because it maximizes wealth (or even prestige) but because it is interesting and challenging, that is, intrinsically rewarding; and there is no reason to doubt that this response would be correct. The statistical evidence, he points out, suggests that "if *very* high income is your goal, and you have a high I.Q., do not waste your time with formal education beyond high school." Thus if you are an economic maximizer, don't bother with a college education, given a high IQ. Few follow this advice, quite probably because they prefer interesting work to mere material reward. The assumption that people will work only for gain in wealth and power is not only unargued but quite probably false, except under extreme deprivation. But this degrading and brutal assumption, common to capitalist ideology and the behaviorist view of human beings (excepting, again, the tautological behaviorism of Skinner), is fundamental to Herrnstein's argument.

There are other ideological elements in Herrnstein's argument, more peripheral but still worth noting. He invariably describes the society he sees evolving as a "meritocracy," thus expressing the value judgment that the characteristics that yield reward are a sign of merit, that is, positive characteristics. He considers specifically IQ, but of course recognizes that there might very well be other factors in the attainment of "social success." One might speculate, rather plausibly, that wealth and power tend to accrue to those who are ruthless, cunning, avaricious, self-seeking, lacking in sympathy and compassion, subservient to authority and willing to abandon principle for material gain, and so on. Furthermore, these traits might very well be as heritable as IQ, and might outweigh IQ as factors in gaining material reward. Such qualities might be just the valuable ones for a war of all against all. If so, then the society that results (applying Herrnstein's "syllogism") could hardly be characterized as a "meritocracy." By using the word "meritocracy" Herrnstein begs some interesting questions and reveals implicit assumptions about our society that are hardly self-evident.

Teachers in ghetto schools commonly observe that students who are self-reliant, imaginative, energetic, and unwilling to submit to authority are often regarded as troublemakers and punished, on occasion even driven out of the school system. The implicit assumption that in a highly discriminatory society, or one with tremendous inequality of wealth and power, the "meritorious" will be rewarded is a curious one indeed.

Consider further Herrnstein's assumption that in fact social rewards accrue to those who perform beneficial and needed services. He claims that the "gradient of occupations" is "a natural measure of value and scarcity," and that "the ties among I.Q., occupation, and social standing make practical sense." This is his way of expressing the familiar theory that people are automatically rewarded in a just society (and more or less in our society) in accordance with their contribution to social welfare or "output." The theory is familiar, and so are its fallacies. Given great inequalities of wealth, we will expect to find that the "gradient of occupations" by pay is a natural measure of service to wealth and power—to those who can purchase and compel—and only by accident "a natural measure of value." The ties among IQ, occupation, and social standing that Herrnstein notes make "practical sense" for those with wealth and power, but not necessarily for society or its members in general.[22]

The point is quite obvious. Herrnstein's failure to notice it is particularly surprising given the data on which he bases his

observations about the relation between social reward and
occupation. He bases these judgments on a ranking of occupations which shows, for example, that accountants, specialists in
public relations, auditors, and sales managers tend to have
higher IQs (hence, he would claim, receive higher pay, as they
must if society is to function effectively) than musicians,
riveters, bakers, lumberjacks, and teamsters. Accountants were
ranked highest among 74 listed occupations, with public relations fourth, musicians 35th, riveters 50th, bakers 65th, truck
drivers 67th, and lumberjacks 70th. From such data, Herrnstein concludes that society is wisely "husbanding its intellectual resources"[23] and that the gradient of occupation is a
natural measure of value and makes practical sense. Is it
obvious that an accountant helping a corporation to cut its tax
bill is doing work of greater social value than a musician,
riveter, baker, truck driver, or lumberjack? Is a lawyer who
earns a $100,000 fee to keep a dangerous drug on the market
worth more to society than a farm worker or a nurse? Is a
surgeon who performs operations for the rich doing work of
greater social value than a practitioner in the slums, who may
work much harder for much less extrinsic reward? The gradient of occupations that Herrnstein uses to support his claims
with regard to the correlation between IQ and social value
surely reflects, in part at least, the demands of wealth and
power; a further argument is needed to demonstrate Herrnstein's claim that those at the top of the list are performing
the highest service to "society," which is wisely husbanding its
resources by rewarding accountants and public-relations experts and engineers (e.g., designers of antipersonnel weapons)
for their special skills. Herrnstein's failure to notice what his
data immediately suggest is another indication of his uncritical
and apparently unconscious acceptance of capitalist ideology
in its crudest form.

Notice that if the ranking of occupations by IQ correlates
with ranking by income, then the data that Herrnstein cites
can be interpreted in part as an indication of an unfortunate
bias in material reward towards occupations that serve the
wealthy and powerful and away from work that might be more
satisfying and socially useful. At least, this would certainly
seem a plausible assumption, one that Herrnstein never dis-

cusses, given his unquestioning acceptance of the prevailing ideology.

There is, no doubt, some complex of characteristics conducive to material reward in a state capitalist society. This complex may include IQ and quite possibly other more important factors, perhaps those noted earlier. To the extent that these characteristics are heritable (and a factor in choosing mates) there will be a tendency towards stratification in terms of these qualities. This much is obvious enough.

Furthermore, people with higher IQs will tend to have more freedom in selection of occupation. Depending on their other traits and opportunities, they will tend to choose more interesting work or more remunerative work, these categories being by no means identical. Therefore one can expect to find some correlation between IQ and material reward, and some correlation between IQ and an independent ranking of occupations by their intrinsic interest and intellectual challenge. Were we to rank occupations by social utility in some manner, we would probably find at most a weak correlation with remuneration or with intrinsic interest, and quite possibly a negative correlation. Unequal distribution of wealth and power will naturally introduce a bias towards greater remuneration for services to the privileged, thereby causing the scale of remuneration to diverge from the scale of social utility in many instances.

From Herrnstein's data and arguments, we can draw no further conclusions about what would happen in a just society, unless we add the assumption that people labor only for material gain, for wealth and power, and that they do not seek interesting work suited to their abilities—that they would vegetate rather than do such work. Since Herrnstein offers no reason why we should believe any of this (and there is certainly some reason why we should not), none of his conclusions follow from his factual assumptions, even if these are correct. The crucial step in his "syllogism" in effect amounts to the claim that the ideology of capitalist society expresses universal traits of human nature, and that certain related implicit assumptions of behaviorist psychology are correct. Conceivably, these unsupported assumptions are true. But once it is recognized how critical their role is in his argument and what empirical support they in fact have, any further interest in this argument would seem to evaporate.

I have assumed so far that prestige, respect, and so on might be factors in causing people to work (as Herrnstein implies). This seems to me by no means obvious, though even if it is true, Herrnstein's conclusions clearly do not follow. In a decent society, socially necessary and unpleasant work would be divided on some egalitarian basis, and beyond that people would have, as an inalienable right, the widest possible opportunity to do work that interests them. They might be "reinforced" by self-respect, if they do their work to the best of their ability, or if their work benefits those to whom they are related by bonds of friendship and sympathy and solidarity. Such notions are commonly an object of ridicule—as it was common, in an earlier period, to scoff at the absurd idea that a peasant has the same inalienable rights as a nobleman. There always have been and no doubt always will be people who cannot conceive of the possibility that things could be different from what they are. Perhaps they are right, but again, one awaits a rational argument.

In a decent society of the sort just described—which, one might think, becomes increasingly realizable with technological progress—there should be no shortage of scientists, engineers, surgeons, artists, craftsmen, teachers, and so on, simply because such work is intrinsically rewarding. There is no reason to doubt that people in these occupations would work as hard as those fortunate few who can choose their own work generally do today. Of course, if Herrnstein's assumptions, borrowed from capitalist ideology and behaviorist belief, are correct, then people will remain idle rather than do such work unless there is deprivation and extrinsic reward. But no reason is offered to explain why we should accept this strange and demeaning doctrine.

Lurking in the background of the debate over Herrnstein's syllogism is the matter of race, though he himself barely alludes to it. His critics are disturbed, and rightly so, by the fact that his argument will surely be exploited by racists to justify discrimination, much as Herrnstein may personally deplore this fact. More generally, Herrnstein's argument will be adopted by the privileged to justify their privilege on grounds that they are being rewarded for their ability and that such reward is necessary if society is to function properly. The situation is reminiscent of nineteenth-century racist anthropology, discussed at the outset. Marvin Harris notes:

> Racism also had its uses as a justification for class and caste hierarchies; it was a splendid explanation of both national and class privilege. It helped to maintain slavery and serfdom; it smoothed the way for the rape of Africa and the slaughter of the American Indian; it steeled the nerves of the Manchester captains of industry as they lowered wages, lengthened the working day, and hired more women and children.[24]

We can expect Herrnstein's arguments to be used in a similar way, and for similar reasons. When we discover that his argument is without force, unless we adopt unargued and implausible premises that happen to incorporate the dominant ideology, we quite naturally turn to the question of the social function of his conclusions and ask why the argument is taken seriously, exactly as in the case of nineteenth-century racist anthropology.

Since the issue is often obscured by polemic, it is perhaps worth stating again that the question of the validity and scientific status of a particular point of view is of course logically independent from the question of its social function; each is a legitimate topic of inquiry, and the latter becomes of particular interest when the point of view in question is revealed to be seriously deficient, on empirical or logical grounds.

The nineteenth-century racist anthropologists were no doubt quite often honest and sincere. They may have believed that they were simply dispassionate investigators, advancing science, following the facts where they led. Conceding this, we might nevertheless question their judgment, and not merely because the evidence was poor and the arguments fallacious. We might take note of the relative lack of concern over the ways in which these "scientific investigations" were likely to be used. It would have been a poor excuse for the nineteenth-century racist anthropologist to plead, in Herrnstein's words, that "a neutral commentator . . . would have to say that the case is simply not settled" (with regard to racial inferiority) and that the "fundamental issue" is "whether inquiry shall (again) be shut off because someone thinks society is best left in ignorance." The nineteenth-century racist anthropologist, like any other person, was responsible for the effects of what he did, insofar as they could be clearly foreseen. If the likely consequences of his "scientific work" were those that Harris describes, he had the responsibility to take this likelihood into account. This would be true even if the work had real scientific merit—more so, in fact, in this case.

Similarly, imagine a psychologist in Hitler's Germany who thought he could show that Jews had a genetically determined tendency towards usury (like squirrels bred to collect too many nuts) or a drive towards antisocial conspiracy and domination, and so on. If he were criticized for even undertaking these studies, could he merely respond that "a neutral commentator . . . would have to say that the case is simply not settled" and that the "fundamental issue" is "whether inquiry shall (again) be shut off because someone thinks society is best left in ignorance"? I think not. Rather, I think that such a response would have been met with justifiable contempt. At best, he could claim that he is faced with a conflict of values. On the one hand, there is the alleged scientific importance of determining whether in fact Jews have a genetically determined tendency towards usury and domination (an empirical question, no doubt). On the other, there is the likelihood that even opening this question and regarding it as a subject for scientific inquiry would provide ammunition for Goebbels and Rosenberg and their henchmen. Were this hypothetical psychologist to disregard the likely social consequences of his research (or even his undertaking of research) under existing social conditions, he would fully deserve the contempt of decent people. Of course, scientific curiosity should be encouraged (though fallacious argument and investigation of silly questions should not), but it is not an absolute value.

The extravagant praise lavished on Herrnstein's flimsy argument and the widespread failure to note its implicit bias and unargued assumptions[25] suggest that we are not dealing simply with a question of scientific curiosity. Since it is impossible to explain this acclaim on the basis of the substance or force of the argument, it is natural to ask whether the conclusions are so welcome to many commentators that they lose their critical faculties and fail to perceive that certain crucial and quite unsupported assumptions happen to be nothing other than a variant of the prevailing ideology. This failure is disturbing—more so, perhaps, than the conclusions Herrnstein attempts to draw from his flawed syllogism.

Turning to the question of race and intelligence, we grant too much to the contemporary investigator of this question when we see him as faced with a conflict of values: scientific curiosity versus social consequences. Given the virtual certainty that even the undertaking of the inquiry will reinforce some of the most despicable features of our society, the seriousness of the presumed moral dilemma depends critically on the scientific significance of the issue that he is choosing to investigate. Even if the scientific significance were immense, we should certainly question the seriousness of the dilemma, given the likely social consequences. But if the scientific interest of any possible finding is slight, then the dilemma vanishes.

In fact, it seems that the question of the relation, if any, between race and intelligence has little scientific importance (as it has no social importance, except under the assumptions of a racist society). A possible correlation between mean IQ and skin color is of no greater scientific interest than a correlation between any two other arbitrarily selected traits, say, mean height and color of eyes. The empirical results, whatever they might be, appear to have little bearing on any issue of scientific significance. In the present state of scientific understanding, there would appear to be little scientific interest in the discovery that one partly heritable trait correlates (or not) with another partly heritable trait. Such questions might be interesting if the results had some bearing, say, on some psychological theory, or on hypotheses about the physiological mechanisms involved, but this is not the case. Therefore the investigation seems of quite limited scientific interest, and the zeal and intensity with which some pursue or welcome it cannot reasonably be attributed to a dispassionate desire to advance science. It would, of course, be foolish to claim, in response, that "society should not be left in ignorance." Society is happily "in ignorance" of insignificant matters of all sorts. And with the best of will, it is difficult to avoid questioning the good faith of those who deplore the alleged "anti-intellectualism" of the critics of scientifically trivial and socially malicious investigations. On the contrary, the investigator of race and intelligence might do well to explain the intellectual significance of the topic he is studying, and thus enlighten us as to the moral dilemma he perceives. If he perceives none, the conclusion is obvious, with no further discussion.

As to social importance, a correlation between race and mean IQ (were this shown to exist) entails no social consequences except in a racist society in which each individual is assigned to a racial category and dealt with not as an individual in his own right, but as a representative of this category. Herrnstein mentions a possible correlation between height and IQ. Of what social importance is that? None, of course, since our society does not suffer under discrimination by height. We do not insist on assigning each adult to the category "below six feet in height" or "above six feet in height" when we ask what sort of education he should receive or where he should live or what work he should do. Rather, he is what he is, quite independent of the mean IQ of people of his height category. In a nonracist society, the category of race would be of no greater significance. The mean IQ of individuals of a certain racial background is irrelevant to the situation of a particular individual, who is what he is. Recognizing this perfectly obvious fact, we are left with little, if any, plausible justification for an interest in the relation between mean IQ and race, apart from the "justification" provided by the existence of racial discrimination.

The question of heritability of IQ might conceivably have some social importance, say, with regard to educational practice. However, even this seems dubious, and one would like to see an argument. It is, incidentally, surprising to me that so many commentators should find it disturbing that IQ might be heritable, perhaps largely so.[26] Would it also be disturbing to discover that relative height or musical talent or rank in running the one-hundred-yard dash is in part genetically determined? Why should one have preconceptions one way or another about these questions, and how do the answers to them, whatever they may be, relate either to serious scientific issues (in the present state of our knowledge) or to social practice in a decent society?

VI

Returning to Skinner, we have noted that his "science" neither justifies nor provides any rational objection to a totalitarian state or even a well-run concentration camp. The libertarians and humanists whom Skinner scorns object to totalitarianism out of respect for freedom and dignity. But, Skinner argues, these notions are merely the residue of traditional mystical beliefs and must be replaced by the stern scientific concepts of behavioral analysis. However, there exists no behavioral science incorporating nontrivial, empirically supported propositions that apply to human affairs or support a behavioral technology. It is for this reason that Skinner's book contains no clearly formulated substantive hypotheses or proposals We can at least begin to speculate coherently about the acquisition of certain systems of knowledge and belief on the basis of experience and genetic endowment, and can outline the general nature of some device that might duplicate aspects of this achievement. But as to how a person who has acquired systems of knowledge and belief then proceeds to use them in his daily life, we are entirely in the dark, at the level of scientific inquiry. If there were some science capable of treating such matters, it might well be concerned precisely with freedom and dignity and might suggest possibilities for enhancing them. Perhaps, as the classical literature of freedom and dignity sometimes suggests, there is an intrinsic human inclination towards free creative inquiry and productive work, and humans are not merely dull mechanisms shaped by a history of reinforcement and behaving predictably with no intrinsic needs apart from the need for physiological satiation. Then humans are not fit subjects for manipulation, and we will seek to design a social order accordingly. But we cannot, at present, turn to science for insight into these matters. To claim otherwise is pure fraud. For the moment, an honest scientist will admit at once that we understand virtually nothing, at the level of scientific inquiry, with regard to human freedom and dignity.

There is, of course, no doubt that behavior can be controlled, for example, by threat of violence or a pattern of deprivation and reward. This much is not at issue, and the conclusion is quite consistent with a belief in "autonomous man." If a tyrant has the power to demand certain acts, whether by threat of punishment or by allowing only those who perform these acts to escape from deprivation (e.g., by restricting employment to such people), his subjects may choose to obey—though some may have the dignity to refuse. They will be aware that they are submitting under compulsion. They will understand the difference between this compulsion and the laws that govern falling bodies. Of course, they are not free. Sanctions backed by force restrict freedom, as does differential reward. An increase in wages, in Marx's phrase, "would be nothing more than a better *remuneration of slaves,* and would not restore, either to the worker or to the work, their human significance and worth." But it would be absurd to conclude, merely from the fact that freedom is limited, that "autonomous man" is an illusion, or to overlook the distinction between a person who chooses to conform in the face of threat, or force, or deprivation and differential reward and a person who "chooses" to obey Newtonian principles as he falls from a high tower. The inference remains absurd even where it is possible to predict the course of action that most "autonomous men" would select, under conditions of duress and limited opportunity for survival. The absurdity merely becomes more obvious when we consider the real social world, in which determinable "probabilities of response" are so slight as to have virtually no predictive value. And it would be not absurd, but grotesque, to argue that since circumstances can be arranged under which behavior is quite predictable—as in a prison, for example, or the concentration-camp society "designed" above—therefore there need be no concern for the freedom and dignity of "autonomous man." When such conclusions are taken to be the result of a "scientific analysis," one can only be amazed at human gullibility.

Skinner confuses science with terminology. He apparently believes that if he rephrases commonplace "mentalistic" expressions with terminology drawn from the laboratory study of behavior, but deprived of its precise content, then he has achieved a scientific analysis of behavior. It would be hard to conceive of a more striking failure to comprehend even the rudiments of scientific thinking. The public may well be deceived, given the prestige of science and technology. It may even choose to be misled into agreeing that concern for freedom and dignity must be abandoned. Perhaps it will choose this course out of fear and insecurity with regard to the consequences of a serious concern for freedom and dignity. The tendencies in our society that lead towards submission to authoritarian rule may prepare individuals for a doctrine that can be interpreted as justifying it.

The problems that Skinner discusses—it would be more proper to say "circumvents"—are often real enough. Despite his curious belief to the contrary, his libertarian and humanist opponents do not object to "design of a culture," that is, to creating social forms that will be more conducive to the satisfaction of human needs, though they differ from Skinner in the intuitive perception of what these needs truly are. They would not, or at least should not, oppose scientific inquiry or, where possible, its applications, though they will no doubt dismiss the travesty that Skinner presents.

If a physical scientist were to assure us that we need not concern ourselves over the world's sources of energy because he has demonstrated in his laboratory that windmills will surely suffice for all future human needs, he would be expected to produce some evidence, or other scientists would expose this pernicious nonsense. The situation is different in the behavioral sciences. A person who claims that he has a behavioral technology that will solve the world's problems and a science of behavior that supports it and reveals the factors that determine human behavior is required to demonstrate nothing. One waits in vain for psychologists to make clear to the general public the actual limits of what is known. Given the prestige of science and technology, this is a most unfortunate situation.

Notes

This chapter is expanded from an essay published in *Cognition*, vol. 1, no. 1 (1972). Parts appeared, in a slightly different form, as a review of B. F. Skinner, *Beyond Freedom and Dignity*, in the *New York Review of Books*, December 30, 1971. The discussion of Herrnstein's work appeared in part in *Social Policy*, 1972, vol. 3, no. 1 (1972), and in *Ramparts*, July 1972. For Herrnstein's response, with further comments of mine (in part incorporated here), see *Cognition*, vol. 1, nos. 2–3, 4 (1972).

1 *Economist*, October 31, 1862. Cited by Frederick F. Clairmonte in his review of *The Race War*, by Ronald Segal, *Journal of Modern African Studies*, forthcoming.

2 Marvin Harris, *The Rise of Anthropological Theory*, pp. 100–1. By the 1860s, he writes, "anthropology and racial determinism had become almost synonyms."

3 B. F. Skinner, *Beyond Freedom and Dignity*, p. 82. Subsequent references will be to page number only.

4 W. V. O. Quine, "Linguistics and Philosophy," in Sidney Hook, ed., *Language and Philosophy*, p. 97.

5 We can, of course, design circumstances under which behavior can be predicted quite closely, as any military interrogator in the field is aware. And we can reduce the issue to triviality by regarding a person's wishes, intentions, purposes, and so on as part of the circumstances that elicit behavior. If we are really intent on deluding ourselves, we might go on to "translate" wishes, intentions, and purposes into the terminology of operant conditioning theory, along the lines that we will explore in a moment.

6 L. Breger and J. L. McGaugh, "Critique and Reformulation of 'Learning-Theory' Approaches to Psychotherapy and Neurosis," *Psychological Bulletin*, May 1965.

7 Aubrey J. Yates, *Behavior Therapy*, p. 396. Skinner also points out, irrelevantly to any rational consideration, that "the speaker does not feel the *grammatical rules* he is said to apply in composing sentences, and men spoke grammatically for thousands of years before anyone knew there were rules" (p. 16).

8 Jacques Monod, *Choice and Necessity*.

9 See, e.g., Kenneth MacCorquodale, "On Chomsky's Review of Skinner's *Verbal Behavior*," *Journal of the Experimental Analysis of Behavior*, vol. 13, no. 1 (1970).

10 As Koestler points out, in remarks Skinner quotes, Skinner's approach represents "question-begging on a heroic scale" (p. 165). It will not do to respond, as Skinner does, by claiming that this is "name-calling" and a sign of emotional instability. Rather it will be necessary to show that this is not the literal and obvious truth (as indeed it is).

11 See his *Verbal Behavior*, which incorporates and extends these lectures.

12 In reviewing Skinner's *Verbal Behavior* (*Language*, vol. 35, no. 1 [1959], pp. 26–58), I stated that there did appear to be one result, namely, with regard to modifying certain aspects of the speaker's behavior (say, production of plural nouns) by "reinforcement" with such expressions as "right" and "good," without the speaker's awareness. The result is at best of marginal interest, since evidently the speaker's behavior in such respects could be far more "effectively" modified by a simple instruction, a fact that cannot be incorporated into the Skinnerian system, if the latter is interpreted at all strictly. Of course, if the subject is aware of what the experimenter is doing, the result is of no interest at all. It turns out that this may very well be the case. See D. Dulany, "Awareness, Rules and Propositional Control: A Confrontation with S-R Behavior Theory," in Theodore R. Dixon and David Horton, eds., *Verbal Behavior and General Behavior Theory*. Therefore it seems that there are no clear nontrivial results that have been achieved in the study of normal human speech by application of the operant-conditioning paradigm.

Interesting reading, in this connection, is MacCorquodale, "On Chomsky's Review of Skinner." I cannot take the space here to correct the many errors (such as his misunderstanding of the notion of "function," which leads to much confusion). The major confusion in the article is this: MacCorquodale assumes that I was attempting to disprove Skinner's theses, and he points out that I present no data to disprove them. But my point was, rather, to demonstrate that when Skinner's assertions are taken literally, they are false on the face of it (MacCorquodale discusses none of these examples accurately) or else quite vacuous (as when we say that the response "Mozart" is under the control of a subtle stimulus), and that many of his false statements can be converted into uninteresting truths by employing such terms as "reinforce" with the full imprecision of "like," "want," "enjoy," and so on (with a loss of accuracy in transition, of course, since a rich and detailed terminology is replaced by a few terms that are divorced entirely from the setting in which they have some precision). Failing to understand this, MacCorquodale "defends" Skinner by showing that quite often it is possible to give a vacuous interpretation to his pronouncements; exactly my point. The article is useful, once errors are eliminated, in revealing the bankruptcy of the operant-conditioning approach to the study of verbal behavior.

13 See MacCorquodale, "On Chomsky's Review of Skinner," for a revealing example of complete inability to understand this point.

14 Note the shift in Skinner's account from the discussion of things that taste good to value judgments about things that we call good (pp. 103–5).

15 One way out would be to deny that these are facts. This is the approach taken by Patrick Suppes, in remarks that MacCorquodale quotes. Suppes refers to several books that contain a variety of facts such as these and explore the problem of accounting for them by an explanatory theory, and he asserts simply that these books contain no data. Apparently, Suppes would have us believe that these facts become "data" only when someone conducts an experiment in which he "proves" that the facts are what we know them to be, on

a moment's thought. It would, of course, be a straightforward matter to devise such experiments (adjusting them, in the typical fashion of such experimental work, until they give what we antecedently know to be the right results), were anyone willing to waste his time in such ways. Then the books would contain "data," in Suppes' sense.

[16] Libertarian thinkers have often been "radical environmentalists," mistakenly so, in my opinion, for reasons discussed elsewhere (see my Problems of Knowledge and Freedom).

[17] Richard Herrnstein, "I.Q.," Atlantic Monthly, September 1971.

[18] He does not specifically mention this assumption, but it is necessary to the argument. I will not discuss here two factual matters central to Herrnstein's argument: heritability of IQ, and the significance of IQ as a factor in determining economic reward. On the former, see Christopher Jencks et al., Inequality, Appendix A; this extensive analysis suggests that Herrnstein accepts an estimate of heritability that is far too high. On IQ as a factor in determining "social reward," Herrnstein presents no serious evidence for his claim that it is a major factor, but the matter has been carefully investigated by others (see Jencks et al., and Samuel Bowles and Herbert Gintis, "I.Q. in the U.S. Class Structure," mimeographed, Harvard University, July 1972). Bowles and Gintis conclude that IQ, social class, and education "contribute independently to economic success, but that IQ is by far the least important"; "a perfect equalization of IQs across social classes would reduce the intergenerational transmission of economic status by a negligible amount." Jencks et al. give as their "best estimate" that there is "about 3 percent less income inequality in genetically homogenous subpopulations than in the entire American population" (p. 221). In short, empirical investigations indicate that IQ is a minor factor determining income, and the genetic component in IQ a negligible factor. Thus there is nothing to support Herrnstein's belief that in a society like ours, a genetic component in IQ will tend to produce a stable hereditary "meritocracy." These observations suffice to dismiss Herrnstein's rather careless discussion. But my concern here is not its empirical inadequacies but rather its ideological assumptions, and in particular, the question why there has been such interest in and acclaim for work so lacking in substance.

[19] Note again Herrnstein's failure to distinguish remuneration from social approval, though the argument collapses if the only reward is approval.

[20] Atlantic Monthly, November 1971. See p. 110, first paragraph, for his rejoinder.

[21] See, e.g., Harry W. Blair, "The Green Revolution and 'economic man': Some Lessons for Community Development in South Asia," Pacific Affairs, vol. 44, no. 3 (1971).

[22] To assume that society tends to reward those who perform a social service is to succumb to essentially the same fallacy (among others) that undermines the argument that a free market, in principle, leads to optimal satisfaction of wants—whereas when wealth is badly distributed, the system will tend to produce luxuries for the few who can pay rather than necessities for the many who cannot.

[23] Misleadingly, Herrnstein states that "society is, in effect, husbanding

its intellectual resources by holding engineers in greater esteem and paying them more." But if he really wants to claim this on the basis of the ties between IQ and social standing that his data reveal, then he should conclude as well that society is husbanding its intellectual resources by holding accountants and PR men in greater esteem and paying them more. Quite apart from this, it is not so obvious as he apparently believes that society is wisely husbanding its intellectual resources by employing most of its scientists and engineers in military and space R-and-D.

²⁴ Harris, *Anthropological Theory*, p. 106.

²⁵ See the correspondence in the *Atlantic Monthly*, November 1971.

²⁶ An advertisement in the *Harvard Crimson*, November 29, 1971, signed by many faculty members, refers to the "disturbing conclusion that 'intelligence' is largely genetic, so that over many, many years society might evolve into classes marked by distinctly different levels of ability." Since the conclusion does not follow from the premise, as already noted, it may be that what disturbs the signers is the "conclusion that 'intelligence' is largely genetic." Why this should seem disturbing remains obscure.

CHAPTER 8

Notes on Anarchism

A French writer, sympathetic to anarchism, wrote in the 1890s that "anarchism has a broad back, like paper it endures anything"—including, he noted, those whose acts are such that "a mortal enemy of anarchism could not have done better."[1] There have been many styles of thought and action that have been referred to as "anarchist." It would be hopeless to try to encompass all of these conflicting tendencies in some general theory or ideology. And even if we proceed to extract from the history of libertarian thought a living, evolving tradition, as Daniel Guérin does in *Anarchism*, it remains difficult to formulate its doctrines as a specific and determinate theory of society and social change. The anarchist historian Rudolf Rocker, who presents a systematic conception of the development of anarchist thought towards anarchosyndicalism, along lines that bear comparison to Guérin's work, puts the matter well when he writes that anarchism is not

a fixed, self-enclosed social system but rather a definite trend in the historic development of mankind, which, in contrast with the intellectual guardianship of all clerical and governmental institutions, strives for the free unhindered unfolding of all the individual and social forces in life. Even freedom is only a relative, not an absolute concept, since it tends constantly to become broader and to affect wider circles in more manifold ways. For the anarchist, freedom is not an abstract philosophical concept, but the vital concrete possibility for every human being to bring to full development all the powers, capacities, and talents with which nature has endowed him, and turn them to social account. The less this natural development of man is influenced by ecclesiastical or political guardianship, the

more efficient and harmonious will human personality become, the more will it become the measure of the intellectual culture of the society in which it has grown.[2]

One might ask what value there is in studying a "definite
trend in the historic development of mankind" that does not
articulate a specific and detailed social theory. Indeed, many
commentators dismiss anarchism as utopian, formless, primitive, or otherwise incompatible with the realities of a complex
society. One might, however, argue rather differently: that at
every stage of history our concern must be to dismantle those
forms of authority and oppression that survive from an era
when they might have been justified in terms of the need for
security or survival or economic development, but that now
contribute to—rather than alleviate—material and cultural
deficit. If so, there will be no doctrine of social change fixed
for the present and future, nor even, necessarily, a specific and
unchanging concept of the goals towards which social change
should tend. Surely our understanding of the nature of man or
of the range of viable social forms is so rudimentary that any
far-reaching doctrine must be treated with great skepticism,
just as skepticism is in order when we hear that "human
nature" or "the demands of efficiency" or "the complexity of
modern life" requires this or that form of oppression and
autocratic rule.

Nevertheless, at a particular time there is every reason to
develop, insofar as our understanding permits, a specific realization of this definite trend in the historic development of
mankind, appropriate to the tasks of the moment. For Rocker,
"the problem that is set for our time is that of freeing man
from the curse of economic exploitation and political and
social enslavement"; and the method is not the conquest and
exercise of state power, nor stultifying parliamentarianism, but
rather "to reconstruct the economic life of the peoples from
the ground up and build it up in the spirit of Socialism."

But only the producers themselves are fitted for this task,
since they are the only value-creating element in society out
of which a new future can arise. Theirs must be the task
of freeing labor from all the fetters which economic exploitation has fastened on it, of freeing society from all the
institutions and procedure of political power, and of open-

ing the way to an alliance of free groups of men and women based on co-operative labor and a planned administration of things in the interest of the community. To prepare the toiling masses in city and country for this great goal and to bind them together as a militant force is the objective of modern Anarcho-syndicalism, and in this its whole purpose is exhausted. [P. 108]

As a socialist, Rocker would take for granted "that the serious, final, complete liberation of the workers is possible only upon one condition: that of the appropriation of capital, that is, of raw material and all the tools of labor, including land, by the whole body of the workers."[3] As an anarcho-syndicalist, he insists, further, that the workers' organizations create "not only the ideas, but also the facts of the future itself" in the prerevolutionary period, that they embody in themselves the structure of the future society—and he looks forward to a social revolution that will dismantle the state apparatus as well as expropriate the expropriators. "What we put in place of the government is industrial organization."

> Anarcho-syndicalists are convinced that a Socialist economic order cannot be created by the decrees and statutes of a government, but only by the solidaric collaboration of the workers with hand and brain in each special branch of production; that is, through the taking over of the management of all plants by the producers themselves under such form that the separate groups, plants, and branches of industry are independent members of the general economic organism and systematically carry on production and the distribution of the products in the interest of the community on the basis of free mutual agreements. [p. 94]

Rocker was writing at a moment when such ideas had been put into practice in a dramatic way in the Spanish Revolution. Just prior to the outbreak of the revolution, the anarchosyndicalist economist Diego Abad de Santillan had written:

> . . . in facing the problem of social transformation, the Revolution cannot consider the state as a medium, but must depend on the organization of producers.
>
> We have followed this norm and we find no need for the hypothesis of a superior power to organized labor, in order to establish a new order of things. We would thank anyone to point out to us what function, if any, the State can have in an economic organization, where private property has

been abolished and in which parasitism and special privilege have no place. The suppression of the State cannot be a languid affair; it must be the task of the Revolution to finish with the State. Either the Revolution gives social wealth to the producers in which case the producers organize themselves for due collective distribution and the State has nothing to do; or the Revolution does not give social wealth to the producers, in which case the Revolution has been a lie and the State would continue.

Our federal council of economy is not a political power but an economic and administrative regulating power. It receives its orientation from below and operates in accordance with the resolutions of the regional and national assemblies. It is a liaison corps and nothing else.[4]

Engels, in a letter of 1883, expressed his disagreement with this conception as follows:

The anarchists put the thing upside down. They declare that the proletarian revolution must *begin* by doing away with the political organization of the state. . . . But to destroy it at such a moment would be to destroy the only organism by means of which the victorious proletariat can assert its newly-conquered power, hold down its capitalist adversaries, and carry out that economic revolution of society without which the whole victory must end in a new defeat and in a mass slaughter of the workers similar to those after the Paris commune.[5]

In contrast, the anarchists—most eloquently Bakunin—warned of the dangers of the "red bureaucracy," which would prove to be "the most vile and terrible lie that our century has created."[6] The anarchosyndicalist Fernand Pelloutier asked: "Must even the transitory state to which we have to submit necessarily and fatally be the collectivist jail? Can't it consist in a free organization limited exclusively by the needs of production and consumption, all political institutions having disappeared?"[7]

I do not pretend to know the answer to this question. But it seems clear that unless there is, in some form, a positive answer, the chances for a truly democratic revolution that will achieve the humanistic ideals of the left are not great. Martin Buber put the problem succinctly when he wrote: "One cannot in the nature of things expect a little tree that has been turned into a club to put forth leaves."[8] The question of conquest or destruction of state power is what Bakunin regarded as the primary issue dividing him from Marx.[9] In one form or another, the problem has arisen repeatedly in the century since, dividing "libertarian" from "authoritarian" socialists.

Despite Bakunin's warnings about the red bureaucracy, and their fulfillment under Stalin's dictatorship, it would obviously be a gross error in interpreting the debates of a century ago to rely on the claims of contemporary social movements as to their historical origins. In particular, it is perverse to regard Bolshevism as "Marxism in practice." Rather, the left-wing critique of Bolshevism, taking account of the historical circumstances of the Russian Revolution, is far more to the point.[10]

> The anti-Bolshevik, left-wing labor movement opposed the Leninists because they did not go far enough in exploiting the Russian upheavals for strictly proletarian ends. They became prisoners of their environment and used the international radical movement to satisfy specifically Russian needs, which soon became synonymous with the needs of the Bolshevik Party-State. The "bourgeois" aspects of the Russian Revolution were now discovered in Bolshevism itself: Leninism was adjudged a part of international social-democracy, differing from the latter only on tactical issues.[11]

If one were to seek a single leading idea within the anarchist tradition, it should, I believe, be that expressed by Bakunin when, in writing on the Paris Commune, he identified himself as follows:

> I am a fanatic lover of liberty, considering it as the unique condition under which intelligence, dignity and human happiness can develop and grow; not the purely formal liberty conceded, measured out and regulated by the State, an eternal lie which in reality represents nothing more than the privilege of some founded on the slavery of the rest; not the individualistic, egoistic, shabby, and fictitious liberty extolled by the School of J.–J. Rousseau and the other schools of bourgeois liberalism, which considers the would-be rights of all men, represented by the State which limits the rights of each—an idea that leads inevitably to the reduction of the rights of each to zero. No, I mean the only kind of liberty that is worthy of the name, liberty that consists in the full development of all of the material, intel-

lectual and moral powers that are latent in each person; liberty that recognizes no restrictions other than those determined by the laws of our own individual nature, which cannot properly be regarded as restrictions since these laws are not imposed by any outside legislator beside or above us, but are immanent and inherent, forming the very basis of our material, intellectual and moral being—they do not limit us but are the real and immediate conditions of our freedom.[12]

These ideas grow out of the Enlightenment; their roots are in Rousseau's *Discourse on Inequality*, Humboldt's *Limits of State Action*, Kant's insistence, in his defense of the French Revolution, that freedom is the precondition for acquiring the maturity for freedom, not a gift to be granted when such maturity is achieved (see chapter 9, pp. 392–3). With the development of industrial capitalism, a new and unanticipated system of injustice, it is libertarian socialism that has preserved and extended the radical humanist message of the Enlightenment and the classical liberal ideals that were perverted into an ideology to sustain the emerging social order. In fact, on the very same assumptions that led classical liberalism to oppose the intervention of the state in social life, capitalist social relations are also intolerable. This is clear, for example, from the classic work of Humboldt, *The Limits of State Action*, which anticipated and perhaps inspired Mill and to which we return below (chapter 9, pp. 397–402). This classic of liberal thought, completed in 1792, is in its essence profoundly, though prematurely, anticapitalist. Its ideas must be attenuated beyond recognition to be transmuted into an ideology of industrial capitalism.

Humboldt's vision of a society in which social fetters are replaced by social bonds and labor is freely undertaken suggests the early Marx (see chapter 9, note 15), with his discussion of the "alienation of labor when work is external to the worker . . . not part of his nature . . . [so that] he does not fulfill himself in his work but denies himself . . . [and is] physically exhausted and mentally debased," alienated labor that "casts some of the workers back into a barbarous kind of work and turns others into machines," thus depriving man of his "species character" of "free conscious activity" and "productive life." Similarly, Marx conceives of "a new type of human being who *needs* his fellow-men. . . . [The workers' association becomes] the real constructive effort to create the social texture of future human relations."[13] It is true that classical libertarian thought is opposed to state intervention in social life, as a consequence of deeper assumptions about the human need for liberty, diversity, and free association. On the same assumptions, capitalist relations of production, wage labor, competitiveness, the ideology of "possessive individualism"— all must be regarded as fundamentally antihuman. Libertarian socialism is properly to be regarded as the inheritor of the liberal ideals of the Enlightenment.

Rudolf Rocker describes modern anarchism as "the confluence of the two great currents which during and since the French revolution have found such characteristic expression in the intellectual life of Europe: Socialism and Liberalism." The classical liberal ideals, he argues, were wrecked on the realities of capitalist economic forms. Anarchism is necessarily anticapitalist in that it "opposes the exploitation of man by man." But anarchism also opposes "the dominion of man over man." It insists that *socialism will be free or it will not be at all. In its recognition of this lies the genuine and profound justification for the existence of anarchism.*"[14] From this point of view, anarchism may be regarded as the libertarian wing of socialism. It is in this spirit that Daniel Guérin has approached the study of anarchism in *Anarchism* and other works.[15]

Guérin quotes Adolph Fischer, who said that "every anarchist is a socialist but not every socialist is necessarily an anarchist." Similarly Bakunin, in his "anarchist manifesto" of 1865, the program of his projected international revolutionary fraternity, laid down the principle that each member must be, to begin with, a socialist.

A consistent anarchist must oppose private ownership of the means of production and the wage slavery which is a component of this system, as incompatible with the principle that labor must be freely undertaken and under the control of the producer. As Marx put it, socialists look forward to a society in which labor will "become not only a means of life, but also the highest want in life,"[16] an impossibility when the worker is driven by external authority or need rather than inner impulse: "no form of wage-labor, even though one may be less obnoxious than another, can do away with the misery of wage-labor itself."[17] A consistent anarchist must oppose not only alienated labor but also the stupefying specialization of labor that takes place when the means for developing production

> mutilate the worker into a fragment of a human being, degrade him to become a mere appurtenance of the machine, make his work such a torment that its essential meaning is destroyed; estrange from him the intellectual potentialities of the labor process in very proportion to the extent to which science is incorporated into it as an independent power. . . .[18]

Marx saw this not as an inevitable concomitant of industrialization, but rather as a feature of capitalist relations of production. The society of the future must be concerned to "replace the detail-worker of today . . . reduced to a mere fragment of a man, by the fully developed individual, fit for a variety of labours . . . to whom the different social functions . . . are but so many modes of giving free scope to his own natural powers."[19] The prerequisite is the abolition of capital and wage labor as social categories (not to speak of the industrial armies of the "labor state" or the various modern forms of totalitarianism or state capitalism). The reduction of man to an appurtenance of the machine, a specialized tool of production, might in principle be overcome, rather than enhanced, with the proper development and use of technology, but not under the conditions of autocratic control of production by those who make man an instrument to serve their ends, overlooking his individual purposes, in Humboldt's phrase.

Anarchosyndicalists sought, even under capitalism, to create "free associations of free producers" that would engage in militant struggle and prepare to take over the organization of production on a democratic basis. These associations would serve as "a practical school of anarchism."[20] If private ownership of the means of production is, in Proudhon's often quoted phrase, merely a form of "theft"—"the exploitation of the weak by the strong"[21]—control of production by a state bureaucracy, no matter how benevolent its intentions, also does not create the conditions under which labor, manual and intellectual, can become the highest want in life. Both, then, must be overcome.

In his attack on the right of private or bureaucratic control over the means of production, the anarchist takes his stand with those who struggle to bring about "the third and last emancipatory phase of history," the first having made serfs out of slaves, the second having made wage earners out of serfs, and the third which abolishes the proletariat in a final act of liberation that places control over the economy in the hands of free and voluntary associations of producers (Fourier, 1848).[22] The imminent danger to "civilization" was noted by de Tocqueville, also in 1848:

> As long as the right of property was the origin and ground-work of many other rights, it was easily defended—or rather it was not attacked; it was then the citadel of society while all the other rights were its outworks; it did not bear the brunt of attack and, indeed, there was no serious attempt to assail it. But today, when the right of property is regarded as the last undestroyed remnant of the aristocratic world, when it alone is left standing, the sole privilege in an equalized society, it is a different matter. Consider what is happening in the hearts of the working-classes, although I admit they are quiet as yet. It is true that they are less inflamed than formerly by political passions properly speaking; but do you not see that their passions, far from being political, have become social? Do you not see that, little by little, ideas and opinions are spreading amongst them which aim not merely at removing such and such laws, such a ministry or such a government, but at breaking up the very foundations of society itself?[23]

The workers of Paris, in 1871, broke the silence, and proceeded

> to abolish property, the basis of all civilization! Yes, gentlemen, the Commune intended to abolish that class property which makes the labor of the many the wealth of the few. It aimed at the expropriation of the expropriators. It wanted to make individual property a truth by transforming the means of production, land and capital, now chiefly the means of enslaving and exploiting labor, into mere instruments of free and associated labor.[24]

The Commune, of course, was drowned in blood. The nature of the "civilization" that the workers of Paris sought to overcome in their attack on "the very foundations of society itself" was revealed, once again, when the troops of the Versailles government reconquered Paris from its population. As Marx wrote, bitterly but accurately:

> The civilization and justice of bourgeois order comes out in its lurid light whenever the slaves and drudges of that order rise against their masters. Then this civilization and justice stand forth as undisguised savagery and lawless revenge . . . the infernal deeds of the soldiery reflect the innate spirit of that civilization of which they are the mercenary vindicators. . . . The bourgeoisie of the whole world, which looks complacently upon the wholesale massacre after the battle, is convulsed by horror at the desecration of brick and mortar. [*Ibid.*, pp. 74, 77]

Despite the violent destruction of the Commune, Bakunin wrote that Paris opens a new era, "that of the definitive and complete emancipation of the popular masses and their future true solidarity, across and despite state boundaries . . . the next revolution of man, international and in solidarity, will be the resurrection of Paris"—a revolution that the world still awaits.

The consistent anarchist, then, should be a socialist, but a socialist of a particular sort. He will not only oppose alienated and specialized labor and look forward to the appropriation of capital by the whole body of workers, but he will also insist that this appropriation be direct, not exercised by some elite force acting in the name of the proletariat. He will, in short, oppose

> the organization of production by the Government. It means State-socialism, the command of the State officials over production and the command of managers, scientists, shop-officials in the shop. . . . The goal of the working class is liberation from exploitation. This goal is not reached and cannot be reached by a new directing and governing class substituting itself for the bourgeoisie. It is only realized by the workers themselves being master over production.

These remarks are taken from "Five Theses on the Class Struggle" by the left-wing Marxist Anton Pannekoek, one of the outstanding theorists of the council communist movement. And in fact, radical Marxism merges with anarchist currents.

As a further illustration, consider the following characterization of "revolutionary Socialism":

> The revolutionary Socialist denies that State ownership can end in anything other than a bureaucratic despotism. We have seen why the State cannot democratically control industry. Industry can only be democratically owned and controlled by the workers electing directly from their own ranks industrial administrative committees. Socialism will be fundamentally an industrial system; its constituencies will be of an industrial character. Thus those carrying on the social activities and industries of society will be directly represented in the local and central councils of social administration. In this way the powers of such delegates will flow upwards from those carrying on the work and conversant with the needs of the community. When the central administrative industrial committee meets it will represent every phase of social activity. Hence the capitalist political or geographical state will be replaced by the industrial administrative committee of Socialism. The transition from the one social system to the other will be the *social revolution*. The political State throughout history has meant the government *of men* by ruling classes; the Republic of Socialism will be the government *of industry* administered on behalf of the whole community. The former meant the economic and political subjection of the many; the latter will mean the economic freedom of all—it will be, therefore, a true democracy.

This programmatic statement appears in William Paul's *The State, its Origins and Function*, written in early 1917—shortly before Lenin's *State and Revolution*, perhaps his most libertarian work (see note 9). Paul was a member of the Marxist–De Leonist Socialist Labor Party and later one of the founders of the British Communist Party.[25] His critique of state socialism resembles the libertarian doctrine of the anarchists in its principle that since state ownership and management will lead to bureaucratic despotism, the social revolution must replace it by the industrial organization of society with direct workers' control. Many similar statements can be cited.

What is far more important is that these ideas have been realized in spontaneous revolutionary action, for example in Germany and Italy after World War I and in Spain (not only in the agricultural countryside, but also in industrial Barcelona) in 1936. One might argue that some form of council communism is the natural form of revolutionary socialism in an industrial society. It reflects the intuitive understanding that democracy is severely limited when the industrial system is controlled by any form of autocratic elite, whether of owners, managers and technocrats, a "vanguard" party, or a state bureaucracy. Under these conditions of authoritarian domination the classical libertarian ideals developed further by Marx and Bakunin and all true revolutionaries cannot be realized; man will not be free to develop his own potentialities to their fullest, and the producer will remain "a fragment of a human being," degraded, a tool in the productive process directed from above.

The phrase "spontaneous revolutionary action" can be misleading. The anarchosyndicalists, at least, took very seriously Bakunin's remark that the workers' organizations must create "not only the ideas but also the facts of the future itself" in the prerevolutionary period. The accomplishments of the popular revolution in Spain, in particular, were based on the patient work of many years of organization and education, one component of a long tradition of commitment and militancy. The resolutions of the Madrid Congress of June 1931 and the Saragossa Congress in May 1936 foreshadowed in many ways the acts of the revolution, as did the somewhat different ideas sketched by Santillan (see note 4) in his fairly specific account of the social and economic organization to be instituted by the revolution. Guérin writes: "The Spanish revolution was relatively mature in the minds of the libertarian thinkers, as in the popular consciousness." And workers' organizations existed with the structure, the experience, and the understanding to undertake the task of social reconstruction when, with the Franco coup, the turmoil of early 1936 exploded into social revolution. In his introduction to a collection of documents on collectivization in Spain, the anarchist Augustin Souchy writes:

> For many years, the anarchists and syndicalists of Spain considered their supreme task to be the social transformation of the society. In their assemblies of Syndicates and groups, in their journals, their brochures and books, the problem of the social revolution was discussed incessantly and in a systematic fashion.[26]

All of this lies behind the spontaneous achievements, the constructive work of the Spanish Revolution.

The ideas of libertarian socialism, in the sense described, have been submerged in the industrial societies of the past half-century. The dominant ideologies have been those of state socialism or state capitalism (of an increasingly militarized character in the United States, for reasons that are not obscure).[27] But there has been a rekindling of interest in the past few years. The theses I quoted by Anton Pannekoek were taken from a recent pamphlet of a radical French workers' group (*Informations Correspondance Ouvrière*). The remarks by William Paul on revolutionary socialism are cited in a paper by Walter Kendall given at the National Conference on Workers' Control in Sheffield, England, in March 1969. The workers' control movement has become a significant force in England in the past few years. It has organized several conferences and has produced a substantial pamphlet literature, and counts among its active adherents representatives of some of the most important trade unions. The Amalgamated Engineering and Foundryworkers' Union, for example, has adopted, as official policy, the program of nationalization of basic industries under "workers' control at all levels."[28] On the Continent, there are similar developments. May 1968 of course accelerated the growing interest in council communism and related ideas in France and Germany, as it did in England.

Given the general conservative cast of our highly ideological society, it is not too surprising that the United States has been relatively untouched by these developments. But that too may change. The erosion of the cold-war mythology at least makes it possible to raise these questions in fairly broad circles. If the present wave of repression can be beaten back, if the left can overcome its more suicidal tendencies and build upon what has been accomplished in the past decade, then the problem of how to organize industrial society on truly democratic lines, with democratic control in the workplace and in the community, should become a dominant intellectual issue for those who are alive to the problems of contemporary society, and, as a mass movement for libertarian socialism develops, speculation should proceed to action.

In his manifesto of 1865, Bakunin predicted that one element in the social revolution will be "that intelligent and truly noble part of the youth which, though belonging by birth to the privileged classes, in its generous convictions and ardent aspirations, adopts the cause of the people." Perhaps in the rise of the student movement of the 1960s one sees steps towards a fulfillment of this prophecy.

Daniel Guérin has undertaken what he has described as a "process of rehabilitation" of anarchism. He argues, convincingly I believe, that "the constructive ideas of anarchism retain their vitality, that they may, when re-examined and sifted, assist contemporary socialist thought to undertake a new departure . . . [and] contribute to enriching Marxism."[29] From the "broad back" of anarchism he has selected for more intensive scrutiny those ideas and actions that can be described as libertarian socialist. This is natural and proper. This framework accommodates the major anarchist spokesmen as well as the mass actions that have been animated by anarchist sentiments and ideals. Guérin is concerned not only with anarchist thought but also with the spontaneous actions of popular forces that actually create new social forms in the course of revolutionary struggle. He is concerned with social as well as intellectual creativity. Furthermore, he attempts to draw from the constructive achievements of the past lessons that will enrich the theory of social liberation. For those who wish not only to understand the world, but also to change it, this is the proper way to study the history of anarchism.

Guérin describes the anarchism of the nineteenth century as essentially doctrinal, while the twentieth century, for the anarchists, has been a time of "revolutionary practice."[30] *Anarchism* reflects that judgment. His interpretation of anarchism consciously points towards the future. Arthur Rosenberg once pointed out that popular revolutions characteristically seek to replace "a feudal or centralized authority ruling by force" with some form of communal system which "implies the destruction and disappearance of the old form of State." Such a system will be either socialist or an "extreme form of democracy . . . [which is] the preliminary condition for Socialism inasmuch as Socialism can only be realized in a world enjoying the highest possible measure of individual freedom." This ideal, he notes, was common to Marx and the anarchists.[31] This natural struggle for liberation runs counter to the prevailing tendency towards centralization in economic and political life.

A century ago Marx wrote that the workers of Paris "felt there was but one alternative—the Commune, or the empire —under whatever name it might reappear."

> The empire had ruined them economically by the havoc it made of public wealth, by the wholesale financial swindling it fostered, by the props it lent to the artificially accelerated centralization of capital, and the concomitant expropriation of their own ranks. It had suppressed them politically, it had shocked them morally by its orgies, it had insulted their Voltairianism by handing over the education of their children to the *frères Ignorantins*, it had revolted their national feeling as Frenchmen by precipitating them headlong into a war which left only one equivalent for the ruins it made—the disappearance of the empire.[32]

The miserable Second Empire "was the only form of government possible at a time when the bourgeoisie had already lost, and the working class had not yet acquired, the faculty of ruling the nation."

It is not very difficult to rephrase these remarks so that they become appropriate to the imperial systems of 1970. The problem of "freeing man from the curse of economic exploitation and political and social enslavement" remains the problem of our time. As long as this is so, the doctrines and the revolutionary practice of libertarian socialism will serve as an inspiration and a guide.

Notes

This essay is a revised version of the introduction to Daniel Guérin's *Anarchism: From Theory to Practice*. In a slightly different version, it appeared in the *New York Review of Books*, May 21, 1970.

1 Octave Mirbeau, quoted in James Joll, *The Anarchists*, pp. 145–6.
2 Rudolf Rocker, *Anarchosyndicalism*, p. 31.
3 Cited by Rocker, *ibid.*, p. 77. This quotation and that in the next sentence are from Michael Bakunin, "The Program of the Alliance," in Sam Dolgoff, ed. and trans., *Bakunin on Anarchy*, p. 255.

4 Diego Abad de Santillan, *After the Revolution*, p. 86. In the last chapter, written several months after the revolution had begun, he expresses his dissatisfaction with what had so far been achieved along these lines. On the accomplishments of the social revolution in Spain, see my *American Power and the New Mandarins*, chap. 1, and references cited there; the important study by Broué and Témime has since been translated into English. Several other important studies have appeared since, in particular: Frank Mintz, *L'Autogestion dans l'Espagne révolutionnaire* (Paris: Editions Bélibaste, 1971); César M. Lorenzo, *Les Anarchistes espagnols et le pouvoir, 1868–1969* (Paris: Editions du Seuil, 1969); Gaston Leval, *Espagne libertaire, 1936–1939: L'Oeuvre constructive de la Révolution espagnole* (Paris: Editions du Cercle, 1971). See also Vernon Richards, *Lessons of the Spanish Revolution*, enlarged 1972 edition.

5 Cited by Robert C. Tucker, *The Marxian Revolutionary Idea*, in his discussion of Marxism and anarchism.

6 Bakunin, in a letter to Herzen and Ogareff, 1866. Cited by Daniel Guérin, *Jeunesse du socialisme libertaire*, p. 119.

7 Fernand Pelloutier, cited in Joll, *Anarchists*. The source is "L'Anarchisme et les syndicats ouvriers," *Les Temps nouveaux*, 1895. The full text appears in Daniel Guérin, ed., *Ni Dieu, ni Maître*, an excellent historical anthology of anarchism.

8 Martin Buber, *Paths in Utopia*, p. 127.

9 "No state, however democratic," Bakunin wrote, "not even the reddest republic—can ever give the people what they really want, i.e., the free self-organization and administration of their own affairs from the bottom upward, without any interference or violence from above, because every state, even the pseudo-People's State concocted by Mr. Marx, is in essence only a machine ruling the masses from above, through a privileged minority of conceited intellectuals, who imagine that they know what the people need and want better than do the people themselves. . . ." "But the people will feel no better if the stick with which they are being beaten is labeled 'the people's stick'" (*Statism and Anarchy* [1873], in Dolgoff, *Bakunin on Anarchy*, p. 338)—"the people's stick" being the democratic Republic.

  Marx, of course, saw the matter differently.

  For discussion of the impact of the Paris Commune on this dispute, see Daniel Guérin's comments in *Ni Dieu, ni Maître*; these also appear, slightly extended, in his *Pour un marxisme libertaire*. See also note 24.

10 On Lenin's "intellectual deviation" to the left during 1917, see Robert Vincent Daniels, "The State and Revolution: a Case Study in the Genesis and Transformation of Communist Ideology," *American Slavic and East European Review*, vol. 12, no. 1 (1953).

11 Paul Mattick, *Marx and Keynes*, p. 295.

12 Michael Bakunin, "La Commune de Paris et la notion de l'état," reprinted in Guérin, *Ni Dieu, ni Maître*. Bakunin's final remark on the laws of individual nature as the condition of freedom can be compared with the approach to creative thought developed in the rationalist and romantic traditions, discussed in chapter 9. See my *Cartesian Linguistics* and *Language and Mind*.

13 Shlomo Avineri, *The Social and Political Thought of Karl Marx*, p. 142, referring to comments in *The Holy Family*. Avineri states that within the socialist movement only the Israeli *kibbutzim* "have perceived that the modes and forms of present social organization will determine the structure of future society." This, however, was a characteristic position of anarchosyndicalism, as noted earlier.

14 Rocker, *Anarchosyndicalism*, p. 28.

15 See Guérin's works cited earlier.

16 Karl Marx, *Critique of the Gotha Programme*.

17 Karl Marx, *Grundrisse der Kritik der Politischen Ökonomie*, cited by Mattick, *Marx and Keynes*, p. 306. In this connection, see also Mattick's essay "Workers' Control," in Priscilla Long, ed., *The New Left*; and Avineri, *Social and Political Thought of Marx*.

18 Karl Marx, *Capital*, quoted by Robert Tucker, who rightly emphasizes that Marx sees the revolutionary more as a "frustrated producer" than a "dissatisfied consumer" (*The Marxian Revolutionary Idea*). This more radical critique of capitalist relations of production is a direct outgrowth of the libertarian thought of the Enlightenment.

19 Marx, *Capital*, cited by Avineri, *Social and Political Thought of Marx*, p. 83.

20 Pelloutier, "L'anarchisme."

21 "Qu'est-ce que la propriété?" The phrase "property is theft" displeased Marx, who saw in its use a logical problem, theft presupposing the legitimate existence of property. See Avineri, *Social and Political Thought of Marx*.

22 Cited in Buber's *Paths in Utopia*, p. 19.

23 Cited in J. Hampden Jackson, *Marx, Proudhon and European Socialism*, p. 60.

24 Karl Marx, *The Civil War in France*, p. 24. Avineri observes that this and other comments of Marx about the Commune refer pointedly to intentions and plans. As Marx made plain elsewhere, his considered assessment was more critical than in this address.

25 For some background, see Walter Kendall, *The Revolutionary Movement in Britain*.

26 *Collectivisations: L'Oeuvre constructive de la Révolution espagnole*, p. 8.

27 For discussion, see Mattick, *Marx and Keynes*, and Michael Kidron, *Western Capitalism Since the War*. See also discussion and references cited in my *At War with Asia*, chap. 1, pp. 23–6.

28 See Hugh Scanlon, *The Way Forward for Workers' Control*. Scanlon is president of the AEF, one of Britain's largest trade unions. The institute was established as a result of the sixth Conference on Workers' Control, March 1968, and serves as a center for disseminating information and encouraging research.

29 Guérin, *Ni Dieu, ni Maître*, introduction.

30 *Ibid*.

31 Arthur Rosenberg, *A History of Bolshevism*, p. 88.

32 Marx, *Civil War in France*, pp. 62–3.

CHAPTER 9

Language and Freedom

When I was invited to speak on the topic "language and freedom," I was puzzled and intrigued. Most of my professional life has been devoted to the study of language. There would be no great difficulty in finding a topic to discuss in that domain. And there is much to say about the problems of freedom and liberation as they pose themselves to us and to others in the mid-twentieth century. What is troublesome in the title of this lecture is the conjunction. In what way are language and freedom to be interconnected?

As a preliminary, let me say just a word about the contemporary study of language, as I see it. There are many aspects of language and language use that raise intriguing questions, but—in my judgment—only a few have so far led to productive theoretical work. In particular, our deepest insights are in the area of formal grammatical structure. A person who knows a language has acquired a system of rules and principles—a "generative grammar," in technical terms—that associates sound and meaning in some specific fashion. There are many reasonably well-founded and, I think, rather enlightening hypotheses as to the character of such grammars, for quite a number of languages. Furthermore, there has been a renewal of interest in "universal grammar," interpreted now as the theory that tries to specify the general properties of these languages that can be learned in the normal way by humans. Here too, significant progress has been achieved. The subject is of particular importance. It is appropriate to regard universal grammar as the study of one of the essential faculties of mind. It is, therefore, extremely interesting to discover, as I believe we do, that the principles of universal grammar are rich, abstract, and restrictive, and can be used to construct principled explanations for a variety of phenomena. At the present stage of our understanding, if language is to provide a springboard for the investigation of other problems of man, it is these aspects of language to which we will have to turn our attention, for the simple reason that it is only these aspects that are reasonably well understood. In another sense, the study of formal properties of language reveals something of the nature of man in a negative way: it underscores, with great clarity, the limits of our understanding of those qualities of mind that are apparently unique to man and that must enter into his cultural achievements in an intimate, if still quite obscure, manner.

In searching for a point of departure, one turns naturally to a period in the history of Western thought when it was possible to believe that "the thought of making freedom the sum and substance of philosophy has emancipated the human spirit in all its relationships, and . . . has given to science in all its parts a more powerful reorientation than any earlier revolution."[1] The word "revolution" bears multiple associations in this passage, for Schelling also proclaims that "man is born to act and not to speculate"; and when he writes that "the time has come to proclaim to a nobler humanity the freedom of the spirit, and no longer to have patience with men's tearful regrets for their lost chains," we hear the echoes of the libertarian thought and revolutionary acts of the late eighteenth century. Schelling writes that "the beginning and end of all philosophy is—Freedom." These words are invested with meaning and urgency at a time when men are struggling to cast off their chains, to resist authority that has lost its claim to legitimacy, to construct more humane and more democratic social institutions. It is at such a time that the philosopher may be driven to inquire into the nature of human freedom and its limits, and perhaps to conclude, with Schelling, that with respect to the human ego, "its essence is freedom"; and with respect to philosophy, "the highest dignity of Philosophy consists precisely therein, that it stakes all on human freedom."

We are living, once again, at such a time. A revolutionary ferment is sweeping the so-called Third World, awakening enormous masses from torpor and acquiescence in traditional authority. There are those who feel that the industrial societies as well are ripe for revolutionary change—and I do not refer only to representatives of the New Left. See for example, the remarks of Paul Ricoeur cited in chapter 6, pages 308–9.

The threat of revolutionary change brings forth repression and reaction. Its signs are evident in varying forms, in France, in the Soviet Union, in the United States—not least, in the city where we are meeting. It is natural, then, that we should consider, abstractly, the problems of human freedom, and turn with interest and serious attention to the thinking of an earlier period when archaic social institutions were subjected to critical analysis and sustained attack. It is natural and appropriate, so long as we bear in mind Schelling's admonition, that man is born not merely to speculate but also to act.

One of the earliest and most remarkable of the eighteenth-century investigations of freedom and servitude is Rousseau's *Discourse on Inequality* (1755), in many ways a revolutionary tract. In it, he seeks to "set forth the origin and progress of inequality, the establishment and abuse of political societies, insofar as these things can be deduced from the nature of man by the light of reason alone." His conclusions were sufficiently shocking that the judges of the prize competition of the Academy of Dijon, to whom the work was originally submitted, refused to hear the manuscript through.[2] In it, Rousseau challenges the legitimacy of virtually every social institution, as well as individual control of property and wealth. These are "usurpations . . . established only on a precarious and abusive right. . . . having been acquired only by force, force could take them away without [the rich] having grounds for complaint." Not even property acquired by personal industry is held "upon better titles." Against such a claim, one might object: "Do you not know that a multitude of your brethren die or suffer from need of what you have in excess, and that you needed express and unanimous consent of the human race to appropriate for yourself anything from common subsistence that exceeded your own?" It is contrary to the law of nature that "a handful of men be glutted with superfluities while the starving multitude lacks necessities."

Rousseau argues that civil society is hardly more than a conspiracy by the rich to guarantee their plunder. Hypocritically, the rich call upon their neighbors to "institute regulations of justice and peace to which all are obliged to conform, which make an exception of no one, and which compensate in some way for the caprices of fortune by equally subjecting the powerful and the weak to mutual duties"—those laws which, as Anatole France was to say, in their majesty deny to the rich and the poor equally the right to sleep under the bridge at night. By such arguments, the poor and weak were seduced: "All ran to meet their chains thinking they secured their freedom. . . ." Thus society and laws "gave new fetters to the weak and new forces to the rich, destroyed natural freedom for all time, established forever the law of property and inequality, changed a clever usurpation into an irrevocable right, and for the profit of a few ambitious men henceforth subjected the whole human race to work, servitude and misery." Governments inevitably tend towards arbitrary power, as "their corruption and extreme limit." This power is "by its nature illegitimate," and new revolutions must

> dissolve the government altogether or bring it closer to its legitimate institution. . . . The uprising that ends by strangling or dethroning a sultan is as lawful an act as those by which he disposed, the day before, of the lives and goods of his subjects. Force alone maintained him, force alone overthrows him.

What is interesting, in the present connection, is the path that Rousseau follows to reach these conclusions "by the light of reason alone," beginning with his ideas about the nature of man. He wants to see man "as nature formed him." It is from the nature of man that the principles of natural right and the foundations of social existence must be deduced.

> This same study of original man, of his true needs, and of the principles underlying his duties, is also the only good means one could use to remove those crowds of difficulties which present themselves concerning the origin of moral inequality, the true foundation of the body politic, the

reciprocal rights of its members, and a thousand similar questions as important as they are ill explained.

To determine the nature of man, Rousseau proceeds to compare man and animal. Man is "intelligent, free . . . the sole animal endowed with reason." Animals are "devoid of intellect and freedom."

> In every animal I see only an ingenious machine to which nature has given senses in order to revitalize itself and guarantee itself, to a certain point, from all that tends to destroy or upset it. I perceive precisely the same things in the human machine, with the difference that nature alone does everything in the operations of a beast, whereas man contributes to his operations by being a free agent. The former chooses or rejects by instinct and the latter by an act of freedom, so that a beast cannot deviate from the rule that is prescribed to it even when it would be advantageous for it to do so, and a man deviates from it often to his detriment. . . . it is not so much understanding which constitutes the distinction of man among the animals as it is his being a free agent. Nature commands every animal, and the beast obeys. Man feels the same impetus, but he realizes that he is free to acquiesce or resist; and it is above all in the consciousness of this freedom that the spirituality of his soul is shown. For physics explains in some way the mechanism of the senses and the formation of ideas; but in the power of willing, or rather of choosing, and in the sentiment of this power are found only purely spiritual acts about which the laws of mechanics explain nothing.

Thus the essence of human nature is man's freedom and his consciousness of his freedom. So Rousseau can say that "the jurists, who have gravely pronounced that the child of a slave would be born a slave, have decided in other terms that a man would not be born a man."[3]

Sophistic politicians and intellectuals search for ways to obscure the fact that the essential and defining property of man is his freedom: "they attribute to men a natural inclination to servitude, without thinking that it is the same for freedom as for innocence and virtue—their value is felt only as long as one enjoys them oneself and the taste for them is lost as soon as one has lost them." In contrast, Rousseau asks rhetorically "whether, freedom being the most noble of man's faculties, it is not degrading one's nature, putting oneself on the level of beasts enslaved by instinct, even offending the author of one's being, to renounce without reservation the most precious of all his gifts and subject ourselves to committing all the crimes he forbids us in order to please a ferocious or insane master"—a question that has been asked, in similar terms, by many an American draft resister in the last few years, and by many others who are beginning to recover from the catastrophe of twentieth-century Western civilization, which has so tragically confirmed Rousseau's judgment:

> Hence arose the national wars, battles, murders, and reprisals which make nature tremble and shock reason, and all those horrible prejudices which rank the honor of shedding human blood among the virtues. The most decent men learned to consider it one of their duties to murder their fellowmen; at length men were seen to massacre each other by the thousands without knowing why; more murders were committed on a single day of fighting and more horrors in the capture of a single city than were committed in the state of nature during whole centuries over the entire face of the earth.

The proof of his doctrine that the struggle for freedom is an essential human attribute, that the value of freedom is felt only as long as one enjoys it, Rousseau sees in "the marvels done by all free peoples to guard themselves from oppression." True, those who have abandoned the life of a free man

> do nothing but boast incessantly of the peace and repose they enjoy in their chains. . . . But when I see the others sacrifice pleasures, repose, wealth, power, and life itself for the preservation of this sole good which is so disdained by those who have lost it; when I see animals born free and despising captivity break their heads against the bars of their prison; when I see multitudes of entirely naked savages scorn European voluptuousness and endure hunger, fire, the sword, and death to preserve only their independence, I feel that it does not behoove slaves to reason about freedom.

Rather similar thoughts were expressed by Kant, forty years later. He cannot, he says, accept the proposition that certain people "are not ripe for freedom," for example, the serfs of some landlord.

> If one accepts this assumption, freedom will never be achieved; for one can not arrive at the maturity for freedom without having already acquired it; one must be free to learn how to make use of one's powers freely and usefully. The first attempts will surely be brutal and will lead to a state of affairs more painful and dangerous than the former condition under the dominance but also the protection of an external authority. However, one can achieve reason only through one's own experiences and one must be free to be able to undertake them. . . . To accept the principle that freedom is worthless for those under one's control and that one has the right to refuse it to them forever, is an infringement on the rights of God himself, who has created man to be free.[4]

The remark is particularly interesting because of its context. Kant was defending the French Revolution, during the Terror, against those who claimed that it showed the masses to be unready for the privilege of freedom. Kant's remarks have contemporary relevance. No rational person will approve of violence and terror. In particular, the terror of the postrevolutionary state, fallen into the hands of a grim autocracy, has more than once reached indescribable levels of savagery. Yet no person of understanding or humanity will too quickly condemn the violence that often occurs when long-subdued masses rise against their oppressors, or take their first steps towards liberty and social reconstruction.

Let me return now to Rousseau's argument against the legitimacy of established authority, whether that of political power or of wealth. It is striking that his argument, up to this point, follows a familiar Cartesian model. Man is uniquely beyond the bounds of physical explanation; the beast, on the other hand, is merely an ingenious machine, commanded by natural law. Man's freedom and his consciousness of this freedom distinguish him from the beast-machine. The principles of mechanical explanation are incapable of accounting for these human properties, though they can account for sensation and even the combination of ideas, in which regard "man differs from a beast only in degree."

To Descartes and his followers, such as Cordemoy, the only sure sign that another organism has a mind, and hence also lies beyond the bounds of mechanical explanation, is its use of language in the normal, creative human fashion, free from control by identifiable stimuli, novel and innovative, appropriate to situations, coherent, and engendering in our minds new thoughts and ideas.[5] To the Cartesians, it is obvious by introspection that each man possesses a mind, a substance whose essence is thought; his creative use of language reflects this freedom of thought and conception. When we have evidence that another organism too uses language in this free and creative fashion, we are led to attribute to it as well a mind like ours. From similar assumptions regarding the intrinsic limits of mechanical explanation, its inability to account for man's freedom and consciousness of his freedom, Rousseau proceeds to develop his critique of authoritarian institutions, which deny to man his essential attribute of freedom, in varying degree.

Were we to combine these speculations, we might develop an interesting connection between language and freedom. Language, in its essential properties and the manner of its use, provides the basic criterion for determining that another organism is a being with a human mind and the human capacity for free thought and self-expression, and with the essential human need for freedom from the external constraints of repressive authority. Furthermore, we might try to proceed from the detailed investigation of language and its use to a deeper and more specific understanding of the human mind. Proceeding on this model, we might further attempt to study other aspects of that human nature which, as Rousseau rightly observes, must be correctly conceived if we are to be able to develop, in theory, the foundations for a rational social order.

I will return to this problem, but first I would like to trace further Rousseau's thinking about the matter. Rousseau diverges from the Cartesian tradition in several respects. He defines the "specific characteristic of the human species" as man's "faculty of self-perfection," which, "with the aid of circumstances, successively develops all the others, and resides among us as much in the species as in the individual." The faculty of self-perfection and of perfection of the human species through cultural transmission is not, to my knowledge, discussed in any similar terms by the Cartesians. However, I think that Rousseau's remarks might be interpreted as a development of the Cartesian tradition in an unexplored direction, rather than as a denial and rejection of it. There is no inconsistency in the notion that the restrictive attributes of mind underlie a historically evolving human nature that develops within the limits that they set; or that these attributes of mind provide the possibility for self-perfection; or that, by providing the consciousness of freedom, these essential attributes of human nature give man the opportunity to create social conditions and social forms to maximize the possibilities for freedom, diversity, and individual self-realization. To use an arithmetical analogy, the integers do not fail to be an infinite set merely because they do not exhaust the rational numbers. Analogously, it is no denial of man's capacity for infinite "self-perfection" to hold that there are intrinsic properties of mind that constrain his development. I would like to argue that in a sense the opposite is true, that without a system of formal constraints there are no creative acts; specifically, in the absence of intrinsic and restrictive properties of mind, there can be only "shaping of behavior" but no creative acts of self-perfection. Furthermore, Rousseau's concern for the evolutionary character of self-perfection brings us back, from another point of view, to a concern for human language, which would appear to be a prerequisite for such evolution of society and culture, for Rousseau's perfection of the species, beyond the most rudimentary forms.

Rousseau holds that "although the organ of speech is natural to man, speech itself is nonetheless not natural to him." Again, I see no inconsistency between this observation and the typical Cartesian view that innate abilities are "dispositional," faculties that lead us to produce ideas (specifically, innate ideas) in a particular manner under given conditions of external stimulation, but that also provide us with the ability to proceed in our thinking without such external factors. Language too, then, is natural to man only in a specific way. This is an important and, I believe, quite fundamental insight of the rationalist linguists that was disregarded, very largely, under the impact of empiricist psychology in the eighteenth century and since.[6]

Rousseau discusses the origin of language at some length,

though he confesses himself to be unable to come to grips with the problem in a satisfactory way. Thus

> if men needed speech in order to learn to think, they had even greater need of knowing how to think in order to discover the art of speech. . . . So that one can hardly form tenable conjectures about this art of communicating thoughts and establishing intercourse between minds; a sublime art which is now very far from its origin. . . .

He holds that "general ideas can come into the mind only with the aid of words, and the understanding grasps them only through propositions"—a fact which prevents animals, devoid of reason, from formulating such ideas or ever acquiring "the perfectiblity which depends upon them." Thus he cannot conceive of the means by which "our new grammarians began to extend their ideas and to generalize their words," or to develop the means "to express all the thoughts of men": "numbers, abstract words, aorists, and all the tenses of verbs, particles, syntax, the linking of propositions, reasoning, and the forming of all the logic of discourse." He does speculate about later stages of the perfection of the species, "when the ideas of men began to spread and multiply, and when closer communication was established among them, [and] they sought more numerous signs and a more extensive language." But he must, unhappily, abandon "the following difficult problem: which was most necessary, previously formed society for the institution of languages, or previously invented languages for the establishment of society?"

The Cartesians cut the Gordian knot by postulating the existence of a species-specific characteristic, a second substance that serves as what we might call a "creative principle" alongside the "mechanical principle" that determines totally the behavior of animals. There was, for them, no need to explain the origin of language in the course of historical evolution. Rather, man's nature is qualitatively distinct: there is no passage from body to mind. We might reinterpret this idea in more current terms by speculating that rather sudden and dramatic mutations might have led to qualities of intelligence that are, so far as we know, unique to man, possession of language in the human sense being the most distinctive index of these qualities.[7] If this is correct, as at least a first approximation to the facts, the study of language might be expected to offer an entering wedge, or perhaps a model, for an investigation of human nature that would provide the grounding for a much broader theory of human nature.

To conclude these historical remarks, I would like to turn, as I have elsewhere,[8] to Wilhelm von Humboldt, one of the most stimulating and intriguing thinkers of the period. Humboldt was, on the one hand, one of the most profound theorists of general linguistics, and on the other, an early and forceful advocate of libertarian values. The basic concept of his philosophy is *Bildung*, by which, as J. W. Burrow expresses it, "he meant the fullest, richest and most harmonious development of the potentialities of the individual, the community or the human race."[9] His own thought might serve as an exemplary case. Though he does not, to my knowledge, explicitly relate his ideas about language to his libertarian social thought, there is quite clearly a common ground from which they develop, a concept of human nature that inspires each. Mill's essay *On Liberty* takes as its epigraph Humboldt's formulation of the "leading principle" of his thought: "the absolute and essential importance of human development in its richest diversity." Humboldt concludes his critique of the authoritarian state by saying: "I have felt myself animated throughout with a sense of the deepest respect for the inherent dignity of human nature, and for freedom, which alone befits that dignity." Briefly put, his concept of human nature is this:

> The true end of Man, or that which is prescribed by the eternal and immutable dictates of reason, and not suggested by vague and transient desires, is the highest and most harmonious development of his powers to a complete and consistent whole. Freedom is the first and indispensable condition which the possibility of such a development presupposes; but there is besides another essential—intimately connected with freedom, it is true—a variety of situations.[10]

Like Rousseau and Kant, he holds that

> nothing promotes this ripeness for freedom so much as freedom itself. This truth, perhaps, may not be acknowledged by those who have so often used this unripeness as an excuse for continuing repression. But it seems to me to

follow unquestionably from the very nature of man. The incapacity for freedom can only arise from a want of moral and intellectual power; to heighten this power is the only way to supply this want; but to do this presupposes the exercise of the power, and this exercise presupposes the freedom which awakens spontaneous activity. Only it is clear we cannot call it giving freedom, when bonds are relaxed which are not felt as such by him who wears them. But of no man on earth—however neglected by nature, and however degraded by circumstances—is this true of all the bonds which oppress him. Let us undo them one by one, as the feeling of freedom awakens in men's hearts, and we shall hasten progress at every step.

Those who do not comprehend this "may justly be suspected of misunderstanding human nature, and of wishing to make men into machines."

Man is fundamentally a creative, searching, self-perfecting being: "to inquire and to create—these are the centres around which all human pursuits more or less directly revolve." But freedom of thought and enlightenment are not only for the elite. Once again echoing Rousseau, Humboldt states: "There is something degrading to human nature in the idea of refusing to any man the right to be a man." He is, then, optimistic about the effects on all of "the diffusion of scientific knowledge by freedom and enlightenment." But "all moral culture springs solely and immediately from the inner life of the soul, and can only be stimulated in human nature, and never produced by external and artificial contrivances." "The cultivation of the understanding, as of any of man's other faculties, is generally achieved by his own activity, his own ingenuity, or his own methods of using the discoveries of others. . . ." Education, then, must provide the opportunities for self-fulfillment; it can at best provide a rich and challenging environment for the individual to explore, in his own way. Even a language cannot, strictly speaking, be taught, but only "awakened in the mind: one can only provide the thread along which it will develop of itself." I think that Humboldt would have found congenial much of Dewey's thinking about education. And he might also have appreciated the recent revolutionary extension of such ideas, for example, by the radical Catholics of Latin America who are concerned with the "awakening of consciousness," referring to "the transformation of the passive exploited lower classes into conscious and critical masters of their own destinies"[11] much in the manner of Third World revolutionaries elsewhere. He would, I am sure, have approved of their criticism of schools that are

> more preoccupied with the transmission of knowledge than with the creation, among other values, of a critical spirit. From the social point of view, the educational systems are oriented to maintaining the existing social and economic structures instead of transforming them.[12]

But Humboldt's concern for spontaneity goes well beyond educational practice in the narrow sense. It touches also the question of labor and exploitation. The remarks, just quoted, about the cultivation of understanding through spontaneous action continue as follows:

> . . . man never regards what he possesses as so much his own, as what he does; and the labourer who tends a garden is perhaps in a truer sense its owner, than the listless voluptuary who enjoys its fruits. . . . In view of this consideration,[13] it seems as if all peasants and craftsmen might be elevated into artists; that is, men who love their labour for its own sake, improve it by their own plastic genius and inventive skill, and thereby cultivate their intellect, ennoble their character, and exalt and refine their pleasures. And so humanity would be ennobled by the very things which now, though beautiful in themselves, so often serve to degrade it. . . . But, still, freedom is undoubtedly the indispensable condition, without which even the pursuits most congenial to individual human nature, can never succeed in producing such salutary influences. Whatever does not spring from a man's free choice, or is only the result of instruction and guidance, does not enter into his very being, but remains alien to his true nature; he does not perform it with truly human energies, but merely with mechanical exactness.

If a man acts in a purely mechanical way, reacting to external demands or instruction rather than in ways determined by his own interests and energies and power, "we may admire what he does, but we despise what he is."[14]

On such conceptions Humboldt grounds his ideas concerning the role of the state, which tends to "make man an instrument to serve its arbitrary ends, overlooking his individual purposes." His doctrine is classical liberal, strongly opposed to all but the most minimal forms of state intervention in personal or social life.

Writing in the 1790s, Humboldt had no conception of the forms that industrial capitalism would take. Hence he is not overly concerned with the dangers of private power.

> But when we reflect (still keeping theory distinct from practice) that the influence of a private person is liable to diminution and decay, from competition, dissipation of fortune, even death; and that clearly none of these contingencies can be applied to the State; we are still left with the principle that the latter is not to meddle in anything which does not refer exclusively to security. . . .

He speaks of the essential equality of the condition of private citizens, and of course has no idea of the ways in which the notion "private person" would come to be reinterpreted in the era of corporate capitalism. He did not foresee that "Democracy with its motto of *equality of all citizens before the law* and Liberalism with its *right of man over his own person* both [would be] wrecked on realities of capitalist economy."[15] He did not foresee that in a predatory capitalist economy, state intervention would be an absolute necessity to preserve human existence and to prevent the destruction of the physical environment—I speak optimistically. As Karl Polanyi, for one, has pointed out, the self-adjusting market "could not exist for any length of time without annihilating the human and natural substance of society; it would have physically destroyed man and transformed his surroundings into a wilderness."[16] Humboldt did not foresee the consequences of the commodity character of labor, the doctrine (in Polanyi's words) that "it is not for the commodity to decide where it should be offered for sale, to what purpose it should be used, at what price it should be allowed to change hands, and in what manner it should be consumed or destroyed." But the commodity, in this case, is a human life, and social protection was therefore a minimal necessity to constrain the irrational and destructive workings of the classical free market. Nor did Humboldt understand that capitalist economic relations perpetuated a form of bondage which, as early as 1767, Simon Linguet had declared to be even worse than slavery.

It is the impossibility of living by any other means that compels our farm laborers to till the soil whose fruits they will not eat, and our masons to construct buildings in which they will not live. It is want that drags them to those markets where they await masters who will do them the kindness of buying them. It is want that compels them to go down on their knees to the rich man in order to get from him permission to enrich him. . . . What effective gain has the suppression of slavery brought him? . . . He is free, you say. Ah! That is his misfortune. The slave was precious to his master because of the money he had cost him. But the handicraftsman costs nothing to the rich voluptuary who employs him. . . . These men, it is said, have no master—they have one, and the most terrible, the most imperious of masters, that is *need*. It is this that reduces them to the most cruel dependence.[17]

If there is something degrading to human nature in the idea of bondage, then a new emancipation must be awaited, Fourier's "third and last emancipatory phase of history," which will transform the proletariat to free men by eliminating the commodity character of labor, ending wage slavery, and bringing the commercial, industrial, and financial institutions under democratic control.[18]

Perhaps Humboldt might have accepted these conclusions. He does agree that state intervention in social life is legitimate if "freedom would destroy the very conditions without which not only freedom but even existence itself would be inconceivable"—precisely the circumstances that arise in an unconstrained capitalist economy. In any event, his criticism of bureaucracy and the autocratic state stands as an eloquent forewarning of some of the most dismal aspects of modern history, and the basis of his critique is applicable to a broader range of coercive institutions than he imagined.

Though expressing a classical liberal doctrine, Humboldt is no primitive individualist in the style of Rousseau. Rousseau extols the savage who "lives within himself"; he has little use for "the sociable man, always outside of himself, [who] knows how to live only in the opinion of others . . . from [whose] judgment alone . . . he draws the sentiment of his own existence."[19] Humboldt's vision is quite different:

. . . the whole tenor of the ideas and arguments unfolded in this essay might fairly be reduced to this, that while they would break all fetters in human society, they would attempt to find as many new social bonds as possible. The isolated man is no more able to develop than the one who is fettered.

Thus he looks forward to a community of free association without coercion by the state or other authoritarian institutions, in which free men can create and inquire, and achieve the highest development of their powers—far ahead of his time, he presents an anarchist vision that is appropriate, perhaps, to the next stage of industrial society. We can perhaps look forward to a day when these various strands will be brought together within the framework of libertarian socialism, a social form that barely exists today though its elements can be perceived: in the guarantee of individual rights that has achieved its highest form—though still tragically flawed—in the Western democracies; in the Israeli *kibbutzim*; in the experiments with workers' councils in Yugoslavia; in the effort to awaken popular consciousness and create a new involvement in the social process which is a fundamental element in the Third World revolutions, coexisting uneasily with indefensible authoritarian practice.

A similar concept of human nature underlies Humboldt's work on language. Language is a process of free creation; its laws and principles are fixed, but the manner in which the principles of generation are used is free and infinitely varied. Even the interpretation and use of words involves a process of free creation. The normal use of language and the acquisition of language depend on what Humboldt calls the fixed form of language, a system of generative processes that is rooted in the nature of the human mind and constrains but does not determine the free creations of normal intelligence or, at a higher and more original level, of the great writer or thinker. Humboldt is, on the one hand, a Platonist who insists that learning is a kind of reminiscence, in which the mind, stimulated by experience, draws from its own internal resources and follows a path that it itself determines; and he is also a romantic, attuned to cultural variety, and the endless possibilities for the spiritual contributions of the creative genius. There is no contradiction in this, any more than there is a contradiction in the insistence of aesthetic theory that individual works of genius are constrained by principle and rule. The normal, creative use of language, which to the Cartesian rationalist is the best index of the existence of another mind, presupposes a system of rules and generative principles of a sort that the rationalist grammarians attempted, with some success, to determine and make explicit.

The many modern critics who sense an inconsistency in the belief that free creation takes place within—presupposes, in fact—a system of constraints and governing principles are quite mistaken; unless, of course, they speak of "contradiction" in the loose and metaphoric sense of Schelling, when he writes that "without the contradiction of necessity and freedom not only philosophy but every nobler ambition of the spirit would sink to that death which is peculiar to those sciences in which that contradiction serves no function." Without this tension between necessity and freedom, rule and choice, there can be no creativity, no communication, no meaningful acts at all.

I have discussed these traditional ideas at some length, not out of antiquarian interest, but because I think that they are valuable and essentially correct, and that they project a course we can follow with profit. Social action must be animated by a vision of a future society, and by explicit judgments of value concerning the character of this future society. These judgments must derive from some concept of the nature of man, and one may seek empirical foundations by investigating man's nature as it is revealed by his behavior and his creations, material, intellectual, and social. We have, perhaps, reached a point in history when it is possible to think seriously about a society in which freely constituted social bonds replace the fetters of autocratic institutions, rather in the sense conveyed by the remarks of Humboldt that I quoted, and elaborated more fully in the tradition of libertarian socialism in the years that followed.[20]

Predatory capitalism created a complex industrial system and an advanced technology; it permitted a considerable extension of democratic practice and fostered certain liberal values, but within limits that are now being pressed and must be overcome. It is not a fit system for the mid-twentieth century. It is incapable of meeting human needs that can be expressed only in collective terms, and its concept of competitive man who seeks only to maximize wealth and power, who subjects himself to market relationships, to exploitation and external authority, is antihuman and intolerable in the deepest sense. An autocratic state is no acceptable substitute; nor can the militarized state capitalism evolving in the United States or the bureaucratized, centralized welfare state be accepted as the goal of human existence. The only justification for repressive institutions is material and cultural deficit. But such institutions, at certain stages of history, perpetuate and produce such a deficit, and even threaten human survival. Modern science and technology can relieve men of the necessity for specialized, imbecile labor. They may, in principle, provide the basis for a rational social order based on free association and democratic control, if we have the will to create it.

A vision of a future social order is in turn based on a concept of human nature. If in fact man is an indefinitely malleable, completely plastic being, with no innate structures of mind and no intrinsic needs of a cultural or social character, then he is a fit subject for the "shaping of behavior" by the state authority, the corporate manager, the technocrat, or the central committee. Those with some confidence in the human species will hope this is not so and will try to determine the intrinsic human characteristics that provide the framework for intellectual development, the growth of moral consciousness, cultural achievement, and participation in a free community. In a partly analogous way, a classical tradition spoke of artistic genius acting within and in some ways challenging a framework of rule. Here we touch on matters that are little understood. It seems to me that we must break away, sharply and radically, from much of modern social and behavioral science if we are to move towards a deeper understanding of these matters.[21]

Here too, I think that the tradition I have briefly reviewed has a contribution to offer. As I have already observed, those who were concerned with human distinctiveness and potential repeatedly were led to a consideration of the properties of language. I think that the study of language can provide some glimmerings of understanding of rule-governed behavior and the possibilities for free and creative action within the framework of a system of rules that in part, at least, reflect intrinsic properties of human mental organization. It seems to me fair to regard the contemporary study of language as in some ways a return to the Humboldtian concept of the form of language: a system of generative processes rooted in innate properties of mind but permitting, in Humboldt's phrase, an infinite use of finite means. Language cannot be described as a system of organization of behavior. Rather, to understand how language is used, we must discover the abstract Humboldtian form of language—its generative grammar, in modern terms. To learn a language is to construct for oneself this abstract system, of course unconsciously. The linguist and psychologist can proceed to study the use and acquisition of language only insofar as he has some grasp of the properties of the system that has been mastered by the person who knows the language. Furthermore, it seems to me that a good case can be made in support of the empirical claim that such a system can be acquired, under the given conditions of time and access, only by a mind that is endowed with certain specific properties that we can now tentatively describe in some detail. As long as we restrict ourselves, conceptually, to the investigation of behavior, its organization, its development through interaction with the environment, we are bound to miss these characteristics of language and mind. Other aspects of human psychology and culture might, in principle, be studied in a similar way.

Conceivably, we might in this way develop a social science based on empirically well-founded propositions concerning human nature. Just as we study the range of humanly attainable languages, with some success, we might also try to study the forms of artistic expression or, for that matter, scientific knowledge that humans can conceive, and perhaps even the range of ethical systems and social structures in which humans can live and function, given their intrinsic capacities and needs. Perhaps one might go on to project a concept of social organization that would—under given conditions of material and spiritual culture—best encourage and accommodate the fundamental human need—if such it is—for spontaneous initiative, creative work, solidarity, pursuit of social justice.

I do not want to exaggerate, as I no doubt have, the role of investigation of language. Language is the product of human intelligence that is, for the moment, most accessible to study. A rich tradition held language to be a mirror of mind. To some extent, there is surely truth and useful insight in this idea.

I am no less puzzled by the topic "language and freedom" than when I began—and no less intrigued. In these speculative and sketchy remarks there are gaps so vast that one might question what would remain, when metaphor and unsubstantiated guess are removed. It is sobering to realize—as I believe we must—how little we have progressed in our knowledge of man and society, or even in formulating clearly the problems that might be seriously studied. But there are, I think, a few footholds that seem fairly firm. I like to believe that the intensive study of one aspect of human psychology—human language—may contribute to a humanistic social science that will serve, as well, as an instrument for social action. It must, needless to say, be stressed that social action cannot await a firmly established theory of man and society, nor can the validity of the latter be determined by our hopes and moral judgments. The two—speculation and action—must progress as best they can, looking forward to the day when theoretical inquiry will provide a firm guide to the unending, often grim, but never hopeless struggle for freedom and social justice.

Notes

This essay was presented as a lecture at the University Freedom and the Human Sciences Symposium, Loyola University, Chicago, January 8–9, 1970. It is to appear in the Proceedings of the Symposium, edited by Thomas R. Gorman. It also was published in *Abraxas*, vol. 1, no. 1 (1970), and in *TriQuarterly*, nos. 23–24 (1972). A number of the topics mentioned here are discussed further in my *Problems of Knowledge and Freedom*.

1 F. W. J. Schelling, *Philosophical Inquiries into the Nature of Human Freedom*.

2 R. D. Masters, introduction to his edition of *First and Second Discourses*, by Jean-Jacques Rousseau.

3 Compare Proudhon, a century later: "No long discussion is necessary to demonstrate that the power of denying a man his thought, his

will, his personality, is a power of life and death, and that to make a man a slave is to assassinate him."

4 Cited in Lehning, ed., Bakunin, *Etatisme et anarchie*, editor's note 50, from P. Schrecker, "Kant et la révolution française," *Revue philosophique*, September–December 1939.

5 I have discussed this matter in *Cartesian Linguistics* and *Language and Mind*.

6 See the references of note 5, and also my *Aspects of the Theory of Syntax*, chap. 1, sec. 8.

7 I need hardly add that this is not the prevailing view. For discussion, see E. H. Lenneberg, *Biological Foundations of Language*; my *Language and Mind*; E. A. Drewe, G. Ettlinger, A. D. Milner, and R. E. Passingham, "A Comparative Review of the Results of Behavioral Research on Man and Monkey," Institute of Psychiatry, London, unpublished draft, 1969; P. H. Lieberman, D. H. Klatt, and W. H. Wilson, "Vocal Tract Limitations on the Vowel Repertoires of Rhesus Monkey and other Nonhuman Primates," *Science*, June 6, 1969 and P. H. Lieberman, "Primate Vocalizations and Human Linguistic Ability," *Journal of the Acoustical Society of America*, vol. 44, no. 6 (1968).

8 In the books cited above, and in *Current Issues in Linguistic Theory*.

9 J. W. Burrow, introduction to his edition of *The Limits of State Action*, by Wilhelm von Humboldt, from which most of the following quotes are taken.

10 Compare the remarks of Kant, quoted above. Kant's essay appeared in 1793; Humboldt's was written in 1791–1792. Parts appeared but it did not appear in full during his lifetime. See Burrow, introduction to Humboldt, *Limits of State Action*.

11 Thomas G. Sanders, "The Church in Latin America," *Foreign Affairs*, vol. 48, no. 2 (1970).

12 *Ibid.* The source is said to be the ideas of Paulo Freire. Similar criticism is widespread in the student movement in the West. See, for example, Mitchell Cohen and Dennis Hale, eds., *The New Student Left*, chap. 3.

13 Namely, that a man "only attains the most matured and graceful consummation of his activity, when his way of life is harmoniously in keeping with his character"—that is, when his actions flow from inner impulse.

14 The latter quote is from Humboldt's comments on the French Constitution, 1791—parts translated in Marianne Cowan, ed., *Humanist Without Portfolio*.

15 Rudolf Rocker, "Anarchism and Anarcho-syndicalism," in Paul Eltzbacher, *Anarchism*. In his book *Nationalism and Culture*, Rocker describes Humboldt as "the most prominent representative in Germany" of the doctrine of natural rights and of the opposition to the authoritarian state. Rousseau he regards as a precursor of authoritarian doctrine, but he considers only the *Social Contract*, not the far more libertarian *Discourse on Inequality*. Burrow observes that Humboldt's essay anticipates "much nineteenth century political theory of a populist, anarchist and syndicalist kind" and notes the hints of the early Marx. See also my *Cartesian Linguistics*, n. 51, for some comments.

[16] Karl Polanyi, *The Great Transformation.*

[17] Cited by Paul Mattick, "Workers' Control," in Priscilla Long, ed., *The New Left*, p. 377. See also chapter 8, p. 000.

[18] Cited in Martin Buber, *Paths in Utopia*, p. 19.

[19] Yet Rousseau dedicates himself, as a man who has lost his "original simplicity" and can no longer "do without laws and chiefs," to "respect the sacred bonds" of his society and "scrupulously obey the laws, and the men who are their authors and ministers," while scorning "a constitution that can be maintained only with the help of so many respectable people . . . and from which, despite all their care, always arise more real calamities than apparent advantages."

[20] See chapter 8.

[21] See chapter 7 for a discussion of the fraudulent claims in this regard of certain varieties of behavioral science.

Bibliography

Abaya, Hernando J. *The Untold Philippine Story*. Quezon City: Malaya Books, 1968.

Ackland, Len. "No Place for Neutralism: The Eisenhower Administration and Laos." In *Laos: War and Revolution*, edited by Nina S. Adams and Alfred W. McCoy. New York: Harper & Row, 1970.

———. "Hue." Unpublished article.

Adams, Nina S., and Alfred W. McCoy, eds. *Laos: War and Revolution*. New York: Harper & Row, 1970.

Ahmad, Eqbal. "Revolutionary War and Counterinsurgency." *Journal of International Affairs*, vol. 25, no. 1 (1971).

Allison, Graham T., and Morton H. Halperin. "Bureaucratic Politics." *World Politics*, vol. 24, no. 3 (1972).

Allman, T. D. "Search in Earnest." *Far Eastern Economic Review*, July 24, 1971.

———. "Landscape Without Figures." *Far Eastern Economic Review*, January 8, 1972.

———. "The Blind Bombers." *Far Eastern Economic Review*, January 29, 1972.

———. "Once More for Victory." *Far Eastern Economic Review*, February 18, 1972.

Alperovitz, Gar. *Cold War Essays*. Garden City, N.Y.: Doubleday & Co., Anchor Books, 1970.

Alves, Marcio Moreira. "Brazil: What Terror Is Like." *The Nation*, March 15, 1971.

Apple, R. W. "Calley: The Real Guilt." *New Statesman*, April 2, 1971.

Arendt, Hannah. *On Revolution*. New York: Viking Press, 1965.

———. "Lying in Politics: Reflections on the Pentagon Papers." *New York Review of Books*, November 18, 1971. Reprinted in her *Crisis of the Republic*. New York: Harcourt Brace Jovanovich, 1972.

Aronson, James. "The Media and the Message." In *The Pentagon Papers*, Senator Gravel Edition, vol. 5, *Critical Essays*, edited by Noam Chomsky and Howard Zinn. Beacon Press, 1972.

Austin, Anthony. *The President's War*. Philadelphia: J. B. Lippincott Co., 1971.

Avineri, Shlomo. *The Social and Political Thought of Karl Marx*. London: Cambridge University Press, 1968.

Bakunin, Michael. *Etatisme et anarchie*. Edited by Arthur Lehning. Leiden: E. J. Brill, 1967.

————. "La Commune de Paris et la notion de l'état." In *Ni Dieu, ni Maître*, edited by Daniel Guérin. Lausanne: La Cité Editeur, n.d.

————. *Bakunin on Anarchy*. Edited and translated by Sam Dolgoff. New York: Alfred A. Knopf, 1972.

Ball, George. "Top Secret: The Prophecy of the President Rejected." *Atlantic Monthly*, July 1972.

Barker, Charles A., ed. *Power and Law: American Dilemma in World Affairs*. Baltimore: Johns Hopkins University Press, 1971.

Barnet, Richard. *Intervention and Revolution*. New York: World Publishing Co., 1968.

————. *The Economy of Death*. New York: Atheneum Publishers, 1969.

————. *Roots of War*. New York: Atheneum Publishers, 1972.

Bell, Daniel. "The Scholar Cornered." *American Scholar*, vol. 37, no. 3 (1968).

Bergsten, C. Fred. "Crisis in U.S. Trade Policy." *Foreign Affairs*, vol. 49, no. 4 (1971).

Berle, A. A. "The Formulation and Implementation of American Foreign Policy." In *America's Future in the Pacific*, by J. C. Vincent *et al.* New Brunswick, N.J.: Rutgers University Press, 1947.

Blair, Harry W. "The Green Revolution and 'Economic Man': Some Lessons for Community Development in South Asia." *Pacific Affairs*, vol. 44, no. 3 (1971).

Bodenheimer, Susanne. "Inside a State of Siege: Legalized Murder in Guatemala." *Ramparts*, June 1971.

Bourne, Randolph. *The World of Randolph Bourne*, edited by Lillian Schlissel. New York: E. P. Dutton Co., 1965.

Bowles, Samuel, and Herbert Gintis. "I.Q. in the U.S. Class Structure." Harvard University, July 1972. Mimeographed.

Boyd, James. "Following the Rules with Dita and Dick." *Washington Monthly*, July 1972.

Branfman, Fred. "Presidential War in Laos." In *Laos: War and Revolution*, edited by Nina S. Adams and Alfred W. McCoy. New York: Harper & Row, 1970.

————, ed. *Voices from the Plain of Jars*. New York: Harper & Row, 1972.

Breger, Louis, and James L. McGaugh. "Critique and Reformulation of 'Learning-Theory' Approaches to Psychotherapy and Neurosis." *Psychological Bulletin*, May 1965.

Brodine, Virginia, and Mark Selden, eds. *Open Secret: The Kissinger-Nixon Doctrine in Asia; Why We Are Never Leaving.* New York: Harper & Row, 1972.

———. "Henry Kissinger's Diplomacy of Force," in *Open Secret: The Kissinger-Nixon Doctrine in Asia; Why We Are Never Leaving.* New York: Harper & Row, 1972.

Brown, Michael Barratt. *After Imperialism.* Rev. ed. New York: Humanities Press, 1970.

Browne, Malcolm W. *The New Face of War.* Indianapolis: Bobbs-Merrill Co., 1965.

Browning, Frank, and Banning Garrett. "The New Opium War." *Ramparts*, May 1971.

Bruce, William. "The United States and the Law of Mankind." In *Power and Law*, edited by Charles A. Barker. Baltimore: Johns Hopkins University Press, 1971.

Brzezinski, Zbigniew. "Japan's Global Engagement." *Foreign Affairs*, vol. 50, no. 2 (1972).

Buber, Martin. *Paths in Utopia.* Boston: Beacon Press, 1958.

Buckley, Kevin P. "Pacification's Deadly Price." *Newsweek*, June 19, 1972.

Bundy, McGeorge. "End of Either/Or." *Foreign Affairs*, vol. 45, no. 2 (1967).

Burchett, Wilfred. "The Receiving End." In *The Pentagon Papers*, Senator Gravel Edition, vol. 5, Critical Essays, edited by Noam Chomsky and Howard Zinn. Boston: Beacon Press, 1972.

Buttinger, Joseph. *Vietnam: A Dragon Embattled.* New York: Frederick A. Praeger, 1967.

Caldwell, Malcolm. "Oil and Imperialism in East Asia." *Journal of Contemporary Asia*, vol. 1, no. 3 (1971).

Chaffard, Georges. *Les Deux Guerres du Vietnam.* Paris: La Table Ronde, 1969.

Chai, Nam-Yearl. "Law as a Barrier to Change." In *Power and Law*, edited by Charles A. Barker. Baltimore: Johns Hopkins University Press, 1971.

Chang Hsin-hai. *America and China: A New Approach to Asia.* New York: Simon & Schuster, 1965.

Chapelier, G., and J. Van Malderghem. "Plain of Jars: Social Changes Under Five Years of Pathet-Lao Administration." *Asia Quarterly* [Brussels], 1971/1.

Cherry, Benjamin. "Balance of Weakness." *Far Eastern Economic Review*, July 1, 1972.

Chi, Hoang Van. *From Colonialism to Communism: A Case*

History of North Vietnam. New York: Frederick A. Praeger, 1964.

Cho, Soon Sung. Korea in World Politics, 1940–1950: United States Policy in the Unification of Korea. Berkeley: University of California Press, 1967.

Chomsky, Noam. Current Issues in Linguistic Theory. New York: Humanities Press, 1964.

———. Cartesian Linguistics. New York: Harper & Row, 1966.

———. Aspects of the Theory of Syntax. Cambridge, Mass.: M.I.T. Press, 1969. (Reproduction of 1965 ed.)

———. American Power and the New Mandarins. New York: Pantheon Books, 1969.

———. At War with Asia. New York: Pantheon Books, 1970.

———. "Revolt in the Academy." Modern Occasions, vol. 1, no. 1 (1970).

———. "Mayday: The Case for Civil Disobedience." New York Review of Books, June 17, 1971.

———. Problems of Knowledge and Freedom: The Russell Lectures. New York: Pantheon Books, 1971.

———. "The Pentagon Papers as Propaganda and as History." In The Pentagon Papers, Senator Gravel Edition, vol. 5, Critical Essays, edited by Noam Chomsky and Howard Zinn. Boston: Beacon Press, 1972.

———. "Nixon's Peace Offer." Ramparts, April 1972.

———. "Indochina: The Next Phase." Ramparts, May 1972.

———. "Vietnam: How Government Became Wolves." New York Review of Books, June 15, 1972.

———, and Howard Zinn, eds. Critical Essays. Vol. 5 of The Pentagon Papers: The Defense Department History of United States Decisionmaking on Vietnam. The Senator Gravel Edition. Boston: Beacon Press, 1972.

Chronology of the Vietnam War. Distributed by Association d'Amitié Franco-Vietnamienne, 5 rue Las Cases, Paris 75.

Citizens' Commission of Inquiry. The Dellums Committee Hearings on War Crimes in Vietnam. New York: Vintage Books, 1972.

Clifford, Harold B. Exploring New England. New Unified Social Studies. Chicago: Follett Publishing Co., 1966.

Cohen, Mitchell, and Dennis Hale, eds. The New Student Left. Rev. ed. Boston: Beacon Press, 1967.

Collectivisations: L'Oeuvre constructive de la révolution espagnole. 2nd ed. Toulouse: Editions C.N.T., 1965. First edition, Barcelona, 1937.

Committee of Concerned Asian Scholars. The Indochina Story: A Fully Documented Account. New York: Pantheon Books, 1970.

Connell-Smith, Gordon. The Inter-American System. New York: Oxford University Press, 1966.

Conroy, Hilary. "Japan's War in China: Historical Parallel to Vietnam?" *Pacific Affairs*, vol. 43, no. 2 (1970).

Cooper, Chester. *The Lost Crusade: America in Vietnam*. New York: Dodd, Mead & Co., 1970.

————. "The CIA and Decision-making." *Foreign Affairs*, vol. 50, no. 2 (1972).

Cooper, Jon. "Operation Phoenix." Department of History, Dartmouth College. Mimeographed.

Corbett, Percy E. "The Vietnam Struggle and International Law." In *The International Law of Civil War*, edited by Richard A. Falk. Baltimore: Johns Hopkins University Press, 1971.

Corson, William R. *The Betrayal*. New York: W. W. Norton & Co., 1968.

Critchfield, Richard. *The Long Charade: Political Subversion in the Vietnam War*. New York: Harcourt, Brace & World, 1968.

Daniels, Robert Vincent. "The State and Revolution: A Case Study in the Genesis and Transformation of Communist Ideology." *American Slavic and East European Review*, vol. 12, no. 1 (1953).

Darling, Frank C. *Thailand and the United States*. Washington, D.C.: Public Affairs Press, 1965.

Davies, Derek. "The Region." In *Far Eastern Economic Review Yearbook*. Hong Kong, 1971 and 1972.

Dellums Committee Hearings. *See* Citizens' Commission of Inquiry.

Devillers, Philippe, and Jean Lacouture. *End of a War: Indochina Nineteen Fifty-four*. New York: Frederick A. Praeger, 1969.

Domhoff, G. William. *The Higher Circles: The Governing Class in America*. New York: Random House, 1970.

Dommen, Arthur. *Conflict in Laos: The Politics of Neutralization*. Rev. ed. New York: Praeger Publishers, 1971.

Donovan, James A. *Militarism, U.S.A.* New York: Charles Scribner's Sons, 1970.

Dower, John. "Occupied Japan and the American Lake." In *America's Asia*, edited by Edward Friedman and Mark Selden. New York: Pantheon Books, 1971.

————. "The Superdomino in Postwar Asia: Japan in and out of the Pentagon Papers." In *The Pentagon Papers*, Senator Gravel Edition, vol. 5, *Critical Essays*, edited by Noam Chomsky and Howard Zinn. Boston: Beacon Press, 1972.

Draper, Theodore. *The Abuse of Power*. New York: Viking Press, 1967.

Drewe, E. A., G. Ettlinger, A. D. Milner, and R. E. Passingham. "A Comparative Review of the Results of Behavioral Research on Man and Monkey." Institute of Psychiatry, London, 1969. Unpublished draft.

Du Boff, Richard B. "Business Ideology and Foreign Policy: The National Security Council and Vietnam." In *The Pentagon Papers*, Senator Gravel Edition, vol. 5, *Critical Essays*, edited by Noam Chomsky and Howard Zinn. Boston: Beacon Press, 1972.

Dudman, Richard. *Forty Days with the Enemy*. New York: Liveright, 1971.

Duffett, John, ed. *Against the Crime of Silence*. Flanders, N.J.: O'Hare Books, 1968.

Dulany, D. "Awareness, Rules, and Propositional Control: A Confrontation with S-R Behavior Theory." In *Verbal Behavior and General Behavior*, edited by Theodore R. Dixon and David Horton. Englewood Cliffs, N.J.: Prentice-Hall. 1968.

Duncanson, Dennis J. *Government and Revolution in Vietnam*. New York: Oxford University Press, 1968.

Egan, Jean. "South Korea: Time to Face Facts." *Far Eastern Economic Review*, January 15, 1972.

Elliot, William Y., ed. *The Political Economy of American Foreign Policy*. New York: Holt, Rinehart & Winston, 1955.

Ellsberg, Daniel. "The Quagmire Myth and the Stalemate Machine." *Public Policy*, spring 1971.

———. *Papers on the War*. New York: Simon & Schuster, 1972.

Eltzbacher, Paul. *Anarchism: Exponents of the Anarchist Philosophy*. London: Freedom Press, 1960.

Emerson, Gloria. "Vietnam Diary." *McCall's*, August 1971.

Emerson, Thomas. *Toward a General Theory of the First Amendment*. New York: Random House, 1966.

Enthoven, Alain C., and K. Wayne Smith. *How Much Is Enough? Shaping the Defense Program, 1961–1969*. New York: Harper & Row, 1971.

Ervin, Sam. "Executive Privilege: Secrecy in a Free Society." *The Nation*, November 8, 1971.

Everingham, John. "Decimation of the Meo." National Anti-War Conference, Sydney, Australia, February 1971.

Facts on Foreign Aid. United States Embassy, Laos, 1971.

Falk, Richard A. *Legal Order in a Violent World*. Princeton, N.J.: Princeton University Press, 1968.

———. "The Circle of Responsibility." *The Nation*, January 26, 1970.

———, ed. *The Vietnam War and International Law*. Princeton, N.J.: Princeton University Press, 1968.

———, ed. *The International Law of Civil War*. Baltimore: Johns Hopkins University Press, 1971.

Fall, Bernard. *The Two Viet-Nams: A Political and Military Analysis*. Rev. ed. New York: Frederick A. Praeger, 1964.

———. "This Isn't Munich, It's Spain." *Ramparts*, December

1965. Reprinted in his *Last Reflections on a War*. Garden City, N.Y.: Doubleday & Co., 1967.

———. "Vietcong—the Unseen Enemy in Vietnam." *New Society*, April 22, 1965. Reprinted in *The Vietnam Reader*, edited by Bernard Fall and Marcus G. Raskin. New York: Vintage Books, 1965.

———. "Vietnam—the Agonizing Appraisal." *Current History*, February 1965. Reprinted in *The Vietnam Reader*, edited by Bernard Fall and Marcus G. Raskin. New York: Vintage Books, 1965.

———. *Vietnam Witness, 1953–66*. New York: Frederick A. Praeger, 1966.

———. *Last Reflections on a War*. Garden City, N.Y.: Doubleday & Co., 1967.

———. *Street Without Joy*. Rev. ed. Harrisburg, Pa.: Stackpole Books, 1967.

———. "Vietnam Blitz." *New Republic*, October 9, 1965. Reprinted in *In The Name of America*, edited by Seymour Melman. Annandale, Va.: Turnpike Press, 1968.

———, and Marcus G. Raskin, eds. *The Vietnam Reader*. New York: Vintage Books, 1965.

Fallaci, Oriana. "Working Up to Killing." *Washington Monthly*, February 1972.

Farer, Thomas J. "Intervention in Civil Wars: A Modest Proposal." In *The Vietnam War and International Law*, edited by Richard A. Falk. Princeton, N.J.: Princeton University Press, 1968.

Feingold, David. "Opium and Politics in Laos." In *Laos: War and Revolution*, edited by Nina S. Adams and Alfred W. McCoy. New York: Harper & Row, 1970.

Feldman, Herbert. "Aid as Imperialism?" *International Affairs*, vol. 43, no. 2 (1967).

Ferrell, Robert H. "The Merchants of Death: Then and Now." *Journal of International Affairs*, vol. 26, no. 1 (1972).

FitzGerald, Frances. *Fire in the Lake: The Vietnamese and the Americans in Vietnam*. Boston: Little, Brown & Co., 1972.

Franck, Thomas M. "Who Killed Article 2(4)? or: Changing Norms Governing the Use of Force by States." *American Journal of International Law*, vol. 64, no. 4 (1970).

———, and Edward Weisband. *Word Politics: Verbal Strategy Among the Superpowers*. Oxford: Oxford University Press, 1971.

Freeland, Richard M. *The Truman Doctrine and the Origins of McCarthyism*. New York: Alfred A. Knopf, 1972.

Friedman, Edward, and Mark Selden, eds. *America's Asia: Dissenting Essays on Asian-American Relations*. New York: Pantheon Books, 1971.

Garrett, Banning. "Vietnam: How Nixon Plans to Win." *Ramparts*, February 1971.

Gelb, Leslie H. "Lessons of the Pentagon Papers." *Life*, September 17, 1971.

——. "On Schlesinger and Ellsberg: A Reply." *New York Review of Books*, December 2, 1971.

——. "Vietnam: The System Worked." *Foreign Policy*, vol. 1, no. 3 (1971).

Gennard, John. *Multinational Corporations and British Labour*. London: British–North American Committee, 1972.

Gettleman, Marvin E., ed. *Vietnam: History, Documents and Opinions*. New York: Fawcett World Library, 1965.

Gitlin, Todd. "Counter-insurgency: Myth and Reality in Greece." In *Containment and Revolution*, edited by David Horowitz. Boston: Beacon Press, 1967.

Gittings, John. "The Great Asian Conspiracy." In *America's Asia*, edited by Edward Friedman and Mark Selden. New York: Pantheon Book, 1971.

Glazer, Nathan. " 'Student Power' in Berkeley." *Public Interest*, no. 13 (fall 1968).

Gold, Gerald, Allan M. Siegal, and Samuel Abt, eds. *The Pentagon Papers*. New York: Bantam Books (for the New York Times), 1971.

Goldstein, Walter. "The American Political System and the Next Vietnam." *Journal of International Affairs*, vol. 25, no. 1, (1971).

Goodman, Allan E. "Diplomatic and Strategic Outcomes of the Conflict." In *Vietnam: Issues and Alternatives*, edited by Walter Isard. Cambridge, Mass.: Schenkman Publishing Co., 1969.

——. "The Ending of the War as a Setting for the Future Development of South Vietnam." *Asian Survey*, vol. 11, no. 4 (1971).

Goodstadt, Leo. "Might and Right." *Far Eastern Economic Review*, April 10, 1971.

Goodwin, Richard. *Triumph or Tragedy: Reflections on Vietnam*. New York: Random House, 1966.

Goulden, Joseph C. *Truth Is the First Casualty; The Gulf of Tonkin Affair: Illusion and Reality*. Chicago: Rand-McNally & Co., 1969.

Goulet, Denis, and Michael Hudson. *The Myth of Aid: The Hidden Agenda of the Development Reports*. New York: Orbis Books and IDOC, North America, 1971.

Grant, Jonathan S., L. A. G. Moss, and J. Ungar, eds. *Cambodia: The Widening War in Indochina*. New York: Washington Square Press, 1971.

Gray, Colin S. "What RAND Hath Wrought." *Foreign Policy*,

vol. 1, no. 4 (1971).

Griffiths, Philip Jones. *Vietnam Inc.* New York: Macmillan Co., 1971.

Guérin, Daniel. *Jeunesse du socialisme libertaire.* Paris: Librairie Marcel Rivière, 1959.

——. *Anarchism: From Theory to Practice,* translated by Mary Klopper. New York: Monthly Review Press, 1970.

——. *Pour un marxisme libertaire.* Paris: Robert Laffont, 1969.

——, ed. *Ni Dieu, ni Maître.* Lausanne: La Cité Editeur, n.d.

Halliday, Jon. "The Korean Revolution." *Socialist Revolution,* vol. 1, no. 6 (1970).

——, and Gavan McCormack. *Japanese Imperialism Today.* New York: Monthly Review Press, 1972.

Halperin, Ernst. Introduction to *Cuba: Castroism and Communism,* by Andrés Suárez. Cambridge, Mass.: M.I.T. Press, 1967.

Haney, Walter. "The Pentagon Papers and U.S. Involvement in Laos." In *The Pentagon Papers,* Senator Gravel Edition, vol. 5, *Critical Essays,* edited by Noam Chomsky and Howard Zinn. Boston: Beacon Press, 1972.

Harris, Marvin. *The Rise of Anthropological Theory: A History of Theories of Culture.* New York: Thomas Y. Crowell Co., 1968.

Henderson, Gregory. *Korea: The Politics of the Vortex.* Cambridge, Mass.: Harvard University Press, 1968.

Herman, Edward S. *Atrocities in Vietnam: Myths and Realities.* Boston: Pilgrim Press, 1970.

Herrnstein, Richard. "I.Q." *Atlantic Monthly,* September 1971.

Hersh, Seymour. *My Lai Four: A Report on the Massacre and Its Aftermath.* New York: Random House, 1970.

——. *Cover-up.* New York: Random House, 1972.

Hilsman, Roger. *To Move a Nation.* Garden City, N.Y.: Doubleday & Co., 1967.

——. "Two American Counterstrategies to Guerrilla Warfare." In *China in Crisis,* edited by Tang Tsou. Chicago: University of Chicago Press, 1968.

Hobsbawm, Eric. *Industry and Empire: The Making of Modern English Society, Vol. II 1750 to the Present Day.* New York: Pantheon Books, 1968.

Honda, Katsuichi. *The National Liberation Front and Vietnam: A Voice from the Villages.* Privately translated and reprinted from *Asahi Simbun,* Tokyo, 1967.

Hook, Sidney. "Lord Russell and the War Crimes 'Trial.'" *New Leader,* October 24, 1966.

——. "The Knight of the Double Standard." *The Humanist,* vol. 21, no. 1 (1971).

Hoopes, Townsend. *The Limits of Intervention.* New York: David McKay Co., 1969.

Horowitz, David. "The Foundations." *Ramparts*, April 1969.

————. "The Making of America's China Policy." *Ramparts*, October 1971.

————, ed. *Containment and Revolution.* Bertrand Russell Centre for Social Research (London), Studies in Imperialism and the Cold War, vol. 1 Boston: Beacon Press, 1967.

————, ed. *Corporations and the Cold War.* New York: Bertrand Russell Peace Foundation and Monthly Review Press, 1969.

Houghton, Neal D., ed. *Struggle Against History: U.S. Foreign Policy in an Age of Revolution.* New York: Washington Square Press, 1968.

Howard, Michael. "Realists and Romantics: On Maintaining an International Order." *Encounter*, April 1972.

Hudon, Edward G. *Freedom of Speech and Press in America.* Washington, D.C.: Public Affairs Press, 1963.

Humboldt, Wilhelm von. *Humanist Without Portfolio: An Anthology.* Translated and edited by Marianne Cowan. Detroit: Wayne State University Press, 1963.

————. *The Limits of State Action.* Edited by J. W. Burrow. Cambridge Studies in the History and Theory of Politics. London: Cambridge Press, 1969.

Huntington, Samuel P. "The Bases of Accommodation." *Foreign Affairs*, vol. 46, no. 4 (1968).

International Military Tribunal for the Far East. Calcutta: Sanyal & Co., 1953.

Isard, Walter, ed. *Vietnam: Issues and Alternatives.* Cambridge, Mass.: Schenkman Publishing Co., 1969.

Jackson, J. Hampden. *Marx, Proudhon and European Socialism.* New York: Collier Books, 1962.

Jacobson, Julius. "In Defense of the Young." *New Politics*, vol. 8, no. 1 (1970).

Jencks, Christopher, and David Riesman. *The Academic Revolution.* Garden City, N.Y.: Doubleday & Co., 1968.

———— et al. *Inequality: A Reassessment of the Effect of Family and Schooling in America.* New York and London: Basic Books, 1972.

Johnson, Lyndon. *The Vantage Point: Perspectives of the Presidency.* New York: Holt, Rinehart & Winston, 1971.

Johnstone, L. Craig. "Ecocide and the Geneva Protocol." *Foreign Affairs*, vol. 49, no. 4 (1971).

Joll, James. *The Anarchists.* Boston: Little, Brown & Co., 1964.

Kahin, George McT. "Nixon's Peace Plan." *New Republic*, February 12, 1972.

————, and John W. Lewis. *The United States in Vietnam.* Rev. ed. New York: Dial Press, 1969.

Kendall, Walter. *The Revolutionary Movement in Britain 1900–1921*. London: Weidenfeld & Nicolson, 1969.

Kidron, Michael. *Western Capitalism Since the War*. London: Weidenfeld & Nicolson, 1968.

Kindleberger, Charles. "United States Economic Foreign Policy Is Unrelievedly Evil," review of *The Age of Imperialism*, by Harry Magdoff. *Public Policy*, summer 1971.

King, Peter. "The Political Balance in Saigon." *Pacific Affairs*, vol. 44, no. 3 (1971).

Kissinger, Henry A. *The Necessity for Choice*. New York: Harper & Row, 1961.

———. *Nuclear Weapons and American Foreign Policy*. Abridged ed. Edited by Philip Quigg. New York: W. W. Norton & Co., 1969.

Knoll, Erwin, and Judith N. McFadden, eds. *War Crimes and the American Conscience*. New York: Holt, Rinehart & Winston, 1970.

Kolko, Gabriel. *The Politics of War: The World and U.S. Foreign Policy 1943–1945*. New York: Random House, 1969.

———. *The Roots of American Foreign Policy: An Analysis of Power and Purpose*. Boston: Beacon Press, 1969.

———. "The American Goals in Vietnam." In *The Pentagon Papers*, Senator Gravel Edition, vol. 5, *Critical Essays*, edited by Noam Chomsky and Howard Zinn. Boston: Beacon Press, 1972.

———, and Joyce Kolko. *The Limits of Power: The World and United States Foreign Policy, 1945–1954*. New York: Harper & Row, 1972.

Komer, Robert. "Pacification: A Look Back." *Army*, June 1970.

———. "Impact of Pacification on Insurgency in South Vietnam." *Journal of International Affairs*, vol. 25, no. 1 (1971).

———. "Epilogue." *Journal of International Affairs*, vol. 25, no. 2 (1971).

Krause, Lawrence B. "Why Exports Are Becoming Irrelevant." *Foreign Policy*, vol. 1, no. 3 (1971).

Kristol, Irving. "A Different Way to Restructure the University." *New York Times Magazine*, December 8, 1968.

Kunen, James S. *Standard Operating Procedure*. New York: Avon Books, 1971.

Lacouture, Jean. *Vietnam: Between Two Truces*. New York: Random House, 1966.

Lake, Anthony, and Roger Morris. "The Human Reality of Realpolitik." *Foreign Policy*, vol. 1, no. 4 (1971).

Lam, Truong Buu. *Patterns of Vietnamese Response to Foreign Intervention: 1858–1900*. Southeast Asia Studies Monograph no. 11. New Haven, Conn.: Yale University Press, 1967.

Langer, Paul F., and Joseph Zasloff. *North Vietnam and the*

Pathet Lao. Cambridge, Mass.: Harvard University Press, 1970.

Langguth, A. J. "Vietnam—1964: Exhilaration—1968: Frustration—1970: Hopelessness." *New York Times Magazine*, October 4, 1970.

Lawyers Committee on American Policy Towards Vietnam, Consultative Council (Richard A. Falk, chairman; John E. Fried, rapporteur.) *Vietnam and International Law: An Analysis of the Legality of the U.S. Military Involvement*. Flanders, N.J.: O'Hare Books, 1967.

Lazarsfeld, Paul, and Robert Merton. "Mass Communications, Popular Taste, and Organized Social Action." In *Mass Communications*, edited by Wilbur Schramm. Urbana: University of Illinois Press, 1949.

Lee, Daniel. "Blank Coup in Thailand." *New Left Review*, January-February 1972.

Lenneberg, Eric H. *Biological Foundations of Language*. New York: John Wiley & Sons, 1967.

Letwin, William. "The Past and Future of the American Businessman." *Daedalus*, winter 1969.

Lieberman, P. H. "Primitive Vocalizations and Human Linguistic Ability." *Journal of the Acoustical Society of America*, vol. 44, no. 6 (1968).

———, D. H. Klatt, and W. H. Wilson. "Vocal Tract Limitations on the Vowel Repertoires of Rhesus Monkey and Other Nonhuman Primates." *Science*, June 6, 1969.

Lindholm, Richard W., ed. *Viet-nam: The First Five Years: An International Symposium*. East Lansing: Michigan State University Press, 1959.

Littauer, Rafael, *et al. The Air War in Indochina*. Preliminary Report, Cornell University Center for International Studies, October 1971.

Long, Ngo Vinh. "Leaf Abscission." In *Ecocide in Indochina*, edited by Barry Weisberg. San Francisco: Canfield Press (Harper & Row), 1970.

———. *Before the August Revolution*. Cambridge, Mass.: M.I.T. Press, forthcoming.

Lyon, Peter. *War and Peace in South-east Asia*. Oxford: Royal Institute of International Affairs, 1969.

Magdoff, Harry, and Paul Sweezy. "The Mind of the Ruling Class." *Monthly Review*, June 1972.

Maneli, Mieczyslaw. *War of the Vanquished: A Polish Diplomat in Vietnam*. New York: Harper & Row, 1971.

Marr, David G. *Vietnamese Anti-colonialism: 1885–1925*. Berkeley: University of California Press, 1971.

Marx, Karl. *The Civil War in France, 1871*. New York: International Publishers, 1941.

May, Herbert K. *The Effects of United States and Other Foreign Investments in Latin America*. Council of the Americas, 1971.

Mattick, Paul. *Marx and Keynes: The Limits of the Mixed Economy*. Extending Horizons Series. Boston: Porter Sargent, 1969.

———. "Workers' Control." In *The New Left: A Collection of Essays*, edited by Priscilla Long. Boston: Porter Sargent, 1969.

McAlister, John T., Jr., and Paul Mus. *The Vietnamese and Their Revolution*. New York: Harper & Row, 1970.

MacCorquodale, Kenneth. "On Chomsky's Review of Skinner's *Verbal Behavior*." *Journal of the Experimental Analysis of Behavior*, vol. 13, no. 1 (1970).

McCoy, Alfred W., with Cathleen B. Read and Leonard P. Adams II. *The Politics of Heroin in Southeast Asia*. New York: Harper & Row, 1972.

McKeithen, Edwin T. *Life Under the P.L. in the Xieng Khouang Ville Area*. Undated.

———. *The Role of North Vietnamese Cadres in the Pathet Lao Administration of Xieng Khouang Province*. American Embassy, Vientiane, April 1970.

McNamara, Robert S. *The Essence of Security: Reflections in Office*. New York: Harper & Row, 1968.

McWilliams, Wilson C. Review of *Washington Plans an Aggressive War*, by Ralph Stavins *et al*. *New York Times Book Review*.

Melman, Seymour, ed. *In the Name of America*. Annandale, Va.: Turnpike Press, 1968.

———. *Pentagon Capitalism: The Management of the New Imperialism*. New York: McGraw-Hill Book Co., 1970.

Meyer, Charles. *Derrière le sourire khmer*. Paris: Plon, 1971.

Michigan Brain Mistrust Collective. "Southeast Asia: American Power versus Regionalism." *American Report*, December 10, 1971.

Mirsky, Jonathan. "High Drama on Foggy Bottom." *Saturday Review*, January 1, 1972.

———, and Stephen Stonefield. "The United States in Laos, 1945–1962." In *America's Asia*, edited by Edward Friedman and Mark Selden. New York: Pantheon Books, 1971.

Monod, Jacques. *Chance and Necessity: An Essay on the Natural Philosophy of Modern Biology*. New York: Alfred A. Knopf, 1971.

Nakamura, Koji. "The Okinawa Payoff." *Far Eastern Economic Review*, August 21, 1971.

National Planning Association. *U.S. Foreign Economic Policy for the 1970s: A New Approach to New Realities*. Planning Pamphlet no. 130, Washington, D.C., November 1971.

Nighswonger, William A. *Rural Pacification in Vietnam*. New York: Frederick A. Praeger, 1967.

Nivolon, François. "Profit and Honour." *Far Eastern Economic Review*, April 24, 1971.

Nulty, Timothy, and Leslie Nulty. "Pakistan: The Busy Bee Route to Development." *Trans-action*, February 1971.

Nussbaum, Bruce. "Aid Watershed in 1972." *Far Eastern Economic Review*, July 3, 1971.

Oberdorfer, Don. *Tet*. Garden City, N.Y.: Doubleday & Co., 1971.

Pannekoek, Anton. *Lenin as Philosopher: A Critical Examination of the Philosophical Basis of Leninism*. New York: New Essays, 1948. Translated from German edition of 1938.

Paranzino, Dennis. "Inequality and Insurgency in Vietnam: A Further Reanalysis." *World Politics*, vol. 24, no. 4 (1972).

Partan, Daniel G. "Legal Aspects of the Vietnam Conflict." In *The Vietnam War and International Law*, edited by Richard A. Falk. Princeton, N.J.: Princeton University Press, 1968.

Paul, William. *The State, Its Origins and Function*. Glasgow: Socialist Labour Press, n.d.

Pearson, Jeff, and Jessica Smilowitz. "Biting the Fishhook." *Bulletin of Concerned Asian Scholars*, vol. 2, no. 4 (1970).

Pelloutier, Fernand. "L'Anarchisme et les syndicats ouvriers." *Les Temps nouveaux*, 1895. Reprinted in *Ni Dieu, ni Maître*, edited by Daniel Guérin. Lausanne: La Cité Editeur, n.d.

The Pentagon Papers: The Defense Department History of United States Decisionmaking on Vietnam. 5 vols. The Senator Gravel Edition. Boston: Beacon Press, 1971–2.

Pfaff, William. *Condemned to Freedom: The Breakdown of Liberal Society*. New York: Random House, 1971.

Pfeffer, Richard M., ed. *No More Vietnams? The War and the Future of American Policy*. New York: Harper & Row, 1968.

Phi Bang. "Land: Theory and Practise." *Far Eastern Economic Review*, April 23, 1970.

———. "Screws on Thieu." *Far Eastern Economic Review*, March 27, 1971.

———. "South Vietnam: A Hand-to-Mouth Economy." *Far Eastern Economic Review*, January 15, 1972.

———. "Leading the Field." *Far Eastern Economic Review*, March 4, 1972.

Pike, Douglas. *Viet Cong: The Organization and Techniques of the National Liberation Front in South Vietnam*. Cambridge, Mass.: M.I.T. Press, 1966.

———. *War, Peace, and the Viet Cong*. Cambridge, Mass.: M.I.T. Press, 1969.

Polanyi, Karl. *The Great Transformation: The Political and Economic Origins of Our Time*. Boston: Beacon Press, 1957.

Pomonti, Jean-Claude. "The Other South Vietnam." *Foreign Affairs*, vol. 50, no. 2 (1972).

———, and Serge Thion. *Des courtisans aux partisans*. Paris: Plon, 1971.

Pool, Ithiel de Sola. "Village Violence and International Violence." In *Reprints of Publications on Vietnam, 1966–1970*, edited by Ithiel de Sola Pool. Privately printed, May 1971.

Porter, D. Gareth. "The Diemist Restoration." *Commonweal*, July 11, 1969.

———. "After Geneva: Subverting Laotian Neutrality." In *Laos: War and Revolution*, edited by Nina S. Adams and Alfred W. McCoy. New York: Harper & Row, 1970.

———. *The Myth of the Bloodbath: North Vietnam's Land Reform Reconsidered*. International Relations of East Asia, IREA Project, Cornell University, Interim Report no. 2, September 1972, Ithaca, N.Y.

Quine, W. V. O. "Linguistics and Philosophy." in *Language and Philosophy*, edited by Sidney Hook. Proceedings of New York University Institute of Philosophy Symposium. New York: New York University Press, 1969.

Race, Jeffrey. "How They Won." *Asian Survey*, August 1970.

———. *War Comes to Long An*. Berkeley: University of California Press, 1971.

Reich, Michael, and David Finkelhor. "Capitalism and the Military-Industrial Complex: The Obstacles to Conversion." *Review of Radical Political Economics*, vol. 2, no. 4 (1970).

Richards, Vernon. *Lessons of the Spanish Revolution (1936–1939)*. Enlarged ed. London: Freedom Press, 1972.

Ridgeway, James. *The Closed Corporation. American Universities in Crisis*. New York: Random House, 1968.

Roberts, Chalmers M. "How Containment Worked." *Foreign Policy*, vol. 2, no. 3 (1972).

Roberts, John G. "The American Zaibatsu." *Far Eastern Economic Review*, July 24, 1971.

Roche, John P. "The Pentagon Papers." *Political Science Quarterly*, vol. 87, no. 2 (1972).

Rocker, Rudolf. *Nationalism and Culture*. London: Freedom Press, 1937.

———. *Anarchosyndicalism*. London: Secker & Warburg, 1938.

———. "Anarchism and Anarcho-syndicalism." Appended essay in *Anarchism: Exponents of the Anarchist Philosophy*, by Paul Eltzbacher. London: Freedom Press, 1960.

Rogin, Michael. "Liberal Society and the Indian Question." *Politics and Society*, May 1971.

Rosenberg, Arthur. *A History of Bolshevism from Marx to the First Five Years' Plan*. Translated by Ian F. Morrow. New York: Russell & Russell, 1965.

Rostow, Walt W., and Richard W. Hatch. *An American Policy in Asia*. Cambridge, Mass.: M.I.T. Press, 1955.

Rousseau, Jean-Jacques. *First and Second Discourses*. Edited by R. D. Masters. New York: St. Martin's Press, 1964.

Russell, Bertrand. *Power: A New Social Analysis*. New York: W. W. Norton & Co., 1938.

Russo, Anthony. "Inside the RAND Corporation and Out: My Story." *Ramparts*, April 1972.

Sanders, Thomas G. "The Church in Latin America." *Foreign Affairs*, vol. 48, no. 2 (1970).

Sansom, Robert L. *The Economics of Insurgency in the Mekong Delta of Vietnam*. Cambridge, Mass.: M.I.T. Press, 1970.

Santillan, Diego Abad de. *After the Revolution*. New York: Greenberg Publishers, 1937.

SarDesai, S. R. *Indian Foreign Policy in Cambodia, Laos, and Vietnam, 1947–1964*. Berkeley: University of California Press, 1968.

Scanlon, Hugh. *The Way Forward for Workers' Control*. Institute for Workers' Control Pamphlet Series, no. 1, Nottingham, England, 1968.

———. "International Combines Versus the Unions." *Bulletin of the Institute for Workers' Control*, vol. 1, no. 4 (1969).

Schell, Jonathan. *The Village of Ben Suc*. New York: Alfred A. Knopf, 1967.

———. *The Military Half: An Account of Destruction in Quang Ngai and Quang Tin*. New York: Alfred A. Knopf, 1968.

Schelling, F. W. T. *Philosophical Inquiries into the Nature of Human Freedom*. Translated and edited by James Gutmann. Chicago: Open Court Publishing Co., 1936.

Schlesinger, Arthur M., Jr. *A Thousand Days: John F. Kennedy in the White House*. Boston: Houghton Mifflin Co., 1965.

Schurmann, Franz, Peter Dale Scott, and Reginald Zelnik. *The Politics of Escalation in Vietnam*. New York: Fawcett World Library, 1966.

Scigliano, Robert. *South Vietnam: Nation Under Stress*. Boston: Houghton Mifflin Co., 1964.

Scott, Peter Dale. *The War Conspiracy*. Indianapolis: Bobbs-Merrill Co., 1972.

———. "Vietnamization and the Drama of the Pentagon Papers." In *The Pentagon Papers*, Senator Gravel Edition, vol. 5, *Critical Essays*, edited by Noam Chomsky and Howard Zinn. Boston: Beacon Press, 1972.

Scott, Rebecca. "Economic Aid and Imperialism in Bolivia." *Monthly Review*, May 1972.

Selden, Mark. "People's War and the Transformation of Peasant Society: China and Vietnam." In *America's Asia*, edited by Edward Friedman and Mark Selden. New York: Pantheon Books, 1971.

Shaplen, Robert. *The Lost Revolution: The United States in Vietnam*. New York: Harper & Row, 1965.

———. "The Challenge Ahead." *Columbia Journalism Review*,

vol. 9, no. 4 (1970–1).

———. "Cambodia Is Sihanouk." In *Cambodia: The Widening War in Indochina*, edited by Jonathan S. Grant *et al.* New York: Washington Square Press, 1971.

———. "We Have Always Survived." *New Yorker*, April 15, 1972.

———. "Letter from Vietnam." *New Yorker*, June 24, 1972.

Skinner, B. F. *Verbal Behavior*. New York: Appleton-Century-Crofts, 1957.

———. *Beyond Freedom and Dignity*. New York: Alfred A. Knopf, 1971.

Smith, George E. *P.O.W.: Two Years with the Viet Cong*. Berkeley, Calif.: Ramparts Press, 1971.

Smythe, D. W., and M. H. Wilson. "Cold War-mindedness and the Mass Media." In *Struggle Against History: U.S. Foreign Policy in an Age of Revolution*, edited by Neal D. Houghton. New York: Washington Square Press, 1968.

"South Asia in Turmoil." *Bulletin of Concerned Asian Scholars*, vol. 4, no. 1 (1972).

Standard, William L. *Aggression: Our Asian Disaster*. New York, Random House, 1971.

Starner, Frances. "I'll Do It My Way." *Far Eastern Economic Review*, November 6, 1971.

Stavins, Ralph, Richard J. Barnet, and Marcus G. Raskin. *Washington Plans an Aggressive War*. New York: Random House, 1972.

Stavrionos, L. S. "Greece's Other History." *New York Review of Books*, June 17, 1971.

Stein, Jeffrey. "Bloodbath Over the Rainbow." *The Phoenix* [Boston], May 10, 1972.

Stevenson, Charles A. *The End of Nowhere: American Policy Toward Laos Since 1954*. Boston: Beacon Press, 1972.

Stone, I. F. "The Hidden Traps in Nixon's Peace Plan." *New York Review of Books*, March 9, 1972.

Strock, Carl. "No News from Laos." *Far Eastern Economic Review*, January 30, 1971.

Sumida, Gerald A. "The Right of Revolution." In *Power and Law*, edited by Charles A. Barker. Baltimore: Johns Hopkins University Press, 1971.

Takeyama, Yasuo. "Don't Take Japan for Granted." *Foreign Policy*, vol. 1, no. 2 (1971–2).

Tanham, George K., and Dennis J. Duncanson. "Some Dilemmas of Counterinsurgency." *Foreign Affairs*, vol. 48, no. 1 (1969).

Taylor, G. E. *The Philippines and the United States: Problems of Partnership*. Council on Foreign Relations Publications Series. Mystic, Conn.: Lawrence Verry, 1964.

Taylor, Maxwell D. *Swords and Plowshares*. New York: W. W. Norton & Co., 1972.

Taylor, Telford. *Nuremberg and Vietnam: An American Tragedy*. Chicago: Quadrangle Books, 1970.

Thompson, Robert. *Defeating Communist Insurgency: The Lessons of Malaya and Vietnam*. New York: Frederick A. Praeger, 1966.

———. *No Exit from Vietnam*. London: Chatto & Windus, 1969.

———. "A Successful End to the War in Vietnam." *Pacific Community*, vol. 2, no. 3 (1971).

Thorne, David, and George Butler, eds. *The New Soldier*. New York: Collier Books, 1971.

Toye, Hugh. *Laos: Buffer State or Battleground*. New York: Oxford University Press, 1968.

Tregaskis, Richard. *Vietnam Diary*. New York: Holt, Rinehart & Winston, 1963.

Tsou, Tang, ed. *China in Crisis*. Vol. 2: *China's Policies in Asia and America's Alternatives*. Chicago: University of Chicago Press, 1968.

Tucker, Robert C. *The Marxian Revolutionary Idea*. New York: W. W. Norton & Co., 1969.

Tucker, Robert W. *Nation or Empire? The Debate over American Foreign Policy*. Studies in International Affairs, no. 10. Baltimore: Johns Hopkins University Press, 1968.

———. *The Radical Left and American Foreign Policy*. Baltimore: Johns Hopkins University Press, 1971.

Van Dyke, Jon M. *North Vietnam's Strategy for Survival*. Santa Barbara, Calif.: Pacific Press, 1972.

Vernon, Raymond. *Sovereignty at Bay*. New York: Basic Books, 1971.

Vien, Nguyen Khac. *South Vietnam: Realities and Prospects*. Vietnamese Studies, nos. 18/19. Hanoi, 1968.

Vietnam 1967–1971: Toward Peace and Prosperity. Saigon Ministry of Information, 1971.

Vietnam Veterans Against the War, eds. *Winter Soldier Investigation*. Boston: Beacon Press, 1972.

Vu, Tam, and Nguyen Khac Vien. *A Century of National Struggle: 1847–1945*. Vietnamese Studies, no. 24. Hanoi, 1970.

Wald, George. "Our Bombs Fall on People." *Washington Monthly*, May 1972.

Weisband, Edward, and Thomas M. Franck. "The Brezhnev-Johnson Two-World Doctrine." *Trans-action*, October 1971.

Weisberg, Barry, ed. *Ecocide in Indochina*. San Francisco: Canfield Press, 1970.

West, Richard. *Sketches from Vietnam*. New York: International Publishers Service, 1968.

————. "Vietnam: The Year of the Rat." *New Statesman*, February 25, 1972.

Westing, Arthur. "Poisoning Plants for Peace." *Friends Journal*, vol. 16 (1970).

————. "Ecocide in Indochina." *Natural History*, March 1971.

————. "Leveling the Jungle." *Environment*, November 1971.

Whiting, Allen S. "Scholar and Policy-maker." *World Politics*, vol. 24, no. 3 (1972).

Wiles, Peter. "The Declining Self-confidence of the Super-Powers." *International Affairs*, vol. 47, no. 2 (1971).

Windchy, Eugene G. *Tonkin Gulf*. Garden City, N.Y.: Doubleday & Co., 1971.

Woodside, Alexander. "Ideology and Integration in Post-colonial Vietnamese Nationism." *Pacific Affairs*, vol. 44, no. 4 (1971–2).

Wulff, Eric. "Le Crime de Song My: Avec les félicitations du commandant en chef." *Africasia* [Paris], April 26–May 9, 1971.

Yale, Wesley W. "On Ignorance of Armies." *Army*, June 1972.

Yates, Aubrey J. *Behavior Therapy*. New York: John Wiley & Sons, 1970.

Zagoria, Donald. "The Strategic Debate in Peking." In *China in Crisis*, edited by Tang Tsou. Vol. 2. Chicago: University of Chicago Press, 1968.

Zasloff, Joseph J. *Political Motivation of the Viet Cong: The Vietminh Regroupees*. RAND Memorandum RM-4703-2—ISA/ARPA, May 1968.

Zeitlin, Maurice, and Robert Scheer. *Cuba: Tragedy in Our Hemisphere*. New York: Grove Press, 1963.

Zinn, Howard. *Vietnam: The Logic of Withdrawal*. Boston: Beacon Press, 1967.

United States Government Documents

U.S., Congress, House. Hearings on Department of Defense Appropriations Before a Subcommittee of the Committee on Appropriations, 88th Cong., 1st sess., 1963.

U.S., Congress, Senate. *Vietcong Motivation and Morale*. Hearings Before the Committee on Armed Services and the Subcommittee on the Department of Defense of the Committee on Appropriations, 89th Cong., 2nd sess., January 20, 21, 24, 25, and February 2, 1966.

U.S., Congress, Senate. Hearings Before the Committee on Armed Services, 92nd Cong., 1st sess., July 1971.

U.S., Congress, Senate, Committee on Foreign Relations. Hearings Before the [Symington] Subcommittee on United States

Security Agreements and Commitments Abroad, 91st Cong., 1st sess., October 1969, pt. 2: "Kingdom of Thailand"; pt. 3: "Kingdom of Laos."

U.S., Congress, Senate, Committee on Foreign Relations. Hearings Before the [Symington] Subcommittee on United States and Security Agreements and Commitments Abroad, 91st Cong., 2nd sess., 1970, pt. 2: "Kingdom of Laos."

U.S., Congress, Senate, Committee on Foreign Relations. *Laos: April 1971.* Staff Report of the [Symington] Subcommittee on United States Security Agreements and Commitments Abroad, 92nd Cong., 1st sess., April 1971.

U.S., Congress, Senate, Committee on Foreign Relations. Hearings Before the [Church] Subcommittee on Western Hemisphere Affairs, 92nd Cong., 1st sess., May 1971.

U.S., Congress, Senate. *The United States and Vietnam: 1944–47.* Staff Study for the Foreign Relations Committee by Robert Blum *et al.*, 92nd Cong., 2nd sess., April 3, 1972.

U.S., Congress, Senate, Committee on the Judiciary. Hearings Before the [Kennedy] Subcommittee on Refugees and Escapees, 91st Cong., 2nd sess., May 7, 1970.

U.S., Congress, Senate, Committee on the Judiciary. *Refugee and Civilian War Casualty Problems in Indochina.* Staff Report for the [Kennedy] Subcommittee on Refugees and Escapees, 91st Cong., 2nd sess., September 28, 1970.

U.S., Congress, Senate, Committee on the Judiciary. *War-Related Civilian Problems in Indochina.* Hearings Before the [Kennedy] Subcommittee on Refugees and Escapees, 92nd Cong., 1st sess., April 21–22, 1971, pt. 3: "Laos and Cambodia."

U.S., Congress, Senate, Committee on the Judiciary. Hearings Before the [Kennedy] Subcommittee on Refugees and Escapees, 92nd Cong., 1st sess., July 22, 1971, app. 2: "A Survey of Civilian War Casualties Among Refugees from the Plain of Jars," by Walter Haney.

U.S., Congress, Senate, Committee on the Judiciary. *Problems of War Victims in Indochina.* Hearings Before the [Kennedy] Subcommittee on Refugees and Escapees, 92nd Cong., 2nd sess., May 9, 1972, pt. 2: "Cambodia and Laos," app. 2: "A Survey of Civilian Fatalities Among Refugees from Xieng Khouang Province, Laos," by Walter Haney.

U.S., Department of the Army. *The Law of Land Warfare.* Field Manual FM 27-10, 1956.

U.S., Department of Defense. *United States–Vietnam Relations, 1945–67.* 12 vols. Washington, D.C., Government Printing Office, 1971.

U.S., Department of State. *Kingdom of Laos: Background Notes.* Washington, D.C.: Government Printing Office, March 1969.

Index

About the author

Professor Noam Chomsky, an eminent and revolutionary scholar in the field of linguistics, has in recent years become a figure of national attention through his leadership in Resist, a national draft-resistance movement, and through his brilliant criticism of American political life. He received his B.A., M.A., and Ph.D. from the University of Pennsylvania and was a Fellow at Harvard from 1951 to 1955. In 1955 he was appointed to the faculty of the Massachusetts Institute of Technology, and in 1961 he became a full professor. In addition he has served as a visiting professor at the University of California, Los Angeles, and at Berkeley, and as a Research Fellow at the Institute for Advanced Study at Princeton and the Center for Cognitive Studies at Harvard.

Among the many works Professor Chomsky has written in his field are *Syntactic Structures, Aspects of the Theory of Syntax, Cartesian Linguistics, Language and Mind,* and with Morris Halle, *Sound Pattern of English*. Recently his articles on political and historical themes have attracted widespread attention. Professor Chomsky is a member of the American Academy of Arts and Sciences, as well as of numerous professional societies of the Council of the International Confederation for Disarmament and Peace. His most recent books are *American Power and the New Mandarins* and *Problems of Freedom and Knowledge: The Russell Lectures*.